THE PHILOSOPHY OF BRENTANO

THE PHILOSOPHY
OF BRENTANO

Edited by

Linda L. McAlister

HUMANITIES PRESS
Atlantic Highlands, N.J.

© 1976 Linda L. McAlister
First published in the United States of America in 1977
by Humanities Press Inc.
Atlantic Highlands, New Jersey 07716
Library of Congress Cataloging in Publication Data

Library of Congress Cataloging in Publication Data
Main entry under title:

The Philosophy of Brentano.

  Bibliography: p.
  Includes index.
  1. Brentano, Franz Clemens, 1838-1917 – Addresses,
essays, lectures. I. McAlister, Linda L.
B3212.Z7P48   1976b   193   76-28290
ISBN 0-391-00653-3
ISBN 0-391-00654-1 pbk.

CONTENTS

In memoriam

Myrtle Saxe Jacobson

Editor's Introduction

While writing a doctoral dissertation on the philosophy of Franz Brentano in the late 1960s, I discovered that, despite the fact that I was working in an excellent research library, the secondary literature concerning Brentano was sometimes difficult to obtain. Although, as the bibliography to this volume indicates, there is a considerable body of material, it is often scattered in rather obscure journals and long-out-of-print books. Later, when teaching a graduate course on Brentano, the additional problem arose that articles that I wanted students to read were often in German or French, and I could not assume sufficient or uniform knowledge of two foreign languages from my students. I decided that what was needed was a collection of the most interesting of the essays written, to date, about Brentano and his philosophy – translated into English when necessary – and I set about to make such a collection.

As I was plodding slowly through the first of the translations I had the good fortune to meet *Dipl.-Dolmetscherin* Margarete Schättle of the Institute of Translation and Interpretation of the University of Vienna. Supported by the generous assistance of the Franz Brentano Foundation we undertook the translating chores jointly. The combination of a professional philosopher and a professional translator seems to me to be the optimal one for such an undertaking, and, at the very least, the translations that have resulted were far more efficiently done and are far better than those I could have produced working alone. Any errors that may occur – especially where philosophical interpretation of the texts was necessary – are, however, ultimately my responsibility.

Although this collection was originally motivated by the need for a volume of secondary literature to be used in connection with a course of Brentano's philosophy, I believe that it will also serve a broader purpose. In the last decade several of Brentano's major works have appeared in English translation: *The True and the Evident* (1966), *The Origin of our Knowledge of Right and Wrong* (1969); *The Foundation and Construction of Ethics* (1972); and *Psychology From An Empirical Standpoint* (1973). Translations of other of Brentano's major works are also in progress under the auspices of the Franz Brentano Foundation. These translations are arousing considerable interest in Brentano's philosophy among Anglo-American philosophers, and it is hoped that this volume will help further this interest and the critical discussion of Brentano's ideas which the translations have initiated.

Because I believe that it is very helpful, if not essential, to have a knowledge of the life, times and personality of a philosopher when trying to understand his work, this collection begins with three essays of a biographical nature. The first is a biographical sketch by Brentano's friend and editor Oskar Kraus; the second is a memoir by Carl Stumpf, who was particularly close to Brentano during his Würzburg years, 1866–1873; the third is by Brentano's most famous (although certainly not his most faithful) student, Edmund Husserl, who studied with Brentano at the University of Vienna during the 1880s.

Among the essays which deal with Brentano's philosophy proper, I have chosen to begin with Etienne Gilson's paper on Brentano's interpretation of medieval philosophy because it contains a relatively full exposition of Brentano's doctrine of the four phases of philosophy, and thus provides us with the background necessary to understand Brentano's rejection of the still-prevailing German Idealism of his time, and his efforts to establish a new, scientific mode of philosophizing. Another Gilson – Lucie – then explores in depth Brentano's notion of a philosophy whose method is that of the natural sciences and whether and in what sense Brentano remained true to this conception of philosophy throughout his long philosophical development.

These essays are followed by a group of three (by Titchener, Chisholm, and de Boer) concerning Brentano's descriptive psychology – what it is, how it differs from experimental psychology, especially that of Wundt, and its significance for phenomenology.

The central thesis of Brentano's psychology is that all mental acts are intentional. Herbert Spiegelberg's paper presents an historical comparison of the concepts of 'intention' and 'intentionality' as employed in scholastic philosophy and by Brentano and Husserl, while the paper by Ausonio Marras challenges Spiegelberg's interpretation. Roderick M. Chisholm's extremely influential chapter entitled 'Intentional Inexistence' from his book *Perceiving* gives an account in logico-linguistic terms of Brentano's intentionality doctrine; I argue in my paper that the doctrine that Chisholm describes – however interesting or correct it may be – is not that of Brentano, and I suggest an alternative interpretation and approach to the problem Brentano was trying to solve.

Then follows a group of three articles (Chisholm, Moore and Franks) concerning Brentano's ethics: first a description of the psychological bases on which his ethical theory is constructed, then G.E. Moore's favorable yet extremely puzzling review of Brentano's *The Origin of the Knowledge of Right and Wrong*, and, thirdly, Franks' attempt to clear up some of the puzzling aspects of Moore's review.

During his later years Brentano gradually developed a philosophical position sometimes called 'Reism' or '*Reismus*', the main tenet of which is that only *things* can be the objects of thought. A similar position was developed independently by the Polish philosopher Kotarbinski, who here discusses the two doctrines. D.B. Terrell then takes a closer look at the argument which forms the basis of Brentano's *Reismus*.

The collection ends with two papers which do not fit into the above groups, one on Brentano's theory of induction, and one – essentially a compilation of letters and lecture notes of Brentano and Anton Marty – depicting Brentano's views on the nature of our consciousness of time.

Roderick M. Chisholm has recently compiled a comprehensive bibliography of all of Brentano's published works, and I am very pleased that he has offered it to me for inclusion in this volume. I have compiled the bibliography of secondary literature about Brentano, and have attempted to make it a comprehensive one, although there are undoubtedly omissions.

I wish to express my thanks to the Franz Brentano Foundation, its Trustees and its Director for their generous support and encouragement; to the contributors, journals and publishers who have granted me permission to reprint these essays; and to Richard Sorabji for a very helpful suggestion.

Linda L. McAlister

Würzburg
May, 1975

1 Biographical Sketch of Franz Brentano[1]

Oskar Kraus

Franz Brentano (1838–1917), who was active at the University of Vienna for twenty years, is one of the most important figures in all philosophy, and one of the most congenial personalities in German intellectual history . . .

Franz Clemens Honoratus Hermann Brentano was born on 16 January 1838, in Marienberg near Boppard on the Rhine, in what had once been a cloister. He was the second child of the Catholic writer Christian Brentano and his wife Emilie, neé Genger, from Braubach on the Rhine. He was the grandson of Peter Anton Brentano and Maximiliane de la Roche, who was, in her youth, a friend of Goethe's. He was also the nephew of Clemens Brentano, and the child listened to fairy tales at his knee.[2]

In the same year, soon after the birth of his son, Christian Brentano was expelled from Prussia for having actively supported Archbishop von Droste-Vischering of Cologne in his conflict with the Prussian government. The family then moved to Aschaffenburg. Joseph Merkel, the Lyceum professor and Court Librarian, had a great influence on Franz's education. In 1861 Christian Brentano died.[3]

Franz Brentano's youngest sister Claudine describes her brother, in the 1918 issue of *Monatshefte für pädagogische Reform* dedicated to him, as follows:

> He was wonderfully gifted at everything. As a boy he sang so beautifully that people passing the house would compliment my mother on his beautiful voice; it developed into a rich, sonorous voice when he grew up. His violin teacher used to praise his progress at every lesson, even though he did not practise very much. He could

1. Translated from the German by Linda L. McAlister. Reprinted from *Neue Österreichische Biographie, 1815–1918*, vol. 3 (Vienna, 1926).

2. Peter Anton Brentano had emigrated from Tremezzo, Italy to Frankfurt, and had twenty children – six from his first marriage, twelve from his second, and two from his third. Christian was born of the second marriage, and he in turn had five children: Maria Ludovica Cäcilia, who married the famous Egyptologist Sir Peter Le Page Renouf; Franz; Sophie, who married the French historian Theophil Funck; Claudine, who is a nun and lives in Zangberg near Ampfing; and Lujo, the well known professor of political economy. (From a genealogy in the possession of Lujo Brentano.)

3. Compare the article 'Christian Brentano' in *Allgemeine deutsche Biographie*. See also his posthumous religious writings published in 1851 by the *Literarisch-artistischen Anstalt* in Munich. There is considerable material about Christian in Bettina Brentano's *Frühlingskranz* and in *Briefwechsel eines Kindes mit Goethe*. *Das Haus Brentano* by Müller-Königswinter is a chronicle of the Brentano family, in the form of a novel.

skilfully draw or paint whatever he wanted to. For a time he took painting lessons with the Countesses Geldern in Munich. After his death one of them wrote to me how happy they had been there. I still remember the last stanza of a light-hearted verse he wrote at that time:

> *Und müßte ich wie Seneca zum Tode mich bequemen*
> *Ich würde vor dem Tode noch zwei Malerstunden nehmen.*
> *Ich stürbe nicht am Anderlaß, ich würde tot mich lachen*
> *Und würde es viel besser noch als jener Weise machen.*[4]

He loved games and was very good at them . . . especially at chess, his favourite hobby . . . A chess set held such fascination for him, that once when he went to visit his favourite aunt, Antonie Schoeff-Brentano, in Frankfurt, he found a chess set in the entry hall, and completely forgot why he had come. His aunt discovered him much later completely absorbed in the game . . . He could compete with the best of them in swimming and in gymnastics . . . He loved children, and children – as well as grown-ups – loved him.

Franz attended the Royal Bavarian Gymnasium in Aschaffenburg. According to the philosopher, he had his first religious doubts at the age of seventeen. They were caused by the doctrine of indeterminism. He thought that contemporary philosophy was just so much talk. In 1855–6 he took the required general education courses in Aschaffenburg at the Lyceum so that 'the dangerous university years could be postponed', as he himself put it. In 1856 he entered the University of Munich. In his old age he still had words of praise for Ernst Lasaulx's lectures and his appearance.

Brentano's relationship with his mother, a woman of great agility of mind and deep religious feeling, was very close. She was deeply involved in the publication of devotional literature, and to please her he translated numerous poems, including one of the famous sonnets which some attribute to St Theresa and others to Xavier.[5] His zeal and enthusiasm for Thomas Aquinas in his youth was so great that, under Aquinas' influence, he succeeded in converting a young Jewish friend named Adler to Christianity. Adler joined the Dominican Order in Graz and later became Prior.

Besides studying in Munich (1856–7), Brentano spent one semester in Würzburg (1858), and then went to Berlin (1858–9), where he worked under Trendelenburg and undertook an intensive study of Aristotle. There he was stimulated by his contact with his aunt, Bettina Brentano von Arnim, and the household of von Savigny, his Aunt Kunigunde's husband. Then he spent two semesters (1859–60) at the Academy in Münster where

4. Translated somewhat freely: 'And if I had, like Seneca, to come to terms with dying,/ Before my death I could be found in painting classes – trying./ I would not have to slit my wrists, I'd kill myself with laughter,/ And I would do a better job than that old Roman master.'

5. Reprinted in the *Historisch-politischen Blättern*, vol. 72, p. 924, and later in Brentano's *On the Origin of our Knowledge of Right and Wrong*, trans. Roderick M. Chisholm, p. 86.

he studied the medieval Aristotelians under Professor Clemens. The poems he wrote during these years express deep melancholy and longing.

In 1862 Brentano's first book, *Von der mannigfachen Bedeutung des Seienden nach Aristoteles*, appeared, published by Herber in Freiburg. It is dedicated to Trendelenburg. In this work he shows that Aristotle's Table of Categories is not just an arbitrary conglomeration of grammatical concepts, but is actually derived from a single basic thought, and he gives a consistent deduction and classification of the categories. Trendelenburg was convinced: 'He has attempted a most ingenious new interpretation of the Aristotelian doctrine, against which no important objections can be raised.' This is what Trendelenburg reported to the young Georg von Hertling.[6] The expert on the subject was astounded by the intellectual maturity of this twenty-four-year old.

On 17 July 1862, Franz Brentano received his doctorate from the University of Tübingen *in absentia*. In the autumn of the same year he was in residence for a short time at the Dominican monastery in Graz. He was there at the same time as Denifle, a close friend who was very much pained by Brentano's early departure. After that Brentano went to Munich to study theology. Döllinger was already teaching that the Council takes precedence over the Pope. Then Brentano attended the Theological Seminar in Würzburg, and took the examination in theology. He once told me that one of the questions asked was, 'Why is the Church visible?' The answer they expected was, 'Because Christ, its head, was visible.' Brentano's answer, however, was, 'Because it is a society made up of people, and they, in the interests of social unity, must perceive each other.'

On 6 August 1864 he was ordained by Bishop Stahl. In July 1866 he habilitated as a *Privatdozent* in the Philosophical Faculty of the University of Würzburg. In his written thesis he treated the topic, *'Darstellung und Kritik der Lehre Schellings in den drei Stadien'* ('Exposition and Critique of Schelling's Teachings in their Three Phases'). Philosophy was always Brentano's main interest, but he also studied mathematics, natural sciences, philology, history and theology.

For the public disputation in the *Aula* (something still practised at that time) on 15 July, Brentano proposed twenty-five theses, among which the fourth was the, later famous, proposition, *'Vera philosophiae methodus nulla alia nisi scientiae naturalis est'* ('The true method philosophy is none other than that of the natural sciences'). By 'philosophy' he means, above all, metaphysics, in which he was already employing the inductive method of hypothesis formation. Psychology, too, was for him strictly an empirical science.

The first two theses are also characteristic:

(1) 'Philosophy must protest against the distinction between speculative and exact sciences; its very right to existence provides the justification for this protest.' He thus claimed for philosophy the strictest scientific principles and attacked the speculative-mystical

6. Brentano's cousin, who later became the German chancellor. Compare his *Erinnerungen*, p. 51.

philosophy of the Romantics Fichte, Schelling and Hegel.[7]

(2) 'Philosophy must protest against the assumption that it derives its principles from theology, and against the claim that without the existence of supernatural revelation a scientific philosophy is impossible.'

These basic principles, and especially the fourth thesis and the way he subsequently worked it out in his lectures, were exciting to young people and brought him numerous students and followers.

His habilitation thesis was the book *Die Psychologie des Aristoteles insbesondere seine Lehre vom* Nous Poietikos (*Aristotle's Psychology, In Particular his Doctrine of* Nous Poietikos) which was published in 1867 by Kirchheim in Mainz, and dedicated to Dr Joseph Merkel ('In memory of my dear, fatherly friend, in true gratitude'). His guiding principle was already something that he later recommended to historians of philosophy in an unpublished essay on methods of Aristotelian research: Let yourself become completely immersed in the spirit of the philosopher being studied; try to understand his train of thought – if not logically then at least psychologically – through the philosopher's spirit and his characteristic thought-patterns. Based on this, try to reconstruct his system, as in Cuvier's method, even when the data are incomplete, by taking into consideration what his predecessors and successors, teachers and students teach about a subject. Brentano's masterful lectures on the history of philosophy followed this principle. It is not possible to comment further at this point on the contents of this work. It has been eclipsed, especially in Protestant circles, on the authority of Eduard Zeller. This is particularly true of the appendix, *'Uber das Wirken des aristotelischen Gottes'* in which Brentano proves that when the Aristotelian God thinks about himself this includes thinking of himself as the cause of the world and, therefore, indirectly, thinking of and consciously governing the world; this, in contrast to the prevailing view, makes a full understanding of Aristotelian metaphysics possible.

Brentano began his lectures in 1866. They included history of philosophy, metaphysics, logic and psychology. One of his first students was Carl Stumpf, whose life was twice greatly influenced by Brentano. The powerful impression that Brentano's personality made is described by Stumpf in his *Selbstdarstellung*.[8] Under his influence Stumpf left the study of law and devoted himself completely to philosophy and theology. 'Everything was overshadowed by the great tasks of philosophical and religious rebirth.' Soon, in 1867, they were joined by Anton Marty, who, after Stumpf, is among the most devoted and important of Brentano's students.

Hermann Schell, later a leader of the German Catholic Modernist movement, as well as Commer, Schell's future opponent, joined this circle, as did Georg von Hertling, who later became Chancellor of Germany, and whose first philosophical steps were taken with Brentano's guidance.

7. For a discussion of Brentano's first and fourth theses, and his views on the relationship between science and philosophy, see the essay by Lucie Gilson below, pp. 68–79.

8. See also Stumpf's memoir of Brentano, ch. 2 below.

Hertling's dissertation at the University of Berlin, *De Aristotelis notione Unius* (Freiburg, 1864), was greatly influenced by Brentano, as was his book *Materie und Form bei Aristotles*. At the time he wrote to his mother about his teacher: 'I have never seen a person who had such a sharp mind and such deep speculative gifts. But even if this were not true, his efforts would still be blessed because he does not look for anything for himself but does everything out of purest enthusiasm for the truth. You would have to look long and hard to find another who goes to church before each lecture to seek strength and concentration.'

Brentano's collaboration on Möhler's *Kirchengeschichte*, edited by Gams in 1867 (vol. 2, pp. 328–484), was during this period. Brentano wrote the history of medieval philosophy 'according to Möhler's format.' He was already basing his presentation on his theory of the four phases of philosophy, as he did his lectures on the history of philosophy at that time. On this theory, the development of philosophy in the ancient, medieval and modern periods exhibits four successive stages in each phase – one ascending stage (the epoch in which pure theoretical interest dominates), and three descending stages of decay (in which practical and extra-scientific motives become the norm). The first of these is a phase of dogmatisation and popularisation, in reaction to which there follows a sceptical phase, and, finally, one of mysticism. In the modern period this mystical epoch of decay is represented by speculative Idealist philosophy.

In *Chilianeum* (n.s. vol. 2, 1869), Brentano published a treatise entitled 'Auguste Comte und die positive Philosophie'. Repulsed by contemporary [German] philosophy, Brentano had been introduced to Comte by John Stuart Mill, with whom he later corresponded. In this essay, Brentano augments Comte's theory of phases with his own, and interprets Comte as what we would now call a 'critical realist'. He considers the speculative decadence of Schelling and Hegel to have been overcome. 'It is the task of our time to return to a positive treatment of philosophy.' 'Positive' here is to be understood in Comte's sense rather than in the sense of positive religion, the churchly positivism.

The dogma of papal infallibility was being prepared at this time and with it Brentano's resistance to its promulgation, and his apostasy. It was then that von Hertling wrote to his mother, 'I do not want to be the Melanchthon to this Luther' (*Erinnerungen*, p. 174).

On behalf of Bishop Ketteler, Brentano wrote a position paper for the German bishops against infallibility; in it he proved that this doctrine contradicts the Gospels, the Church fathers, and all history. His arguments were favourably received at the conference of German bishops in Fulda (cp. Fritz Vegener, *Ketteler und das Vaticanum*, Fischer, 1915) [cp. also T. Freudenberger, *Quelle und Beiträge zur Geschichte der Universität Würzburg*, vol. 1 (1969)].

Brentano's inner break with the Church came in 1870, but only after he had first accepted the invitation of Abbot Haneberg, 'a priest honourable almost to the point of saintliness', and had again examined the paper and its origins, in seclusion in the Benedictine Abbey of St Boniface in Munich.

In the meantime, Stumpf had entered a seminary and Marty had been ordained into the priesthood. Brentano persuaded Stumpf to leave the seminary, while Marty, who had just taken holy orders, followed the example of his teacher spontaneously.

In 1872, Brentano, while on a trip to England, where he visited Spencer, was made a professor (*extraordinarius*) of philosophy. The Senate had wanted to appoint F.A. Lange, even though Lotze, when asked, had definitely spoken in favour of Brentano.[9]

The following year Brentano left the priesthood and resigned from his professorship, which he had accepted under different circumstances. New travels took him to France and England. Following an invitation from John Stuart Mill he travelled to Avignon, but found that Mill had died. Döllinger's attempt to win Brentano over to the Old Catholic faith foundered, for his new point of view was unshakeable.

In 1874 Brentano was appointed to the University of Vienna by Minister Stremayr. His inaugural lecture, 'Über die Gründe der Entmutigung auf philosophischem Gebiete,' was received by the audience – despite their initial distrust of the 'clerical obscurantist' – with great enthusiasm. 'That was the one work of mine that had the greatest impact, and yet it was relatively unoriginal (Comte) and unimportant.' In May, *Psychologie vom empirischen Standpunkt* appeared. This work established Brentano's reputation and made him one of the most influential thinkers of the second half of the nineteenth century and of the present.

In the same year Brentano contracted smallpox, and was nursed by Anton Marty, and later by his mother as well. T.G. Masaryk, also a member of Brentano's circle of friends, visited the patient, too. During the First World War, forty years later, two of Brentano's former students, von Hertling and Masaryk, were opponents in their respective governmental positions.[10] Among other students of Brentano's from his Viennese period were Alexius Meinong, Alois Höfler, Edmund Husserl, Kasimir Twardowski, Franz Hillebrand, Christian von Ehrenfels, Alfred Berger, A. Olzelt, Baron von Pidoll. Sometimes even the largest lecture halls could not accommodate his audience, which included such scholars as the zoologist Claus and others.

Brentano became caught up in Viennese social life, to which his exotic appearance and fascinating personality added special glitter and charm. The true solemnity of his nature, which always basically tended toward the otherworldly, manifested itself in his behaviour – in speech and gestures which somehow always retained a slightly priestly air. This contrasted

9. Stumpf's account (below, p. 10), is somewhat more accurate on this point. The archives of the University Senate show that Brentano was being considered for an *extraordinarius* at the same time a search was being made for a second *ordinarius*. Brentano was not in serious contention for the latter, apparently because strong factions in the philosophy faculty objected to a priest holding such a position. Lotze, did, however, write a letter saying he would recommend Brentano as *ordinarius*. Lange was offered and declined the *ordinarius*; Brentano eventually got his *extraordinarius*, and Carl Stumpf was finally appointed the second professor *ordinarius* in philosophy at Würzburg.

10. Von Hertling was, of course, on the German side, having been chancellor of Germany, and Masaryk was to become, after the war, the first president of Czechoslovakia.

wonderfully with the happy, childlike quality and playfulness which his sister mentioned, and which stayed with him all his life.

Chess became an all-consuming passion at times. He even invented, among other things, a new defence of the Spanish Game, which was published in a chess magazine.[11]

An extensive volume of poems that he had intended to call *Himmlische und irdische Liebe*, which has never been published, reveals that exceptional poetic talent which characterised his book of riddles, *Änigmatias* (first edition entitled *Neue Rätsel*, 1876). That riddle book, written 'for a highly talented friend, the Baroness Dora von Gagern', will soon appear in its fourth edition. Bettelheim is right to call it 'a classic in the literature riddles'. Brentano's artistic inclinations, which extended into all spheres, were an obstacle to his scholarly production, because they made him a perfectionist and took time away from his academic endeavours. Superficial or envious observers catch only a glimpse of one or another side of his many-faceted nature. Some see Adolf Wilbrandt's book *Gast vom Abendstern* as a true portrait of Brentano, whereas I have already pointed out in my book on Brentano[12] that he only caught some of Brentano's gestures and external features and used them to paint a picture which stands in the most glaring contrast to Brentano's manly, courageous, sometimes even rash nature (of which he all too often gave unwelcome demonstrations).

In 1880, when Brentano decided he wanted to marry Ida Lieben, 'one of Vienna's most noble daughters', friends of the family, Glaser and Unger, called attention to the fact that certain court decisions, especially those of the Supreme Court, declared marriages of former priests void, contrary to the letter and the spirit of the law. In order to escape these dangers Brentano acquired Saxon citizenship and was married in a civil ceremony in Leipzig on 16 September. Before doing this he resigned his professorship, having been given firm confirmation by the government that he would be reappointed shortly.

Section 63 of the Austrian Legal code says: 'Clerics who have taken holy orders cannot enter into a valid marriage.' The most important lawyers in Austria, Lemayer and Schmerling, as well as Glaser and Unger, said that the Supreme Court was wrong, for the marriage of a man who had left the clergy was no longer subject to that paragraph, because of the inter-denominational laws. But, taking cognisance of the incorrect interpretation of the law, Brentano wished to take steps to render his marriage above reproach. In the autumn of 1881 Brentano became a *Privatdozent* at the University of Vienna. But, despite repeated recommendations by the faculty, repeated pledges from the government, and continued successful teaching on his part, the professorship failed to materialise. A direct petition from Brentano to the Kaiser requesting re-appointment was never delivered because Minister Gautsch was afraid that he would have problems with the clergy if the permission were granted. Angered by the delay that continued for a decade, Brentano began to entertain thoughts of leaving Austria. All

---

11. See 'Neue Verteidigung der Spanischen Partie', *Wiener Schachzeitung*, 1900.

12. Oskar Kraus, *Franz Brentano: Zur Kenntnis seines Lebens und seiner Lehre* (Munich, 1919).

too soon these thoughts were to become a reality. Ida Brentano died at the beginning of 1893. A new recommendation by the faculty was ignored. The Minister of Education, a Pole named Madeyski, maintained that Brentano's claim had expired. In his final lecture on *Die vier Phasen der Philosophie* Brentano explained to the Viennese Literary Society why he was leaving. In December he published *Letzten Wünsche für Österreich* which appeared in the *Neue Freie Presse*. The first article described the disgraceful way he had been treated after twenty years of active service, the outrageous details of which I cannot describe here. The third discussed the inexplicable rejection of his proposal to establish an Institute for Experimental Psychology, which he had supported from the beginning; the second dealt with the unlawful interpretation of Section 63, which the Supreme Court unjustifiably gave when it adopted the Catholic Church's position on the *character indelibilis* of holy orders. The public was very much interested in Brentano's case. The liberal-minded took Brentano's side, but some pro-clerical publications such as *Das Vaterland* were abusive of him; he, for his part, always refrained, in a gentlemanly way, from attacking the Church.

Professor H. Krasnopolski from Prague defended the position of the courts that Brentano had attacked (in Vering's *Archiv für Kirchenrecht*, vol. 83). Brentano responded to this work with an essay entitled 'Zur eherechtlichen Frage in Österreich' (Cotta, Stuttgart, 1895). Krasnopolski's reply produced a counter-reply, 'Krasnopolski's lezter Versuch' (J.J. Arndt, Leipzig, 1896, reprinted from the weekly magazine *Die Zeit*, 17 and 24 October 1896). At this time it became necessary for Brentano to sue Krasnopolski for libel, but the treatment of the case was a complete travesty of justice, since the *Ratskammer* and the *Oberlandesgericht* in Prague refused to hear the case.

Chief Justice Josef Unger, unfortunately, remained silent on the question of Section 63 until 1910; then, in an essay entitled 'Priesterehen und Mönchsehen' (cp. the *Festschrift* paper he wrote on the occasion of the centennial celebration of the Austrian legal code, the *Allgemeines Österreichisches Gesetzbuch*), he explained that he had always agreed with Brentano, and he gave his reasons.

In April 1895 Brentano left an ungrateful Vienna to take up residence in Italy (Rome, Palermo, Florence), after a brief stay in Switzerland. He spent summers at his house in Schönbühel in the Wachau on the Danube, which he had bought in 1887.

He took part in the Third International Congress of Psychology in Munich (1896) and delivered a paper, 'Über Individuation, multiple Qualitäten und Intensität sinnlicher Erscheinungen'.

In 1897 Brentano married Emilie Rueprecht, who was not only a second mother to his son Johannes Christian Michael, who had been born in 1888, but also a devoted helper to him. A sacroiliac ailment prompted him to exchange Florence for Palermo temporarily in 1899.

In 1905 he wrote a paper for the Psychology Congress in Rome entitled 'Von der psychologischen Analyse der Tonqualitäten in ihre eigentlich letzten Elemente' . . . The two lectures given at the Congresses in 1896 and 1905 appeared, together with two papers concerning 'phenomenal green' as *Untersuchungen zur Sinnespsychologie* in 1907.

In 1911 Brentano wrote a treatise on Aristotle for the series *Grosse Denker*. *Aristotles und seine Weltanschauung* was published by Quelle und Meyer, while Veit published *Aristoteles Lehre vom Ursprung des menschlichen Geistes*, a new, much enlarged edition of his early work *Über den Creatianismus des Aristoteles*. It contains corrections and additions to his polemic against Zeller.

During the same year the book *Von der Klassifikation der psychischen Phänomene* appeared, published by Duncker and Humblot; this was a new and expanded edition of the relevant chapters of his *Psychology*.

In 1914 Brentano went to Prague to visit the grave of his friend and student Anton Marty, who had just died. Two eye operations in 1903 had not been able to forestall Brentano's almost complete blindness. Before Italy declared war he left Florence and went to Zurich, where he took an apartment on the Zürichberg. In 1916 he had attack of appendicitis; the following spring he had a relapse, and died on 17 March 1917. He was buried in Sihlfeld Cemetery. The last two decades of his life were filled with intense and fruitful work which had important results; these Brentano wrote down mostly in letters to friends, students and his students' students, and in numerous dictations . . .

Throughout his life Brentano exchanged ideas with important people and had personal contact with them. Some of these have been mentioned above; others who should be noted are the painter Führich; the sculptor Zumbusch; Ignaz Plener; the Slavicist Miklosich; the psychiatrist Meynert; Hermann Grimm; Ewald Hering; Ernst Mach; W. Dilthey; Josef Breuer; Boltzmann, who was a guest of Brentano's in Florence shortly before his death; the Gomperz and Wertheimstein families, especially Franzisca von Wertheimstein, whose beauty and spirit made a deep impression on Brentano; Isolde Kurz; Marie von Ebner-Eschenbach; Anton Bettelheim; Ferdinand von Saar; Minister Hartel; Dr Heinrich Glücksmann. In Florence and Palermo he was in more or less close touch with countless Italian philosophers, young and old, especially with Amato and Faggi in Palermo, as well as with Guastala, Tocco, Calderoni, Desarlo and others. Mario Puglisi, editor of the magazine *Progresso Religioso* deserves to be singled out for special attention. In Schönbühel, Brentano used to receive scholars and philosophers in the summertime. There were often several guests under his hospitable roof at one time. The Pole Lutoslavski, the Serb Petroniewicz, the Hungarian Revezs, all sought him out there. He corresponded with the mathematicians Vailati and Enriques, and the Aristotelian Eugen Rolfes and the Platonist Gustav Schneider. In Lausanne in 1895, he was in contact with Alexander Herzen, and contributed a foreword to his book on sexual ethics. In Florence he befriended the Russian General Zoubow, a successor of Euler's, and J.B. Stallo. But no one was as close to him throughout his life as Anton Marty.

2 Reminiscences of Franz Brentano[1]

Carl Stumpf

What the reader expects from me here is factual material about Brentano's life and personality, as well as about the history of the origin of his philosophical theories. Yet first of all, I wish to express the love and gratitude which I owe to my great teacher and which I will retain until the day I die. The close relationships he established with his students and which he was so eager to maintain played a more important part in his inner life than is the case with many other thinkers. I have already deeply regretted that the restlessness and over-work of my years in Berlin have kept me from maintaining the close contact we had established in our youth. My friend Marty and his students were more fortunate in that respect. But I am convinced that at present no one is in a better position than I to report about the most important years of Brentano's development and about his years in Würzburg. Therefore I shall gladly undertake the task. I am happy to have an opportunity after half a century to relive, in a flight of memory, a time which was a decisive one for me as well as for him.

Habilitation, 1866: Brentano as teacher: our association in Würzburg and Aschaffenburg

I first saw and heard Brentano on 14 July 1866, at the well-attended public disputation for his habilitation in Würzburg. These were very troubled times. On the same day the battle of Aschaffenburg raged; that was home to both of us. It was a strange coincidence that a well-known Austrian historian, Karl Friedrich Stumpf-Brentano, not only combined both names, but also had the same first name as I. He was related to the Brentano family by marriage to one of the Frankfurt Brentanos (the same one to whom Franz Brentano had written a pretty little poem during his student days in Munich). My family, however, was related neither to the Brentanos nor to the Austrian Stumpfs in any way. In my first two semesters at Würzburg (the autumn of 1865 and the spring of 1866), I took some general courses, as required in Bavaria, including philosophy with the Baader scholar Franz Hoffman, whose prating style could arouse nobody's interest, and with the philologian Urlichs, who gave elegant but philosophically rather superficial lectures on aesthetics, based largely on Kant's *Critique of Judgement*. In the

1. Translated from the German by Linda L. McAlister and Margarte Schättle. Reprinted from the Appendix to Oskar Kraus' *Franz Brentano, zur Kenntnis seines Lebens und seiner Lehre* (Munich, 1919).

spring term of 1866 I began to major in law, and I was particularly impressed by Köpper's Pandekten and his careful and sharp-witted elaboration of controversial cases. The notice about Brentano's disputation enticed me and my elder brother to attend the battle of wits. Brentano had submitted no less than twenty-five Latin theses covering the whole range of philosophy, which were, however, to be argued in German. Hoffmann and Urlichs opposed him, and perhaps some others as well. The way in which Brentano defended and explained his theses revealed him to be so superior to his attackers that I decided then and there to attend his lectures in the autumn. Behind each of these theses was a thoroughly thought-out theory; this became clear in part during the disputation and in part later on in his lectures. We were especially happy that the method he claimed for philosophy was none other than that of the natural sciences, and that he based his hopes for a rebirth of philosophy on this method. It was a new, incomparably deeper and more serious way of understanding philosophy.

Not only the green students, but also the faculty and Senate members present were considerably impressed by Brentano; this is shown by the report made by the Senate Commission to the Senate on 15 July, which Professor Chroust in Würzburg discovered in the archives and communicated to me recently. The report praises

> his mental acuity, the clarity and precision of his concepts, the ease
> with which he grasps other ideas, the certainty with which he
> develops his ideas, the genuinely scientific character of his method,
> not to mention his diversified knowledge of the field of philosophy and
> exact inquiry . . . He combines the power of conviction with a proper
> manner, the dignity of the man of science with a becoming modesty.
> Calm, clarity, precision, and thoroughness must be mentioned as the
> essential characteristics of his discussions.

Of Brentano's habilitation thesis (*The Psychology of Aristotle*), the Dean said that of all the works that had been submitted to the Faculty of Arts and Sciences of his university in the course of a half century this was definitely the outstanding one. The theme of the inaugural lecture on 15 July was very remote from Brentano's interests and he certainly did not choose it himself; it must have been set by Hoffmann: 'On the Main Stages of Development in Schelling's Philosophy and the Scientific Value of the Last Phase of its Formation'.

Two weeks later, not just the fortress but Würzburg itself was shelled by the Prussian forces, and the university closed its doors. Brentano is said to have gone home on foot through the Spessart and to have been taken into custody as a suspected spy.

In the autumn, then, I attended his first course of lectures on the history of philosophy, and he was already teaching the doctrine of the four phases at that time. The first time Brentano was struck by this idea, as he later told me, was during his convalescence from a serious illness (Easter 1860). Having almost lost his faith in philosophy, he thought for a long time about the significance of the systems of speculative philosophy which make such high claims, and which are at times so widely admired and then again wholly rejected. Then he was struck by the illuminating and saving idea of an analogy in the course of philosophical development within each of the three main periods (which he naturally did not consider valid for all time). In the presentation itself Brentano dwelt in great detail on Greek philosophy. He presented each individual system of the older and the newer natural philosophy with utmost conscientiousness in the interpretation of the preserved fragments, and he turned it into a work of art, with every fragment connected to the whole, and exhibiting the continual progress. Instead of a dry series of doctrines, a living development appeared before our very eyes. The ingenious presentation of Heracleitus, the solutions of apparent contradictions in the fragments, and the writings of Xenophon, wherein at the same time the transition from the old Ionians to the Eleatics became understandable, the portrayal of the personality of Socrates, the reproduction of the Aristotelian system by this most competent expert – in short, everything – filled me with admiration. All this was enhanced by the personal impression of the teacher, who was inspired by the consciousness of a high mission, who became wholly absorbed in the great task of a reconstruction of philosophy, whose thinking and feeling merged in this one focus and then once again emanated from it. Add to this the outward appearance of the tall ascetic figure in priestly garb with the very finely modelled, magnificent head of a thinker; the high, beautiful forehead; and the keen eyes hidden under a high brow and somewhat drooping lids, which noticed every expression of doubt or questioning on the face of a student. His soft but very clear and well-formulated speech compelled the listeners to breathless silences and rapt attention during the abstract investigations; it was the force of the firmly structured logic of his thought rather than any special art that fascinated his students, although he did occasionally employ an appropriate anecdote. What a contrast to old Hoffman! The lecture hall was filled to the last chair and stayed that way; admittedly not everyone was registered officially. The figures sent me by the Registrar at Würzburg are far below the actual number of people in attendance, as was the case with Lotze, too.

The power that Brentano exercised over susceptible students is shown by the metamorphosis that he produced in me. After a few weeks my interest in jurisprudence began to wane, and before Christmas I sought him out to inform him of my intention of choosing philosophy and theology as my life's work. I even wanted to follow him into the priesthood, so much of an example had he set for me. To be sure, I had been religious from childhood, but being always of a cheerful disposition I had never thought of renouncing the world, and nothing of the sort had happened in my family as far back as we can remember. My father, as a doctor, was mostly interested in the natural sciences and medicine. I had chosen to study law because a job in law or public administration seemed to leave the most leisure time after office hours for my beloved music. Apart from that, my main passion was for hiking in the mountains and valleys. And now I was willing to withdraw behind cloistered walls for years and take upon myself a lifetime of the strictest internal and external limitations, so that I might gain, in return, inner peace.

Brentano advised me, as was his duty, to undergo a long period of contemplation and examination. After all, he did not yet know me. But from then on I accompanied him more and more frequently on his walks in Würzburg and Aschaffenburg, and enjoyed his personal concern and care in every further phase of my spiritual development. I have never met an academic, neither in my student days nor since I have been a professor, who dedicated himself to such an extent, both verbally and in writing, to his task as a teacher. In this he followed the example of the great Greek thinkers whom he ranked above all others. The friendly relations with his students, based upon an equally absolute devotion to the highest purposes, was one of the strongest needs of his life. Even in his last letter to me, a few weeks before his death, he spoke of this need in a very moving way, lamenting the fact that our scientific contacts and our correspondence had decreased so much.

Thousands of students since my time have had the valuable experience, as beginners, of having logical training under this penetrating and exact thinker. Just as he himself was schooled by the greatest masters of syllogistic, Aristotle and Aquinas, so he, too, trained his students, above all, in self-discipline and a critical attitude with respect to the logical requisites of thought. He would interrupt long discourses and demand concise syllogistic summaries of the thoughts expressed, whose premises and inferences were then subjected to a rigorous examination. *Concedo majorem, distinguo majorem, nego minorem, probo minorem* – even if these old formulae were not used, the forms were, and I consider it an advantage even today, just as John Stuart Mill had said that he would like to see the re-introduction of courses in this area. In the second semester, Autumn 1867, Brentano also introduced some special, open classes in which objections to the developments in his metaphysics lectures were formulated and examined. Again many students attended these classes, but actually only a few ventured objections, for it was no fun to be convicted of a logical blunder, even though Brentano was always very considerate in doing so. You could not come there for the purpose of expressing vague feelings. I remember that one person once took the line that he could not be happy with a certain thesis; the reply was that it really did not matter whether he was happy or not.

Along with his students' philosophical development, Brentano was also much concerned with their deeper understanding of religious problems. He placed extraordinary emphasis on meditation – on the calm, thoughtful concentration on the mysteries and on traditional religious doctrines, as was common practice among the medieval ascetics and mystics. Such meditation forms a part of the training of the Catholic clergy to this day. The contemplative and the active life, like Mary and Martha, should supplement one another, but the contemplative has a higher value insofar as it approaches the final goal of the blissful vision of God in the next world.

Brentano wrote to me in Göttingen on New Year's Eve 1867,

The person who is not contemplative seems to me hardly to be alive, and a philosopher who does not use and practice contemplation does not deserve the name; he is no philosopher but a scientific artisan and the most philistine of philistines. For heaven's sake, let nothing shake

your resolve to dedicate a little time each day to contemplation.
Unfaithfulness to the purposes which God inspires in you would take
its bitter revenge. Perhaps your most beautiful flower of life, only half
opened, would wither away for ever. If I could only express to you how
immeasurable this loss would be! I cannot, but the one thing I can say
truly is that I would rather throw my whole profession of learning to
the wind, I would even rather die, than give up contemplation.

We must, however, not overlook the fact that even this contemplative
thought had its roots in Greek philosophy: in Plato's doctrine of the
apprehension of the Idea of the Good as the highest end of man and
especially of the philosopher who, having walked in this light, is as though
blinded to the lower things of this world, and in Aristotle's praise of the
theoretical life.

At my departure for Göttingen he sent me a small New Testament from
the Bible Society in Greek in which he had written the motto (in Greek):

'Come forward, you who are thirsty, accept the water of life, a free gift
to all who desire it' (Revelations 22, 17).

The appearance of the little book shows how the thirsty one, to whom he
gave it, quenched his thirst. Among the works for meditation which
Brentano treasured in addition to the Gospels I remember one other little
booklet, the German edition of the touchingly naive descriptions of the life
of Jesus by St Bonaventure.

For philosophical walks, the beautiful areas of Würzburg and
Aschaffenburg in Franconia were very well suited. In Würzburg Brentano
lived in a large apartment house on the upper quay on the Main across from
the fortress. From there it was only a few steps to the 'Glacis', the beautiful
wooded grounds which surrounded the city where the old fortress walls had
been. That was the ideal Academy garden, and I was permitted to
accompany him there, though in fact we did not notice the external beauties
which would have distracted us from our subtle abstractions. The thinker in
the black clerical robe walking about with long strides and an upright
bearing, deep in thought, was soon a well-known figure in Würzburg. Later,
somebody told me that he was fairly regularly accompanied by an equally
pale and thin student with whom he often stood on the same spot,
immersed in conversation, for long periods of time.

The site in Aschaffenburg was even better. The Brentano family home
stood on a secluded side street on the hilly banks of the Main. Through a
door which was built into an old archway one came first into a courtyard
surrounded by walls; the yard was rather overgrown, with a few trees, and
the grass was allowed to grow up between the stones however it wanted. Then
you came into a comfortable old-fashioned house with spacious rooms
and halls. The living room and drawing room were up a flight of stairs.
From a balcony there was a lovely view of the Main, which curved to the
palace and to the 'Pompeii House', and also a view of the plains across the
river to the west. When I later visited Brentano at Schönbühel on the
Danube, I was immediately aware of a certain resemblance between his

house and its surroundings and the Aschaffenburg home, and I do not doubt that in choosing and renovating the house he actually had this in mind. As I saw subsequently, he himself refers in a postcard to the house that he had built there as 'new Aschaffenburg'. And just as in Schönbühel, where you climbed down through a romantic tunnel and footpath to the Danube and walked along its banks philosophising, there was a similar exit in Aschaffenburg through which you left the courtyard to walk to the park along the Main and over the bridge to the open bank on the other side, where, in a good half an hour, one could walk through a rectilinear row of poplars to 'Schönen Busch', a large park dating from the time of the Elector. That was the real philosophy walk. In addition to this, it was just a few steps from the house to the palace garden which surrounded the magnificent and massive red sandstone Renaissance palace, where the people of rank in the city went for solitary walks. From there one came to the *Schöntal*, another gently sloping park from which a grove of plane trees led into an extended wooded area called the *Fasanerie*. All this may have now changed somewhat, due to the industrial development of the area; at that time it was idyllicly beautiful. For philosophical studies, moreover, the library, the *Königliche Schloßbibliotek* in Aschaffenburg, was a very great help; its directors – until 1866 the good old Lyceum Professor Merkel, a friend of the Brentano family, and later my family friend the Gymnasium Professor Englert – gladly satisfied our occasional desires for new acquisitions. The considerable philosophy collection owed its existence to the fact that at the beginning of the century Aschaffenburg, which was the winter residence of the Elector of Mainz, also accommodated the University of Mainz until the city united with Bavaria (1814), and the well-known physician-philosopher Windischmann, then librarian, had seen to the expansion of the collection during this very active period in philosophy. Schelling had writings by Plotinus, Giordano Bruno, Kepler, and Lamark sent to Würzburg from Aschaffenburg.[2]

The Brentanos' house, in which Clemens and his brother Christian, the philosopher's father, died and where the five children grew up, had now become very quiet. It was occupied only by his venerable mother, with whom I also became acquainted, and who remained attached to me and my family by the bonds of true friendship until her death in 1882. She, too, had a striking appearance; she was a beautiful, dark-eyed old woman with expressive features, who was dear, sympathetic and lively in her behaviour, and not insensitive to the beauty of the world, but who was also imbued to her inmost core with a religious disposition and religious interests. Day after day, winter and summer, she could be seen walking to 6 o'clock mass in the Capuchin Church, which was quite a distance away. She was at the centre of all Catholic charitable activities in the city, but also had many connections elsewhere. I often heard the names of the Mainz canons, Moufang and Heinrich; the latter, especially, was very close to the Brentanos. How much freedom the children must have enjoyed, despite the religious tradition of the house, is seen in their varied development, especially in that of Lujo, the

2. See A. Dyroff, *C.J. Windischmann und sein Kreis* (1919), pp. 19ff., 71.

economist, whose natural disposition was focused very early in completely different and worldly directions.

Brentano now also came to visit our family frequently. He felt at home there and was excellent company. His storytelling blood would come to the fore, and he knew the funniest and most comical stories, at which he himself would laugh heartily. He had a good tenor voice and would give singularly pathetic but diverse performances of gruesome ballads such as the one about the Grandmother Snake-Cook from *Des Knaben Wunderhorn* that gave everyone the creeps.[3]

Lectures, life and influence, 1866–70

Let us now return to his teaching activities at Würzburg. The history of philosophy was followed in the spring of 1867 by metaphysics; autumn 1867, history of philosophy; spring 1868, metaphysics (five hours a week); autumn 1868, history of philosophy, metaphysics I (transcendental philosophy and ontology); spring 1869, metaphysics II (theology and cosmology) plus public lectures on August Comte and positivism in present-day France; autumn 1869, deductive and inductive logic, history of philosophy I (ancient); spring 1870, metaphysics, history of philosophy II (medieval and modern).

One can already see from this survey how wrong it would be to view psychology as the starting point of his systematic philosophising. Metaphysics was the beginning and end of his thought. This, of course, would not keep psychology from at times assuming a place in the foreground of his work, and this was in fact what happened. But in his innermost soul metaphysical interests predominated over all others. 'I am at the moment wholly a metaphysician,' he wrote to me from Vienna in 1886. 'I must confess that, after having been exclusively a psychologist for a few years, the change makes me happy.' I still have a good set of notes in shorthand from the first metaphysics lectures. Here it is not the Scholastics such as St Thomas Aquinas who are his point of departure, but Aristotle, whom he also praised in his inaugural thesis, along with Dante, as the master of those who know. As highly as he esteemed St Thomas, and as well as he knew the other Scholastics, they were to him only fellow students and their opinions carried no authoritative weight for him. His attitude toward Aristotle was different. He knew that authority, as such, may play no role in philosophy, and he maintained that with regard to Aristotle too, but he had found so much truth and profundity in the Aristotelian doctrines that he granted them a certain *prima facie* probability, a certain right to be heard, which did not rule out examination and rejection. Many people today have a similar attitude toward Kant. In this sense and in this sense only was the Stagirite his highest authority, and his admiration for him did not lessen in the course of time despite the fact that he diverged more and more from Aristotle's doctrines, but became even greater, as can be seen in his very last writings.

3. By his uncle, Clemens Brentano, and his uncle by marriage, Achim von Arnim, the Romantic poets.

His association with Aristotle and the process of freeing himself from it can be closely observed in his first metaphysics lectures. The beginning, definition, value, and place among the sciences is like a commentary on the first chapter of Aristotle's *Metaphysics*. He speaks briefly, too, about the relationship to belief. Supernatural theology is described as *stella rectrix* but not as the indispensible prerequisite and help of metaphysics. But we immediately encountered a new creation of Brentano's own in the first part of the metaphysics lectures ('On Transcendental Philosophy'). The name and its general tendency are reminiscent of Kant, but Brentano himself had in mind Aristotle's defence of the principles of reason in *Metaphysics* IV, 3ff. He first collected the most penetrating objections of the new sceptics, which he rendered even more incisive, against external and inner perception, the axioms, derived knowledge, and against knowledge in general; he then showed the internal impossibility of absolute scepticism, stated the positive basis for knowledge, and finally gave the solution to the objections. This procedure, which he followed in more or less the same way for all of the larger investigations, is reminiscent first of all of St Thomas, who, in every article, first sets out the objections, then the '*sed contra*', then the positive formulation in the *corpus articuli*, and finally the solution to the objections. But the High Scholastics themselves did nothing but imitate Aristotle who, in the investigations he carried out, started from *aporiai*, then established the foundation, developed the theory, and finished with the answers to the *aporiai*. In fact, this procedure has much to be said for it, as a method of research as well as of exposition, provided it is not used in the stereotyped Scholastic manner, but only occasionally for larger investigations and always varied to fit the subject-matter and the requirements of the present context. Through the vivid illustration of difficulties interest is aroused, the ground broken, and the whole subject-matter is filled with that dramatic tension that Brentano's listeners always experienced.

During these first metaphysics lectures this inner tension was present not only in the listeners but also in the teacher. While we were still in Würzburg, Brentano admitted to me that he had prepared the lectures from hand to mouth, so to speak, and put a tremendous strain on his nerves in so doing. He would raise the sharpest objections against the possibility of knowledge, without knowing exactly how he was going to answer them, trusting only that he would.

Of special interest from his epistemological point of view is the most general *aporia* about knowledge, and its solution. It runs as follows: 'My ability to know is not something I can blindly trust, but neither is it something I can prove. In order to prove it I would have to make use of the same ability to know whose reliability I want to prove. Therefore, I can never be reliably certain of any knowledge.' The answer runs: 'I can also trust my insight. If a proposition is directly evident, one does not need to prove the knowledge nor the ability to know. To a certain extent it is true, however, that we fall back on the reliability of our powers of knowledge, insofar as we use them; but we do not use them as a premise, so there is no question of circular reasoning here.'

Brentano designated the logical axioms and the facts of inner perception as directly evident knowledge. The necessity of concurring with them stems not from a blind psychological compulsion, but from their own inner self-illuminating *Evidenz*. To say, 'I could be so constructed that I must agree with what is false', is the same thing as saying, 'I am uncertain whether that which I am certain of might not be false'. In his large lecture class on metaphysics in 1869 this was further explained: 'We could boldly say that neither nature nor God deceived us here. Even God cannot make it evident to us that red is a sound or $2 + 1 = 4$. His will would thereby contradict itself. He who denies Him this power does not deny His perfection but rather His imperfection.' Brentano here alludes to a well-known scholastic controversy on which Descartes took an affirmative and Leibniz a negative position. Brentano, therefore, is in agreement with Leibniz. He infers, in addition, that the evident is true not only for our intellects but for any possible intellect because it is only the illumination of the matter itself. Thus he was worlds away from psychologism, which tries to derive logical necessity from psychological necessity.

Brentano, then, in the ontology section, thoroughly justified his deviations from Aristotle as regards the doctrine of the categories, the distinction between matter and form, and others. In every case he deviated from his point of departure only little by little, and only if there were compelling reasons for doing so. He devoted special attention to proofs for the existence of God, in order to establish in a logically compelling manner the conclusiveness of tracing all phenomena back to a Godly source, in spite of Kant's verdict, which had been ignored by his successors and by Lotze and Fechner as well.

Because I plunged with the greatest intensity into philosophy and the natural sciences, during the first half of 1867, Brentano considered me already mature enough to become acquainted with other important philosophers, and he advised me to go to Lotze at Göttingen in order further to pursue and take a degree in the natural sciences there. This I proceeded to do and I came back in August 1868 with a doctorate. A more important gain was the personal friendship of Lotze. In the meantime, Brentano and I continued to correspond. Even when away I felt the guiding hand, the watchful eye, and the deep concern of my teacher. We have demonstrated this already. Lotze's views, with which Brentano agreed only in part, were a major subject of our scientific correspondence. He also reported, however, on further developments in his own metaphysical lectures, especially with regard to space and to causality. The letters contain nothing more detailed on this subject, however. On the other hand, I have detailed notes on the lectures of 1868 to 1870, which I once again personally attended.

Before I characterise these lectures, there are some students who should be mentioned who established closer contact with Brentano during these and the following years at Würzburg. The autumn of 1868 found Anton Marty from Schwyz in Switzerland among his students and thus began the lifelong friendship between us and our teacher. A third member of the group at that time was the Rhinelander van Endert, a clever man with a pleasantly dry sense of humour. Later on, I believe, he became Canon of Cologne Cathedral, but we lost touch with each other. Because the three of us always sat together during the two-semester-long metaphysics course (in which the participants exhibited much less endurance than before in the face of the difficult detailed investigations which were extended to extraordinary lengths), Brentano called us The Three Kings. He loved to make such good-natured little jokes from time to time. Later, in Vienna, he introduced one of his students, who was especially enthused about the evident nature of consciousness of the self, as 'His Evidenz the Inner Perception'.

It was not until some years later, probably in 1870, that Herman Schell, a serious and thorough intellect and later the leader of German Modernism, came to study with Brentano. It is Brentano to whom he owes his philosophical education and his free though not fully worked-out mode of thought, and to whom he dedicated his book on the unity of the soul in Aristotle. They kept in touch both in person and through correspondence.

Johannes Wolff, too, joined Brentano at the beginning of the 1870s and was sent by him to Göttingen, when I was teaching there. He wrote, under my direction, his work on Plato's dialectic, and later published a work in psychology, *Das Bewußtsein und sein Objekt* (Consciousness and its Object), which was not without merit, and he was appointed instructor of philosophy at Trier and later at Freiburg (Switzerland). Several letters from Brentano to me about Wolff testify to the degree and extent to which Brentano concerned himself with the further education of his young friend. He inquired into and gave advice about the most minute details.

Other students of Brentano from that time who later became known as writers and teachers were Schütz (Trier), Kirschkamp (Bonn), and Commer (Vienna), Schell's opponent.

Our seventh Chancellor, Count Georg von Hertling, was also one of Brentano's students at that time and was always considered as such by him, although I do not know whether he had ever attended his lectures. He was a cousin of Brentano and often came to Aschaffenburg at that time, where a branch of the von Hertling family lived, and thus he associated a lot with Brentano both there and in Würzburg. He studied philosophy just as Brentano had done, but two or three years after him, in Münster, Munich, and in Berlin with Trendelenburg. He got his degree with a dissertation on Aristotle's ontology (*De notione unius*) and in 1871 published a thorough book *Materie und Form und die Definition der Seele bei Aristotles* (*Matter and Form and the Definition of the Soul in Aristotle*), which is directly connected with and is based upon Brentano's *Psychologie des Aristotles*. There is no doubt about the fact that Brentano's example and intellectual work during the time he was in the Church exerted a very great influence on von Hertling. The promulgation of the dogma of papal infallibility in 1870 presented von Hertling with a difficult choice, and from then on he and Brentano went their separate ways. I have only fragmentary knowledge of how their personal relationship later developed, and am not in a position to speak about it.

In the autumn of 1868, Brentano again lectured on the history of philosophy, and in these lectures the detailed elaborations of Aristotle and the Scholastics were particularly valuable to me. Brentano ventured to penetrate far deeper into the subtlest details of these already very subtle systems than is usually the case in lectures. The considerably elaborated metaphysics course, which he was now giving for the third time, captivated us above all. He divided the material into two semesters, and lectured five hours a week each term. My notes comprise a quarto volume, in shorthand, of 822 pages. The erudition and the acuteness öf the presentation always astounds me, even now. The entire course was designed and arranged with the skill of an architect – every detail expanding itself into a completed whole; in this it was remiscent of the great Scholastic *Summa*, and, along with them, of the masterpieces of medieval architecture. Among his investigations only the most important should be mentioned, namely, those of space, time and motion, especially the exemplary exposition of Zeno's paradoxes; the theory of the Euclidian parallel axioms, a theme which was not as current among philosophers then as it is today; the debates over physical, metaphysical and logical parts; the original justification of the Law of Causality by means of 'immanent induction' (infinite probability derived from the concept of change). In addition should be mentioned the extremely careful elaboration of the teleological mode of thought, where he distinguished sharply between the purely factual, for example, the appearance of an all-penetrating experience, and attempts at explanation. He discussed the dysteleologians by giving a destructive critique of Vogt's superficialities with regard to the eye and Lange's with regard to the waste of seed; he then went on to the theory of evolution which he agreed with in principle but rejected in Darwin's form, and employed the principles of probability as regards the positive formulation and inferences in a much more extensive way than had been the case in his first metaphysics lectures. The decisive importance which Brentano attributed to the mathematical laws of probability, to which he then granted an important place in logic too, dates from this period.

Incidental to the concept of reality, Brentano cast side glances at the theological problems of the Trinity and Incarnation, and sought to show how one could cope with them without direct internal contradictions; but still it came very close to that.

I do not know what induced Brentano to give an additional public lecture on Comte and positivism in the spring of 1869. Perhaps English empiricism (his metaphysics lectures showed that he had studied Mill's *Logic* thoroughly) and Mill's piece on Comte are what spurred him on. This could be seen as an initial step in his interest in foreign endeavours which soon was to assume even greater dimensions. Furthermore, Comte's personality and the history of its development, as well as the doctrine of positivism, which was as yet not so well known in Germany, deserved such attention. Obviously there was no lack of critical opposition.

In October 1869 I actually entered the Würzburg Seminary and began theological studies, but at the same time I continued to attend Brentano's lectures. In the Autumn of 1869 he lectured on logic for the first time and, in addition, on the history of philosophy I, which was now also divided into two large lectures. The announced logic lectures did not begin, however, until after Christmas; in the preceeding months he devoted twenty-eight lecture hours to the treatment of the immortality of the soul. He argued there (I have almost verbatim notes of this, too) first on the foundations of Atomism, but only *ad hominem* because he did not agree with them; then he moved on to a comparison of human and animal functions which led him for the first time in his lectures to extended psychological investigations, and finally he came to the conclusion that a part of the human soul is to be viewed as something spiritual, much like Aristotle had represented it. It was precisely from the essential similarity of the structure of the brain in men and in anthropoids, on which the materialists rely, that he drew the conclusion that the undeniably powerful differences between mental lives, whose roots he sought, along with Aristotle, in conceptual thought, must have an immaterial substrate.

It was a beautifully finished exposition, although he later gave up this standpoint in several essential regards in that he no longer ascribed the sensory functions to the body as subject, and in that, on the other hand, he switched from the indeterminism he advocated here to determinism. Both of these changes may have occurred as early as his first years in Vienna. It is noteworthy that the separation of affirmation from mere presentation, and the threefold division of mental functions into presentation, judgement, and desire (as he then called the fundamental class comprising the emotions, following Aristotle) had already been put forward here. This was probably his conviction by 1866–7, when he had special words of praise in his history of philosophy lectures for William of Ockham and his distinction between the *actus judicandi* and the *actus apprehendendi*.

Then came the logic: and here Brentano plunged head-first into a complete revision of the old traditions. He took as his point of departure considerations about thoughts and their expression in language, and distinguished, with regard to both names and statements, what they express (the mental functions which are made known through them) from what they mean. A statement means that something is to be affirmed or denied. Brentano called this the content of judgement. It can be expressed linguistically in the infinitive form or in that-clauses. This concept, which I later designated as 'fact', is important, among other things, because the whole class of indirect judgements ('It is possible, necessary, probable, true, false, that . . .') relates, as Brentano then expressed it, to properties of such contents of judgements. Brentano called the totality of the presentations upon which the judgement was based the matter of judgement. The form or quality of the judgement, finally, is affirmation or denial, i.e. acceptance or rejection of the matter of the judgement. On this Brentano based his doctrine of the existential proposition as the simplest form of statement to which categorical statements and all others can be reduced. We get then only universal negative and particular affirmative judgements, there being no contrast between judgements except this contradictory one, and all judgements, when correctly expressed (therefore, for example, the so-called universal affirmative as universal negative) are simply convertible. So Brentano was led to an overthrow and an extraordinary simplification of logical theory as a whole, which we in the audience listened to with growing astonishment and with admiration for the inexorable consequences of the presentation.[4] He went no further this time because the semester had come to an end.

4. There is a noteworthy similarity to Leibniz here, who (as has already been pointed out by W. Freytag in *Archiv für die gesammte Psychologie*, vol. 33, p. 140), in his *Generales inquisitiones de analysi notionum et veritatum* sect. 11321, of 1686, had already shown the convertability of all categorical statements into existential propositions in exactly the same way. This work, which was only brought to light by Couturat, and

1870: The transformation of his religious convictions

During the spring of 1870 Brentano experienced a revolution of another sort, which was to be of even greater consequence to him: the transformation of his religious convictions.

In this regard we must make a clear separation between the events in his religious life and the logical and metaphysical considerations which made him aware of the internal impossibilities in the teachings of the Church, at which he surely would have arrived sooner or later, even without any external stimulus.

Brentano had never been a supporter of the Jesuit movement in the Church, either in theory or in practice. The sophistical interpretations of 'probability' in moral matters, already scourged by Pascal in the *Lettres Provinciales*, were rejected by him in the same way as were the attempts to mediate in the theological disputes over God's knowledge ·and influence. Above all, however, he objected to the Order's thirst for power. In the late summer of 1869, papal infallibility had become a burning question. The Jesuits used all their influence and power to bring about its formal declaration. In Germany there was strong opposition, and not merely from Döllinger and his supporters, but also from the bishops such as Ketteler in Mainz and Hefele in Rottenburg, as well as from the learned Benedictine Abbot Haneberg in Munich. No less opposed were prominent foreign Catholics such as Montalembert, Gratry, Bishop Strossmayer in Hungary, and Lord Acton, among others. The German bishops held a conference in Fulda. Brentano was prevailed upon by Ketteler, Bishop of Mainz, to work up a position paper on the subject. He read this paper, for which he had made detailed historical studies, to me in Aschaffenburg on the *Buschweg* during the summer vacation in 1869. It treated in a concise but impressive way the blunders made in earlier times by popes speaking *ex cathedra*, as well as other arguments against the doctrine of infallibility. It is said to have been highly influential. Obviously these Church matters aroused Brentano very much, as they did all Catholics who took an interest in the fate of the Church, and the news of the incidents at the Council in Rome (Ketteler is even said to have prostrated himself) were received with the greatest attention.

Certainly these external circumstances provided a psychological motivation for Brentano to become absorbed anew in the logical difficulties posed by the mysteries of the Church, which he, as we mentioned before, had just managed to skirt in his latest metaphysics lectures. In fact believing Catholics are generally prohibited from doubting, and the sinfulness of any

---

published in 1903, to which Leibniz himself appended the remark 'hic egregie progressus sum', was unknown to Brentano. With his respect for Leibniz, he would have certainly approached him for support of his bold doctrine, just as in the case of his doctrine of judgement as a basic function along with presentation and feeling, he looked to Descartes. Couturat is wrong, however (*La Logique Leibniz*, pp. 19, 350) when he attributes the re-discovery of this doctrine, as well as the explanation of the invalidity of the modes Darapti, Felapton, Bramantip, and Fesapo, to MacColl in 1878; both had previously been taught by Brentano and had been published in 1874.

such doubt which is not immediately removed from one's soul constitutes one of the strongest bulwarks with which the Church surrounds itself. But sometimes there comes a point when inner necessity becomes too great, and then the rule of reason prevails. This must have happened to Brentano in the spring of 1870. At first I did not know of these inner battles, since I was living behind seminary walls and had only occasional visits from Brentano. I am certain that the reason he did not tell me was that he did not want to disturb my peace of mind. Yet on 15 March 1870 I received a peculiar letter from Aschaffenburg in which he suggested my leaving the seminary, explaining that in the light of recent developments I could not count on getting a state professorship if I became a priest. But this made no impression on me whatsoever. I am inclined to believe now that by this time Brentano's inner crisis had developed to such an extent that he wanted to deter me at all costs from the decisive step. But he had not yet broken with the faith; this is clear from the rest of the letter.

On the other hand, on 29 April, having come back from a vacation in Aschaffenburg, he visited me and raised certain doubts about the dogmas of the Trinity and Incarnation which seemed insoluble to him despite all the usual distinctions between substance, subsistence, substitution, nature, person and hypostasis. On 3 May he voiced further doubts about the concept of faith itself, as it was defined by the Church. I did not know how to resolve them either. What I felt when I saw that this time he was serious, and what I went through during the following days and nights, does not belong here. But I can understand his own condition during this time; he had had, after all, from childhood on, even stronger ties to religious convictions than I had, he was the hope and pride of his orthodox mother, and the bearer of that frightful *character indelibilis* which was yet to cause so many difficulties for him. In order to facilitate the transition both for him and myself, I did not leave the seminary until 18 July 1870, and the only reason I gave was that I no longer felt the call to the priesthood, which, after all, was not difficult for others to understand. Fortunately, I had not as yet taken any kind of vows, and so I could go as I had come. Because Lotze, who was informed of all this, warmly welcomed my intention of joining the faculty at Göttingen, I wrote a habilitations thesis on the mathematical axioms during the vacation in Munich, and became a *Dozent* by October.

Later, when Brentano's defection became known, all possible suspicions or theories about his motives were put forward. There are always rumours in the Church in such cases, because, according to the Church's view, the loss of God's grace, which forms the very basis of the condition of faith, must somehow stem from one's disposition and way of life. He was said to have intended to marry, which in some cases of this sort is undeniably true; he was said to be pursuing ambitious plans to curry favour with those in power, etc. Others started the rumour that he was insane, and this even appeared in the newspapers. Somehow the scandal had to be alleviated.

But the truth was that it happened just as I have described it here. Brentano's motives were of a theoretical nature, they were simply the result of internal contradictions in the Church's doctrine which even his penetrating mind, after years of wrestling with the problem, could not resolve. For quite a while after his decision he did not tire of carefully reexamining the inferences which had brought it about, nor of trying every conceivable possibility for a way out. On 19 November he wrote to me in Göttingen of an *enneakilemma*, a nine-termed disjunction, in which he had summarised the contradictions in the dogma of the Trinity. He also talked to me about it later. For myself these many-faceted considerations were not as convincing as the simpler ones regarding the concept of faith, the reason being that the continual exertions necessary to maintain the absolute certainty, claimed to be essential for the condition of faith, particularly in view of the rather deficient and contradictory records we have about historical events, represented for me, like so many other believers, a psychological experience which continued to disturb me. But Brentano was of a thoroughly intellectual nature. His disposition and self-training had completely subjugated his emotions and his will to the rule of reason. I have never known anyone who was like this to such an extent. However, he in no way lacked tenderness or intensity of feeling; on the contrary, all of us who associated with him knew how soft-hearted he was. What he was to individuals, what he was to whole families, how he committed himself whole-heartedly to help those suffering need or injustice – about this much could be said, if it were not that he preferred to remain silent about it. And so religion, above all, had taken possession of him. But no matter how much he allowed its mysteries to affect him, he never dropped the reins of *Logistikon* whose function it is to guide the chariot of the soul. Here too remained the disciple of Socrates, Plato and Aristotle, whose examples guided him no less than those of the Christian saints.

None of the things that alienate thousands of people, during their early youth, from the Church and religion in general – such as the daily spectacle of worldly and all-too-human clerics, the horrors of the persecution of heretics, and the scandalous doings of the popes in centuries past – none of these would have had any power over him. One could still manage to cope with them by drawing distinctions as they are taught in school. Nor were the historical difficulties of the threatening dogma of infallibility the primary reason for this defection. They did not carry the decisive weight with him that they did with many thinking Catholics at that time; had this not been the case he would have waited with his inner decision until the dogma was actually declared, which was not until 2 August. Those who were more historically than philosophically minded saw themselves forced to renounce the Pope and to turn to Old Catholicism, but remained, for the rest, on Christian and Catholic grounds, while Brentano's considerations led him to an inner break not just with Catholicism but with Christianity in general. The following year he was asked to sign the letter to Döllinger and to join the reform movement. He declined. Protestantism, too, seemed only a half-way measure; as far as I know he never considered converting to it.

Döllinger, too, was certainly of a theoretical nature; one can even say he was a man dominated by reason. But for him the weight of the arguments tipped the scale in the opposite direction. He was by nature not a philosopher but an historian. In the case of Old Catholicism, the philosopher prevailed over the historian even in historical matters: the new Church could not sustain itself, its vitality diminished with the abatement of the *Kulturkampf* and of governmental good will. An essentially Catholic Church without the papacy as a unifying force seemed to be impossible after all.

Brentano spent the vacation in 1870 in Munich where he opened his heart to the noble Haneberg, whom I also met through him. Haneberg advised him provisionally not to make public his altered views for the time being, and this is what happened. To my knowledge Brentano did not seek out Döllinger at this time, whose student Brentano had been and whom he knew personally as well.

The war, with its battles and the victories of our troops in France during these months did not, I must admit, inspire in us such great feelings of patriotism as they did in the large majority of the people. There were still people in southern Germany who could not forget 1866. Both my father and I were among them. Even though we admired the offensive strength of our troops under Prussian leadership, we deplored the political dominance of Prussia and we had nothing more than a certain affection for Bismarck. Only later did I begin gradually to change my attitude. For Brentano, however, Bismarck was always Germany's evil spirit. He was and remained a supporter of the 'greater Germany solution'. He could never get over the exclusion of Austria and saw in Bismarck nothing but the representative of contemptible power politics. The memory of the way his father was treated by the Prussian government during the bishop's conflict in Cologne (the details of which I do not know), may well have played a part in it, for he had a·very strong feeling for the history and tradition of his family. That his cousin and student, von Hertling, would take over Bismark's office in the most difficult times no one then would ever have imagined.

According to the laws of the Church, Brentano could not resign from his spiritual offices without at the same time leaving the Church altogether. This formal resignation and declaration of withdrawal he postponed for a full three years. It was not until the early part of 1873, in Würzburg, that he did it. Until then he wore priestly garb and for a long time he behaved in the prescribed manner. When he had no other choice he said mass, the ceremonies of which he performed in a way similar to that in which the more liberal Protestant ministers approach the traditional church formulas – inwardly extolling the Highest in spirit and in truth, without worrying too much about the spoken word. For a time he even forced himself to do the prescribed daily reading in his breviary, even though he could have given this up without anyone noticing it. He had always regarded the breviary as a very difficult burden, and he considered it to be one of the strongest ties with which the Church binds the clergy, in that it imposes the strict obligation that they, day by day, regardless of mood and external hinderances, immerse themselves in the prescribed material or, following a general pious intention, fill up the time with mere lip motions. In order now to be able to say to himself that he did not regard the release from this bond as the direct reward of his transformation, and that this in no way was one of the motives for his change, he continued to bear these obligations of his own free will for a considerable time afterward.

There are two main reasons why he waited so long before he submitted his formal notice of withdrawal: consideration for his mother and for his spiritual mother the Church. The effect this step must have had on his mother we need not stress, at least not to those who know the strong

Catholic views concerning apostates. In addition, there were some friends of his such as Haneberg who were favourably disposed toward the Church and with whom he had talked about the problem. They exerted some pressure on him because they feared the scandal, the harm that could be done to the Church, which at this time was already experiencing such a great loss of esteem and members due to the conflict over infallibility and the consequences thereof. But what facilitated and enabled Brentano to persevere in this situation, and what made it possible for him to come to terms to some extent with Church customs, were the religious values that remained. All his life he continued to be deeply religious and had complete trust in God. But he also continued to preserve a high esteem for Christianity and the Catholic Church in particular, as regards the contributions that its institutions and doctrines have made toward the formation of character, despite all the abuses and superstitions. For this reason, even later he never attacked or scorned the Church, and the Church authorities, on their part, for political reasons avoided solemn excommunication or any such measures which would have challenged him to battle, a challenge which he would have doubtless taken up fearlessly and with all his might. For nothing was more foreign to him than human fear.

Connected with this interest he still had in religious affairs was the extraordinary importance that Brentano ascribed all his life to the elaboration of the philosophical concept of God and the proof of His reality. In view of the enormous differences among the views of God within which men can be good or even pious, agreement on these last questions of knowledge seemed to me, later on, not only harder and harder to achieve, but also no longer all that necessary. I do not want to imply that to develop the concept as sharply as possible, to the furthest attainable boundaries of the scientific standpoint, is not an important goal. The metaphysical treatises he left behind will teach us how far his untiring contemplation carried him in this direction. Brentano's conception of the high mission of philosophy for the education of mankind was intensified by his renunciation of positive faith. He hoped, like Cicero in his time, that the development of philosophy would create, if not exactly a new religion, then at least a renewal of religious consciousness without the admixture of the statutory and the confessional. He hoped that the impressions of philosophical knowledge in the consciousness of the educated would be transmitted through them to the consciousness of the masses. We both continued to be convinced for years that the philosopher whose whole thought, feeling and will is directed toward this task must forego even the thought of marriage. Brentano was the first one to break, theoretically at first, with this self-imposed dogma. I remember that he admitted having some hesitation on this point on an excursion in the *Bergstraße* in 1874 or 1875; this time, however, I cannot say that it was painful to agree with him.

From the shipwreck of his faith Brentano also salvaged the habit of contemplation, of which we have heard him say he would rather die than be without. Now it was no longer specifically Christian ideas and events, but the whole area of religious, great and noble thoughts and deeds of humanity in general to which it extended. He still liked to base his contemplation on the familiar writings of a Thomas à Kempis (who was also a favourite of

Paulson and was the last thing he read), of a Pascal, and a Fenelon, and even descriptions of the lives of the saints such as that of Vincent du Paul; he also recommended to me the continuation of these exercises. 'With Fenelon's simple, beautiful meditations I refresh myself daily. Today his considerations "*De l'emploi du temps*" have once again clearly shown my carelessness' (8 November 1871). To me, the *Confessions* and *Soliloquies* of St Augustine, Epictetus and Plato were dear companions; the hours of meditation were soon replaced by the general state of mind in which every one who is serious in his philosophising must find himself every hour of the day. And Brentano will have had the same experience, I am sure.

It seemed a difficult question whether Marty, too, who had returned to his home in Schwyz at Easter 1870, in order to enter the priesthood there in compliance with his own, his family's and his bishop's wishes, should be informed of the changes in Brentano's views. We often spoke of this, and it seemed to me the right thing to do to tell him everything; but Brentano had reservations because Marty's case could not be kept as inconspicuous as mine, and his future would be completely called into question (he had already become a Lyceum professor in Schwyz). Furthermore, it was possible that he would not succeed in convincing Marty by letter of the new ideas and would only precipitate a crisis of conscience. These were, at least as I remember them, the operative considerations. It was not until 1873 – I do not know exactly whether with or without suggestions from Brentano's side, but at any rate after he had learned of Brentano's change – that Marty himself was led to doubt and to the renunciation of his religious standpoint. He came to Aschaffenburg for some time where, however, Brentano's mother was not allowed to see him; he took his doctoral examination in Göttingen in 1875, and in the same year he received an appointment at the · University of Chernovtsy in the Ukraine. Brentano's reserve with regard to Marty is to me even today not wholly understandable, and certainly if he had foreseen what Marty would later become to him and to our science, he would not have hesitated to spare him the tremendous complications which his entrance into the priesthood caused him for the rest of his life. How much Marty suffered under them, how heroically he bore the renunciations and the external restraints which were connected with it, is well known to his friends. He himself must have well appreciated the importance of Brentano's practical considerations; in any case he never reproached him.

Experiences in Würzburg, autumn 1870 to summer 1873

We will now pursue Brentano's life in Würzburg from 1870 to 1873. I can no longer report as an eye-witness because during these years I taught in Göttingen. But a lively correspondence and frequent visits during vacations preserved our relationship. First, in order to make his position and the difficulties with it more comprehensible, something should be mentioned about the composition of the faculty and student community at Würzburg at that time, as I myself came to know it after 1873 when I became a professor there.

Würzburg attracted medical students and Catholic theologians in particular. The latter constituted a large part of the student body in the philosophy lectures because Catholic theology always placed great value on philosophical preparation – of course only if it did not contradict Church doctrine. Also, the already mentioned governmental requirement that one had to take certain general courses in the first year helped to provide a large audience. As far as the medical students were concerned, even then they did not usually study philosophy in the narrow sense, but preferred the natural sciences. But Brentano succeeded, then as well as later, even in attracting medical students occasionally, and he considered it an especially desirable achievement to win them over to his convictions.

Among the faculty members he established friendly relations with the physiologist Fick, an amiable character with a philosophical mind who actually esteemed Schopenhauer and Kant above all but who had an interest in every meaningful human and scientific phenomenon. Almost the same was true of the chemist Wislicenus, that wonderful, religious and yet free-thinking human who later became a very close friend of mine; he, however, did not work at Würzburg prior to 1872. Also the Germanist Lexer, the jurist Risch, who was the head of' the administration of the university, and the mathematician Prym took an objective and benevolent position toward Brentano. Kölliker, who headed the medical school and was especially influential in the Senate and in the Ministry as well, seems to have taken an essentially wait-and-see attitude; he was of a cool, pondering nature and had no natural bent for philosophy. In the faculty of theology Brentano had a good friend, the honourable, mild, exegete Schegg, who later, even after Brentano's public withdrawal from the Church, continued to respect and trust him. The imposing apologist Hettinger, a papal prelate, was also very astute in worldly matters and would have gladly acted as a mediator. He was quite conscious of the difficulties in the dogmas even if, for his part, he overcame them with more elegance and literary embellishment than thoroughness. But naturally that good work could not succeed. As for the rest, the faculty of theology, among whom we find the tall, thin and thoroughly learned Hergenröther, who later became a cardinal and the director of the Vatican Library, was essentially influenced by the Roman-Jesuitical trend. As Brentano's friends, let me mention, in addition, the history professor, Ludwig; the library director, Ruland, a man of great character although clerical-minded; and, in particular, the teacher of constitutional law, Edel, the well-known parliamentarian who had for decades exerted great influence on the internal political life of Bavaria. Brentano had very close personal ties with him, which most likely went back to their Aschaffenburg relations. All his life he remained a true and devoted friend of one of Edel's daughters, Frau Hauser, and her whole family.

The majority of Würzburg professors, however, were certainly either hostile or mistrustful of Brentano. In predominantly Catholic cities in Germany there is, as a rule, a Protestant and a radical anti-religious party, both of which are spurred on to action by their opposition to the ruling majority. These parties at first considered Brentano a Scholastic who had to be opposed. When I passed a scholarship examination in 1867 with the botanist Schenk, he warned me in a well-meaning way against Brentano, the Scholastic. Later, when Brentano's altered views became known, a more or less strong mistrust of him remained alive in these liberal circles, and because he only associated with a few, and opened up to even fewer, it could not have been otherwise. To Hoffman, who was very much opposed to the Ultramontanists (*Blitzstrahlen wider den Vatkian*) he was nothing but a kind of Jesuit in disguise.

The Bishop of Würzburg, Stahl, was no fanatic and acted, as far as I know, with great restraint throughout. In Aschaffenburg Brentano found friendly sympathy, though no agreement, from Hessler, the prefect of the seminary, and from the religion teacher Schlör, who later became the Bishop of Würzburg; the excellent chaplain Huhn, a thoroughly practical man who later became a pastor in Munich, could not bring himself to understand how one could torture one's reason so, since, after all, the blessed influence of the Church, its survival of all storms, and so many other obvious facts testified to its divinity.

It was felt at the University of Würzburg – all the more in view of Brentano's great success as a teacher – that Hoffman, whose effectiveness had decreased tremendously, or rather had vanished completely, was no longer sufficient as the only permanently employed philosopher, and people began to come up with suggestions. Lotze, and then Überweg and F.A. Lange, were possible choices for *professor ordinarius*; Brentano's appointment as *professor extraordinarius* was the subject of much discussion.[5] Lotze himself warmly endorsed Brentano's appointment. But they did not want to go so far as to propose a cleric as *ordinarius* in philosophy. Brentano's letters show that he was thinking, as early as the end of the winter of 1870–1, of leaving Würzburg if they did not give him a professorship. At Easter he saw Döllinger, whom he liked more than he had expected, and he also met Lord Acton. 'I did not associate with the Anti-infallibilists who were there at the same time. Naturally they know how infinitely far I am from the infallibility dogma. But I do not trust these men. And I am equally annoyed by governmental despotism which is in no way inferior to the Church's brand.' But these very reservations toward the anti-infallibility letter to Döllinger aroused suspicions that he believed in infallibility. He found, however, that even if the suspicion were correct, it would be no hindrance to

---

5. I draw upon Brentano's letter for this and the following information about the question of his appointment. It has, however, been confirmed by the comparison with the files of the faculty and the Senate, which Professor Chroust was kind enough to undertake at my request. The details of these discussions seem peculiar enough, but I do not want to go into them here, for such things are not uncommon in university proceedings. Only one remark of the faculty should be mentioned, which forms a strange contrast to the above-quoted enthusiastic praise of Brentano. On 20 December 1870, the faculty declared by a vote of 6 to 5 that Brentano's candidacy for appointment as *professor extraordinarius* could not be supported, 'because he has neither received an offer nor exhibited eminent scientific or practical achievements'. Five faculty members, however, submitted minority opinions in his favour. The Senate majority took the position of one of these reports; certain reservations did indeed exist concerning his spiritual position, but the Senate stressed his 'independent, anti-Ultramontanist attitude, for which there was ample testmony'. It would support his appointment, but only after a new *ordinarius* had been appointed.

his appointment. 'They wouldn't hold it against me if I believed in the Dalai Lama!'

A letter of 14 July 1871 shows that we planned a trip to Switzerland together during the summer vacation, where we wanted to visit Marty, who had just recovered from a serious illness at Easter. These plans never materialised. In November 1871, Brentano was studying English and looked forward to going to England at Easter, primarily to meet Mill. It became increasingly harder for him to hide his convictions. 'Fénelon continues to be my true friend. I could be satisfied if I did not have, from time to time, the powerful longing for the confession of the truth which makes my heart heavy' (5 January 1872).

He asked, then, for a summer vacation to take a trip to England. The government was appealed to because the request threw the university into a great dilemma, particularly because Hoffman, too, had declared that he would not teach for reasons of health. The Senate unanimously supported his appointment. But a friendly colleague, in a great rush, called in an opponent by persuading a certain Dr L., about whom the histories of philosophy are today completely silent, to prepare as quickly as possible for his habilitation in philosophy. Brentano wrote to me on 25 February 1872, in great detail, about his participation in the disputation; and because the report gives a vivid picture of his extraordinary superiority in verbal battles, it should be repeated here verbatim. We will allow the victor his moment of triumph. The effect was that the pathetic tool of intrigue was turned away.

In all haste, bypassing all antecedents, his habilitation was announced for yesterday. He did not visit me, he did not even send me his theses. As a result, I thought at first that I would not go at all. Then I changed my mind. The audience, who knew nothing of the preceeding impoliteness, could have interpreted my absence as hostility. I decided to oppose him. I seized upon two theses, one about the task of logic, the other about the applicability of mathematics to psychology, which the candidate sought to deny in every way and for all eternity. Although I – as I later heard acknowledged on all sides – showed myself in no way aroused or of ill-will, the result was his complete defeat, and I celebrated a more brilliant triumph than I could have anticipated or desired. The students, who attended in great numbers, gradually came alive during the disputation, and sometimes broke into noisy applause, sometimes into laughter. And there's even more. The professors and *Dozents* themselves (and there were rather a lot of them, too, especially from the natural sciences, arts and sciences, and medicine) forgot their decorum to such an extent that they gave the clearest signs of approval. The somewhat lively Fick called over the bench to the physicist Kundt, 'Excellent!' in such a loud voice that even the students in the back of the auditorium heard it, and he replied with equally vigorous gestures. The same was true of Hofrat Wagner. The *Privatdozents* from the medical school looked completely bewildered at first. People had tried very hard indeed to spread the rumour that I am a mystic, that I am a Scholastic, that I am a one-sided Aristotelian, and the like, and both of the theses were such that they offered me the opportunity to destroy their prejudice at its very roots. It was as if all those who had formerly showed enmity toward me suddenly recognised in me an ally, and gloated with unconcealed joy at my victory. Hoffmann himself, who sat in the middle of the people expressing their approval, began to nod approvingly and to smile ... After the final act Fick came up to me and paid me the most flattering compliments, while the poor candidate, abandoned by his friends, stood like a wretched sinner on the podium, so utterly confused that he could not even move. I felt sorry for him and if I had not been occupied with Fick and thus hindered from doing so, I would have gone to him, despite his previous unfriendliness, to say a couple of kind words to him. Hoffman had heaped extravagant praise on the man in his critique of the thesis he had handed in. But after the impression made by this public disputation, according to what I hear, he will most likely be rejected in spite of that.

When I went to Würzburg some weeks later during the Easter holidays, the impression made by this disputation was still the talk of the town. It had won Brentano the great appreciation even of his enemies. But they still considered him a wholly black Ultramontanist, now as before.

Brentano did not actually lecture in the spring of 1872. At Easter he travelled to London. During his absence, on 13 May 1872, he was named *professor extraordinarius*.

The letters from London extend from 22 April to 5 June. First he completed his knowledge of the language and the English philosophical literature. He associated, too, with anti-infallibility Catholics. Letters of introduction from my Göttingen friend William Robertson Smith, who was later to become such a famous free theologian, and who was equally at home in mathematics and in philosophy, led to further acquaintances. He also wanted to visit Newman, the spirited leader of the English Catholics; whether that ever came about is not revealed in the letters. He met Herbert Spencer and later corresponded with him. He became acquainted too with Mivart, the important anti-Darwinian, with whom he concurred in one of the main objections (that the first beginnings of an organ could have no useful value). Mivart told him of Darwin's remark that his book had caused him sleepless nights and that he himself considered his hypothesis inadequate in its exclusivity. (Something similar to this effect can be found in the writings and letters of this almost ideally honest great scientist.)

He now considered the possibility that I might be appointed at Würzburg and we could work together there. During the summer an offer was made to Dilthey, but he declined. Brentano did not agree with the *Kulturkampf* that had broken out in the meantime, nor with the expulsion of the Jesuits, despite his opposition to them.

In the middle of June 1872, he returned to Aschaffenburg, making a brief stop-over on the way to visit Lotze and Baumann in Göttingen. We were invited together to both their homes. Lotze was friendly but taciturn, as he so often was. At the end of June in Aschaffenburg Brentano heard that both there and in Würzburg and in Munich the rumour had begun to spread that he not only rejected Ultramontanism, but the Church and Christianity as well. The minister had remarked to an acquaintance that Brentano was full of hate for the Pope, the Church and Christianity. He now saw that he could not remain for long in Würzburg, and he began to work for my appointment there. At the end of April 1872, I had begun the work on the psychological origin of the idea of space, and with the high degree of concentration that was permitted me I had made such quick progress that in August I was already in the midst of publication. But while the first part was being printed, the second part was still being written, and was much discussed with Brentano during his vacation stop-over in Aschaffenburg in September. By the beginning of November the whole work was finished.

Brentano's inner withdrawal was now gradually becoming known in narrow circles. The *Privatdozent* in theology, Stahl, a cousin of the bishop, held philosophical lectures and agitated against Brentano, whom he represented as an atheist, even though the bishop himself did nothing against him and had not even barred the theologians from his classes. He had submitted his reasons to Hettinger and to Heinrich of Mainz, and they did not know how to refute them. On the other hand, however, the liberals did not trust him either.

The Ministry demanded new suggestions for the position of *professor ordinarius*. People in Vienna, where likewise a *professor ordinarius* had to be appointed, were made aware of Brentano, and private negotiations were already in progress. 'Now as before I wished that I were far away from Würzburg and only your coming here could make it somewhat more bearable for me, because now, even more than before, I shut myself up within my four walls' (19 November 1872). To this there was a postscript: 'My seminar consists of thirteen students, among them philosophers, law students, medical students and theologians.' Then on 30 November 1872:

> At the moment it is quite bearable here, yet the thunderclouds always hover above my head. For you yourself know how many Ultramontanists live in the delusion that I have usurped an Ultramontanist post, and finally the appointment at Giessen (which was likewise much discussed) would be a step further toward emancipation and perhaps also would pave the way for another appointment. As long as I live here and do not express my views in public, and here I may not do otherwise, people elsewhere will take me, if not for an Ultramontanist, at least for a priest.

At Christmas Sigwart had been offered a position at Würzburg, but declined. Later, Lasson from Berlin was suggested but the Ministry declined. In the *Kreuzzeitung* there appeared a pietistic lamentation about Brentano, and Ultramontanist newspapers as well (*Volksfreund, Bonner Reichszeitung*) polemicised against his 'Deism'.

In the meantime we corresponded about problems concerning space, about the observations of cross-eyed people, Nagel's theory, the power of imagination as regards the idea of space. Brentano reported that he had seen unmistakeably binocular colour mixtures, described the details and thought of a kind of mental chemistry. He came back to that in several letters. Thus we see how early his experiments and studies of colour had begun. At the end of January my book came out.

He considered resigning and formally breaking with the Church at Easter. But there were things to be said against it; it could feed the rumours that he had gone insane. On 6 February 1873, he made a definite decision and told Lotze about it. In Giessen as well as in Vienna we were, so to speak, competitors, but the reader can imagine the sense in which we ourselves understood and treated this. In February Brentano reviewed the situation with people in the Ministry in Munich, and informed them of his decision; they tried to disuade him by holding out hopes for a position as *professor ordinarius*, and he referred them to me. The Ministry requested an opinion from the Senate, which, during the course of the summer, recommended my appointment. Lotze, in particular, had endorsed it warmly.

At the beginning of March 1873 Brentano requested that he be relieved of his position. According to the report of the Senate of 17 March, several conversations with him showed the irrevocability 'of his long contemplated decision, the motivation for which he purposely did not spell out in detail'.

The compelling reason doubtless lay in the fact that he was thinking of announcing his departure from the Church shortly, and after that he could no longer remain in this position given the circumstances that prevailed in Würzburg, to which he had come as the hope and pride of Church-oriented circles. Although he was in no way indebted to these people for his professorship, he wanted to cut off any pretext for unjustified reproaches in this regard. But above all he wanted to pursue further his scientific life's goal in positive work and did not want to see himself caught up in a continual battle with the Church faction, which, in all probability, was unavoidable in Würzburg.

That they wanted to appoint an *ordinarius* besides him did not contribute to the decision, at least not to any great extent. For apart from the fact that he himself was given hope, on this occasion, of being appointed *ordinarius*, the person to be appointed *ordinarius*, regardless of who it was, would have had to fear much more for his effectiveness in light of Brentano's teaching abilities than Brentano himself. Neither did hurt feelings play a role, for he would have even been satisfied, if his student had become *ordinarius*, to take second rank as *professor extraordinarius* as long as it served the cause.

On 24 March he was discharged from his responsibilities, 'with positive acknowledgement of his excellent achievements in the area of science as well as of teaching'.

On Good Friday, 11 April 1873, Brentano left the Church. I have not been informed of the detailed circumstances of this decisive step. It seems to have taken place in private, before the bishop alone, and appears not to have been made public at first. The date is only known to me indirectly, conveyed through Professor Kraus from Brentano's oral communication.

The next letter, dated 9 May, came from Paris. The trip came about partially because he wished to remain out of sight in his homeland after the great reversal in his fate, but also partially because of his increasing desire to acquaint himself with the intellectual currents abroad, and to come into contact with the important thinkers of the time. He had written a long letter to Mill on 29 November 1872, concerning the theory of knowledge, to which Mill replied on 6 February 1873 (Brentano communicates a section of the reply in his *Psychology*).[6] Mill invited him to Avignon in early summer and Brentano wanted to travel there from Paris. Unfortunately, Mill died and the meeting never took place. From Paris Brentano had at first almost nothing but favourable things to report. He praised family life, the honesty of the people, the free and yet tolerant attitude toward belief. He was enchanted by the collections of art and science. On 9 June, however, he wrote that he had got to know Paris from more or less all sides, and must now tone down his first favourable judgement to a considerable extent. It is certainly no place for quiet scholarship; also, the use of the library is difficult. He did not as yet know where he would go next, Aschaffenburg being no fit place for him to stay. 'What is happening with the new Old Catholic bishop? Will he be chosen soon and where will his seat be? "By the Grace of God and Bismarck" is a straightforwardly contradictory title, yet at least as far as the latter part is concerned, quite appropriate in this case.'

On 23 June, he was in Roodt, Luxemburg. The heat had driven him out of Paris. He longed to work in Leipzig or some place like that. He had news of Marty, that he had already begun to waver in his religious views. On 8 July he congratulated me from Aschaffenburg on my appointment at Würzburg, and had, for his part, good news from Vienna. Lotze had interceded there emphatically in favour of his appointment. Cardinal Rauscher protested (later he is said to have taken the protest back); on the other hand, Brentano had personal support from von Gagern, who had befriended him and who pacified the objections of the emperor. In July 1873, Brentano was himself in Vienna. The faculty had recommended Lange first and Stumpf second; the minister expressed to Zimmerman his astonishment that Brentano was passed over. In November 1873 he spent some time in Leipzig where he visited Fechner, Drobisch, E.H. Weber, and the young philosopher Schuster, and where he also got acquainted with Strümpell and Windelband; but the library conditions disappointed him very much, the English literature was lacking completely and the German was represented very spottily. Because he was writing his *Psychology* he regretted that very much. He then had me send books from Würzburg to Aschaffenburg. He looked forward to my coming at Christmas. 'For the lack of any scientific conversation and any exchange of ideas about the things that occupy us is, for someone of my nature, not merely something I feel strongly about, but it is a genuine hindrance.' Something like this appears in another letter: 'The lack of association with people to talk to is always felt by someone like me who is naturally inclined to be friendly. Now, when there are so many scientific questions which provide material for discussion, even more so.' He concerned himself with the question of

6. *Psychology from an Empirical Standpoint*, English edition ed. Linda L. McAlister (London and New York, 1973), pp. 219–20. All of Mill's extant letters to Brentano, plus translations of excerpts from Brentano's letters to Mill, appear in *The Later Letters of John Stuart Mill 1849–1873*, ed. Francis E. Mineka and Dwight N. Lindley (Toronto and London, 1972).

innate associations, and had doubts about the psycho-physical law, for the reasons given in his book.

On 22 January 1874, Brentano was named *professor ordinarius* in philosophy at Vienna. The *Sektionschef* communicated this to him in a flattering letter.

The Preface of his book is dated 7 March 1874. While it was being printed I had many discussions with him about questions of form. He was at that time excessively conscientious about such things. The proof-reading was a painful experience for him for that reason. Stylistic arrangements, the choice of a word – even in more or less insignificant cases – the placement of a comma, all entailed long periods of deliberation. Yet these changes concerned only unimportant externals. Otherwise, Brentano's thoughts were expressed in such a way that all the words seemed to be 'tailor-made'. The form was derived, in its essentials, directly from the thought and no fitting was necessary. And if it is often somewhat involved and not as elegant or full of metaphors as is the writing of some philosophical stylists, this is a reflection of his way of thinking. Because any ambiguity or unclarity was unbearable to him, so were pretty metaphors, jokes, and verbal embellishments, which would be very appropriate for the author of a little book of riddles[7] but which were of no value at all to him in the difficult problems of philosophy. Indeed, he stopped everyone who tried to get by with such things and forced him to express himself in a wholly factual way. And thus self-discipline had become second nature to him even in this respect.

Lectures 1870 to 1873

Now I shall report, insofar as I was informed of them, about Brentano's lectures from 1870 to 1873. The information I have comes primarily from sections of his lecture notes that he shared with me in September 1873 (see below, p. 39). The notes that Brentano used in his lectures consisted only of key words or short phrases, but these were arranged with the utmost care, and the train of thought was rendered so clear by the use of numerals and Roman and Greek letters that someone familiar with Brentano's ideas in general could usually follow these notes quite easily. The notebooks he left behind are, for that reason, an invaluable aid to all future interpreters of his theories.

The subjects of the lectures during this period were: autumn 1870, deductive and inductive logic (five hours a week); spring 1871, psychology; autumn 1871, history of philosophy from its beginnings to the present (five hours a week), seminar on selected philosophical writings; autumn 1872, psychology, on the existence of God, seminar. For the spring of 1872, metaphysics (five hours weekly) was announced, and for the spring of 1873, deductive and inductive logic with explanatory applications to the history of the natural sciences and the humanities (five hours weekly).

In the course on logic, 1870–1 (the course with the largest attendance in

7. *Neue Rätsel von Änigmatias* (Vienna, 1879).

the university, he informed me), Brentano continued to develop the theory of judgement and concentrated, among other things, on the new formulation of the doctrine of modality. He distinguished sharply between the concepts of the evident, sureness, certainty, and exactness, which people had more or less conflated in the 'apodictic' judgement. The distinction between sureness (including degrees of probability) as one of the characteristics rooted in the content of the judgement, and certainty or conviction as a subjective characteristic of judgement 'that is also dependent upon feelings, was, among other things, important for the theory of religious belief. Then followed the detailed theory of inference, especially of categorical syllogisms, as we know it from the brief treatment in the *Psychology* of 1874 and from Hillebrand's book. Brentano had developed it while in seclusion in Aschaffenburg. I still remember how wholly and completely taken up he was with these logical investigations, and every day he arrived at new conclusions from his basic assumptions. This was an area in which he was completely at home. In fact, it still seems to me that his theory of inference, the reduction of all so-called simple categorical conclusions to the two basic existential forms, one for the affirmative, one for the negative conclusions, based upon the principle that in affirmative judgements one may reduce at will without harming the truth value, and in negative judgements increase at will, as well as the derivation of three rules of inference in place of the complicated old doctrine of modes, are grand achievements. The rigorousness of the derivations and the simplicity and invariable inner harmony of the results are admirable. Yet I can no longer consider them the last word on the subject because their bases in the theory of judgement, namely, the interpretation of universal affirmative assertions as negative judgements or judgements containing a negation, have seemed incorrect to me for a long time. Brentano himself, of course, later modified them when he recognised so-called double judgements, which are at the same time predicative.

When evaluating Brentano's very controversial theory of judgement, which exercised the greatest influence on contemporary philosophy, one must always bear in mind that he used the term 'judgement' in a much more general way than do most people in ordinary usage. One must remember that for him every perception, inner as well as external, is a judgement, that this already constitutes for him an elementary affirmation, and that he is of the opinion that any kind of mental act, from the very beginning, is bound up with an evident self-affirmation, that is a judgement in this broadest sense' of the word. This is all, of course, far removed from the standpoint that there are only verbally formulated judgements and then only those composed of subject and predicate.

In the last decade of his life, Brentano, always moving forward supplemented and modified his theory through the thesis that only a *Reales*, a thing, could be made the object of presentation and judgement; as a consequence, even the above mentioned 'indirect judgements' had to be interpreted differently. About this change, which is only briefly sketched in 'The Classification of Mental Phenomena', Marty and his students Kraus and Kastil reported in more detail.[8] Even though the interpretation of the

8. See Oskar Kraus, *Franz Brentano: zur Kenntnis seines Lebens und seiner Lehre*, and Kastil in the Foreword to Anton Marty's *Gesammelte Schriften II*, Part 1, 1918.

statements becomes thus much more complicated, we must not, on the other hand, fail to appreciate that the whole theory of judgement thereby achieves an even higher degree of uniformity. Obviously a factual opinion cannot be expressed here.

A further consequence of the new logic was the inclusion of the mathematical-philosophical theory of probability; Brentano used Laplace's definition as a basis and quoted the seven first rules from his *Essai Philosophique*, gave an elementary derivation of the formula $\frac{n+1}{n+2}$ and reduced incomplete induction in part to (infinite) probability. Some years later, in 1874, Stanley Jevons' *Principles of Science* appeared, in which the theory of induction and causality was essentially based upon the mathematical laws of probability. Brentano himself had, unfortunately, published nothing on this topic. The theories of both thinkers are rooted in Laplace's sixth principle, and, further back, in Bayes' formula. My own later work on the concept of mathematical probability (1892) stemmed mainly from the question whether such applications are themselves logically free from error. For, if the widespread conception were correct, according to which, conversely speaking, causal relations or inductions form the presuppositions of probability statements, then we would have come in a beautiful circle. In addition, von Kries had thought certain material assumptions, a certain scope (*Spielräume*), to be necessary. Thus a thorough-going investigation seemed necessary in order to determine whether the mathematical concept of probability is bound up with any limitations or assumptions not mentioned in Laplace's definition. Brentano sent me a number of critical remarks after having received the treatise, and I must admit that some of them were justified, but in essentials he was naturally in agreement.

Psychology entered the list of lecture topics for the first time in 1871. At that time Brentano divided it into two main sections, the first concerning mental phenomena and their laws, the second concerning the bearer of mental phenomena and the immortality of the soul. I have detailed information on the repetition of the lecture course in the autumn of 1872–3 only from fragments of his notebook, because I have never studied psychology with him. In the first section he discussed the tripartite divison of the basic functions and their mutual relations. He dealt thoroughly with the doctrine of association, and the works of the English psychologists were considered in detail. He recognised only one basic law, which he formulated approximately as follows: 'Any idea leaves behind a disposition toward the appearance of a similar idea under similar mental circumstances.' By means of this formula, which already takes into consideration what have lately been called the facts of substitution, all cases of so-called similarity reproduction are to be understood. I consider it even today the most correct and comprehensive one. Brentano had also anticipated some of the results of later experimental research on memory, for example Jost's Law (by which, of course, I do not mean to say that the experimental confirmation was superfluous). He compared the way in which older, strongly grounded associations prevailed over newer ones in the course of time, with the behaviour of two sources of light of objectively different intensities, of which the weaker one is nearer the eye and for that reason at first seems subjectively lighter, but if you move both of them further and further away without changing their distance from each other, a point must come when the stronger one. becomes subjectively the lighter. Also, abnormal and pathological phenomena such as 'double consciousness' and hypermnesia were discussed and related to the basic law. .

To the question of the origin of the idea of space Brentano devoted no less then twenty hours of lectures in January and February 1873. It had occupied him a great deal since the discussions occasioned by my book.

At that time Brentano described time consciousness as follows: At every moment of an (inner or external) perception, a presentation is produced of the content of the perception which is qualitatively the same but which is temporally more remote to a certain extent. For him the characteristic of time was a determination of content whose regular alterations are subject to the very laws of consciousness. He called the process an 'original association' as opposed to the 'acquired associations' of memory. If several impressions, *a, b, c, d,* follow one after another, we see that at the entrance of the second one the first has already been pushed back in the above-stated manner, and so on. Brentano illustrated this as shown in figure 2.1 in which the horizontal refers to the objective passage of time and the vertical to the presentation as it exists at each point. This clear initial description of the facts he later 'modified' in the literal sense of the word, in that he defined the transformation not as one of content, but as a change in the mode of the presentation. His reason was that the past is not real, and that *irrealia* cannot be the objects of presentations.

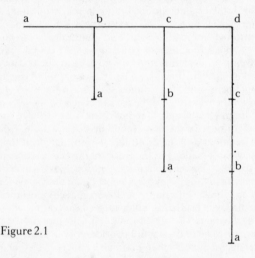

Figure 2.1

This first theory of time was also connected with the logical doctrine that the temporal differences in our assertions, as they are present in the tenses of verbs, have nothing to do with the judgement function (John Stuart Mill), but only affect the object of the judgement. Thus if I say, 'Yesterday a storm raged', then my affirmation is no different from one in the present tense, but that which is affirmed is different, similar to the situation when a judgement at one time concerns an object which is spatially distant, and, at another time, one which is spatially near.

In his Würzburg lectures Brentano had not yet begun to deal with ethics. But I would like to remark, with reference to the development of his thought in this direction, that at that time essentially he advocated the standpoint of the greatest good. He considered the insight that the totality of what is best for all individuals is more desirable than any of its component parts, to be a satisfactory basis for ethics, even though he recognised that Mill's proof of this proposition contains a fallacious inference. The carrying over of the distinction between blind and insightful judgements into the emotional life, the formulation of the concept of a 'love and hate experienced as being correct', and also of a preference similarly characterised which guarantees for us the principle of summation among other things, only came about during his Viennese period.[9]

Our meetings and relations after 1873

Unfortunately I can relate in a few words when and where we saw each other again in later life.. In the summer of 1874, Brentano came back to Franconia after he finished his lectures in Vienna. Because he wished to avoid Würzburg, we met at a station outside the city, in Rottendorf. He was worn out, having found the Viennese summer climate debilitating, and he complained about the dustiness of the air. He was satisfied with his success as a teacher. We were together again in September for two weeks in the Belgian seaside resort of Heyst, and for another two weeks in Klausen near Luxemburg as guests of his brother-in-law, Theophil Funck-Brentano (later at the University of Paris). Brentano had brought a section of his lecture notes on logic and psychology with him to Heyst for me. Funck-Brentano was a well educated and philosophically well read man, and an elegant writer, and the whole family was amiable and very hospitable. In 1875, at the end of September, I visited Brentano in Vienna (at Erdbergstr. 19) after a convention of natural scientists. He had already established pleasant social relations and took me to the home of the bookdealer Gerold, whose wife Rosa liked to entertain writers and artists. I also got to know his close friend Zumbusch, the sculptor, who was just then working on the imposing Maria-Theresa monument, and I was invited to his pleasant home. In 1876, I again visited him for a week at the same apartment in Vienna, and then again for a few days on the occasion of my appointment at Prague. In 1881, I was Brentano's guest for a week in Vienna (at Oppolzergasse 6), and I satisfied myself that he was happy and that he had a very large circle of acquaintances. I had the opportunity of meeting several of his current students, among them von Meinong and Masaryk, who shortly after that came to the newly founded Czech University in Prague.[10]

9. See Roderick M. Chisholm, 'Brentano's Theory of Correct and Incorrect Emotion', Ch. 13 below, and G.E. Moore's review of Brentano's *On the Origin of our Knowledge of Right and Wrong*, ch. 14 below.

10. And much later became the first president of Czechoslovåkia.

Intermittently I had considerable correspondence with Brentano from Prague concerning a question in the psychology of auditory tones, namely of the unity or plurality of simultaneous tones. At that time he still believed that they were a unity, a position which I had abandoned as incompatible with musical consciousness. I suspect that his later view was to some extent influenced by this correspondence.

April of 1884 brought a short reunion when Brentano stopped in Prague on his way to Paris. In the autumn of this year I accepted a position at Halle, of which Brentano did not approve. He regarded this as a kind of ingratitude toward Austria, where I had been treated so well by the government. I believed, however, that I had sufficiently fulfilled my duties to the state, and I was mentally and physically exhausted by life in Prague, so that I welcomed the return to regular and calm circumstances. People in Vienna or in Germany simply had no real idea of what the situation was for Germans in Prague. I cannot deny, furthermore, that the appointment at the University of Halle-Wittenburg, precisely because its statutes excluded non-Protestant teachers on principle, filled me with a special satisfaction and joy in virtue of earlier experiences, about which I do not want to speak here.

In 1885, I sought out Brentano in St Gilgen. Those were stimulating, friendly days spent with him and his spirited wife in beautiful surroundings. Among the people with whom he associated there were his student Franz Hillebrand, the phsyiologist von Fleischl and the psychiatrist Meynert. In the autumn of 1886, Husserl, recommended by Brentano, came to Halle for the purpose of habilitation and became my student and friend. After I transferred to Munich in 1888, we saw Brentano and his wife there for some time in spring 1891, but then there came another long interruption. I moved to Berlin in 1894, in the same year that Brentano's wife died. In 1896 I was with him at the International Congress of Psychologists in Munich, to which, at my request, he contributed a paper 'On the Theory of Sensation'. He did not like such conventions very much, in which major questions, of necessity, must be dealt with very superficially. I only learned later that my own introductory speech on body and soul met with certain reservations on his part. It seemed· to him not to take a strong enough stand against materialism.

For me difficult years of work followed, but also years in which our close relations twice underwent temporary disturbances, especially in 1903. This was a result of the long personal separation and insufficient ability to correspond on my part. As a result of my publications, but especially due to false personal information which had come to him (he was always somewhat credulous about such things), dark thoughts about my whole inner and external relation to him became fixed in his mind, and he expressed them in rather strong words; I could do nothing but reply in kind. But the first moment we saw each other again – the first handshake at the station in Melk – dispersed all of the bad feelings at one stroke and we were both doubly happy to see that we really had not changed. I am convinced that it would have been just the same with others had they been willing to decide to have a personal reunion with him.

In September 1905 I was guest for the first time of Brentano and his second wife at Schönbühel, and then again in the autumn of 1911 and 1913. It is now hard for me to understand how eighteen years could have gone by before I sought out Brentano in his 'new Aschaffenburg'. But each year brought new obstacles. Each of these visits I can only remember with the deepest feelings of gratitude. Brentano used to meet his guests at Melk and take them on the steamer down the Danube to the village of Schönbühel, from which it was still a quarter of an hour trip to his home. The unceasing care with which his wife Emilie surrounded her husband who, because of his eye trouble, was more and more dependent upon her for help, did not stop her from also looking after the well-being of her guests in an exemplary manner. Their hospitality was such that one could not imagine anything better. Along with all the attention and care, one had complete freedom of movement. In good weather we had breakfast and afternoon coffee in the front garden, which was full of trees and overlooked the Danube. With Brentano or his son I roamed around the beautiful region and, just as in the old days, we took many philosophical walks on the forest path to Aggsbach or down on the banks of the Danube.

The subjects of our conversations were preferably the metaphysical questions which then occupied him, such as space and time; the concept of infinity, especially Cantor's theory of the actual infinite, which he rejected; questions about contingency and necessity and the consequences for the concept of God; optimism; Laplace's and Darwin's theories of evolution; the problem of probability (among other things Bertand's paradox); the so-called megethology; things phenomenological, especially the theory of colour which he later published; and things psychological such as the doctrine of presentations which was published in the new edition of the 'Classification'. I wrote down the contents of all of these conversations, but I must admit that in many points I found it more difficult than before to follow his development, because our world of thought and, in part, even our habits of thought had, after all, developed in different directions over the years. And so, for the most part, we did not succeed in convincing each other. But for me it was of great value once more to enjoy his widely ranging and profound manner and to learn of the results of his never-tiring thought. Since our paths had outwardly parted, I had developed resigned and almost Spinoza-like thoughts which had very early impressed themselves upon me in view of the insoluble riddle of the world; and it was one of Brentano's major concerns in his relation to me to bring my thoughts into closer proximity to his own unconditional optimism. In this respect he remained true to the Leibnizian standpoint, which he tried to comprehend more deeply and to prove. Once he decided, however, that one could call the world the worst of all possible as well as the best of all possible, because it follows directly from the doctrine of absolute necessity, which he now recognised, that there could be only one and only this one, then I could agree with him. His concept of God, too, no longer conformed to the earlier one, particularly insofar as he included absolute necessity and at the same time constant change in the concept. You could almost say that it had now acquired a pantheistic element, even if Brentano himself would certainly have objected to this description of it. The intensity and all-penetrating warmth of his religious feelings remained the same, however – the same old imperturbable trust in God. And when he would regularly be up for a few sleepless hours during the night and turn to solitary meditation on the balcony with the wide, murmuring Danube at his feet, then the mystical, blessed feeling of God's nearness may have rewarded him for his life of hard and keen mental labour. Among the poems he left behind is the translation of an English hymn, 'Nearer my God to Thee', which is said to have been sung on the Titanic in 1913 before the ship sank. It is certain that in it he expresses his own feelings.

Anyone who saw Brentano in these later years can only think with great emotion of the calm, mildness and goodness of his spirit, and of the uncomplaining patience with which he bore the onset of the twilight and then the dark night in which his blindness enveloped him. The only things that called forth his indignation and sharp condemnation, now as before, were moral wickedness, especially large-scale injustice in the relations of peoples toward one another, as, for example, the predatory raids against Tripoli in which his new Italian homeland was engaged, and later Italy's betrayal of its allies.

This is the picture of the man that I have before my eyes, whom, as Aristotle said, 'the bad do not even have the right to praise.' He had his weaknesses, too; his friends know that. But who does not? Let those who thrive on derision look for them. As for me, who had known him longer and better than all of them, I have no doubt but that he deserves a place of honour among the greatest personalities of our time.

Brentano's relations toward his students

By way of an appendix I would like to discuss some points which refer to no definite period of time in his life but to his whole relationship to students and to his philosophical mode of thought, and whose inclusion in the body of this piece would have fragmented the chronological presentation too much.

First, Brentano's relation to the literary work of his students: he went to extraordinary lengths to help them. This is more or less generally the German custom, to be sure. We academicians place our experiences and ideas at the disposal of our students without being overly concerned about property rights. When you take this into consideration, dissertations are often more the work of the teacher than of the student, while the author can still claim that it was completed without outside help, because this help does not count. Brentano, however, could, when a theme was of special interest to him, become so involved in it that he practically snatched it right out of the hands of the student he was dealing with. I experienced this especially with the second part of my work on the idea of space, which he, as mentioned above, talked through with me in September 1872. While the first part was already being printed, I still took an empirical standpoint toward the dimension of depth, which the book fortunately does not reveal. That I also adopted nativistic bases for it in the following part, is due to Brentano's influence. And likewise essential details with regard to binocular vision sprang from his suggestions. Certainly it was give and take on both sides, for my studies had led me more deeply into the area of physiology. Brentano did not participate in developing the basic explanations in the first part, except for the most general thoughts about the inseparability of colour and extention, but here, however, he was only reviving older theories.

But how do I go on, where should I begin or end, if I want to give an adequate characterisation of Brentano's influence on my thought, my teaching, and my literary productions? My whole understanding of philosophy and the correct and mistaken methods of philosophising, essential basic doctrines in logic, theory of knowledge, psychology, ethics, and metaphysics that I still maintain today are his doctrines. On other points I did, of course, believe that I had to diverge from him. But this often happened so slowly that I did not recognise the deviation as such. In general, a third party is a better judge of such questions of ownership; as is well known, it is easier to notice family resemblances if you are not a member of the family. This should also be taken into consideration by other students of Brentano's who might overestimate their own original contributions. I know that Husserl, at least, who in his later work deviated considerably from Brentano's ideas concerning the future and the health of philosophy, by no means underestimates the power and the richness of the seeds sown by his teacher.

A second point which should be discussed touches, on the other hand, on the way students were hindered in their literary production as a result of Brentano's own reservations about publishing his research. It is very awkward to have to refer to lectures or even conversations in order to explain to the reader the assumptions one uses as a starting point; it is even more awkward to attack points of view which came from your teacher and which you can no longer share, if these points of view are not available in printed form. How great is the possibility for misunderstanding and inaccuracy! How far, in any case, does the right to cite another's views extend when they are views that the originator himself has not published or may have even renounced altogether or in part in the meantime? Personal separation for years must necessarily bring about transformations in thought on both sides, which make complete mutual understanding difficult. And so I, and he too, came across factual misunderstandings in the publications of the last decades, which require correction. As the eldest student, convinced that I am speaking in the name of others as well, I have taken the liberty of reminding the teacher, in several letters, of our wishes concerning further, especially comprehensive publications. But the intense desire for inquiry and his own progress was far stronger in him than the desire to see his work in print; this in itself is admirable and anyone who has endured the joyless task of adding the finishing touches, filling in literary and factual details, getting the manuscript ready for printing, and proof-reading will appreciate the importance and attractiveness of this attitude. But it is still a source of inconvenience for his closer friends and students in the field of philosophy. I admit that this was one of my motives for devoting a considerable amount of time to the area of the psychology of sound and acoustical observation. There I could hope to achieve something useful without taking a position of agreement or dissent with regard to a great number of unpublished views of the teacher. It was the same with Marty in philosophy of language and Kraus in philosophy of law.

Yet a third point should finally be alluded to as well: a certain touchiness on Brentano's part toward dissension that he thought to be unfounded. He was, on principle and with every right, against the development of a 'school' that swears by his every word; he had in mind here the sort of thing that so many philosophers perceive as the main goal of their ambition and their major claim to fame. He once told me while he was in Vienna that people there had already begun to talk about 'Brentanians' and that this was most disagreeable to him. He loved to quote Aristotle in that respect, saying that Plato is his friend but truth is even more so. And yet, if he encountered basic intuitions in his students' publications which were considerably different from his own, and which were not thoroughly justified and defended on the spot, he was inclined to consider them at first as unmotivated, arbitrary statements even though they may have been subject to several years' thorough study or may have matured imperceptibly without one's having been expressly aware of it. Occasional ill-feelings were unavoidable in the face of this, just as has happened between other teachers and students; I think, for example of the later relations between Müllenhoff and Wilhelm Scherer. But as long as there was open discussion and an unwavering adherence to the ultimate bases of friendship, it could not lead to an extended or lasting quarrel.

Brentano's deductive turn of mind and his opposition to speculation

Brentano's greatest merit as a thinker was extreme consistency and far-sightedness in viewing lines of thought from top to bottom – premises and conclusions alike – that is to say, thinking vertically. Experience was for him the basis of philosophy; but we know, of course, that the experiential sciences cannot do without deduction and they become increasingly deductive the further they progress. His strength lay precisely in the deductive part of the method, in the conception of the most general points of view and the derivation of all their respective consequences for the interpretation of phenomena. And it was this which interested and fascinated him above all. You see this most clearly in his book on questions of the psychology of the senses[11] where the 'Law of Nonpenetration' led him to very bold even though not impossible interpretations of the facts of perception. His eminently deductive talent made it possible for him quickly to survey even very remote consequences of a statement and in discussions he could immediately recognise contradictions with other intuitions held by his opponent, which the opponent himself had not seen.

In addition to that, there is, however, also a more horizontally directed kind of thought, a prevailing tendency to do justice to the breadth of the factual and its manifold differences. Here one runs the risk of coming across

11. *Untersuchungen zur Sinnespsychologie* (Leipzig, 1907).

different laws in the various factual realms which cannot at first be reduced to common principles, and which even contradict each other. The natural scientist often proceeds in this way; as Lotze once humourously boasted, 'with paws not quite washed clean by logic, and grasping clumsily, he squeezes the seed of knowledge from the prickly shell of fact'. If philosophy is to be pursued as an empirical science, and if a part of it, psychology, comes into ever closer contact with the natural sciences, then here, too, a special treatment of individual areas cannot be avoided and laws may then be revealed which at first seem incompatible.

There is no doubt that the vertical must finally prevail and that this direction of thought, which tries to reduce everything, without contradiction, to common universal principles is the first and foremost characteristic of philosophical minds. Unity, rigorousness and correct inference are requirements of eminent importance in philosophy just as they are in mathematics. The danger is that one tries to unify before the incomplete knowledge of the details permits. Brentano, too, was not faultless in this respect; for example, he had a certain tendency in discussion to bolster his arguments by means of analogies which could easily make a critical opponent mistrustful. But even if not all of the concepts and propositions he formulated can be maintained as such in this form, still, every sharply outlined, deeply thought-through blueprint of great architects is of value for posterity.

The only irreconcilable contrast which remains is between his manner of thinking and that of the speculative systems of German philosophy and similar systems from earlier times which he included all together under the heading of philosophical mysticism. Brentano neither underestimated their great aims nor the outstanding talent of their creators, and he even shared one essential characteristic with them: the incessant striving toward the highest and most ultimate things. But for him concepts are based only on intuition, and complete clarity is the first and most indispensable requirement. Here lies an unbridgable gap. This turning away from intuition, from the patient, never-ending analysis of that which is given, constitutes the root of that ambiguous indistinctness of concepts which we deplore in the so-called idealist systems and which is far more objectionable than the clear contradictions that occasionally appear between various areas of experience and are resolved through new and even more precise propositions. Here there is no choice: either philosophy must give up its claim to be called a science, or it extracts and verifies its concepts by means of conscientious analysis of the data. Here there is no return either to Hegel or to Kant; it is necessary to start from the very foundations again. This is the path Brentano took, and he still has my wholehearted agreement on this as he did when I was a student. Of course, clarity of concepts is not automatically guaranteed by starting from experience, as famous examples of natural scientists who did philosophy or switched to philosophy prove. But the principle cannot be called into question. Bacon's golden rule that truth emerges from falsehood before it emerges from confusion is borne out again and again. The air around us is sharp and cutting and it is no use coddling ourselves; it also does no good to surround yourself with smokescreens if you want to see clearly.

Franz Brentano's most carefully thought-out doctrines deserve careful consideration by those who come after him. But even more than in the factual results, I see his legacy to future German philosophy in these methodological demands.

3 Reminiscences of Franz Brentano[1]

Edmund Husserl

I had for only two years the good fortune of attending Brentano's lectures.
During that time the only full semesters were in the autumn of 1884 and
1885. Both years he gave philosophy seminars, and he lectured on 'practical
philosophy' for five hours a week and on selected philosophical problems for
an additional hour or two. During the corresponding spring semesters he
gave continuations of these smaller classes exclusively for advanced
students, but these were over by the first week in June. Under the title
'Elementary Logic and its Needed Reforms', the first of these classes dealt
with systematically connected basic elements of a descriptive psychology of
the intellect, without neglecting, however, the parallel elements in the
sphere of the emotions, to which a separate chapter was devoted. The other
class, on 'Selected Psychological and Aesthetic Questions', was devoted
mainly to fundamental descriptive analyses of the nature of the imagination.
Somewhere around the middle of June, Brentano went to the Wolfgangsee, of
which he was very fond at the time, and, at his friendly invitation, I
accompanied him there (to St Gilgen). It was especially during these
summer months, when I was free to visit in his hospitable home at any time
and to accompany him on his shorter walks and boat-rides (as well as on the
one longer excursion he took during these two years) that I was allowed to
get closer to him, to the extent that the great difference in age and maturity
would allow. At that time I had just finished my university studies, but was
still a beginner in philosophy. (My doctorate was in mathematics with a
minor in philosophy.)

At a time when my interest in philosophy was increasing and I was
vacillating between staying in mathematics and devoting my life to
philosophy, Brentano's lectures were the deciding factor. I went to them at
first merely out of curiosity, to hear the man who was the subject of so much
talk in Vienna at that time, the man whom some people respected so highly
and admired so much, but whom others (and not so very few) derided as a
Jesuit in disguise, as a rhetoritician, a fraud, a Sophist, and a Scholastic. My
first impression of him was rather striking. This lean figure with the powerful
head framed by curly hair, the manly, prominent nose, the expressive lines in
his face which bespoke not only mental toil but deep spiritual conflict as well
– these lay wholly outside the scope of common life. In every feature, in every
movement, in his soulful, introspective eyes, filled with determination, in his

---

1. Translated from the German by Linda L. McAlister and Margarete Schättle.
Reprinted from the Appendix to Oskar Kraus's *Franz Brentano, zur Kenntnis seines
Lebens und seiner Lehre* (Munich, 1919).

whole manner, was expressed the consciousness of a great mission. The language of his lectures, perfect in form, free from all contrived figures of speech, witty embellishments and rhetorical phrases, was nothing less than the language of dispassionate scientific discourse, though it did have a certain elevated and artistic style through which Brentano could express himself in a completely appropriate and natural way. When he spoke like this, in his characteristically soft, husky undertone, accompanying his speech with priestly gestures, he stood before his young students like a seer of eternal truths and the prophet of an other-worldly realm.

In spite of all my prejudices, I could not resist the power of this personality for long. I was soon fascinated and then overcome by the unique clarity and dialectical accuity of his explanations, by the so to speak cataleptic power of his development of problems and theories. It was from his lectures that I first acquired the conviction that gave me the courage to choose philosophy as my life's work, that is the conviction that philosophy, too, is a field of serious endeavour, and that it too can – and in fact must – be dealt with in a rigorously scientific manner. The pure objectivity with which he tackled all questions, treating them as *aporiai*, his fine dialectical weighing of different possible arguments, his analyses of equivocations, the way he traced all philosophical concepts back to their sources in intuition – all of this filled me with admiration and with great confidence. The tone of solemn earnestness and genuine devotion to the subject ruled out any cheap academic humour or jokes during his lectures. He avoided those clever antitheses that make their vital point usually only by means of a violent over-simplification of thought. Yet in informal conversation and when he was in a good mood he was extremely witty and could bubble over with humour. Most impressive was his effectiveness in those unforgettable philosophy seminars. (I remember the following topics: Hume's *Enquiry Concerning Human Understanding,* and *Enquiry Concerning the Principles of Morals*; Helmholtz's lecture *Die Tatsachen der Wahrnehmung* (*The Facts of Perception*); and Du Bois-Reymond's *Über die Grenzen des Naturerkennens* (*On the Limits of the Knowledge of Nature*). Brentano was a master of Socratic maieutic. He knew so well how to guide the fumbling, unsure beginner by questions and interjections, how to infuse the serious student with courage, and how to turn initially fuzzy perceptions of truth into clear conceptions and insights. On the other hand, he also knew how to silence the empty babblers, without ever being insulting. After these seminars he used to invite the person who had led the discussion and three or four of the other most enthusiastic participants to his house where Mrs Ida Brentano would have prepared dinner. The conversation would never turn to small talk. The themes of the discussion would be continued and Brentano would speak energetically, posing new questions or opening up new perspectives by giving whole discourses. Very often Mrs Brentano, who was so touching in her concern that the shy students get enough to eat (something that Brentano never paid any attention to), disappeared as soon as dinner was over. Once, by chance, the famous politician E. von Plener, a close friend of the family, dropped in when one of these groups of students was there, but Brentano was not to be diverted, and he devoted the evening entirely to his students and the topic of discussion that concerned him.

Brentano was an easy man for students to talk to. He liked to invite them to join him on walks, during which he answered the philosophical questions that were put forward, completely oblivious to the hubbub of the city. He took a very genuine interest not only in his students' scientific problems, but also in their personal ones, and he was their benevolent adviser and teacher. To those whom he considered his trusted friends he also spoke about his political and religious convictions and about his own fate. He stayed aloof from current politics, but the idea of a Greater Germany (in the old South German sense) was dear to his heart; it was something he had grown up with, and something which, along with his antipathy toward Prussia, he retained all his life. In this respect I could never agree with him. It was obvious that he had never had any meaningful experience with the Prussian way, and was not conscious of its valuable social manifestations. I myself was luckier in that respect and learned to value these things a great deal. Accordingly, he lacked all sensitivity to the singular greatness of Prussian history. The same was true of his relationship to Protestantism, which did not improve despite his leaving the Catholic Church. He had freed himself from Catholic dogma as a philosopher; the relationship to Protestant ideas played no role in it, and historico-political understanding and the resultant appreciation of historical values were neither in this instance nor in any other part of Brentano's nature. Yet I never heard Brentano speak of Catholicism itself in other than tones of great respect. From time to time he vigorously defended the ethico-religious forces propagated by Catholicism against foolish derogatory comments. From the philosophical point of view, the theistic *Weltanschauung* which meant so much to him constituted a connection between him and the old Church, and he liked to discuss questions of God and immortality. His two-hour lectures on proofs for the existence of God (a part of the lectures on metaphysics which he had given in previous years in Vienna and in Würzburg) were very carefully thought out, and just as I was leaving Vienna he began to work anew on problems pertaining to this subject. These problems concerned him, I know, all his life.

Principally, however, he was occupied during these years in part with those questions of descriptive psychology which were the theme of the above-mentioned lectures, and in part with the investigations in the psychology of sense perception which were published just a few years ago,[2] the contents of which I remember (at least in broad outline) from conversations in Vienna and St Gilgen. In the lectures on elementary logic, he dealt in great detail with, and was clearly doing a creative re-formulation of, the descriptive psychology of continua, with particular reference to Bolzano's *Paradoxien des Unendlichen (Paradoxes of the Infinite)*; he dealt in like manner with the differences between 'intuitive and unintuitive', 'clear and unclear', 'distinct and indistinct', 'real and unreal', 'concrete and abstract' ideas; during the following summer he attempted a radical investigation of all the descriptive elements underlying the traditional distinctions among judgements, of all the discernible elements in the immanent essence of judgement itself. Directly afterwards, descriptive

2. *Untersuchungen zur Sinnespsychologie* (Leipzig, 1907).

problems concerning imagination were of intense concern to him (as mentioned above, he treated the theme in a separate lecture), in particular the relation between perceptual presentations and those of imagination. These lectures were especially stimulating because they investigated the problems as they developed, while lectures such as those on practical philosophy (or the ones on logic and metaphysics – from which I could use a condensed set of notes) were in a certain sense dogmatic in character despite their critical-dialectical presentation. That is to say, they gave and were meant to give the impression of presenting firmly established truths and definitive theories. I always had the impression at the time as well as later that Brentano, in fact, genuinely thought of himself as the creator of a *philosophia perennis*. Absolutely sure of his method, and constantly striving to achieve the highest standards of an almost mathematical rigour, he believed that in his sharply defined concepts, his tightly woven and systematically ordered theories, and his comprehensive aporetic refutations of opposing points of view, he had arrived satisfactorily at the truth. Yet no matter how determinedly he defended his own theories, he did not, as I used to believe, cling to them at all costs. In later years he gave up many of the theories he had favoured in his youth. He never stood still. Deeply penetrating and often ingenious in his inuitive analyses, he moved relatively quickly from intuition to theory: to the definition of sharp concepts, to theoretical formulations of problems to be worked on, to the construction of a systematic summary of possible solutions, the choice of which was to be made by using critical methods. So, if my judgement of his philosophical style is correct, I would say that at every phase of his development he had, in a like manner, his firmly decided theories, and was armed with a phalanx of thoroughly thought-out arguments which he considered a match for all other theories. He had little regard for thinkers such as Kant and the post-Kantian German Idealists, who place a far higher value on original intuition and premonition as to the future than they do on logical method and scientific theory. That a philosophical thinker could be regarded as great even when all of his theories are, strictly speaking, unscientific and even his basic concepts leave very much to be desired in terms of 'clarity and distinctness'; that his greatness lies not in the logical perfection of his theories but rather in the originality of highly meaningful though vague and hardly clarified basic intuitions, which cannot be integrated into the realm of *logos* but are rather part of a pre-logical striving toward *logos* itself; in short that he is regarded as great because he introduced completely new motives of thinking, ultimately decisive for the aims of all philosophical work, motives which are still too remote to have any effect on rigorous theoretical insights; that is something Brentano would hardly have admitted. He, who was so devoted to the austere ideal of rigorous philosophical science (which was exemplified in his mind by the exact natural sciences), could only see in the systems of German Idealism a kind of degeneration. Having been completely under Brentano's influence when I began in philosophy, it took some time before I arrived at the conviction, which at present is shared by so many researchers who are intent on a rigorously scientific philosophy, that the Idealist systems – basically no different from any of the previous philosophies in the epoch which began with Descartes – should rather be seen as a kind of youthful immaturity, and should, as such, be very highly esteemed. It might be true that Kant and the other German Idealists offered little that was satisfying and tenable for a scientifically rigorous treatment of the problem motives that deeply concerned them: those who are really able to understand these motives and to enter into their intuitive content are certain that in the idealistic systems completely new and extremely radical dimensions of philosophical problems are coming to light, and that it is only through their clarification and through the elaboration of the method of philosophy called for by the very nature of these problems, that the ultimate and highest aims of philosophy will be revealed.

Although the excellence of Brentano's logical theorising is undisputed, we have to realise that the extraordinary and still prevalent effects of his own philosophy are, in the last analysis, due to the fact that he himself, as an original thinker, went back to the sources of intuition and thus provided German philosophy, which had become so unproductive in the 1870s, with new seminal motives. How far his methods and theories will prevail is not for us to decide here. We see that in the fertile minds of other thinkers these motives have developed differently than in Brentano's mind, but this only proves anew their original, seminal vitality. This did not delight Brentano because, as we said, he was convinced of the truth of his philosophy. In fact, his self-confidence was complete. The inner certainty that he was moving in the right direction and was founding a purely scientific philosophy never wavered. To elaborate this philosophy in more detail within the systematic basic theories which he held to be already established was something he felt himself called to do, both from within and from above. I would like to call this absolutely doubt-free conviction of his mission the ultimate fact of his life. Without it one cannot understand nor rightly judge Brentano's personality.

This explains, first, why being a deeply penetrating and effective teacher, indeed, why having a school (in the good sense) was so important to him: not only for the dissemination of the insights achieved, but also for the continued work on his thoughts. It is true, however, that he was very touchy about any deviation from his firmly held convictions, he became excited when he encountered criticisms of them, adhered rather rigidly to the already well defined formulations and aporetic proofs, and held out victoriously, thanks to his masterly dialectic, which, however, could leave the objector dissatisfied if he had based his argument on opposing original intuitions. No one was more conducive to spontaneous, free thought than Brentano, yet no one took it harder when his own firmly entrenched convictions were attacked.

The conviction that he was a pioneer in a new philosophy is doubtless one of the reasons for the great (and for me at that time scarcely understandable) value that Brentano placed upon the recovery of his full professorship at Vienna. He spoke a great deal of the hopes that were always being held out to him and of the promises that were made to him and were never kept. It was simply very difficult for him no longer to be supervising doctoral dissertations and presenting them to the faculty, and, what is worse, having to watch passively the habilitation of instructors of whom he did not approve. He often commented bitterly about this. His teaching activity, however, did not suffer under these circumstances (except for his voluntarily shortening his spring lectures), and he continued to exercise his determining influence not only in Vienna but throughout Austria. His beautiful, almost classically perfect lectures on practical philosophy were attended each winter by hundreds of first-semester law students and by students from all the other faculties – although it is true that the large number shrank quite a bit after a few weeks because the regular additional work that the course required was not to everyone's liking. Moreover, again and again gifted young people came from this course into his seminars, attesting to the fact that his efforts were well applied.

He complained a lot during these years of weak nerves, even in St Gilgen where he went supposedly to strengthen them. His relaxation after intense mental work took the form of other activities which were equally intense and which he pursued with equal enthusiasm. In the Vienna Chess Club he was considered an especially clever player (too clever, I was told, and too prone to pursue an intriguing idea to be able to win very often), and could from time to time become completely engrossed in a game. At other times he did wood-working, or painted and sketched, and he did whatever he was doing wholeheartedly and passionately. He always had to be occupied in some way. On our trip together to St Gilgen he would, as soon as we were underway, take out the handy chess set he had carved for himself, and we would spend the whole long trip in ardent play. In St Gilgen he liked to join in his wife's portrait-painting, she being an able painter, and he would make improvements or even completely take over her pictures in progress, although it is true that she then had to lend a helping hand and do some things over again correctly. This is the way he and his wife together painted me in 1886: 'an amiable picture' says Theodor [sic] Vischer, the discriminating art historian.[3] With equal zeal he spent afternoons in St Gilgen playing boccia (in the 'garden' which was a little piece of land behind the rented cottage near the lake). He was not at all enthusiastic about hiking in the mountains and liked only short walking trips. He lived very simply both in St Gilgen and in Vienna. One really did not need to know him and observe his living habits for long to realise the ridiculousness of the talk that was going around about his having married his first wife for her money. He had no taste for the pleasures of wealth, and he ate and drank in moderation without really being aware of differences in food or drink. I was often at his house at mealtimes and I never heard or noticed any reaction from him about the food or drink that would indicate that he enjoyed it with any special pleasure. Once when we arrived in St Gilgen before his wife did and had to eat in a rather bad restaurant, he was quite satisfied, simply not noticing the difference, for he was always occupied with his thoughts or the conversation. And he allowed himself only the simplest foods, just as, when he travelled alone on the train, he was satisfied to travel

---

3. It was apparently Theodor's son, Robert Vischer, who is quoted here. See Herbert Spiegelberg's 'The Lost Portrait of Edmund Husserl by Franz and Ida Brentano', *Philomathes: Studies and Essays in the Humanities in Memory of Philip Merlan*, ed. Robert B. Palmer and Robert Hamerton Kelly (The Hague, 1971), p. 341 n.

the lowest class. The same was true of his clothing, which was exceedingly simple and often threadbare. Thrifty as he was in all of these respects as far as his own person was concerned, he was nonetheless generous when he could do a good turn for someone else.

In his personal behaviour toward younger people he was, on the one hand dignified, to be sure, but on the other hand extremely gracious and kind, constantly concerned not only with furthering their intellectual development, but with their ethical personality as well. You could not help but surrender yourself completely to this higher guidance, and you felt its ennobling power constantly, even when you were far away from him. Even in his lectures, someone who had once succumbed to him would be very deeply moved, not only on a theoretical level by their content, but by the pure ethos of his personality. And how he could give of himself personally! The quiet summer evenings' walks along the Wolfgangsee, when he would often let himself go and speak freely about himself, are unforgettable to me. He had a kind of childlike openness, as indeed he had in general that childlike quality often found in geniuses.

I have never corresponded very much with Brentano. To the letter in which I asked him to allow me to dedicate the *Philosophy of Arithmetic* (my first philosophical writing) to him, he wrote back and thanked me warmly but tried to dissuade me; he said I should not invite the wrath of his enemies down upon my own head. I dedicated the book to him anyway, but when I sent him the dedication copy I received no reply.[4] It was not until fourteen years later that Brentano noticed that I actually had dedicated the book to him, and then he thanked me in kind and heartfelt terms; he had obviously not looked at it closely, or had, at most, skimmed through it. Of course I had too high a regard for him, and I understood him too well to be really hurt by this.

There were deeper reasons why no active exchange of letters developed. At the beginning I was his enthusiastic pupil, and I never ceased to have the highest regard for him as a teacher; still, it was not to be that I should remain a member of his school. I knew, however, how much it agitated him when people went their own way, even if they used his ideas as a starting point. He could often be unjust in such situations; this is what happened to me, and it was painful. Also, the person who is driven from within by unclarified and yet overpowering motives of thought, or who seeks to give expression to intuitions which are as yet conceptually incomprehensible and do not conform to the received theories, is not inclined to reveal his thoughts to someone who is convinced that his theories are right – and certainly not to a master logician like Brentano. One's own lack of clarity is painful enough, and no new proofs and dialectical refutations are needed to show one's logical inability, which is itself the very force that stimulates

4. Apparently Brentano did reply. Herbert Spiegelberg, in 'The Lost Portrait of Edmund Husserl', p. 344, says: 'Some time in 1891 (the letter has no specific date) Brentano wrote Husserl a brief but warm acknowledgement, but added that he would have to postpone reading the book. Then in 1904, as shown in a letter of 7 October, Brentano re-discovered the volume, and, in the belief that he had not yet acknowledged the dedication, sent him his apologies and renewed thanks.'

philosophical investigation. What they presuppose – methods, concepts, principles – must, unfortunately, be suspect and must at first be eliminated as dubious, and one finds oneself in the unfortunate position of neither being able to produce clear refutations nor being able to set forth anything sufficiently clear and definite. My development was like that and this was the reason for a certain remoteness, although not a personal estrangement, from my teacher, which made close intellectual contact so difficult later on. Never, I must freely admit, was this his fault. He repeatedly made efforts to re-establish scientific relations. He must have felt that my great respect for him had never lessened during these decades. On the contrary, it had only increased. It was in the course of my development that I learned more and more to value the power and worth of the impulses I received from him.

When I was a *Privatdozent* I visited him once during the summer vacation at Schönbühel on the Danube; he had just bought the 'Taverne' and it was being renovated for living purposes. I will never forget the scene in which I found him. As I approached the house I saw a group of bricklayers, among them a lean, tall man wearing an open shirt, lime-spattered trousers and a floppy hat, using a trowel just like the others: an Italian labourer such as you often saw in the streets. It was Brentano. He was very friendly toward me and showed me the plans for the renovation, complaining about the incompetent builders and the masons who had forced him to take matters into his own hands and work along with them. Before long we were in a deep philosophical discussion, he still wearing that outfit.

I did not see Brentano again until the year 1908, in his apartment, magnificently situated on the Via Bellosguardo in Florence. It is only with the greatest emotion that I remember those days. How moving it was when he, almost completely blind, stood on the balcony and described to me the incomparable view of Florence and the surrounding landscape, or guided my wife and me on the prettiest routes to see the two villas that Galileo had lived in, and showed us around. His external appearance, I found, had actually changed very little except that his hair had turned grey and his eyes had lost their gleam and earlier expression. Yet even then, how much those eyes spoke – what radiance and hope in God they expressed. Naturally we talked a great deal of philosophy. That too was sad. How it did his heart good to be able once again to express himself in philosophical terms. He to whom great effectiveness as a teacher had been a necessity of life had to live in isolation in Florence and was not in a position to exercise his personal influence. He was happy just to have someone come down from the North occasionally who could listen to him and understand him. During that visit it seemed to me as though the decades since my student days in Vienna had become nothing but a faint dream; once more I felt like a shy beginner before this towering, powerful intellect. I preferred to listen rather than speak myself. And how great, how beautifully and firmly articulate, was the speech that poured out. Once, however, he himself wanted to listen, and without ever interrupting me with objections, he let me speak about the significance of the phenomenological method of investigation and my old fight against psychologism. We did not reach any agreement. And perhaps some of the fault lies with me. I was handicapped by the inner conviction that he, having become firmly entrenched in his way of looking at things, and having established a firm system of concepts and arguments, was no longer flexible enough to be able to understand the necessity of the changes in his basic intuitions which had been so compelling to me.

Not even the slightest discord marred these lovely days. His second wife, Emilie, who cared for him in such a kind and loving way during his later years and fitted so beautifully into his way of life at that time, was extremely kind and friendly to us. He wanted to be with me as much as possible; he was clearly aware that my gratitude for everything his personality and the vital power of his teaching had meant to me was inextinguishable. In old age he had become even more charming and gentle; I did not find an embittered old man who had been denied the support he deserved in both of his homelands and who had been rewarded for his great gifts with ingratitude. He lived constantly in his world of ideas and for the perfection of his philosophy which, as he said, had undergone a great development in the course of the decades. There was about him a slight aura of transfiguration, as though he no longer belonged entirely to this world and as though he already half lived in that higher world he believed in so firmly, and the theistic philosophical explanation of which occupied him so much during these later years. This last impression of him in Florence has etched itself deeply in my mind: and this is how he lives on in my memory – as a figure from a higher world.

4   Franz Brentano's Interpretation of Medieval Philosophy[1]

Etienne Gilson

The section of J.A. Möhler's *History of the Church* that deals with the history of the ecclesiastical sciences during the Middle Ages, has been compiled from the posthumous notes of Möhler, by Franz Brentano, then a Catholic priest and a professor at the German University of Würzburg.[2] As is usually the case in general histories, Brentano's chapter is a rather short one, but it gives a clear account of what was then known on the subject. Its main interest however does not lie in its remarkable clarity and general accuracy, but rather in the philosophical interpretation of the evolution of medieval thought which it propounds. As will be seen later, there are good reasons to think that the responsible author for that interpretation was not Möhler, but Brentano.

After reviewing the first centuries of medieval philosophy, the so-called Möhler's *History* goes on to say:

> With Saint Thomas, the greatest philosopher of the Middle Ages, theology reaches its highest peak, but it begins to decline as soon as philosophy is in decadence. That decadence, which, as can be seen in the two other great philosophical periods, has its source in a darkening and lessening of the scientific spirit, follows three stages: by ceasing to be scientific, knowledge ushers in scepticism; as scepticism is unable to satisfy the needs of man, it gives rise to a reaction which pretends immediately to reach, by a rapid flight, the summits of intellectual knowledge, and to enjoy its results without going through the long and painful drudgery of investigation, observation and analysis. Thus, do we see in Antiquity, that after Aristotle the Stoics and the Epicureans devote themselves to the exclusive pursuit of practical interests; then come the Sceptics, who succeed in converting such eclectics as Cicero himself; lastly the neo-Platonic mysticism sets in, which gropes its way in the intelligible

1. Reprinted with permission from *Medieval Studies*, vol. 1, no. 1 (1939).
2. The *History of the Church* of J.-A. Möhler will be quoted from the French translation: J.-A. Möhler, *Histoire de l'Eglise*, trans. P. Belet and published by Gams (3 vols, Paris 1868–9). Interesting details on the history of the book will be found in the Preface of Gams. The chapter on the *History of ecclesiastical sciences* is in vol. 2, pp. 467-520. In the German edition of Möhler's *Kirchengeschichte*, the chapter written by Brentano will be found in vol. 2, pp. 526–84.

world. In modern times, we also see that, after Locke and Leibniz, there follows the superficial culture of the French and of the Germans, after which comes critical philosophy, and then, as a reaction against it, the doctrine of identity, the pantheistic mysticism of Schelling and the absolute idealism of Hegel. Now the same phenomenon strikingly manifests itself in the Middle Ages. As soon as the jealousy and the hair-splitting of the schools begin to replace the disinterested quest for knowledge, philosophy declines. Against the faulty dogmatism of the schools, nominalism reacts with a clearly marked sceptical tendency, but scepticism itself gives rise to an excessively bold reaction, largely mystical in its inspiration, which can be observed, under various forms, in the doctrines of Ramon Sibiud, Nicolas of Cues and the disciples of Ramon Lull whose influence then begins to be felt. The chief result of that movement is to lure away from intellectual research great intelligences, which lock themselves into the sanctuary of a truly religious mysticism, in order to achieve the immediate enjoyment of the supreme intelligible beauty.[3]

The essential ideas of that highly suggestive text can be analysed as follows. In the three great periods of its history: the Greek, the medieval and the modern, philosophy has followed a similar evolution. That evolution runs through four successive stages: (1) there is a flowering of purely disinterested and speculative interest for intellectual knowledge; (2) there next comes a period of enthusiasm for essentially practical interests; (3) the theoretical character of true knowledge having thus been forgotten, scepticism sets in; (4) because men cannot abide by scepticism, they turn to mysticism as to its specific remedy.

There is good ground for believing, that when Franz Brentano wrote that chapter, he generously credited Möhler with one of the most important among his own ideas. As a matter of fact, we know for sure that when, in the autumn of 1866, Professor Carl Stumpf, then himself a student at the University of Würzburg, attended the first course of Brentano in the History of Philosophy, the young professor prefixed to his lectures an introduction, where he dealt at some length with the concept and the method of philosophy. To which Professor Carl Stumpf immediately adds: 'The doctrine of the four phases was then already propounded by him.'[4] As Brentano himself was later to say to Professor Carl Stumpf, the idea had struck his mind for the first time in the year 1860,[5] when he was recovering from a serious illness. He had been wondering what was the matter with those pretentious systems, that were so universally admired for some time, and then seemed to be no less universally rejected by all. It then occurred to

3. J.-A. Möhler, *Histoire de l'Eglise*, vol. 2, pp. 479–80.
4. Oskar Kraus, *Franz Brentano. Zur Kenntnis seines Lebens und seiner Lehre, mit Beitragen von Carl Stumpf und Edmund Husserl.* (Munich, 1919) p. 89. See above, p.
5. Franz Brentano was born in Marienberg bei Boppard on 16 January 1838. When he first conceived his doctrine of the 'four phases of philosophy' he was, therefore, twenty-two years old.

his mind that what was happening in his own times with the philosophies of Fichte, Schelling and Hegel, had already taken place in the three main periods for the history of philosophy, but that there was no necessary reason why it should happen again in the future.[6] The very analogy between the histories of the three philosophical decadences pointed to their common cause, and the knowledge of that cause would greatly help in avoiding a repetition of the same tragedy. That consoling thought, which had saved him from philosophical despair, was naturally among the first ones that he wanted to transmit to his students.

In order to find it completely developed however, under Brentano's own name and responsibility, we have to turn to the lecture which he gave much later, on 28 November 1894, for the Literary Society of Vienna, under the title: *The Four Phases of Philosophy and its Present Condition*.[7] After restarting the remarkable parallelism that can be observed between the course of evolution followed by philosophy in Antiquity, in the Middle Ages and in modern times up to the wreck of Hegel's metaphysical domination, Brentano proceeds here to describe each one of the four phases of philosophy with more precision than he had done in Möhler's *History of the Church*.

The first phase is characterised by a lively and pure theoretical interest. Plato and Aristotle have rightly said that 'marvelling', or sheer curiosity has been the first motive which invited men to philosophise. That natural thirst for knowledge immediately gave rise to some elementary methods, which still greatly needed to be perfected, but could already yield truly scientific results.

The second phase is also the first one of the decadence. It is brought about by a weakening, or a deviation of the original interest for theoretical knowledge. From that time on the practical motives are becoming more and more influential in determining intellectual activity, with the necessary consequence that instead of remaining deep, strong and truly scientific in its inspiration, human thought makes itself both broader and more popular in its aims. It is the time of the philosophical sects, where a generalised interest in philosophy hardly makes up for the loss of its pristine scientific character.

There then usually takes place some sort of spiritual revolution, which brings the second period to a close. When knowledge does not keep faith with its own ideal, it does no longer deserve to be respected. Anybody can then see that philosophy does not prove what it preaches, which naturally leads to the conclusion that a truly demonstrated knowledge is an intrinsic impossibility. Hence an age of prevailing scepticism, where men make profession not to know anything, or to know so little that it practically amounts to nothing.

Yet, scepticism is essentially unable to satisfy the human desire for knowledge. 'All men,' says Aristotle at the beginning of his *Metaphysics*,

---

6. Kraus, *Franz Brentano*, pp. 89–90.

7. Franz Brentano, *Die vier Phasen der Philosophie und ihr augenblicklicher Stand,* ed. Oskar Kraus (Leipzig, 1926). Brentano had already given a less complete exposition on the 'four phases' in 1869; cf. note below, p.

'naturally want to know.' Where and when scepticism prevails, that natural desire for knowledge breaks down all obstacles. Since natural knowledge has proved impossible, supernatural knowledge must fill up its place. The times are then ripe for those mystical speculations where everything is immediately intuited and nothing rationally demonstrated. This is the lowest conceivable point of the downfall. People think they know everything, and they know nothing. Nay, they do not even know the only thing which they still knew at the end of the sceptical period, to wit, that they know nothing.[8]

It was easy for Brentano to find historical justifications for his thesis, and he successively proved it for the three great periods which he had first distinguished. To limit ourselves to the Middle Ages, let us say with Brentano that after the magnificent achievements of Thomas Aquinas, all hopes were permitted. Yet the downfall of medieval philosophy began immediately after him. True, Duns Scotus also was a full-blooded metaphysician and a great theologian, but he was a Franciscan, and his own Order was so jealous of the brilliant success of the two Dominican doctors, Albertus Magnus and Thomas Aquinas, that they adopted him as their own champion. His doctrine then became the official Franciscan truth in both philosophy and theology. From that time on, the pure speculative interest which had given rise to the two doctrines was more and more sacrificed to that practical motive: to insure the ultimate triumph of one of the two religious Orders over the other one. It no longer was a quest for truth, but a fight between parties in which neither philosophy nor theology were really interested. Facts were no longer taken into account; observation was progressively replaced by endless and often meaningless distinctions, the whole process culminating in the famous *Actus Sorbonicus* where a harmless candidate had to dispute for twelve hours, with a short midday pause, against the dialectical objections of innumerable opponents. If scholastic philosophy is still today despised on account of its barren subtlety, it owes it to the defects of that age: the Scotist age.

The first stage of its decadence naturally led medieval philosophy to the second one, that of scepticism, which was represented by the nominalism of William of Ockham. According to Ockham, it is not only true to say that the Universals do not exist, but it must be added that all our representations are mere signs which have no more likeness with their objects than smoke with fire. He considered it as impossible rationally to prove that God has created the world, that He knows it, and is Himself an infinite being; or to demonstrate that there is in man a spiritual and immortal principle. Moreover, no room was left for a natural moral order in such a doctrine, for God can prescribe or forbid what He pleases, His infinite will being as free to attach moral merit to lie as to veracity, or to murder as to the love of our neighbour. In point of fact, God could even prescribe us to hate Him, in which case the hatred of man for God would be morally meritorious. As was to be expected, the Church did its utmost to silence the Nominalists, but they took refuge in a very simple distinction. What Ockham and his disciples refused to hold as rationally certain, they made profession

8. Brentano, *Die vier Phasen*, pp. 7–9.

unreservedly to hold it by simple faith. In other words, they would maintain as theologically true what was philosophically unknowable, with the natural result that the very essence of truth itself was wholly annihilated.

Against the nominalistic scepticism there then arose a new and powerful reaction. It is a well-known fact that numerous and eminent mystics appeared around the end of the Middle Ages. Meister Eckhardt, Tauler, Henry Suso, John Ruysbroek and the author of the anonymous *German Theology*, which was to be published by Luther, belong to the group of the religious mystics. But there also were representatives of a more philosophical mysticism, Ramon Lull for instance, and Nicholas of Cues. The so-called *Ars Magna* of Lull, which could have yielded positive results in Logic, was used by him to provide apodictical and purely rational demonstrations of the Trinity, of original sin, as well as of the Incarnation and of the Redemption. Lull had had very few followers during his own lifetime, but his disciples multiplied during the fourteenth century to such an extent that the University of Paris found it necessary to condemn his *Ars Magna*. In spite of that condemnation, Lullism continued to spread and it was condemned again by Paul IV at the times of the Reformation. As to Nicholas of Cues, whose influence, just as that of Lull, can still be felt in the works of Giordano Bruno, he advocated under the name of 'learned ignorance' such an unknowledge as far surpassed all knowledge. He described it as an 'intuition without concepts', or as an 'incomprehensible comprehending' that transcended both sense and reason. For the trouble with reason is, that it is strictly bound by the principle of contradiction, whereas intellectual intuition is able to grasp, by simple sight, the coincidence of the opposites. A truly mystical method indeed, which enabled Nicholas of Cues to gather some insight not only in the mysteries of the human and of the divine natures, but even in the still deeper mystery of their union in the Incarnation of Jesus Christ. Such men as Lull and Nicholas of Cues announced by their irrationalism the end of the Middle Ages, just as the neo-Platonists had announced the end of Greek philosophy, and Hegel the end of modern metaphysics.[9]

The whole doctrine of the four phases of philosophy obviously bears the mark of what was its first origin in the mind of Brentano: a perfectly sound and legitimate reaction against philosophical despair. Instead of the continuous progress that can be observed in the history of sciences, the history of post-Kantian philosophy exhibited a series of wholly discontinuous revolutions, each system flatly contradicting the immediately preceding one until itself destroyed by its successor. Hence his conclusion, which he had already stated in his Thesis of 1866: *Vera philosophia methodus nulla alia nisi scientiae naturalis est*. Brentano wanted to discredit the passionate taste of philosophers for dogmatic systems and to bring them to adopt a truly scientific attitude towards metaphysical problems.[10] His law of the four phases of philosophy was not merely describing the history of the past philosophical decadences, it also pointed out their cause and showed

---

9. *Die vier Phasen*, pp. 13–18.

10. Brentano, *Über die Grunde der Entmutigung auf philosophischem Gebiete*, in *Über die Zukunft der Philosophie*, (Leipzig, 1929), p. 88.

how the recurrence of similar mistakes could be avoided in the future. Once it is well understood that philosophy begins to decline as soon as philosophers forget its purely theoretical nature, the remedy against its periodical diseases is at hand. Philosophy will remain in a healthy condition, and it will follow the same continuous progress as the other branches of human knowledge, provided only it keeps faith with its own nature, which is that of a pure speculative knowledge. In this sense was it true to say, as Brentano said it to Carl Stumpf, that his discovery of the law of the four phases of philosophy had been to him not only a light, but also a liberation.

Let is be added that history was setting at his disposal just as much material as he needed in order to prove that his law was an objective interpretation of observable facts. It can hardly be denied that western philosophy has followed a similar course during the three main periods of its history, and nobody who has achieved a personal survey of its evolution can have failed to notice striking analogies between the doctrinal attitudes of philosophers whose careers have run wholly independent from one another. The telling examples quoted by Brentano could be supplemented by many others of the same kind. It nevertheless remains true to say, that the German philosopher has had the great merit to single out those facts and to realise that their very existence raised an important philosophical problem. He even was clear-sighted enough to perceive that what was there at stake was nothing less than the nature of philosophical knowledge itself, and he should be given full credit for having been the first to see it.

After paying him that well deserved homage, there remains for us a much less pleasant duty, which is to test the truth value of his philosophical interpretation of those historical facts. That his interpretation of them was essentially philosophical seems to be beyond a doubt, for not only did he conceive his idea of the four phases as an answer to a purely philosophical problem, but that answer itself took in his mind the form of a philosophical law. It is not excluded that his early study of the positive philosophy of Auguste Comte, and quite especially of the famous Comtian law of 'the three stages' invited him to such a bold generalisation of some historical facts. It is true that Brentano has rather severely criticised Comte, and that his own four phases are widely different from the three phases of Comte, both in their contents and in their general inspiration. The fact remains however, that 'die drei Phasen' of Auguste Comte might have invited him to conceive the philosophical evolution of mankind in terms of phases, and to systematise the infinite variety of concrete historical experience by means of an exceedingly simple formula.[11]

The main trouble with such simplifications is, that they usually are over-simplifications. In the first place, the sketchy description of medieval

---

11. Brentano, 'Auguste Comte, und die positive Philosophie', *Die vier Phasen der Philosophie*, pp. 99–133. The paper of Brentano on A. Comte was first printed in 1869, when he was still a Catholic priest. His religious crisis took place in 1870 and he openly left the Church on 11 April 1873. Whether or not Brentano was already acquainted with the positivism of Comte when he first conceived his own 'four phases of philosophy', I am not prepared to say.

philosophy which has been given by Brentano begins with Saint Thomas Aquinas. It could not have begun otherwise. If philosophy always begins by a purely speculative and rational phase, the only conceivable starting point of its history in the Middle Ages has necessarily to be the doctrine of Thomas Aquinas. Yet, everybody knows that there has been a medieval philosophy before the middle of the thirteenth century, so much so that Brentano himself had to describe it, from the notes left by Möhler, when he was writing his chapter of Möhler's *History of the Church*. In other words, the speculative phase is bound always to come first, provided only we suppress what would otherwise come before it. A true picture of medieval philosophy should begun with Alcuin, who was by no means a great philosopher, but whose temper was certainly that of a sincere lover of knowledge for its own sake. Almost immediately after him should come the still enigmatic figure of Scotus Erigena, whose doctrine closely resembles that of Plotinus. The opening phase of medieval philosophy was therefore what should have been the last phase of its decadence: a mysticism where intuition is used as a substitute for our powerless abstract reasoning. This obvious fact suffices to prove that the history of the philosophical doctrines cannot be deduced *a priori*. The existence of a given philosopher and the building up of a given philosophy are particular and contingent historical facts, themselves related to innumerable equally particular and contingent other historical facts. In the case under discussion, there were first the person of Erigena, then the probable fact that he knew some Greek when he came from Ireland to France, then the well established fact that, having found at Saint Denis the works of two Greek neo-Platonists: Pseudo-Dionysius and Maxim the Confessor, he translated them into Latin and fell thereby under their influence. It was therefore largely owing to accidental circumstances that medieval philosophy began as a mere continuation of the last phase of Greek philosophy. To express it in Brentano's terminology, one should have to say that medieval philosophy began by the ultimate phase of its own decadence, which is a palpable absurdity.

Another striking fact, which cannot be much more easily reconciled with Brentano's interpretation of medieval philosophy, is that the Middle Ages have completed at least twice the whole course of their evolution. At least, their history could be easily construed to justify that statement. Why not say, for instance, that after the speculative dogmatism of Saint Anselm, the near-nominalism of Abelard resulted in the scepticism of John of Salisbury, to find its ultimate conclusion in the mysticism of the Victorines? The four phases would thus have been completed even before the birth of Thomas Aquinas. Of course, objections could be raised against such an interpretation, but many more, and much more serious ones could be found against the second series of four phases which has been described by Brentano. One does not find in the first series the chronological impossibilities that mar the second one. Thus, for instance, the speculative mysticism of Ramon Lull (1235–1315) cannot possibly have arisen as a reaction against the scepticism of William of Ockham (1300–50). Even Meister Eckhardt (1260–1327) wrote and taught before the times of the English nominalist, so that, in such cases, the mystical reaction would have preceded the sceptical move against which it is supposed to have reacted.

There seems to be, in the doctrine of Brentano, together with a solid nucleus of truth, some fundamental mistake concerning the very nature of that truth.

One of the most notable characters of the four phases of philosophy, such as Brentano conceived them, is that they are an empirical explanation of essentially philosophical relations. To begin with, the so-called first phase does not entail the recognition by the human mind of any principle, or set of principles, which should be received as necessarily true. As soon as a pure intellectual interest for speculative knowledge is there, philosophy also is there. From that point of view, the actual contents of intellectual knowledge is of no importance whatsoever and it plays no part as a determining factor of the evolution of philosophy. So long as men will remain interested in knowledge for knowledge's sake, philosophy will remain in its first phase, the only one in which it keeps faith with its own essence and can fulfil its own destiny. This is so clearly an affair of mere mental attitude, that the whole problem of the transition from the first phase of philosophy to the second one reduces itself, in the mind of Brentano, to what he calls a problem of 'cultural psychology'. Let there be the slightest weakening of the speculative interest of the mind and the practical phase of philosophy shall begin at once. Now to maintain theoretical principles on the strength of purely practical needs is to acknowledge that those principles are without theoretical justification. Hence scepticism, itself soon to be followed by a mystical reaction. Consequently, the remarkable parallelism observed by Brentano between the three great periods of the history of philosophy can be explained away by 'considerations of the simplest sort borrowed from cultural psychology'.[12] Those things do happen and there is nothing more to be said about them.

Such an explanation was quite in keeping with the central inspiration of Brentano's own philosophy. Some of his disciples strongly resent the accusation of psychologism which is often directed against his philosophical attitude. In what measure they are justified in their protest is a difficult problem, whose solution would require a discussion of Brentano's doctrine as a whole. The truth about it seems at least to be, that Brentano often resorted to psychological and more or less empirical explanations, without ever losing the right feeling that, in philosophical problems, psychological necessities are of a more than empirical nature. For instance, where he says that the passage from the first phase to the second one is ascribable to a weakening or to a corruption of the speculative interest, he is using two terms whose respective meanings are altogether different; for indeed the weakening of an interest is a mere psychological fact, whereas the corruption of a notion entails a speculative error about its meaning. It can hardly be doubted that, in Brentano's own mind, the second term was a correction of the first one, or at least was intended to leave open another abstract possibility. The fact remains, however, that he always considered the knowledge of psychological laws as identical with philosophical knowledge itself: *die Kenntnis der psychischen Gesetze, also das philosophische Wissen.*[13] No wonder then if both in Möhler's *History of the Church* and in his

12. Brentano, *Die vier Phasen*, p. 7.   13. Brentano, *Über die Grunde*, p. 100.

own *Four Phases of Philosophy*, he never explicitly resorted to more than psychological explanations of the philosophical evolution.

If this be true, the analysis of the disease of philosophy by Brentano was itself part of that disease, in this sense at least, that having assigned to it an unphilosophical cause he could suggest for it but an unphilosophical remedy. It is rather surprising that he himself never noticed it. If intellectual curiosity is a natural feature of the human mind, if, in Aristotle's own words, all men naturally desire to know, the very weakening of that natural desire is an abnormal phenomenon which claims for some intelligible explanation. Why indeed should men so easily get tired of the normal exercise of reason and regularly turn from its speculative and natural use to another use of it which is both essentially practical and unnatural?

To that question, the only conceivable answer is, that for reason to keep faith with its own nature is not a simple question of good will. Men would never despair of the speculative power of reason if they only knew how to use it. What is the trouble with them is not that they do not want to know, but rather that they do not know how to know. The least mistake made by speculative reason on the nature and meaning of its own principles will unavoidably lead it to speculative impossibilities. Hence philosophical failures which their responsible authors regularly blame on the speculative power of reason itself, instead of looking for their causes at their own inability to make good use of it. Consequently, if there are phases in the evolution of philosophy, their order should be rather different, insofar at least as the three first ones are concerned. Supposing an initial stage of pure speculative interest, philosophy will remain in the same sound condition as long as it succeeds in its speculative undertakings. As soon as, by its own fault, it fails and begins to realise its failure, philosophical reason decrees that the discovery of a pure speculative truth is an intrinsic impossibility; hence one of the many sceptical crises which are recorded by history. But precisely because all men naturally wish to know, scepticism can neither ultimately prevail, nor even last very long even as an heroic intellectual attitude. In order to save themselves from philosophical despair, some men will then ask from mystical intuition the certitudes which they can no longer expect from rational demonstration; while some others, more docile to the urgent requests of moral life, will attempt to legitimise the conclusions of metaphysical speculation as postulates of the practical reason. The mystical escape from scepticism is represented in Antiquity by Plotinus, in the Middle Ages by Nicholas of Cues, and in modern times by Schelling. The ethical escape was preferred in Antiquity by the Stoics and the Epicureans, at the end of the Middle Ages by the Christian school of ascetic life and by Erasmus, in modern times by Immanuel Kant and the various representatives of moralism in philosophy. Sometimes, the same man will try to combine both recipes and do it in a more or less successful way. At any rate, the transition from one of those phases to another, can never be accounted for by some purely psychological reaction; it must always be traced back to some necessary relation between philosophical positions.

The main point however is not there. Before deciding the order according to which the four phases of philosophy follow each other, it seems advisable to make sure that such phases do actually exist. As a matter of fact, nothing would be less sure than their existence, at least if they were to be conceived as the successive and obligatory stages of a temporal evolution. As can be seen from his criticism of Comte, Brentano himself never conceived the four phases of philosophy as the concrete expression of some necessary law. Far from thinking that philosophy is bound to begin as a pure speculation and then to degenerate into moralism, scepticism and mysticism, he felt convinced that his discovery of the four phases would inspire philosophers with a deeper respect for the essentially speculative character of philosophy. This being granted, there nevertheless remains to be seen if the temporal meaning that is inseparable from the word *phase* is not somewhat misleading in the present occasion.

The sometimes remarkable analogy that can be observed between the history of the main philosophical periods is itself a philosophical phenomenon due to essentially philosophical causes. All that which, in the history of philosophy, can be traced back to non-philosophical causes is itself irrelevant to philosophy as such. The Durkheimian notion of a sociological history of philosophy for instance, could lead to an interesting study of the social structure of philosophical schools conceived as collective facts; but philosophical schools can exhibit the same structure as social groups and yet be the vehicles of widely different philosophical doctrines. It may prove interesting to stage a comparative study of the Mohammedan scholasticism with the Jewish and the Christian one from the tenth century to the fourteenth century. Mr Masson-Oursel has attempted to do it[14] and his conclusion is that, taken as a collective social fact, scholasticism is 'the pedagogy of a religion'. A rather vague formula indeed, and probably not the best one even from a purely sociological point of view; but a perfectly empty and meaningless one insofar as philosophy itself is concerned, since it covers wholly antagonistic philosophical positions: Avicenna and Algazel, Maimonides and Gabirol, Thomas Aquinas and William of Ockham. In short, sociology can help in defining some external conditions of the exercise of philosophical thinking; it may succeed in explaining equally external analogies between those conditions, but such interpretations will always leave out philosophy itself because they cannot account for the very contents of the various philosophical positions.

For similar reasons, it is a misleading method to look for phases in the succession of philosophical doctrines, and to account for the existence of analogous phases by the natural play of the simplest psychological laws. Seen from without, those regular consecutions of philosophical events necessarily look like phases, but a closer inspection of the facts always reveals that any one of those so-called phases might have actualised itself at practically any time. In point of fact, it may even happen either that all of them be simultaneously represented, or that, on the contrary, the course of history jump over two or three of the preceding phases in order to reach immediately the last one. In not infrequent cases, the same philosophy will provide room for two or three of those so-called phases, which seem then to co-exist in an indivisible unity. Thus, for instance, after beginning by the

14. Masson-Oursel, 'La Scolastique, Étude de philosophie comparée', in *Revue Philosophique*, 1920, pp. 123–41.

fourth phase with Scotus Erigena, the Middle Ages have witnessed the simultaneous existence of a purely theoretical attitude, with Abelard, and of an essentially practical attitude with Saint Bernard. The first and the second phases were therefore given together. But the fourth phase, the mystical one, was also given together with the practical one in the doctrine of Saint Bernard, just as the sceptical phase was co-existing with the speculative one in the doctrine of Abelard. For Abelard was a highly speculative mind indeed, but he often speculated in the wrong way. In those cases, there is no trace of any transition from the speculative to the practical, or from the practical to the sceptical and to the mystical attitudes. Immediately after, the doctrine of the most famous among the disciples of Abelard, John of Salisbury, has likewise combined the practical with the sceptical phases, each of them being there much less the consequence of the other one than its natural complement. Should we look at the thirteenth century, we would find there the rational attitude of Saint Thomas, given together with the mysticism of Saint Bonaventure and of Ramon Lull, and with the practical, anti-speculative tendencies of the Franciscan Spirituals. From the fourteenth century until the dawn of the Renaissance, there will always be representatives of the purely speculative attitude of Saint Thomas, such as Cajetan for instance, battling against a countless host of sceptics and of practically or mystically minded theologians. Of course, it will be objected that, in the fourteenth century, Thomism was but a survival; to which I beg to answer that, for any living thing, it is an excellent thing to survive, since it is still to live, and the survival of a single truth is of much more value than the new arrival of many errors. Let us therefore conclude that, strictly speaking, it is hardly possible to call 'phases' several different philosophical attitudes, which are, or can always be simultaneously represented.

If the historical analogies quoted by Brentano cannot be defined as the successive stages of a regular consecution in time, what is their nature, and how is it possible to explain their existence? They are necessary relations between philosophical principles and philosophical consequences, and those relations are bound to repeat themselves every time, the same principles being posited, philosophers will think consistently enough to pursue them to their ultimate conclusions. Let the most powerful philosophical genius in the world ask the wrong question, or ask the right question in the wrong way, his philosophical undertaking is bound to be a failure. Now the failures of the masters seldom fail to breed scepticism in the minds of the disciples; not at all by reason of some psychological fatigue, but simply because once it is admitted that a certain method is the only sound philosophical method, and that a certain set of principles is the only receivable set of philosophical principles, the failure of that method and of those principles becomes identical with the failure of philosophy itself. On the other hand, it is true to say, with Kant, that metaphysical questions cannot not be asked, even by those who feel convinced that they cannot be answered. This again is not an empirical necessity of a merely psychological nature; metaphysical questions cannot not be asked, because they arise from the very principles of human knowledge. Unless philosophy lose all interest in its own principles, it cannot fail to find itself confronted with those problems. Unavoidable problems have to be answered, and when speculative reason has failed to justify its own answers to such problems, their answers have to be maintained either as postulates of practical reason, or as objects of some supra-rational intuition.

Thus understood, the nucleus of truth that is contained in the doctrine of the four phases of philosophy reduces itself to the endlessly repeated historical evidence, that there is but one way for philosophy to last, which is for it to be true. There is no other philosophy than perennial philosophy, which always lasts and will always survive the countless failures of its various surrogates. Their number does not much matter, nor their ceaselessly changing order of succession; for just as true philosophy is essentially one, its surrogates are but the manifold expression of one and the same fact, which is its corruption. Thus, philosophy is always there, a standing truth to those who have once recognised its nature, a standing failure to those who mistake it for what it is not. Neither moralism, nor scientism, nor psychologism, nor any conceivable variety of pseudo-mysticism are philosophy; consequently their own failure is not its failure. They failed in the Middle Ages as completely as they had already failed in Antiquity, but no more completely than they are failing in our own times, and, being the same mistakes, they were bound to fail in the same way.

5 Franz Brentano on Science and Philosophy[1]

Lucie Gilson

Can philosophy be saved, and, if so, how? A consideration of these questions marks the starting point of Brentano's work, and the desire to bring about the salvation of philosophy is his principal motivation. It is this desire that inspired the first and fourth of his habilitation theses which he defended in a public disputation at the University of Würzburg one hundred years ago. In the first thesis he stated: 'Philosophy must protest against the distinction between speculative and exact sciences; and the justification for this protest is philosophy's very right to existence.'[2] His fourth thesis read: 'The true method of philosophy is none other than that of the natural sciences.'

According to Brentano, philosophy was in danger of destruction, and in order to survive it had to be saved. To understand this we must bear in mind when it was that Brentano began to engage in philosophical reflection. He started his university studies in 1856, and he was deeply disappointed by the philosophy of his time, dominated by the heritage of Kant and the post-Kantian German Idealists. In contrast to these doctrines, the natural sciences – physics, chemistry, the young science of biology – continued to make progress, and many people were convinced that positive science was destined to supplant philosophy, at least any philosophy that purports to deal with problems which clearly do not belong to the realm of science. Around 1860, Brentano himself was at the point of despairing of philosophy, but his confidence was restored by a liberating intuition, a vision of the history of philosophy which he expressed in the doctrine of the four phases.[3]

This doctrine appears quite frequently in Brentano's teachings and work. Among his published writings it first occurs in the chapter he wrote on the history of the ecclesiastic sciences in the Middle Ages in Möhler's *Kirchengeschichte (Church History)*.[4] But there is a study, published in 1895 as *Die vier Phasen der Philosophie (The Four Phases of Philosophy*, from a lecture

1. Translated from the French by Linda L. McAlister and Margarete Schättle. Reprinted from *Revue Internationale de Philosophie*, vol. 20, no. 78 (1966), pp. 416–33

2. See *Über die Zukunft der Philosophie*, ed. Oskar Kraus (Leipzig, 1929), p. 136 (Latin text) and p. 137 (German text).

3. See Stumpf's memoir of Brentano, pp. 10–46 above.

4. J.A. Möhler, *Kirchengeschichte*, ed. P.B. Gams, 2 vols (Regensburg, 1867), pp. 526–84. See ch. 4 above.

delivered in 1894), whose main object is the explication of this doctrine.[5]

According to Brentano, there is an analogy between the development of philosophical thought in each of the three great periods of history, ancient, medieval, and modern. In each of these periods philosophy actually passes through four phases. At the outset there is an ascending phase in which the studies assume a purely theoretical character and in which the method is essentially in comformity with nature, although, at the beginning, this method must still be perfected considerably. In antiquity it was Aristotle, and in the Middle Ages St Thomas Aquinas who marked the climax of this phase. In modern times it begins with Bacon and Descartes and also includes Locke and Leibniz. Then there follow three stages of decadence. First, interest in theory declines, giving way to interest in practical matters, and research is no longer carried out as rigorously and scientifically as before; this is what happened, for example, after Locke and Leibniz, in the period which was called 'The Enlightenment'. Such a philosophy gives rise to scepticism, which constitutes the second stage of decadence; in modern times this phase is pre-eminently represented by the thought of David Hume. And scepticism itself leads to the final phase, where, as a kind of counter-reaction, the intense need for knowledge emerges anew, and tries in feverish haste to satisfy itself by employing wholly unnatural means, as, for example, immediate intuition and mystical enthusiasm of intellectual life. In the modern period Reid and Kant are among those who begin to fall back on unnatural means in order to save knowledge. But with Fichte, Schelling and Hegel philosophy reaches the most extreme limit of degeneration; their systems, lacking any solid foundations, antagonised thinkers, yet this in itself was a source of hope: a man disappointed by these fragile edifices strives for firmer knowledge, and we can hope to see the beginning of a new period in the evolution of philosophy.

But this doctrine of the four phases could not actually free Brentano of his doubts unless he accepts another premise – namely, that a final rebirth of philosophy is possible, a rebirth not followed by decadence. Philosophy has at its disposal the means necessary for its salvation, but it must take cognisance of the fundamental methodological requirement: to follow the method of natural science. And, as we have said, this is exactly what Brentano stated in his fourth habilitation thesis in 1866, while he objected in his first thesis to the distinction between the speculative and exact sciences and regarded this objection as of vital importance to philosophy.

This was, therefore, a mission which the young Brentano, like the young Descartes before him, felt he must fulfil. Descartes felt himself called upon to reconstruct the edifice of knowledge using a method whose fundamental requirements were revealed to him by reflection on mathematics. Brentano believed he must save philosophy by applying the method of the natural sciences. He had 'the inner certainty that he was moving in the right direction and was founding a purely scientific philosophy'; he felt called to elaborate this philosophy – a calling 'both from within and above'.[6]

5. Franz Brentano, *Die vier Phasen der Philosophie*, ed. Oskar Kraus (Leipzig, 1926). pp. 1–32.

6. See Edmund Husserl's 'Reminiscences of Franz Brentano', pp. 47–9 above.

It seems as though all his life Brentano worked toward the accomplishment of this mission. The meaning of his methodological principle is probably, in reality, more complex, however, than it seemed at the beginning. The question arises, what his exact interpretation was and whether this interpretation remained unchanged throughout his long life.

Over the years his method certainly changed. At the beginning it was much like the method of the natural sciences. Those sciences which are based on the sensible world are the experiential sciences and are based on induction.[7] In the course on the existence of God which he gave from 1868 to 1891 at Würzburg and Vienna,[8] certain essential methodological characteristics resemble those of the natural sciences: the philospher relies on facts which are themselves very often taken from the natural sciences, and he proceeds by the formulation and examination of hypotheses in which frequent use is made of the calculus of probability. The foreword to *Psychology From an Empirical Standpoint*, written in 1874, begins with the words, 'The title which I have given this work characterises both its object and its method. My psychological standpoint is empirical; experience alone is my teacher'.[9] The reliance on what is given in inner perception, the evident grasping of our mental phenomena, their augmentation by means of observation of earlier mental phenomena in memory, and the study of the outward manifestations of the mental lives of others – all of this means that we appeal to experience as a basis of research. And we must go a step further, and then further still, by induction from the patiently observed facts to general laws which then become the starting points for deductions.

Moreover, it is clear that Brentano, in his attempt to apply the method of the natural sciences to metaphysics or psychology, has no intention of imitating the detailed procedures of the physicist, chemist, or physiologist. The difference between the fields does not allow for a complete assimilation of techniques; for example, the study of the ultimate elements of mental life is not a chemical analysis. But the essential requirements of research remain the same.

Here again it is the salvation of philosophy which is at stake. It is essential that the true meaning of the methodological principle be properly discerned. It is this principle which appeared in 1892 when Brentano, in his lecture 'Über die Zukunft der Philosophie' ('On the Future of Philosophy'), defended the view that the humanities can employ the method of the natural sciences, against Exner, then the rector of the University of Vienna. He did not want this affirmation to be misinterpreted; in fact the different branches of the natural sciences do not use exactly the same procesures themselves. What is important in philosophy is 'to proceed in a manner analogous to

---

7. See Franz Brentano, *Versuch über die Erkenntnis*, ed. Alfred Kastil (Leipzig, 1925). Brentano reiterates that the natural sciences are 'experiential sciences' and 'are based on induction'; these affirmations do not seem to have raised any difficulties in his eyes.

8. His lectures have been published by Alfred Kastil, in Franz Brentano, *Vom Dasein Gottes* (Leipzig, 1929), pp. 1–445.

9. *Psychology from an Empirical Standpoint*, English edition ed. Linda L. McAlister (London and New York, 1973), p. xv.

natural science'.[10] Even during that period Brentano rejected certain applications of his principle, which constituted real errors and which, because they led to failure, would have endangered first the method itself and then finally philosophy itself. Among these errors are, above all, the confusion of fields, for example the error of those who take developments typical of physiology and apply them in psychology.[11] Therefore the affirmation of the methodological principle in no way implies a true assimilation of philosophical studies to the natural sciences.

On the other hand, it seems that during the last years of Brentano's life, his method appeared, even less than before, to be a pure and simple utilisation of the procedures of the natural sciences. Certainly, experience continued to play a role, but very often its role was simply to enable the mind to form concepts; the analyses, which can be called *a priori* because they are based only on considerations concerning the content of these notions, then intervene and are the condition for the progress of knowledge. Such analyses, as a matter of fact, were always part of Brentano's philosophy, but their importance has clearly increased. This is shown, for example, in the short treatise of 1915 'Gedankengang beim Beweise für das Dasein Gottes',[12] where we can compare his arguments in favour of Theism with those he had employed in his courses on the existence of God. In the same period Brentano also frequently analysed questions of descriptive psychology, the theory of knowledge, and of ontology. He studied the same problems again and again; he was driven by the desire to examine them repeatedly in detail, and whenever he considered it necessary he changed his earlier views. He never ceased to work with the greatest patience, but the anaology of his method to that of the natural sciences still seems to be somewhat distant.

To give an example indicative of his research work and thereby demonstrate his attitude toward philosophy during his later years, we would like to point out certain aspects of his conception of mental phenomena, as found in the writings of that period. We are not concerned here with a detailed explanation; all we want to show is how this conception is at the point of convergence of several lines of analysis bearing on relations of various types – on the mental relation itself, on the relation of accident to substance, and on the causal relation.

Studying the mental phenomenon or the mental act (or act of thought or mental activity) means, first of all, emphasising its essential characteristic, that is, according to Brentano, its relation to an object. He was of this opinion as early as 1874 and it was always his fundamental thesis in psychology: to think means to think of something. The *Psychology* of 1874 was a conscious attempt to revive a doctrine which dates back to the Scholastics, and even further back, to Aristotle. Like Scholastic philosophy it deals with an intentional existence or a mental existence of the object in

10. Brentano, *Über die Zukunft der Philosophie*, p. 45.
11. *Zukunft*, p. 76.
12. In *Vom Dasein Gottes*, pp 446–89.

the mind.[13] In his later years Brentano dropped the expression 'intentional existence', because he refused to attribute an existence to the thought-of object. But he always believed that the act of thinking is characterised by the relation to an object, or, to use an expression which he himself considered the most exact and precise one, 'the relation to something as an object'.[14] It is this relation which he called a 'mental relation'.

Later on Brentano was even convinced that the concept of thought can exist as a unity only if the expression 'something', which refers to the object of thought, is univocal.[15] The natural fundamental similarity among acts of thought, insofar as they all relate to an object, requires that the *something*, the term of this mental relation, must always be something real, a *thing*[16] which does not mean, however, that it must always be something that exists. Certainly we are not concerned only with material things but with everything to which we can attribute a *being* in the strict sense, that is to say 'every substance, every multiplicity of substances, and every part of a substance' and 'also every accident'.[17] The mental relation cannot have as an object an abstraction as such, or the past or the future as such, or a thought-of thing as such; sometimes we express ourselves as if our thoughts relate to objects which are not things, but linguistic analysis can actually help us to recognise the real things which are the true objects of mental activity behind the expressions we use. For example, whenever we speak about thoughts and acts of thought, mental acts, as we are doing right now, it is always a thinking being with which we are concerned.

On the other hand it would seem that the expressions 'mental act' and 'mental relation' are synonymous. In reality, the mental phenomenon or the mental act is always complex and yet a unity at the same time; it presupposes a multitude of relations, yet those relations in no way impair its fundamental unity. If there is a multitude of relations, this is because the mental act always refers to at least two objects simultaneously and because the reference to one object can manifest itself in a variety of modes; but this still does not result in a multitude of mental acts. In essence these affirmations had already been put forward in the *Psychology* of 1874, but they underwent new developments in Brentano's late writings, with which we are now concerned.

We must recall, first of all, that the mental act always refers to two objects, to its primary object and to itself as secondary object; at a certain moment something is thought by the subject, and this *something* is the primary object; at the same time the mental act or rather the being which performs this mental activity is itself the object of the mental act, it is the secondary object. In other words, mental activity is always conscious and it is a unity in which the thinking being clearly recognises both an object of its mental act and the act itself. The thinking being understands precisely the

---

13. *Psychology from an Empirical Standpoint*, p. 88.
14. *Psychology*, p. 271.
15. *Psychology*, p. 321.
16. *Psychology*, p. xx.
17. Brentano, *Kategorienlehre*, ed. Alfred Kastil (Leipzig, 1933), p. 11.

act's double character as an act which relates to an object, and as a conscious act.[18]

Furthermore, when we think of an object in relation to another one, we think of it *in modo recto* or *in recto* (in the direct mode), and we think of the other part of the relation *in obliquo* (in the oblique mode). If I imagine a being thinking of an object, I am imagining the thinking being *in recto* and that which it thinks *in obliquo*.[19] Since the thinking being is always itself the secondary object of its mental activity, the presentation of that which it is thinking about is always added to the presentation it has of itself as secondary object; therefore the object it thinks of *in recto* as primary object appears here again *in obliquo*. None of this harms the unity of the mental act in the least.

Neither is it impaired by the fact that the relation of the thought to an object may itself assume a multitude of modes. Indeed, the diversity of the modes of this relation provides the very basis for Brentano's classification of mental phenomena. If we consider the relation to an object in its simplest form, the thought is directed toward an object which is apparent to it, and we have a presentation. The mode of the relation of the mental phenomenon to the object can be more complicated but there will never be a mental phenomenon of which one is not conscious; every mental phenomenon is a presentation or is based upon a presentation. If the object is not only presented but also affirmed as being true or rejected as being false, we have a judgement; and if love or hate are also present we have an emotion.[20] A thought can be directed toward an object in these various modes of the mental relation simultaneously, and the secondary object is always an object of a presentation as well as an affirmation. It is this affirmation, or, in other words, this judgement, which constitutes evident inner perception; and sometimes we also feel an emotion toward the secondary object, which then becomes pleasant or unpleasant.[21]

Thus the mental act remains a unity despite its complexity. It is clear that for Brentano the mental act owes its unity to the unity which is implicit in the basic mental relation that relates the thinking being to what is, for it, the primary object in the direct mode.

But several mental acts can take place simultaneously and occur in the same thinking subject. This subject can see and hear at the same time; the two simultaneous acts are clearly recognisable and are accidents of the same substance. We can see here the connection between the study of the mental phenomenon and Brentano's analyses of the accident and its relation to substance. The mental act or rather the being thought of as a being which sees, hears, judges or to use a more general term, thinks, is an accident in relation to a substance, a subject underlying its various accidents. For

18. *Psychology*, pp. 275–6.

19. *Psychology*, p. 281.

20. This method of classification of mental phenomena had already been adopted by Brentano in 1874 and was always retained by him. See *Psychology*, Book 2, chapters V–IX, pp. 177–268.

21. *Kategorienlehre*, p. 222; *Psychology*, p. 276.

Brentano the accident is not, properly speaking, a complementary determination which attaches itself to the substance; it is a whole which envelops the substance as a part. And it is not formed by a second part being added to this substance; for an accident to happen to this substance it is necessary that it is enriched by a new modality: the accident is a whole which results from the increase in the modality of the substance.[22] When we begin to see or hear, our being acquires a new modality which can come to an end, while we remain the same being. We can understand, therefore, that a simultaneous occurrence of accidents is possible without destroying the unity of the substance. Here Brentano's terminology varies, but his doctrine is clear. Without rejecting the notion that a substance can be the subject of several accidents, he prefers to speak of a multiple accident rather than a plurality of accidents. We can see the reason: he certainly wants to emphasise the unity of the being which has simultaneous presentations of different modalities. At the same time, he insists that one part of this multiple accident can disappear without altering the substance as such or the rest of this accident; the being which sees and hears can stop hearing and continue seeing, and yet remain the same individual being and the same seeing being.[23]

Furthermore, because of its connection with the study of the relation between substance and accident, the descriptive analysis of thought cannot, in Brentano's case, be separated from the doctrine of the categories. The accident's dependence on the relation to the substance is itself called 'categorical' and it is in virtue of the different modes of that relation that the accidents can be arranged into different classes which constitute categories.[24] For there are, according to him, two large groups of accidents, the 'qualities' or 'inherent characteristics' on the one hand, and the 'passive affections' on the other hand. The word 'affection' here designates a modification experienced by the being and its meaning is further intensified by the use of the qualification 'passive'. And all the manifestations of thought are included in the second group, that of the passive affections. For a passive affection to persist it is necessary that an active principle continue to be in effect; thus we think of something only as long as we are stimulated to think about it.[25] We can further differentiate among the passive affections; for example, the intensification of an emotion, or the moral

22. See *Kategorienlehre*, p. 271.
23. See *Kategorienlehre*, pp. 222–3.
24. See for example, *ibid.*, pp. 219, 254, 258. These texts indicate, moreover, that substance too has a place in Brentano's table of categories. In order to understand Brentano's concept here it is necessary to recall the relation that he himself established between his doctrine and Aristotle's. 'Aristotle had wanted to distinguish between the categories on the basis of the different ways in which they relate to the first subject. And we can and must remain true to him in this matter . . .' (*ibid.*, p. 259). Now the relation of the accident to the substance which is its subject is different from the relation of that substance to itself, because in the latter case we have a relation of identity. Having established this distinction, Brentano could then distinguish the various classes of accidents from one another according to the differences in the relation of the accident to the subject.
25. *Kategorienlehre*, p. 276.

conversion which makes a virtuous man out of a bad one, are transformations and lead to a result distinct from the passive affection itself; in some cases, on the other hand, the only effect of the action is the passive affection: thoughts are precisely this second type of passive affection. And sometimes the thought itself clearly contains an indication of what it produces; we can therefore immediately recognise, in its particularity, that of which it is the effect. This is true of the conclusion of a rational argument, of the knowledge of an evident axiom *ex terminis*, of a motivated desire or a love which springs from the presentation of the object. It is not always the case, but in every instance the thought presupposes something which caused it; we can say that a thinking being is identical with a 'being which, because of its nature as a thinking being, is caused by something else'.[26] Therefore, if we follow the description of Brentano's conceptions which are here closely intertwined with one another, we are led to the study of causal relations.

Yet for the moment we will not continue with this explanation, but attempt, rather, to make a synthesis at this point. Brentano looks at the thought process from various and complementary points of view – descriptive psychology, epistemology, and ontology being in many respects inseparable. Among other things, he makes it clear that, in his opinion, every thought involves a double relation, a relation to the object and a relation to that which produces it.[27] And we are attempting to show how the study of this double relation is itself closely connected to other analyses of Brentano's, particularly those which concern the relation between substance and accident. Furthermore, being aware of this double relation of our thoughts with respect to their objects on the one hand, and with respect to that which causes them on the other hand, it seems that we can understand the juxtaposition in Brentano's vocabulary of the expressions 'mental act' and 'passive mental affection', expressions which Brentano does not hesitate to use simultaneously to designate the fact of thinking.[28] It seems to us that the expression 'mental act' can be used to refer to the act of thinking when we consider its intentional character, while the expression 'passive mental affection' expresses its character as the effect produced by a cause.

In our opinion, this doctrine raises a certain number of problems. It would be particularly helpful if we could establish precisely the scope of the word 'act' in the expression 'mental act'. At first we will be tempted to emphasise that the thinking subject is directed toward things, in the broad sense in which Brentano uses the word 'thing' as a synonym for 'a reality' or 'being' in the strict sense. But if we look at the relation between the thought and the primary object in Brentano's doctrine, we must remember that the real thing to which this thought refers cannot exist outside of the mind and that, on the other hand, the act of thinking never causes the occurrence of an 'object as object'[29] in the mind, because this would be a thought-of thing,

26. 'Als-Denkend-Bewirktwerdendes', *Kategorienlehre*, p. 217.
27. *Kategorienlehere*, pp. 240–1.
28. *Kategorienlehre*, p. 222.
29. See, for example, *Psychology*, p. 294.

and a thought-of thing is not a being in the strict sense. From the existential point of view, we can affirm only one thing definitely, according to Brentano, and this is the fact that thought always presupposes the existence of a subject which, when thinking, augments itself through an accidental determination; in other words, it enriches itself by means of a modality which takes place, moreover, within the subject in a passive form. Thus we can foresee certain difficulties in these conceptions. We might be surprised, at first, to discover that thought is treated in a very general way as a passive modification, as a state suffered. And when we look at the very heart of this doctrine, are there not two tendencies which are very difficult to reconcile? On the one hand, we are led to regard the thinking subject as a 'being open toward things',[30] but on the other hand, is there not a danger of a simple modality of this subject pushing the object into the background?

Yet we will not try to examine these questions here. What we will attempt to do is discern, by means of these analyses, the attitude which they presuppose when philosophical problems are encountered.

It is clear that this psychology, so completely infused with ontological considerations, hardly seems to conform to that which we expected on the basis of the statements Brentano made about the role the method of the natural sciences plays in philosophy.

Certainly we must avoid excessive generalisation, and we must not claim that in the later part of his life Brentano regarded this kind of analysis as the only mode of philosophical reflection. In his short treatise of 1915 entitled 'Gedankengang beim Beweise für das Dasein Gottes', the important role played by conceptual analyses does not preclude his resorting to a number of observations and discussions pertaining to Darwin's theory, in the study of the teleological argument. We must not forget that in Brentano's mind descriptive psychology, which attempts to establish the characteristics of mental phenomena and to classify them, must precede genetic psychology which uncovers the causal laws that govern them; we can assume that if Brentano had had the time to elaborate his entire genetic psychology, he would have adopted a method in this field which would have resembled the method of the natural sciences more than that of descriptive psychology. On the other hand, a psychological institute, well equipped for experimental research, would be very useful not only for the progress of genetic psychology, but for that of descriptive psychology as well; this was the sort of institute Brentano wanted to see established in Vienna when he left the city in 1894.[31]

Here we should add that the analyses of descriptive psychology, some examples of which we have given, are themselves based on experience, that is, experience which Brentano regards as evident, namely inner perception. The general concepts, the analysis of which leads to the formulation of rationally necessary propositions, are, in effect, themselves formulated on the basis of facts provided by inner perception. By using only a few of his basic teachings we can emphasise that it is through this inner perception

30. M. Cruz Hernandez, *Francisco Brentano* (Salamanca, 1953), p. 122.
31. Brentano, *Meine letzten Wünsche für Österreich* (Stuttgart, 1895) pp. 33–5. (See above, ch. 1, p. 8.)

that we, as a secondary object, are conscious of ourselves as thinking beings and as beings engaging in various kinds of mental activity. It is, therefore, due to this inner perception that we are conscious of ourselves as thinking the primary as well as secondary object simultaneously in the unity of our mental act. It informs us only of our present mental state, although it is true that we can augment it by means of memory, through the analysis of earlier mental facts; thus inner perception of our present mental activity is the only thing that is evident. Therefore, descriptive psychology could be regarded as an experiential science because it tries to employ the data of inner perception and to respect all of its teachings despite the fact that it claims to state the sum total of rationally necessary propositions, analytic certainties, which can, in a sense, be called *a priori*.

One might even be tempted to say that some of the rationally necessary propositions are obtained through induction. Brentano, as a matter of fact, distinguishes between a broader and a narrower sense of the word 'induction'.[32] In the broader sense this word means every thought process starting from more particular and more assertoric propositions and leading toward a general or apodictic judgement. Thus, among the propositions of descriptive psychology certain ones emerge immediately from the analysis of concepts which are themselves elaborated by the fact of inner perception. While the facts of inner perception, the assertoric judgements, are expressed in affirmative propositions, the analytical and apodictic ones, which are imposed universally in the name of the law of contradiction, are negative, according to Brentano's logic. It is true that they are sometimes stated affirmatively, but the exact, strict formulation is negative. Thus there exists no mental act that does not relate to an object, no judgement and no emotion that does not presuppose the presentation of its object. It seems that the essential thesis of Brentano's later doctrine that the mental relation can have as an object only a being in the strict sense, a real thing, can be included among the fundamental rationally evident propositions. If we want to use the word 'induction' here in the broader sense, we can say that we obtain the basic propositions of descriptive psychology through induction; they are then the starting point of analytical deductions which lead to necessary consequences.

According to Brentano, however, and for analogous reasons, one can also say that the fundamental propositions of arithmetic and pure geometry are obtained through induction. Yet the word 'induction' can also be used in a narrower sense; then it refers to a reasoning process by means of which we move from facts to general laws. According to Brentano, this is the most common meaning of the word; this is clearly the meaning he has in mind when he attributes an inductive character to the natural sciences. But if we adopt this more common mode of expression, we cannot say that Brentano's later analyses are based on inductions. Ultimately their method resembles that of mathematics as a purely analytical science despite the role played by experience in the origin of its concepts.

32. On the two sense of the word 'induction', see *Versuch über die Erkenntnis*, pp. 80–2.

But can we discern what is essential for Brentano in his methodological principle, namely the application of the method of the natural sciences to philosophy? As far as we know he never gave up the principle, and yet we see that some of his work does not conform to it very well.

Perhaps we will not find a single answer, but rather two tendencies, in Brentano's writings. And these two tendencies seem to us to be connected with the double meaning of the word 'nature' in this doctrine.

Nature can be the world perceivable by the senses, the object of the natural sciences, i.e. physics, chemistry, physiology. To apply the method of the natural sciences, or at least an analogous method, to philosophy means to take one's inspiration from their procedures when elaborating a philosophy. We are certainly not interested in adopting them in all their details, but we want to rely on experience and learn from it by means of methods of reasoning essentially the same as those in the sciences. As we have seen, this seems to have been Brentano's first conception. It is still the one that comes out in his lecture 'Über Schellings Philosophie'[33] in 1889, where he advocated the elaboration of a 'philosophy of facts' conforming to the requirements of a truly scientific induction and deduction.

But 'nature' can also mean the nature of the object studied, the sum total of its essential characteristics. In order to procede in conformity with nature, it is, therefore, necessary to adapt one's mode of research to the nature of whatever object is being studied.[34] We must furthermore bear in mind the characteristics of the human mind, its actual resources, and this in opposition to the 'anti-natural' procedures of the phase of extreme decadence. It seems, however that it is not a matter of extending the method of one particular science to all fields, but of striving to maintain the same standard of objectivity. If the natural sciences, as the sciences of the sensible world, provide philosophy with an ideal methodology, it is only insofar as they exemplify such objectivity for philosophy. To follow a method analogous to the natural sciences means to rely on the facts and then engage in rigorous research while respecting the requirements inherent in the data, despite diverse modes of reasoning in the various fields. Brentano sometimes seems to have both interpretations of the methodological principle in mind at once, and the transition from the one to the other takes place almost imperceptibly. But it is the second one which seems to form the essential basis for the analyses of mental activity, certain aspects of which were discussed above.

Having pointed out these two tendencies, we can ask whether this basic principle is not in reality less clear than it apears to be. Sometimes Brentano wanted to take it literally, but he was also fully conscious that one must adapt the method to the characteristics of each category of objects. His doctrine seems to have evolved in the direction of a greater autonomy of philosophy from the natural sciences. To the extent to which he seemed to have been unable to fulfil his goal of developing the whole of philosophy through the employment of the method of the natural sciences, it is likely

33. In *Zukunft*, pp. 101–32; see especially p. 123.
34. *Zukunft*, p. 35.

that the methodological hypothesis on which it was based was not completely satisfactory.

But other lessons can be learned from this study. When we put aside the detailed debates that can arise concerning Brentano's conception of philosophical method, what is the basic inspiration that it expresses?

It is his conviction that there are not two radically different types of problem, those which would be the object of pure speculation and those to which a truly scientific method would be applicable. Writing to Bergmann in 1914, he reiterated that philosophy must protest against the notion that there is an opposition between philosophical speculation and science. If it does not do this, it will be unable to regain its place among the sciences, and will be even less able to claim the position of the queen of the sciences, as it did in antiquity. He wants to affirm that there is no fundamental difference between the mental attitude adopted, whether one is working in science or in philosophy. And in expressing this conviction he believes that he is carrying on the tradition of the greatest philosophers of the past, particularly of Aristotle, whom he regarded all his life as his 'great master'. He wants to return to the Aristotelian conception of wisdom as a unity; the distinction between the different branches of knowledge must not make us forget this fundamental unity.

There were other nineteenth-century thinkers who thought they were preserving this Aristotelian conception of the unity of knowledge. Auguste Comte states that he uses 'the word "philosophy" in the sense attributed to it by the ancients, Aristotle above all, as designating the general system of human concepts',[35] and positivism, as the study of the general aspects of the different sciences, owes its unity, in his opinion, to the unity of the method employed by the positive sciences. In certain respects Brentano seems to come very close to positivism; that he knew and studied this school of thought is shown above all by his essay of 1869, *Auguste Comte und die positive Philosophie*.[36] But even though he demands one single method, inspired by the conception of the natural sciences, for the whole area of knowledge, he does not mean to renounce psychology and theistic metaphysics, but merely to provide a firm foundation for them.

What is dead is not metaphysics itself, but the dialectical systems that had usurped its place. Philosophy will profit from the progress of science, and this will serve to renew its ties with the ideal of the great metaphysicians of the past and to realise this ideal more completely than they would have been able to do themselves. The golden age of philosophy is, therefore, not behind us but 'before us'.[37]

Franz Brentano's enthusiasm was an inspiration to others; as Husserl affirmed in 1932 to Maria Brück, 'Without Brentano I would never have written one word of philosophy'.[38]

---

35. Auguste Comte, *Cours de philosophie positive*, author's preface.
36. Reprinted in *Die vier Phasen*, pp. 99–133.
37. *Zukunft*, p. 45.
38. Maria Brück, *Über das Verhältnis E. Husserls zu F. Brentano*, (Würzburg, 1933), p.3.

6   Brentano and Wundt: Empirical and Experimental Psychology[1]

E.B. Titchener

1

The year 1874 saw the publication of two books which, as the event has shown, were of first-rate importance for the development of modern psychology. Their authors, already in the full maturity of life, were men of settled reputation, fired as investigators with the zeal of research, endowed as teachers with a quite exceptional power to influence younger minds, ready as polemists to cross swords with a Zeller or a Helmholtz. Yet one would look in vain for any sign of closer intellectual kinship between them; hardly, indeed, could one find a greater divergence either of tendency or of training. Psychology, seeing how much their work and example have done to assure her place among the sciences, may gladly confess her debt to both. The student of psychology, though his personal indebtedness be also twofold, must still make his choice for the one or the other. There is no middle way between Brentano and Wundt.[2]

Franz Brentano began his career as a Catholic theologian. In 1867 he published an outline of the history of philosophy within the medieval Church which sets forth, as clearly and sharply as the essay of thirty years later, his famous doctrine of the four phases.[3] Early and late, however, his intellectual interest has centred in the philosophy of Aristotle. He came to

---

1. Reprinted from the *American Journal of Psychology*, no. 32 (1921), pp. 108–20.
2. Franz Brentano, *Psychology from an Empirical Standpoint*, ed. Linda L. McAlister (London and New York, 1973). Cf. the biographical note in the C. Hague translation of Brentano's *The Origin of the Knowledge of Right and Wrong*; M. Heinze, *F. Ueberwegs Grundriß der Geschichte der Philosophie*, vol. 4 (1906), pp. 332ff. Wilhelm Wundt, *Grundzüge der physiologischen Psychologie* (henceforth cited as *PP*) (1874). The first ten chapters of Wundt's work were issued in 1873 and are utilised by Brentano. (Titchener himself translated the first six chapters of the fifth German edition (1902) of Wundt's book as *Principles of Physiological Psychology* (London and New York, 1910). References to Wundt's book in this article, however, are to the first German edition.) For a bibliography of Wundt's scientific writings, see *American Journal of Psychology*, vol. xix (1908). C.B. Heinze, pp. 322ff.
3. J.A. Möhler's *Kirchengeschichte*, vol. 2 (1867) pp. 539 f.; F. Brentano, *Die vier Phasen der Philosophie und ihr augenblicklicher Stand* (1895). The four phases, repeated in the three great philosophical periods, are those of scientific construction, failure or perversion of the scientific interest, scepticism and mysticism.

psychology by way of an intensive study of the *De Anima*, and he has made the Aristotelian method his pattern of scientific procedure. We possess, unfortunately, only the first volume of his *Psychologie*.[4] Brentano seems always to have preferred the spoken to the written word: but this volume, like everything else that he has given to the press, is complete in itself, the finished expression of his mature thought.

Wilhelm Wundt started out as a physiologist, interested in the special phenomena of nerve and muscle. In 1862 he had sought to lay the foundations of an 'experimental psychology' (the phrase now appears in print for the first time)[5] in a theory of sense-perception. Here he fell into the mistake to which every student of natural science is liable who turns, without due preparation, to the things of mind: the mistake, namely, of supposing that psychology is nothing more than an applied logic; and the mistake was repeated in a popular work upon human and animal psychology which followed on the heels of the technical volume. By 1874 he had definitely discarded this earlier view for the conception of psychology as an independent science. He still maintained, however, that the path to it leads through the anatomy and physiology of the nervous system.

Such, in briefest outline, were the conditions under which the two psychologies acquired their form and substance. We see, on the one hand, a man who has devoted his 'hours of solitary reflection' to ancient and medieval philosophy; we see, on the other hand, a man who has wrought out in the laboratory his contributions to the latest-born of the experimental sciences. They are both professors of philosophy, and they are both to range widely, in the future, over the varied fields of philosophical enquiry. Yet it would be wrong to suppose that the psychology to which they have now attained, and which, by a happy chance, they give to the world in the same year, represents merely an incident, even if it were the central incident, of their philosophical history. Psychology, on the contrary, has laid strong hands upon them, and is to dominate all their further thinking. Wundt, a generation later, will round off the manifold list of his books with the encyclopedic folk-psychology, and Brentano never gives up the hope of a descriptive – to be followed, perhaps, at long last by a genetic – psychology as the ripe fruit of his studious old age.

2

We shall better understand the nature of this choice which lies before us if we first note the points of resemblance between the two systems. For even in 1874 psychology was not in such bad case that Brentano and Wundt are always at variance. They agree that psychology holds a place of high importance in the fellowship of the sciences, and that it is logically prior to

4. Brentano's original plan was that his *Psychology* would contain six books; Books I and II were published in one volume in 1874. He never fulfilled his intention of publishing the four additional books. See 'Foreword to the 1874 Edition', *Psychology*, p. xv. A posthumous volume of Brentano's later psychological writings was edited by Oskar Kraus and is entitled *Vom sinnlichen und noetischen Bewußtsein, Psychologie III* (Leipzig, 1928); it is not the third book that Brentano had originally planned.

5. W. Wündt, *Beiträge zur Theorie der Sinneswahrnehmung* (1862) p. vi.

natural science.[6] They agree that it may dispense with the concept of substance and confine itself to an account of phenomena.[7] They reject the unconscious as a principle of psychological explanation.[8] They define the unity of consciousness in substantially the same terms.[9] So far there is agreement: and though the agreement is largely of a formal kind, and though a good deal of it has a negative ground in the reaction against Herbart, it serves nevertheless to mark out a common universe of discourse.

On the material side there is also agreement, with such difference of emphasis as the difference of authorship would lead us to expect. We find, for instance, that Brentano deals at length with the general method of psychology, and is at pains to distinguish inner perception from inner observation, while Wundt takes inner observation for granted and describes in detail only those special procedures which raise it to the rank of experiment.[10] We find that Wundt devotes much space to Fechnerian psycho-physics, and interprets the psycho-physical law as a general psychological law of relativity, while Brentano makes only incidental and critical mention of Fechner's work.[11] The differences are striking enough, but behind them lies agreement regarding the subject-matter of psychology. Even in the extreme case, where the one book emphasises what the other omits, difference does not of necessity mean disagreement. We find, again, that Wundt says nothing of a question which for Brentano is the essential problem of psychology as it was the first problem of psycho-physics, the question of 'immortality', of the continuance of our mental life after death', and conversely that Brentano fails to discuss Wundt's cardinal problem of attention. Yet Wundt had touched upon the question of immortality in his earlier writing, and Brentano plainly recognises that there is a problem of attention, although (as we may suppose) he has put off its discussion to his second volume.[12]

So the student of psychology who read these two books in their year of issue might, if he had made due allowance for the training and natural tendencies of the authors, have entertained a reasonable hope for the future of his science; and we ourselves, who see their differences far more plainly than was possible for him, may still hope that the main issue can be taken on common ground and fought out at close quarters.

3

Brentano entitles his book 'psychology from the empirical standpoint', and

6. *Psychology*, pp. 19ff, 91; *PP*, pp. 4, 863.

7. *Psychology*, pp. 8ff; *PP*, pp. 9, 12, 20.

8. *Psychology*, pp. 78ff; *PP*, pp. 644f, 664, 708f, 712, 790ff.

9. *Psychology*, pp. 155ff; *PP*, pp. 715ff, 860ff.

10. *Psychology*, pp. 28ff, 140; *PP*, pp. 1ff.

11. *PP*, pp. 421; *Psychology*, pp. 7f, 66ff.

12. *Psychology*, pp. 14ff, 25f, 72f; Wundt takes up the question of immortality (indirectly it is true) in *Vorlesungen*, etc. vol. 2, (1836), pp. 436, 442; cf. the direct treatment in the later edition (1892), pp. 476ff. Brentano recognises the problem of attention in *Psychology*, pp. 69, 118; cf. p. 199, and C. Stumpf, *Tonpsychologie*, vol. 1 (1883), p. 68; vol. 2 (1890), pp. 279f.

Wundt writes 'physiological psychology' on his title-page and suggests 'experimental psychology' in his text.[13] The adjectives do not greatly help us. For all experimental psychology is in the broad sense empirical, and a psychology which is in the narrow sense empirical may still have recourse to experiment. To show the real difference between the books, the difference that runs through their whole texture and composition, we need at this stage terms that are both familiar and clear; the time has not yet come for technicalities and definitions. We may say, as a first approximation, that Brentano's psychology is essentially a matter of argument, and that Wundt's is essentially a matter of description.

At the end of his discussion of method Brentano refers with approval to Aristotle's use of *aporiai*, of difficulties and objections, wherein a subject is viewed from various sides, and opinion is weighed against opinion and argument against argument, until by comparison of pros and cons a reasonable conclusion is reached.[14] This is, in the large, his own way of working. He appeals but rarely, and then only in general terms, to facts of observation. His rule is to find out what other psychologists have said, to submit their statements to a close logical scrutiny, and so by a process of sifting to prepare the reader's mind for a positive determination. When the ground has thus been cleared Brentano's doctrine, novel though it may be, has the appearance (so to say) of a necessary truth; we feel that we have duly considered the possibilities in the case and have come to the one rational decision; and if for conscience' sake we go on to deduce and to verify, we still are assured beforehand that everything will fit together within the system. Minor points may need to be expanded; even, perhaps, in the light of further *aporiai*, to be corrected; but the whole exposition gives the impression of finality.[15] It is no wonder, then, that many students have

13. *PP*, p.3.

14. *Psychology*, pp. 73f; cf. J.S. Mill, 'Grote's Aristotle', *Fortnightly Review*, N.S. vol. 13 (1873), pp. 48ff. Brentano had earlier noted, with the same approval, the use of *aporiai* by Thomas Aquinas: see J.A. Möhler, *Kirchengeschichte*, vol. 2 (1867), p. 555.

15. I know of only three corrections that Brentano has made to his psychology. (1) in *Psychology*, p. 223, degree of conviction, as intensity of judgement, is declared analogous to degree of intensity of love and hate (cf. p. 154); in the notes to *The Origin of our Knowledge of Right and Wrong* (1889), 1969, pp. 57f, this analogy is denied. (2) In *Psychology*, pp. 153f, feeling is said to be always present along with ideation; the belief to the contrary is due to the mistaken preference of memory over inner perception (p. 35); but in *Untersuchungen zur Sinnespsychologie* (1907), pp. 119, 124, the acts of the two higher senses are not intrinsically emotive. (3) in *Psychology*, p. 88, the object upon which a psychical phenomenon is directed is not to be understood as *eine Realität*; but the notes appended to the reprinted section *Von der Klassifikation der psychischen Phänomene*, p. 149 (*Psychology*, p. 294) lay it down that 'only that which falls under the concept of a thing (*Reales*), can provide an object for mental reference'. There would, no doubt, if the book were rewritten, be many other modifications of detail, and yet others if the second volume were undertaken; the discussion of the modi of ideation in the *Klassifikation* shows that Brentano had not in 1874 thought out the doctrine of his Book III. In the main, nevertheless, the doctrine of 1874 has stood the test of Brentano's own continued reflection and of the attacks of critics.

Such achievement is worthy of all admiration. Only we must add – those of us who judged the author successful in his aim of writing, not Brentano's psychology, nor yet a national psychology, but – psychology.[16]

Wundt's book, on the contrary, abounds in facts of observation: anatomical facts, physiological facts, results of psycho-physical and psychological experiment. Its introductory chapter is brief to the point of perfunctoriness, and criticism of psychological theories is packed away into fine-print paragraphs that, to all intents and purposes, are a series of appendices. There is, to be sure, a great deal of argument. Where the facts are scanty, they must not only be generously interpreted but must also be eked out by hypothesis; if a leading physiologist has mistaken the problem of sense-perception, he must be argued into a better way of thinking; in any case, the new science of experimental psychology must offer a bold front to her elder sisters.[17] The argument, nonetheless, is always secondary and oftentimes plainly tentative; so that the book as a whole gives the impression of incompleteness, of a first essay which can be improved when more work (and a great many suggestions of further work are thrown out[18]) has been accomplished. Hence it is no accident, but rather a direct reflex of the spirit in which the authors approached their task, that Brentano's volume still bears the date 1874 while Wundt's book, grown to nearly triple its original size, has come to a sixth edition.[19]

This thorough-going difference of argument and description means, of course, a radical difference of attitude toward psychology itself. It means that Brentano and Wundt, in spite of formal and material agreement, psychologise in different ways. Our next step, therefore, is to place ourselves inside the sytems and to realise, so far as we may without too much detail, what manner of discipline they intend psychology to be. We have to choose: and the illustrations that follow will show the alternatives of choice in concrete and tangible form.

4

Brentano defines psychology as the science of psychical phenomena. The term may easily be misleading: for the phenomena in question are very far from being static appearances. Generically they are activities; in the individual case they are acts. Hence they can properly be named only by an active verb. They fall into three fundamental classes: those, namely, of Ideating (I see, I hear, I imagine), of Judging (I acknowledge, I reject, I perceive, I recall), and of Loving-Hating (I feel, I wish, I resolve, I intend, I desire). We may use substantives if we will, and may speak of sensation and

challenge Brentano's premises – that even isolated changes are disconcerting. The first statement is so serenely confident, and the changes are again so confidently made!

16. *Psychology*, p. xvi.

17. *PP*, Vorwort.

18. *PP*, pp. 284, 293, 314, 317, 373, 394, 399, etc., etc.

19. See the prefaces to the successive editions of the *PP*. Even the sixth edition, as I have shown elsewhere (*Psych. Rev.*, vol. 24, 1917, pp. 52f.), has not attained to systematic completion, and only in the fifth (*PP*, vol. 1, 1902, p. ix) did Wundt set himself definitely to the task of system-making.

idea, memory and imagination, opinion, doubt, judgement, joy and sorrow, desire and aversion, intention and resolution; but we must always bear in mind that the psychical phenomenon is active, as a sensing or a doubting or a recalling or a willing.

It is true that we never have act without content. When we ideate, we sense or imagine something; when we judge, we perceive something, acknowledge the truth of something, recall something; when we love or hate, we take interest in something, desire or repudiate something. This, however, is precisely the difference between psychical and physical phenomena. The latter are blank and inert: the colour or figure or landscape that I see, the chord that I hear, the warmth or cold or odour that I sense, the like objects that I imagine, all these things are described when their given appearance is described; their appearance sums them up and exhausts them; they have no reference, and do not carry us beyond themselves. Psychical phenomena, on the other hand, are precisely characterised by relation to a content, by reference to an object; they contain an object intentionally within them; and this character of immanent objectivity, in virtue of which they are active, marks them off uniquely from the physical phenomena upon which they are directed or toward which they point. Even in cases where the content of a psychical phenomenon is not physical, but is another psychical phenomenon, the distinction holds good. For the act which becomes content or object of another act is not thereby deprived of its essential character; it is still active in its own right; and it is therefore by no means confusable with bare physical appearance.[20]

These are Brentano's views of the subject-matter of psychology. He begins by considering the alleged differences between physical and psychical, finds an adequate *differentia* of the psychical, and is therefore able to define psychology in terms of the matter with which it deals. He then reviews the principal classifications hitherto made of psychical phenomena, and arrives at a classification of his own, in which judgement is accorded independent rank, and feeling and will are bracketed under a single heading. Throughout the discussion his chief reliance is upon argument. To be sure, he takes the testimony of inner perception; but inner perception is not observation; it is rather a self-evident cognition or judgement; and as such it is, if we may use the phrase, of the same stuff as argument.[21] Psychological observation is possible for Brentano only when past acts are recalled in memory; then indeed, as he admits, even a sort of experimentation becomes possible. Not only, however, is memory subject to gross illusion, but the act of memory, once more, falls under the category of judgement, so that experiment itself takes place in the world of argument.[22] The empirical psychology thus employs the same physical activities to establish the nature of its subject-matter and to discuss the variety of psychological opinion.

20. *Psychology*, pp. 18f, 28, 77ff, 123, 127, 194ff. On the problem of natural science as an explanatory discipline, see pp. 98ff.

21. *Psychology*, pp. 28ff, 138ff (summary 194f), 198-9. Cf. p. 277.

22. *Psychology*, pp. 34ff, 124, 129, 198f, 278.

5

For Wundt, psychology is a part of the science of life. Vital processes may be viewed from the outside, and then we have the subject-matter of physiology, or they may be viewed from within, and then we have the subject-matter of psychology.[23] The data, the items of this subject-matter, are always complex, and the task of experimental psychology is to analyse them into 'the elementary psychical processes'. If we know the elements, and can compare them with the resulting complexes, we may hope to understand the nature of integration, which according to Wundt is the distinguishing character of consciousness.[24]

Analysis of the processes of the inner life brings us, in the last resort, to pure sensations, constituted originally of intensity and quality. Sensations carry no reference; they look neither before nor after; they tell us nothing of their stimuli, whether external or organic, and nothing of their point of excitation, whether peripheral or central, nor do they forecast the ideas in which we find them synthetised. They simply run their course, qualitatively and intensively, and may be observed and described as they proceed.[25] Ideas, in their turn, are originally constituted of these sensations; there is nothing within or upon them to show whether they are ideas of imagination or perceptions.[26] Individual ideas differ psychologically from general ideas solely in the nature of their sensory constituents: in the former the complex of sensations is constant, in the latter it is variable.[27] Concepts are not 'psychical formations' at all; if we psychologise them, we discover only their substitutes in consciousness, spoken or written words, accompanied by a vague and indeterminate feeling.[28] Judgements, in the same way, belong to logic, and not primarily to psychology; logic and psychology approximate only as a result of the parallel growth, long continued, of conceptual thinking and its expression in language; our 'conscious psychological processes' consist originally of nothing more than ideas and their connections.[29]

The trend of all this analysis is clear: Wundt is trying to describe mind, to show the stuff of which it is made, to reduce it to its lowest terms. When, however, he turns from analysis to synthesis, the exposition is less easy to follow. Sensations are integrated into ideas by a 'psychical synthesis' which Wundt himself compares to a chemical synthesis and which critics have assimilated to Mill's 'mental chemistry'.[30] Ideas gain their objective

23. *PP*, pp. 1ff.

24. *PP*, pp. 5, 20, 717.

25. *PP*, pp. 273ff, 484f. When sensations enter into connection with one another, the third attribute of affective tone or sensory feeling is added. Intensity and quality are, however, the 'more original' constituents.

26. *PP*, pp. 464f.

27. *PP*, p. 468.

28. *PP*, p. 672.

29. *PP*, pp. 709ff.

30. *PP*, pp. 484f.; J.S. Mill, *A System of Logic.* (1843), Book VI, chapter 4 (ii, 1856, p. 429); *An Examination of Sir William Hamilton's Philosophy* (1865), pp. 286f.; note in J. Mill, *Analysis of the Phenomena of the Human Mind*, vol. 1 (1869), pp. 106ff. The original

reference by a 'secondary act' which seems to consist, psychologically, in the simple addition of further ideas,[31] yet the objective reference is itself put, later on, to psychological purposes. Concepts and forms of intuition are made 'postulates' of advancing thought,[32] as if the logical and practical aspects of mind were necessarily implied in its given or phenomenal aspect, and as if the psychologist might shift from one aspect to another without breach of scientific continuity. But though we may puzzle over details, there is nothing obscure in the general situation. Wundt, like many others of his generation, is dazzled by the vast promise of the evolutionary principle;[33] 'original' is for him more or less what 'nascent' is for Spencer; the later must derive from the earlier, because that is the way of things, and the later has no other basis. Let us remember, all the same, that Wundt's primary effort is to describe, and that he falls back upon 'genetic explanation' only when some phase of the traditional subject-matter of psychology proves to be indescribable.

That, then, is one of the threads of Wundt's system. Even a descriptive psychology cannot, however, be written simply in terms of sensations and their modes and levels of psychological integration. For the field of consciousness, Wundt, reminds us, is not uniformly illuminated; it shows a small bright area at its centre and a darker region round about; the ideas which occupy it differ in their conscious status. So arises the problem of attention. Descriptively – Wundt takes up the task of description piecemeal, in different contexts, as if it were 'on his conscience' – attention reduces to clearness of ideas and characteristic feelings of effort or strain.[34] It has two concrete manifestations, apperception and voluntary action; we speak of apperception when we are considering the internal course of ideas, and of voluntary action when we are considering the issue of an emotion in external movement.[35] Both forms of the attentional process are subject to conditions, and both are strictly correlated with physiological processes in the cerebral cortex; they therefore fall within the limits of a scientific psychology.[36] Yet psychologists have neglected them, and have paid the penalty of this neglect in inadequate psychology and untenable philosophy.[37]

We need not here trace the doctrine of attention further; nor need we debate whether the problem of attention is included in Wundt's formal statement of the task of experimental psychology. We may, however, as an illustration of the interweaving of the two systematic threads, glance at his treatment of the association of ideas. He begins, as we might expect, with mode of integration; and under this heading declares that the recognised laws, of similarity and of frequency of connection in space and time, are

source is D. Hartley, *Observations on Man* (1749), Part 1, chapter 1, sect. 2, prop. 12, cor 1 (1. 1810, pp. 77f.).

31. *PP*, p. 465.
32. *PP*, pp. 672, 680.
33. *PP*, p. vi.
34. *PP*, pp. 717ff., esp. 724.
35. *PP*, pp. 831, 835.
36. *PP*, pp. 720f., 723f., 834f.
37. *PP*, pp. 792f., 831ff.

imperfect even as empirical generalisations. We find, it is true, two forms of association, distinguishable in the free play of fancy and in reflective thought. But the one is wider than association by similarity, in that the effective resemblance may reside in any and every sensory constituent of the ideas concerned, and especially in their affective tone, while the other reveals itself simply as an affair of habit. Wundt therefore proposes to term them, respectively, 'association by relationship' and 'association by habituation'. The new names, he maintains, are not indifferent; for they do fuller justice than the old to the facts of self-observation, and they also point us to the conditions of association in the central nervous substance.[38]

Here then is an improvement on the side of analysis and synthesis; but that is not enough. For ideas do not associate automatically, as it were of their own motion; the laws of association are, on the contrary, under the universal dominance of attention. And now there opens up, for experimental attack, a whole series of special problems which an empirical psychology, following only the single line of enquiry, must naturally miss. In their light we pass beyond associationism to a more faithful transcript of the 'course and connection of ideas'[39] and in like manner we avoid, in our psychology of will, the philosophical *impasse* of indeterminism.[40]

These paragraphs express, in rough summary, the teaching of the Wundt of 1874. He does not give psychology a distinct and peculiar subject-matter; the difference between physiology and psychology lies simply in our point of view. Wundt had already published a comprehensive work upon physiology, and now that he has turned to psychology he carries his knowledge and method with him; he is convinced that the processes of the inner life are best set forth in close connection with those of the outer life, and that the results of inner observation are surest when the appliances of external observation, the procedures of physiology, are pressed into psychological service. He spends little time upon preliminaries, but gets as quickly as may be to the exposition of facts. Where facts are few or lacking, he seeks to supplement or to supply them by observations of his own. His primary aim in all cases is to describe the phenomena of mind as the physiologist describes the phenomena of the living body, to write down what is there, going on observably before him: witness his treatment of idea, of concept, of attention, of association. There is still great space for argument, and the argument, we must admit, is often influenced by previous habits of thought, by psychological tradition, by a certain tendency to round things off to a logical completeness, by a somewhat naive trust in the principle of evolution. The argument, however, does not impress the reader as anything but secondary: Wundt is at once too dogmatic and too ready to change his views. The recurring need of further facts and the patchwork character of the argument suggest, both alike, that psychology, under his guidance, has still a long systematic road to travel.

38. *PP*, pp. 788ff.
39. *PP*, p. 793; cf. The earlier sections of chapter 19.
40. *PP*, pp. 837f.

6

We have now viewed our two psychologies from within. Brentano, we have found, looks back over the past, weeds out its errors with a sympathetic hand, accepts from it whatever will stand the test of his criticism, and organises old truth and new into a system meant, in all essentials, to last as long as psychology shall be studied; Wundt, after he has acknowledged his debt to the past, turns away from it and plunges into the multifarious and detailed work of the laboratories, producing a psychology that is as much encyclopedia as system, and that bears on its face the need for continual revision. Which of the two books holds the key to a science of psychology?

Brentano has all the advantage that comes with historical continuity. His doctrine of immanent objectivity goes back to Aristotle and the Schoolmen, and the classification of psychical acts into ideas, judgements, and phenomena of love and hate goes back to Descartes.[41] More than this: he can claim kinship with every psychologist, of whatever, school, who has approached his subject from the technically 'empirical' standpoint. For the 'empirical' psychologist means to take mind as he finds it; and like the rest of the world, who are not psychologists, he finds it in use; he finds it actively at work in man's intercourse with nature and with his fellow-man, as well as in his discourse with himself. Terms may change and classifications may vary, but the items of classification are always activities, and the terms employed – faculties, capacities, powers, operations, functions, acts, states – all belong to the same logical universe. Brentano, innovator though he is, takes his place as of right in a great psychological community.[42]

To offset this advantage, and to justify his own break with tradition, Wundt holds out the promise of an experimental method. He should have been more explicit: for technology as well as science – medicine as well as

41. *Psychology*, pp. 88f; *The Origin of our Knowledge of Right and Wrong*, pp. 15-17.

42. It may seem unjust to Brentano if, even in this preliminary sketch of the psychological issue, his interest in experiment is left without record. We note, then, that as early as 1874 he urged the establishment at Vienna of a psychological laboratory (*Über die Zukunft der Philosophie*, 1929, p. 51); that he published *Untersuchungen zur Sinnespsychologie* (1907) and in particular that he brought the Müller-Lyer illusion to the attention of psychologists (*Zeits. f. Psych. u. Phys. d Sinnesorgane*, vol. 3, 1892, p. 349); and that Stumpf, who was his pupil (Überweg-Heinze, vol. 4, 1906, pp. 334f), has given us the experimental *Tonpsychologie*. All this, however, does not prevent his being in the narrow sense, an 'empirical' psychologist. Stumpf tells us that his own work is to 'describe the psychical functions that are set in action by tones' (*Tonpsych.*, vol. 1, 1883, p.v) and declares later that 'there cannot be a psychology of tones; only a psychology of tonal perceptions, tonal judgements, tonal feelings' (*Zur Einleitung der Wissenschaften*, 1907, p. 30). Brentano, even with a laboratory, would not have been, in Wundt's sense, an 'experimental' psychologist. We know, besides, something of Brentano's systematic programme. The empirical psychology is not to be concluded; it is to be supplemented and replaced by a 'descriptive' psychology (*Origin*, vol. 9, p. 56) fragments of which have appeared in *The Origin of our Knowledge of Right and Wrong* (dealing with the phenomena of love and hate and, in the notes, with judgement and in the *Untersuchungen* sense-perception). This in turn is to be followed by an 'explanatory' or 'genetic' psychology, a sample of which is given in *Das Genie* (1892).

physiology, engineering as well as physics – makes use of experiment. His actual purpose, as we trace it in the chapters of this book, is to transform psychology into an experimental science of the strict type, a science that shall run parallel with experimental physiology.[43] He failed, no doubt, to see all that this purpose implied, and his earlier readers may be excused if they looked upon his work as an empirical psychology prefaced by anatomy and physiology and interspersed with psychophysical experiments. There is plenty of empirical psychology in the volume. If, however, we go behind the letter to the informing spirit; if we search out the common motive in Wundt's treatment of the familiar topics; if we carry ourselves back in thought to the scientific atmosphere of the 1870s, and try in that atmosphere to formulate the purpose that stands out sharp and clear to our modern vision; then the real significance of the *Physiological Psychology* cannot be mistaken. It speaks the language of science, in the rigorous sense of the word, and it promises us in this sense a science of psychology.

But Brentano also speaks of a 'science' of psychology. Which of the two authors is in the right?

43. The substitution of folk-psychology for experiment in the study of the more complicated mental processes appears in the fourth edition (*PP*, vol. 1, 1895, p. 4); the reservation in regard to psychophysical parallelism in the fifth edition (*PP*, vol. 3, 1903, pp. 775ff.).

7 Brentano's Descriptive Psychology[1]

Roderick M. Chisholm

1

It is most fitting that one session of an international congress of philosophers meeting in Vienna should be devoted to the topic, 'Brentano, philosophical psychology, and the phenomenological movement'. Franz Brentano's lectures on descriptive psychology were given at the University of Vienna three-quarters of a century ago. Husserl said that without Brentano's researches 'phenomenology could not have come into being at all'.[2] Brentano's descriptive psychology is doubtless very close to what Husserl originally took phenomenology to be. But in the philosophical problems that are central to it, and in the precise analytic manner with which Brentano dealt with them, his descriptive psychology is also very close to the 'philosophy of mind' or 'philosophical psychology', that is now of concern to philosophers in the analytic tradition.

Yet it would not be fiitting, here in Vienna, to look upon Brentano merely as a precursor of subsequent philosophical movements. I shall try to say briefly what he took descriptive psychology to be and I shall comment upon what I take to be its philosophical significance.

2

In the foreword to *Vom Ursprung sittlicher Erkenntnis* (1899), Brentano said that the ethical views he there set forth were a part 'of a "Descriptive Psychology", which I hope to be able to publish in the not too distant future'.[3] Unfortunately he did not publish a work entitled 'Descriptive Psychology', but many of his writings and dictations on the subject have

1. Revised by the author, who notes, 'I have profited by certain criticisms made by D.B. Terrell'. The first version of this paper appeared in the *Proceedings of the XIVth International Congress of Philosophy, 2-9 September 1968* (Vienna, 1968), volume 2, pp. 164–74.

2. See Edmund Husserl, 'Author's Preface to the English Edition', *Ideas — General Introduction to Pure Phenomenology* (London, 1931), p. 23; *Phänomenologische Psychologie* (The Hague, 1962), pp. 31–4, 267–9, 353–4.

3. Franz Brentano, *Vom Ursprung sittlicher Erkenntnis*, ed. Oskar Kraus, 3rd ed. (Leipzig, 1934), pp. 3–4; English edition, *The Origin of our Knowledge of Right and Wrong*, ed. Roderick M. Chisholm, (London and new York, 1969), p. ix.

been published in the various posthumous works edited by Oskar Kraus, Alfred Kastil, and Franziska Mayer-Hillebrand.[4]

He did, however, give a course of lectures on the subject at the University of Vienna. In 1888–9 these were entitled 'Deskriptive Psychologie oder beschreibende Phänomenologie' (although the term 'Phänomenologie' occurred in the title of the lectures, it does not seem to have been used in the lectures themselves). In 1890–1 he entitled the lectures simply 'Psychognosie'. In what follows, I shall refer to the lectures of 1890–1 which I have been able to study, thanks to the kindness of the philosopher's son, Professor J.C.M. Brentano.

The descriptive psychologist, according to Brentano, 'investigates the constituents of human consciousness; he seeks out its elements and attempts to determine as exhaustively as possible their modes of combination'.[5] Unlike genetic or explanatory psychology, descriptive psychology is not concerned with the causal status of psychological phenomena or with the relations that they bear to physical and chemical processes. It is related to genetic or explanatory psychology, according to Brentano, in the way in which anatomy is related to physiology and in the way in which 'geognosy' is related to geology (hence the term 'Psychognosie'). Unlike genetic psychology, descriptive psychology is an exact science. It is the basic discipline of philosophy, according to Brentano; without it, he said, metaphysics, logic, ethics, and the other disciplines of philosophy 'would dry up, like branches cut off from a tree'.[6]

In the Vienna lectures of 1890–1, Brentano formulated several rules for the descriptive psychologist, or 'psychognostician'.[7] For example, the descriptive psychologist must learn to *notice* what is there; moreover, he must fix upon what he has noticed in order to retain it in the corpus of his data. This will involve describing, as accurately as possible, just what it is

---

4. See in particular vol. 2 of the second edition of the *Psychologie von empirischen Standpunkt*, Oskar Kraus (Leipzig,1925); *Psychology from an Empirical Standpoint*, English edition ed. Linda L. McAlister (London and New York, 1973); *Von sinnlichen und noetischen Bewußtsein*, ed. Oskar Kraus (Leipzig, 1938); and *Grundzüge der Ästhetik*, ed. F. Mayer-Hillebrand (Bern, 1959).

5. 'Der Psychognost ... forscht nach den Bestandteilen des menschlichen Bewußtseins; er sucht seine Elemente und deren Verbindungsweisen nach Möglichkeit erschöpfend zu bestimmen.'

6. Franz Brentano, *Meine letzten Wünsche für Österreich* (Stuttgart, 1895), p. 39. Brentano goes on to say: 'All other psychological phenomena are derived from the combinations of ultimate psychological elements, as the totality of words may be derived from the totality of letters: completion of this task would provide the basis for a *Characteristica universalis* of the sort that had been conceived by Leibnitz, and before him by Descartes' (p. 34).

7. 'Damit der Psychognost seine Absicht erreiche, hat er ein Mehrfaches zu leisten. (1) Er muß erleben. (2) Er muß bemerken. (3) Er muß, was er bemerkt, fixieren, um es zu sammeln. (4) Er muß induzierend verallgemeinern. (5) Er muß, wo die Notwendigkeit oder Unmöglichkeit der Vereinigung gewisser Elemente aus den Begriffen selbst erhellt, diese allgemeinen Gesetze intuitiv erfassen. (6) Er muß – können wir endlich hinzufügen – das so Gewonnene deduktiv verwerten, wodurch er manche die Elemente betreffende Fragen, die sonst kaum beachtet werden könnten, zu lösen vermag.'

that he had noticed. (Brentano gives an excellent example of a psychological description, in his lectures on practical philosophy, when he shows how an 'act of will' may be constituted out of elementary psychological phenomena.) These were the lectures, incidentally, that Husserl attended.[8] The descriptive psychologist should make inductive generalisations, according to Brentano, but in addition to this he must intuitively apprehend certain general laws. These laws are the source of all necessary truth.

There are three questions that immediately present themselves, and these are likely to be of especial concern to those who approach philosophy from British and American traditions. (1) What is the difference between merely *having* an experience and *noticing* an experience? (2) How can one arrive at 'apodictic' universal laws by *describing* psychological phenomena? And (3) what *are* the 'elements of consciousness'? By considering these three questions, we may make somewhat more clear just what Brentano took descriptive psychology to be.

3

The first of these questions – 'What is the difference between merely having an experience and noticing an experience?' – is familiar to many British and American philosophers as a result of Wittgenstein's penetrating discussions in Part II, Section xi, of his *Philosophical Investigations*. Brentano's own discussion of noticing, in the lectures of 1890–1, is itself an important contribution to descriptive psychology.[9]

Our question might be put as a puzzle: 'If there is a difference between experience that is noticed and experience that is not noticed, how could it ever be known, unless someone notices an experience that he does not notice?'

To deal with the puzzle, let us first remind ourselves of what it is in our experience that is said to go unnoticed. The clearest examples are to be found in what has traditionally been called 'confused perception', as distinguished from 'distinct perception'. (To be faithful to Brentano, we should note that we are here concerned with 'inner perception'.) The experience of the colour violet, according to Brentano, involves as components the experience of red and the experience of blue. The experience of orange, similarly, involves the experience of red and the experience of yellow. Thus Brentano said: 'A sense experience often comprises in its object a multiplicity of parts. The experience is related to the whole object in its totality, and therefore it must be related to the parts implicitly insofar as they are given with the object; but it may not explicitly

8. See Husserl's 'Reminiscences of Franz Brentano', ch. 3 above. Brentano's lectures on practical philosophy have been edited by Mayer-Hillebrand as *Grundlegung und Aufbau der Ethik* (Bern, 1952); the description of an act of will appears on pp. 218–19; English edition, *The Foundation and Construction of Ethics*, trans. Elizabeth Hughes Schneewind (London and New York, 1973).

9. So, too, is Hugo Bergmann's discussion in his *Untersuchungen zum Problem der Evidenz der inneren Wahrnehmung* (Halle, 1908).

relate to each of its parts'.[10] Another example of such a whole, according to Brentano, would be the hearing of a chord, wherein the particular notes that make up the chord are experienced only 'implicitly' but not noticed 'explicitly'. The distinction between 'explicit' and 'implicit' has its analogue in application to judgement; thus Brentano says that a man may notice what he is judging without noticing everything that is implicit in what he is judging. Still another sense in which experience may be said to escape notice, according to Brentano, is this: one may compare different types of psychological phenomena – for example, seeing and hearing, or (what is of more interest to the philosopher) feeling and judging – and then fail to notice certain respects in which they are alike, or certain respects in which they differ. (Brentano believes that many moral philosophers have failed to notice important analogies that hold between feeling and judging.)

And so how are they to deal with our puzzle? Has the descriptive psychologist noticed, on certain occasions, that something has gone unnoticed? Although Brentano never makes his reasoning on this matter explicit, I think we may reconstruct his reasoning.

Consider the four steps in this example. (1) If we contemplate an experience of the colour violet, we will see that it has components which are experiences of red and components which are experiences of blue. (2) In seeing this, we are also capable of apprehending a more general proposition: *any* experience of violet will contain both an experience of red and an experience of blue; indeed, it is *impossible* for there to be an experience of violet which does not contain an experience of red and an experience of blue. But (3) there are people – other people, or ourselves at other times – who know that they are experiencing violet without knowing that they are experiencing red and experiencing blue. Therefore (4) people have experiences which have components of which they are not aware. And this illustrates what is meant by 'having an experience which is not noticed'.

To see that premise (1) is true, one has only to be a perceptive descriptive psychologist who is acquainted with the three colours, violet, red, and blue. To see that premise (2) is true, it is necessary to have a certain intuitive awareness, or apprehension; I shall return to this concept below. But to see that premise (3) is true, one must go beyond the immediate data of inner perception and appeal either to our memories of our own immediate experience or to what we know about 'other minds'.[11] Brentano's own theory of the evident, however, is very rigid and requires him to say that our judgements about our own previous experiences and our judgements about the experience of other people are 'problematic' or 'blind'. Hence if the descriptive psychologist were to accept Brentano's theory of the evident, he

10. Quoted in Kraus' Introduction to vol. 1 of the 2nd ed. of Brentano's *Psychology*. The importance for metaphysics of the experience of such wholes is also emphasised by Bertand Russell in the chapter entitled 'Analysis' of his *Inquiry into Meaning and Truth* (London and New York, 1940).

11. Brentano emphasises that not all of the data of descriptive psychology is provided by the immediate evidence of inner perception and he notes explicitly that the descriptive psychologist must also appeal to memory (which, according to Brentano, is not a source of immediate evidence). Compare *Grundzüge der Ästhetik*, pp. 37–8.

would have to say that statement (4), the conclusion of the above argument, is as 'problematic' or 'blind' as its weakest premise. And from this it would follow that one of the basic theorems of descriptive psychology – that there is a distinction between noticing and mere experiencing – cannot be known with certainty to be true.

But the descriptive psychologist, I believe, need not, and indeed should not, accept this very rigid theory of the evident.[12] If the third premise of the above argument is not 'blind', then the conclusion is not 'blind' either – provided our theory of the evident countenances the type of intuitive apprehension that must be appealed to in defence of premise (1).

Before turning to the nature of his awareness, we may note briefly certain other things Brentano has to say about noticing in his lectures of 1890–1, for these may be of interest to philosophers associated with the phenomenological movement.

Brentano observes that, although noticing is not easy, there is much of interest that we notice while asleep, in dreaming. But he adds that no one has ever made any significant psychognostic discoveries while asleep. It is not easy, however, for the psychognostician to notice everything he *ought* to notice, and there are various difficulties he must learn to overcome. Thus passion, anxiety, and anger may be distracting – a fact that gives rise to special problems, as Brentano observes, when the psychognostician wishes to study passion, anxiety, and anger themselves. Brentano does not say that the psychognostician should perform an *epoché*, but he does observe that prejudices about the subject-matter being investigated should not be allowed to exert their influence. For, he says, they may prevent the psychognostician from noticing what is there to be noticed, and the result will be that 'noticing is suspended' ('das Bemerken ist suspendiert').

The ways in which language may prejudice the philosopher and distract the psychognostician are well known, and Brentano discusses these in detail in his later writings. We all know, of course, about the damage that can be done by the mere presence of a substantive in the language. In the 1890–1 lectures, Brentano also points out that the *absence* of a term may be harmful, too.

The psychognostician, according to Brentano, must practise noticing. Even more important, he must not allow himself to get into the habit of not noticing. Not noticing will cause him to miss what is there, and prejudice may then cause him to confuse 'not noticing' with 'noticing not': from the fact that he did not notice that A was there, he will later assume mistakenly that he noticed that A was not there. And possibly one may notice and yet not notice that he has noticed. (This fact, Brentano suggests, explains why

12. A. Meinong developed a theory of evidence that was more latitudinarian than Brentano's, but Brentano did not approve of it. See Meinong's 'Zur erkenntnistheoretischen Würdigung des Gedächtnisses', in his *Gesammelte Abhandlungen*, vol. 2 (Leipzig, 1913), pp. 187–213, reprinted as 'Toward an epistemological assessment of memory,' in Chisholm and Schwartz, eds. *Empirical Knowledge* (Englewood Cliffs, N.J., 1973); and his *Über die Erfahrungsgrundlagen unseres Wissens* (Berlin, 1906). I have attempted to carry out such a theory in detail in *Theory of Knowledge* (Englewood Cliffs, N.J., 1966) especially in chapter 3.

it is that philosophers have not been able to agree about the true nature of the evident.)[13]

Brentano also observes that noticing must be distinguished from attending. 'One may speak of "attending well". And there are stages or degrees. But one may not speak of "noticing well". It is a matter simply of what is evident, and there are no degrees.'[14] This point could be put in the terminology of Professor Ryle's *Concept of Mind* by saying that 'noticing' unlike 'attending' is an 'achievement word'.

4

Our second question was: 'How can one arrive at "apodictic" universal laws merely by *describing* psychological phenomena?' This takes us to the 'intuitive apprehension' referred to in connection with premise (2) of the argument set forth above.

In formulating his rules for the psychognostician, Brentano says: 'The descriptive psychologist should intuitively apprehend certain general laws; these are laws that have to do with the necessity or impossibility of uniting certain elements; and they are manifested by the very concepts of these elements.' He assumes, then, that there is a type of knowledge that is 'manifested through concepts'.

So-called analytic judgements present us with one subspecies of this type of knowledge. The statement 'All squares are rectangles' expresses such a judgement. There is a literal sense in which we may say that its predicate term may be 'analysed out' of its subject-term; for the subject-term is synonymous with another expression, viz. 'equilateral rectangles', in which the predicate-term may be seen to be an essential part. Brentano assumes that such statements as 'Whatever is violet is red and blue' are expressive of analytic judgements. He notes that they falsify Kant's assertion that analytic judgements do not extend our knowledge, since one who knows that a certain thing is violet without knowing that it is red and blue may be enlightened when told, analytically, that violet is red and blue. The statement, 'All cubes have twelve edges', which C.H. Langford and others have described as being synthetic *a priori*, would also express an analytic judgement, according to Brentano. Such judgements extend our knowledge since they ennable us to transform a confused perception into one that is clear and distinct.[15]

But Brentano realised that some of the 'apodictic' judgements of descriptive psychology are *not* analytic in the above sense. I believe that the following 'theorems' (Lehrsätze) which Brentano makes to be 'apodictically true' cannot be shown to be synthetic: 'There are no colours other than red, yellow, blue, (possibly) green, white, and their admixtures'. 'There is no conceivable transition from colour to tone, as there is from one colour to another, and from one tone to another'. 'It is impossible for there to be

13. See the discussion of noticing in *Grundzüge der Ästhetik*, esp. p. 38.

14. 'Man kann sagen sich "gut merken". Es gibt hier Stufen. Beim Bemerken nicht. Hier liegt immer Evidenz vot, und sic hat keine Grade.'

15. See Brentano's *Versuch über die Erkenntnis*, ed. Alfred Kastil (Leipzig, 1925), pp. 9ff.

anything such that it may be correctly affirmed and also correctly denied'. 'It is impossible for there to be anything such that it may be incorrectly affirmed and also incorrectly denied'. (The theorems about judgement just cited are among those that constitute the basis of logic, according to Brentano. And certain analogous theorems about the correctness and incorrectness of emotion constitute the basis of ethics.)[16]

The source of what Brentano takes to be our 'apodictic' knowledge of these truths would seem to be what W.E. Johnson described in his *Logic* as 'intuitive induction'.[17] Brentano is perhaps most clear about this type of apprehension when he discusses what he takes to be our knowledge of ethics.

In describing how we come to know, for example, that knowledge as such is worthy of love, he says that when we apprehend ourselves as 'correctly loving' a given act of knowing, 'the goodness or badness of the entire class becomes obvious at a single stroke, so to speak, and without any induction from particular cases'.[18] (In saying that the goodness or badness of 'the entire class' becomes obvious, he means, of course, that it becomes obvious that *all the members* of the class are good or bad. He does not mean that the class itself – that abstract object, if any, which is the *set* – is obviously good or bad.)

It is quite clear, I think, that Brentano would describe our apprehension of the various 'theories' cited above in a similar way. He would say that, in apprehending one confirming instance of the theorem in question, we see *ipso facto* that can be no disconfirming instance. This is the type of apprehension that enables the descriptive psychologist to affirm what is 'apodictically', or necessarily, true, whether what is affirmed is 'analytic' or not.

There has been some controversy about the nature of this apprehension but much of it, so far as I have been able to see, is merely terminological. Brentano does not wish to say that the judgements involved are 'synthetic *a priori*'. For the apprehension does require *some* experience or other ('Der Psychognost muß erleben'), and therefore Brentano feels he can admit the possibility of such apprehension and still call himself an 'empiricist'.[19] But those who *would* call the judgements in question '*a priori*' are concerned, not to deny that a certain experience is involved, but to affirm that we do not have 'induction from particular cases' in the usual sense of this expression, and Brentano concedes that there is no such induction. W.E. Johnson, however, says that one does make an induction here – an 'intuitive induction'. It is 'induction' because it does proceed from a particular case, but 'intuitive' since its conclusion is not 'problematic', but is necessary, or, as Brentano would put it, 'apodictic'.[20] Brentano's followers were insistent

16. One of his clearest statements is in *Vom Ursprung sittlicher Erkenntnis*, 3rd ed., pp. 109–12; *Origin of our Knowledge of Right and Wrong*, pp. 111–13.

17. W.E. Johnson, *Logic*, vol. 2 (Cambridge, 1922), pp. 189–96.

18. *Vom Ursprung sittlicher Erkenntnis*, 3rd ed. p. 82; *Origin*, p. 24.

19. See *Vom Ursprung sittlicher Erkenntnis*, 3rd ed., pp. 109–12; *Origin*, pp. 111–13.

20. Brentano observes in another connection that, in its traditional sense, induction may be said to 'proceed from simple assertoric awareness and conclude with an apodictic assertion'. *Versuch über die Erkenntnis*, ed. Alfred Kastil (Leipzig, 1925), p. 79.

that the apprehension in question involves no *Wesensschau*, or contemplation of essences since, according to Brentano, the requisite experience is of particular things and there *are* no essences. But he would concede that when, say, we have a particular sensation of orange, we are able to contemplate the orange sensation *as such*, and it is in virtue of this fact that we are able to apprehend certain 'theorems' about every orange sensation. And analogously for the other experience of the psychognostician.

I believe that terminological differences are also central to much of the dispute about Brentano's alleged 'psychologism'. We have noted that, according to him, theorems of descriptive psychology are at the basis of logic as well as of ethics. Frege had said, of the general attempt to base mathematics upon psychology: 'It would be strange if the most exact of all sciences had to seek support from psychology, which is still feeling its way none too surely.'[21] But descriptive psychology, if Brentano is right, knows precisely what it is doing and is not feeling its way at all. If by 'psychologism' we mean the doctrine according to which the laws of logic, evidence, and morality are merely contingent or problematic generalisations about the ways in which people happen to think and to feel, then it is not just to charge Brentano with psychologism. For the laws to which he appeals are 'apodictic' or necessary truths about the nature of thinking and feeling. And if by 'psychologism' we mean the attempt to base logic and ethics upon 'empirical psychology', and if by 'empirical psychology', in turn, we mean a psychology that makes only problematic inductions from experience, then, once again, it is not just to charge Brentano with psychologism. For Brentano's descriptive psychology, though it appeals to experience and is therefore 'empirical' in Brentano's sense of the word, is not a psychology that makes only problematic inductions from experience.

5

Our third and final question is: 'What *are* the "elements of consciousness" that constitute the subject-matter of descriptive psychology?' Brentano's answer to this question seems to me to be correct and to be of basic metaphysical importance.

One may wish to say that the 'elements of consciousness' are mere phenomena or appearances. But a phenomenon or appearance is an appearance *to* some thing, or *to* some one. And thus Brentano wrote: 'For what do we understand by a phenomenon? Something that appears to one. It is contradictory to assert that something exists as a phenomenon, but that there is nothing in itself to which it *is* a phenomenon. If one wishes to say, of that *to which* something appears, that it, too, exists only as a phenomenon, then one must say that there is something else to which it, in turn, appears only as a phenomenon, and that this something else exists in itself and is apprehended as such.'[22]

21. Gottlob Frege, *Die Grundlagen der Arithmetik* (Breslau, 1884). sect. 27; trans. J.L. Austin as *The Foundation of Arithmetic* (Oxford, 1950).
22. 'Denn was versteht man unter einem Phänomen? Etwas, was einem erscheint. Die Behauptung, es besteht etwas als Phänomen, es bestehe aver nicht etwas das

Brentano emphasises, moreover, that it is a mistake to suppose we are conscious only of phenomena or sense-impressions. The data of descriptive psychology are not restricted to mere *sense* experience. One is aware of oneself, not only as being appeared to, but also as thinking, judging, desiring, inferring, planning, remembering, endeavouring.

Writing to Stumpf in 1906, Brentano said that no matter what it is that we may be observing as descriptive psychologists, 'every observation may be said to be, in a certain sense, an observation of ourselves. Thus if one analyses a chord one apperceives certain constituents of himself as one who is hearing. He finds that to the extent that he is someone who hears a chord he is at the same time someone who hears this and that particular note.'[23]

Hume had said, notoriously, that 'when I enter most intimately into what I call *myself*, I always stumble upon some particular perception or other, of heat or cold, light or shade, love or hatred, pain or pleasure'. But what he thereby *noticed* was that *he* stumbled upon these perceptions. He had asked: If the idea of the self is of something other than a bundle of perceptions, 'from what impression cou'd this idea be deriv'd?' Brentano's reply would be that one can derive the idea of such a self from any impression whatever. And therefore, he said, we can derive the concept of *substance* from any impression whatever. 'Those who say that this concept is not included in any perception are very much mistaken. Rather, it is given in every perception, as Aristotle had said . . .'[24]

How does one know that it is the *same* thing throughout? How do I now know that the thing that now sees is the same as the thing that now hears – i.e. that the thing that is now appeared in one way to is the same as the thing that is now appeared in some other way to? And how do I know that, in turn, the thing that is thus appeared to is also the same as the thing that now thinks, and the thing that now desires, and the thing that now judges? In his Vienna lectures, Brentano refers back at this point to the chapter on 'The Unity of Consciousness' in his *Psychology from an Empirical Standpoint* (Chapter 4, Book II, 'on the Unity of Consciousness').

Let us consider just one version of the question. How do I know that the one who hears is the same as the one who sees? Suppose, for example, that I am concerned to know whether the dancers are keeping proper time to the music. Then I must be able to *compare* what I see with what I hear, if I am to order the notes of the music with the steps of the dancers. Brentano now asks: If the one who sees is not the same as the one who hears how *is* it possible for the comparison to be made? And who would make the comparison? It couldn't be the one who sees but doesn't hear, nor could it

---

Phänomen Habende als Ding an sich, ist also ein greifbarer Widerspruch. Wollte einer sagen, auch der das Phänomen Habende bestehe nur als Phänomen, so müßte er sagen, daß etwas anderes, das ihn zum Phänomen hat, an sich sei, und als an sich seiend erkannt werde.' Quoted from Brentano's *Nachlaß* by Oskar Kraus, in *Franz Brentano*, p. 28. Compare vol. 1 of the 2nd ed. of the *Psychologie*, pp. 234, 245 (English edition, pp. 165, 172–3) and Brentano's *Die vier Phasen der Philosophie*, ed. Oskar Kraus (Leipzig, 1926), p. 92.

23. Quoted in Kraus' Introduction to vol. 1 of the 2nd ed. of the *Psychologie*, p. lxxxviii (English edition, p. 405).

24. *Versuch über die Erkenntnis*, p. 30.

be the one who hears but doesn't see. Do they somehow do it jointly, then? Brentano says: 'This would be like saying that, although neither a blind man nor a deaf man can compare colours and tones, the two of them can do it together when the one hears and the other sees. And why does this seem absurd to us? Because the awareness of such a comparison involves an actual unity. But when we consider the activities of the deaf man and the blind man together, we have only a mere collective and not a real unitary thing . . . It is only when the colour and the sound are presented to one and the same individual thing that they may conceivably be compared with each other.'[25] And therefore, Brentano concludes: I know directly and immediately that the thing that sees is the same as the one that hears, and the same as the one that desires, and judges, and infers, and remembers.

Here, then, we have a partial exposition of the way in which Brentano deals with the question 'What are the elements of consciousness?' He is led to conclude, correctly, it seems to me, that whatever the nature of the rest of the world, *one* individual thing, or substance, is the person who is the subject of experience. And this confirms an observation that Brentano makes about the value of descriptive psychology: It is of superior value, he says, since unlike the natural sciences it gives us direct knowledge of something as it actually is; it enables us to know directly the nature of ourselves.[26]

25. *Psychologie vom empirischen Standpunkt*, 2nd ed. vol. 1, pp. 226–7; English edition, p. 159.

26. 'Sie macht uns bekannt mit den Bildern unseres eigenen Selbst, und darin des edelsten und höchsten, was das Reich der Erfahrung aufweist. Sie spricht uns vom Dingen, die uns anschaulich sind, wie sie wirklich existieren. Und unterscheidet sich dadurch wesentlich von der gesamten Naturwissenschaft.'

8 The Descriptive Method of Franz Brentano: Its Two Functions and Their Significance for Phenomenology[1]

Theodorus de Boer

When Brentano published his lecture *The Origin of our Knowledge of Right and Wrong*[2] in 1889, he wrote in the foreword that 'this work will develop some of the views that were set forth in my *Psychology from an Empirical Standpoint* and will differ in fundamental respects from everything that has previously been said upon the subject. My readers will then be able to see, I hope, that I have not been idle during the long period of my literary retirement.' There had, in fact, taken place an important change in Brentano's thought during the period between 1874 and 1889. We would like to take this opportunity to direct attention to this and to ask in how far it signifies a further elaboration, a correction, or perhaps even a renunciation of his earlier views. This change in his views is reflected in the position that is now assigned to descriptive psychology. In 1874 it had only a subordinate function: it served as a preliminary for genetic psychology. All this is in line with the natural scientific character of Brentano's philosophy. In 1866 he had defended the well-known thesis, 'The true method of philosophy is none other than that of the natural sciences'.

What was important was explanatory psychology, and descriptive psychology and was only a preliminary stage. Its goal was not to replace explanatory psychology nor to render it superfluous; it merely served a preparatory function. That is one of the fundamental differences between Brentano's descriptive psychology and Dilthey's. In Brentano's case it does not stand in opposition to explanatory psychology, but that is precisely the case with Dilthey. He developed a characteristic method for psychology and the humanities: the understanding of coherences and structures in their human significance from the point of view of the totality of life. That is presented as an alternative to the construction of explanatory psychology. Dilthey's descriptive psychology could be called explanatory psychology

1. Translated from the German by Linda L. McAlister and Margarete Schättle. Reprinted from the *Proceedings of the XIVth International Congress of Philosophy, 2–9 September 1968* (Vienna, 1968), vol. 2, pp. 191–9.
2. Trans. Roderick M. Chisholm (London and New York, 1969).

with an improved method, a method which is better suited to its object. It does not 'explain' the whole by its parts, but the parts by the whole. Dilthey thus wants to introduce a new means of explaining, namely, the understanding. Such an attempt is wholly foreign to Brentano (and was sharply attacked by his student Kraus).[3] Explanation for Brentano had to take place according to the method of the natural sciences and description is only a preliminary step in that direction. But by 1889 descriptive psychology had become an independent, autonomous science. The reason for this is the new function that it had acquired in the meantime – that of providing the foundations for the universally valid laws of the normative sciences: logic, aesthetics, and ethics. This is not psychologism, as Chisholm rightly points out, for Brentano strongly opposes the very attempt to make empirical generalisations the basis of apodictic laws for these sciences. A similar attempt on the part of John Stuart Mill, regarding the laws of logic, he describes as an 'astounding confusion'.[4] It also constitutes a danger in the practical realm if the eternal moral and natural law is reduced to the laws of natural science. Then, for example, a normative science such as criminal law would be derived from psychiatry.[5] The error that one makes is that one wants to derive an absolutely valid norm from a fact. The positivists as well as the historicists are guilty of this. Moore, who thought very highly of Brentano's lecture of 1889, called this 'the naturalistic fallacy'. With this critique Brentano joined in the counter-movement against naturalism at the end of the nineteenth century, which, in a certain respect, desires a return to Kant. Take, for example, Windelband's objection to the unjustified claims of the 'genetic' method, when it comes to providing a foundation for normative science. As an alternative, Windelband advocates the 'critical' method, whose function is analogous to Brentano's descriptive analysis. In this respect Brentano influenced Husserl, who in the *Logical Investigations* and in other writings on logic put forth a brilliant refutation of any attempt to base logical and ethical laws on the inductive generalisations of empirical psychology. Husserl says that we can indeed explain by empirical means how certain empirical forms of moral and legal phenomena arose, but we cannot provide the basis of their 'idea' in this way. When Brentano speaks of the 'origin' of moral knowledge he does not have in mind an explanation of its emergence, a genealogy of morals (Nietzsche) or of law (Ihering, of the historical school of jurisprudence), but rather the discovery of the authoritative source of this knowledge.

The question now arises whether this position does not contradict the slogan of 1866. After all, the method of analysis of origins is hardly identical with that of the natural sciences! In spite of this Brentano continued explicitly to maintain his claim of 1866. When he left Vienna he even went so far as to say that the natural scientific method is the only correct one, and that 'this has now been settled'.[6] Nowhere, therefore, is the method of the

3. *Über die Zukunft der Philosophie* (Leipzig, 1929), pp. 9, 30ff., 44, 46; Oskar Kraus, 'Geisteswissenschaft und Psychologie', *Euphorion* (1927), p. 512.

4. *Versuch über die Erkenntnis* (Leipzig, 1925), pp. 57, 58.

5. *Zukunft*, p. 76.

6. Franz Brentano, *Meine letzten Wünsche für Österreich* (Stuttgart, 1895), p. 32.

natural sciences rejected by Brentano (nor is it later on by Husserl). Yet we can say that Brentano had become conscious of the limited applicability of the inductive method. It is certainly correct, but has a limited validity because it is not in a position to provide the foundations for the *a priori* laws which are at the basis of the normative sciences. He calls the attempt to do this 'an aberration' of scientific method.[7] Brentano, like Husserl, was apprehensive of the relativistic consequences of a monopolisation of the inductive method in naturalism and historicism. This method cannot answer questions about what should be, or, as Husserl said in *Die Krisis der Europäischen Wissenschaften und die transzendentale Phänomenologie*[8] (*The Crisis of European Science and Transcendental Phenomenology*) 'it is not in a position to answer the "highest and most ultimate questions", "the specific questions pertaining to mankind".' It is precisely because this method fails here that descriptive analysis is needed. It is characteristic of Brentano's 'rationalism' that he does not leave the question, 'What should I do?' to the irrational powers of *Weltanschauung* and myth. That which is good and right is not to be an arbitrary dictate of some positive power.[9] These are, after all, typical 'questions of reason', according to Husserl. Practical reason must be subordinated to rational norms. Brentano finds these in an *a priori* descriptive analysis of consciousness.

Science, therefore, will not be diminished in order to make room for the belief in a *Weltanschauung*. No, natural scientific reason must make room in this area for another form of reason. Husserl's logical treatise shows that he was a good student of Brentano's in this respect as well. It is not reason that is to be rejected, says Husserl, but the aberrations of reason under the spell of the natural sciences. Both the positivism and the historicism of the philosophy of *Weltanschauung* are rejected by Husserl when it comes to establishing the foundations of the normative sciences. The correct method here, says Husserl, is the analysis of essences. In this way we can construct a philosophy that is not one of the natural sciences but is still 'a rigorous science'. Now the question arises, what is the relationship between Husserl's analysis of essences and Brentano's descriptive analysis.

Here we come face to face with the problem of Brentano's empiricism. In contrast to Chisholm,[10] I am of the opinion that the dispute on this point between the students of Husserl and Brentano is not of a purely terminological nature. There are substantive problems behind it which are still of great systematic interest.

In what way can we acquire knowledge of apodictic truths? Brentano says we acquire such knowledge 'in a single stroke'. We need no 'long series of inductions'.[11] He does call this induction, but 'induction in the broad sense', and this is because there, too, a transition from a particular to a

7. *Zukunft*, p. 75.
8. (The Hague, 1954), pp. 5ff.
9. *The Origin of our Knowledge of Right and Wrong*, p. 4.
10. See above, p. xx.
11. *Origin*, pp. 9ff., 24n.; *Versuch*, pp. 81, 82; *Vier Phasen*, pp. 118ff.

universal judgement takes place.[12] But now the question arises *how we can justify this generalisation from an empirical standpoint?* From one case a conclusion is drawn about all cases, and that with absolute certainty, which is impossible in empirical science. One can certainly say that in this knowledge 'some experience' (Chisholm) is presupposed, but this does not establish the empirical validity of such knowledge. In my opinion, Brentano's thought here leads to a dead end, and Husserl's doctrine of the intuition of essences (*Wesenschau*) is to be understood as an answer to these difficulties.

There are only two possibilities here: one must either be a consistent empiricist and, as such, reject all *a priori* knowledge, or retain this knowledge (which Husserl wanted to do just as much as Brentano did), and thus renounce the narrow empiricism that recognises only individual experience as the authoritative source of knowledge. Brentano says of *a priori* judgements that they are self-evident simply in virtue of the concepts. ('reine aus den Begriffen einleuchten'), an expression that recurs in Husserl. We are inclined to think of *vérités de raison*. Gilson speaks of an intelligibility inherent in the mind.[13] Yet the analysis of these concepts is not a purely logical one. The judgements that analyse these concepts and which Brentano, therefore, calls 'analytic' judgements increase our knowledge of reality. They are, to speak in Kantian terms, not explanatory judgements, but ampliative judgements. For this reason Brentano does not want to put 'induction in the broad sense'on a par with induction in the ordinary sense which is in reality a syllogism, and therefore purely analytic. The analysis of these concepts claims to enlarge our knowledge of reality. According to Brentano, this is possible because the content of these concepts is itself drawn from reality. Although the judgement that analyses them is *a priori* the concept itself is empirical.[14] Brentano stresses this again in his analysis of the concept number.[15] And this is where some of our questions arise. As a good empiricist Brentano wants to base all knowledge on sensory intuition. To this extent he is a 'positivist' or 'intuitionist'. Husserl later upholds a phenomenological principle according to which intuition alone is acceptable as the authoritative source of knowledge. The reason for conflicts in Brentano's work is that he recognises only sensory experience as the source of knowledge. This causes him some difficulty when it comes to establishing the foundations for the *a priori* sciences, including descriptive psychology. This later caused Husserl to make basic corrections in the empiricist theory of knowledge and to introduce the 'intuition of essences'. How do we know that what is valid for this mental phenomenon has validity for all phenomena and is in no danger of being contradicted by new cases that arise? The validity of an empirical concept is always limited to the perceived cases, and a universal judgement based on these concepts – 'purely from the [inductive] concepts' – is, therefore, always problematic. If in the formation

12. Lucie Gilson, *Méthode et Métaphysique selon Franz Brentano* (Paris, 1955), pp. 114–18.

13. *Méthode et Métaphysique*, p. 160; cp. pp. 141ff.

14. *Origin*, pp. 24, 113; Alfred Kastil, *Die Philosophie Franz Brentanos* (Salzburg, 1951), pp. 57, 199.

15. *Versuch*, pp. 52–3; *Psychology*, p. 28n; *Méthode et Métaphysique*, pp. 68, 95.

of hypotheses such judgements go beyond the contents of the premises, they must again and again be compared with experience. Thus, apodictic judgements are not made on the basis of inductive, but rather of *a priori* concepts. Husserl later speaks of 'purely from the *pure* concepts'.[16]

How does Brentano justify such a concept, if sensory perception is the only form of perception? Is it not necessary for him to fall back on other sources of knowledge, for example on the intuition of an Idea? Yet Brentano decidedly rejects any kind of Platonism. There are only individual things.[17]

One could interject that knowledge of the universal must certainly presuppose the existence of this universal. Brentano himself says that every judgement can be reduced to a negative or a positive existential judgement – an acceptance or a rejection. If this is so, can we not say that the subject of an apodictic judgement, for example 'colour implies extention', presupposes the existential judgement 'the colour (as a universal object) exists'? Yet Brentano decidedly rejects this conclusion. The universal apodictic judgement is, in his opinion, equivalent to a negative existential judgement. In our example: a non-extended colour does not exist. But here the question arises whether negative judgement does not presuppose positive knowledge about the nature of colour. From what reality, then, does this concept come? What is the *fundamentum in re*? Must we not be able to exhibit the reality from which the concept comes, if it has an empirical origin? Yet Brentano steadfastly refuses to move in such a Platonistic direction, a move which would force him to introduce what he considers to be fictitious entities such as 'essences'. (Nor does he accept the doctrine of the *intellectus agens*.) Thus there is an obvious gap in the way Brentano establishes the foundation for 'pure' universal concepts. If these concepts cannot be justified, then the *a priori* sciences that analyse these concepts also lack justification.

Husserl clarifies this issue by stating that the particular instance (possibly that which is common in a number of particular instances), that lies at the basis of the universal apodictic judgement, serves as an example but does not establish validity. The individual is not the fundament of the judgement. All knowledge 'begins with experience', but it does not, therefore, 'arise' from experience, as Kant has said.[18] The basis of the judgement is the universal object as ontic correlate of the universal concept or the universal meaning. When Husserl speaks of knowledge 'purely from the concepts', he means knowledge based upon the essences, the ideal objects.[19] This knowledge is analytic as well, but it analyses essences rather than concepts, and could thus be called ontologically analytic. The logical concept (meaning) originates in the ontological concept (species). Thus Husserl can reject the criticism that his phenomenology is nothing but a Scholastic analysis of the meanings of words. Husserl agrees with Brentano

16. *Erfahrung und Urteil* (Prague, 1939), pp. 409–10.
17. *Psychology*, p. 311; *Von sinnlichen und noetischen Bewußtsein (Psychology III)*, pp. 89, 98; *The True and the Evident*, p. 137.
18. *Logical Investigations*, trans. J.N. Findlay (London and New York, 1970), p. 109.
19. *Logical Investigations*, vol. 1, pp. 352–3.

that no existential judgement can be derived from an apodictic judgement, but in addition to a real being there is also an ideal being. And in the sense of this ideal or 'mathematical' existence, we can say of the universal objects: they truly exist.[20] No 'art of interpreting the world' can talk them away. Has Husserl thereby given up positivism? Not at all, he is the 'true positivist', for true positivism means that one openly recognises every form of experience as legitimate, including the experience of essences.[21] Thus Husserl, through his doctrine of the 'intuition of essences', is in a position to preserve universally valid apodictic truths and uphold intuitionism. These truths could also be called *a posteriori* and synthetic insofar as the intuition of essences is also a form of experience and increases knowledge. They are only *a priori* relative to empirical method in the narrow sense of sensory perception. That is to say, that we can speak of 'empiricism' only if we accept Husserl's very broad concept of experience. Only then is it possible to unite elements of rationalism – rational knowledge – and the intuitionistic point of departure without contradiction. Heidegger was right when he wrote, 'To disclose the *a priori* is not an *aprioristic* construction. Edmund Husserl has not only enabled us to understand once more the meaning of any genuine philosophical empiricism; he has also given us the necessary tools'.[22]

At the outset we wanted to focus attention on the fact that Brentano's lecture on the origin of our moral knowledge displays a development in his thinking. We can now inquire into the relationship between the descriptive analysis of consciousness and the method of the natural sciences which, as he said in 1866, is the true method of philosophy. This descriptive analysis that serves to establish the foundation for the normative sciences Brentano sometimes calls induction, but then he means induction in the broad sense. In reality Brentano here employs a method that is never used in the natural sciences and is more akin to that of mathematics.

By 1889 this descriptive analysis had acquired an independent meaning. The changes of Brentano's standpoint are reflected by the new position of descriptive psychology. In 1874 description was merely a stage preliminary to explanation; by 1889 it had acquired an autonomous position which is connected with its new function: establishing the foundations for the normative sciences. Brentano does not reject the method of the natural sciences, but he now realises that it is not suitable for ascertaining the universally valid norms of morality and law. It is incorrect and, in practical respects, dangerous to trace norms back to laws of nature. In his lecture on the future of philosophy[23] in 1892, he calls this an aberration of scientific method. Thus Brentano came to realise that this method has only limited application.

Secondly, we wanted to ask whether the descriptive analysis that discloses

20. *Logical Investigations*, pp. 352–3, 366. See also Carl Stumpf, *Erkenntnislehre*, vol. 1 (Leipzig, 1939), p. 89.

21. Edmund Husserl, *Ideas – General Introduction to Pure Phenomenology*, trans. W.R. Boyce Gibson (London, 1931), p. 86.

22. Martin Heidegger, *Being and Time*, trans. John Macquarrie and Edward Robinson (London, 1962), p. 490.

23. *Zukunft*.

apodictic truths is compatible with Brentano's 'empiricism'. Brentano says apodictic judgements are certainly *a priori*, while the concepts that are analysed in these judgements are not; they have an empirical origin. The question is, however, whether a universal concept, making an apodictic universal judgement possible, can be grounded in experience, because Brentano does not accept the existence of essences and the perception·of essences. But how can one base an absolutely valid judgement on an experience, which is always limited in scope? Brentano's theory of *a priori* sciences, among which descriptive psychology occupies an important place, leads to a dead-end in this respect. It is this tension between Brentano's adherence to the truths of reason, and his narrow empiricism that only recognises facts, which led Husserl to the doctrine of the intuition of essences. This doctrine makes it possible to give an intuitive basis to apodictic judgements, and at the same time to remain true to the phenomenological 'principle of principles' that all knowledge must be grounded in intuition, while retaining the possibility of the 'judgement of essences' ('Wesensauspruchen'). Husserl thereby extended the concept of empirical method so as to make a philosophical method of knowledge possible, which, as Heidegger says, is *a priori* and yet has nothing to do with construction. The discovery of the *a priori* is not an 'aprioristic' construction.[24]

24. *Being and Time*, p. 490.

9 'Intention' and 'Intentionality' in the Scholastics, Brentano and Husserl[1]

Herbert Spiegelberg

Preface, 1969

This essay originally appeared in Vol. 5 (1936), of the journal *Philosophische Hefte*, edited by Maximillian Beck, first in Berlin and finally in Prague. The inaccessibility of this journal, which ceased publication after the Nazi invasion of Czechoslovakia, and the fact that, to my astonishment, there is still considerable interest in this incidental essay, explains this reprint in almost unaltered form. In the Postscripts a new paragraph is identified and attention is called to the fact that this study needs expanding and updating in several places. The seemingly new title (*'Intention' und 'Intentionalität' in der Scholastik, bei Brentano and Husserl'*) which replaces the earlier one (*'Der Begriff der Intentionalität in der Scholastik, bei Brentano und bei Husserl'*) merely signifies a return to my original choice.

1. Introduction

The attempt at a more thorough investigation of what is designated by the expressions 'intention' and 'intentional' in present-day philosophy needs no special justification at the present stage of philosophy. Brentano and Husserl discovered the strategic role of these phenomena within all mental life, and brought it to the fore. Nevertheless, one can hardly claim that the subject and its context have been sufficiently explored. In several respects more clarity is needed. In many cases unexamined or insufficiently examined preconceptions and anticipations are obstructions to the real understanding of the situation. In part these harken back to conscious or unconscious historical recollections by which one is guided or, rather, misguided, in the study of the phenomena. It is the main purpose of this

---

1. Translated from the German by Linda L. McAlister and Margarete Schättle. The present translation is based on a reprinted version of the German original which appeared in *Studia Philosophica*, vol. 29 (1970), pp. 189–216. However, Professor Spiegelberg, who, together with Professor Donald Sievert, also of Washington University, checked our drafts, wrote to us that after more than thirty-five years he found it difficult to stick to the formulations of his original text. His corrections were, therefore, not always based on disagreements with our translations, but sometimes constituted modifications of the text translated.

essay to render them harmless and at the same time to work out more clearly the systematic problems that stand behind the historical development.

Not everything, however, that goes by the name 'intention' will be dealt with, but only extra-practical intention. 'Intention' is commonly understood in the sense of an intention to do something or a purpose. That is the original *practical* meaning of the term and it has been preserved in ordinary language. This meaning will not be discussed here. By contrast, the extra-practical is secondary; it has been limited to academic philosophy, and is demonstrably derived from the Scholastics of the Middle Ages.

One might be tempted to replace the artificial expression 'extra-practical' by the term 'theoretical'. Actually it does deal, particularly in the Middle Ages, predominantly with theoretical entities. The new meaning, however, also encompasses decidedly atheoretical phenomena such as acts of joy about something or acts of love for something. Even in the practical act of willing we encounter, in addition to the practical intention – the intention to do something – the mere directedness toward the willed object, which is a common characteristic of both this practical act and extra-practical acts. Thus it may be advisable in this context to designate non-practical intention by 'extra-practical' for the time being.

So far, hardly any attention seems to have been devoted to the obvious question whether there is a genus intention that includes both practical and extra-practical intention, i.e. whether the common name 'intention' designates one common referent, or whether it is merely applied equivocally to two totally different things. Thomas Aquinas, when he defined the nature of the *intentio* as a striving toward, an aiming at something else, something beyond the act, was still only thinking of the practical intention, the *actus voluntatis*.[2]

In any case, systematic decision on the question is possible only if, prior thereto, extra-practical and practical intention, as well as the area between the two – for they may be widely separated by a large number of intermediate phenomena – have been thoroughly investigated.

At times the extra-practical meaning of the term has fallen completely into oblivion. Only since Brentano and Husserl has it once again assumed an extremely important role in the theory of acts and meanings, in logic and ontology, psychology and phenomenology. Brentano himself pointed out the connection with the Scholastics. Yet neither Brentano nor others have undertaken more specific studies of this connection. We know very little about the origin and the history of the meaning of the extra-practical intention. For the most part, people have been satisfied with the assertion of terminological agreement. No attempt has been made to investigate in greater detail the question of the basic relationship between the Scholastic

2. *Summa Theologica*, 1, 2q, 12a, 1c. Raymundus Lullus, who offers a comprehensive formula ('Intentio est operatio intellectus et voluntatis, quae se movet ad dandum complementum desideratae et intellectae rei') in his *De Prima et Secunda intentione* (Opera VI), considers only practical intention in the remaining text, especially because this work has a purely ethical character; thus the continuation of the definition reads, 'et intention est actus naturalis appetitus, qui requirit perfectionem quae illi naturaliter convenit'.

and the modern conceptions of extra-practical intention. So far, the relationship has been characterised most accurately by Maximillian Beck (toward the end of his comment on an essay by Oskar Kraus in *Philosophische Hefte*, vol. 1, p. 133). At any rate, opinions on the subject are at present diametrically opposed. Some people believe that the modern theoretical intention is something merely taken over from the Scholastics, which is incontestably true as to the mere term; some regard Brentano, and some regard Husserl, as the discoverer of intentionality. In the present context it is impossible to give a complete history of the problems of intention; not only would this be a very ambitious task, but the necessary material has not yet been made sufficiently accessible. All I shall attempt here is to juxtapose the main types of the old and new extra-practical intention and to bring out the most important differences between them.

In this attempt the two terms 'intention' and 'intentional' (intentionality) will be dealt with separately, despite the fact that in some places this differentiation is at times difficult to maintain. However, the differences between the referents of these terms are much more essential than the grammatical form of the words would suggest. This has been overlooked previously. I shall begin with the investigation of the history of 'intention'.

2. Extra-practical intentio *in the Scholastics*

Throughout ancient philosophy until the beginning of the High Scholastic period, '*intentio*' simply had the practical meaning of 'striving toward', 'intent to do something', 'exertion'. The first passages where the expression has thus far been detected with a divergent, theoretical meaning are the translations of Arabic philosophers from the twelfth and thirteenth centuries, especially the translations of Ibn Sinâ (Avicenna) by Dominicus Gundissalinus and Johannes Hispanus in Toledo.[3] In order fully to understand the meaning and the motives for these translations, one would need to explore Arabic philosophy to an extent not possible for me. There, '*intentio*' seems to correspond, principally, to the word '*ma'na*,' which denotes sense, meaning, idea, concept, matter.[4] The Latin expression seems to be just as ambiguous. But throughout, intention is understood as something which is the object of an act, never as something act-like or mental (intentio sumitur pro eo quod intenditur'; *Metaphysica* IX, 8). Furthermore, the intentions are always cognitive constructs, *intentiones intellectae*, i.e. something that the cognising subject grasps in the sense-given objects ('Id, quod apprehendit anima de sensibili', *De Anima*, in *Opera, Venet*, 1518f. 4a–5a, Pars I c. 5). The whole of the area so designated becomes clear through the distinction, so important later on, between *intentiones primae* and *intentiones secundae*; Avicenna (*Metaphysica* 1, 2), too, speaks in the most important passage, of *intentio primo* and *secundo intellecta*. By *primae intentiones* the objects of knowledge themselves are meant, while *intentiones secundae*

3. Ueberweg-Geyer, *Geschichte der Philosophie*, vol. 2, 11th ed. (1928), p. 343.

4. Another relevant expression besides *Ma'na* is *Maqsad* especially in combinations such as *Qsad Tani* (i.e. *secunda intentio*) (Averroes, *Compendio de Metafisica*, Madrid, 1919, p. 800) and *maqsad alkalam* (aim of speech); I am indebted for the reference to the late Max Mayerhof in Cairo.

refers to the so-called *intentiones logicae* such as the universal, genus, species, differentia, and, in general, the logical concepts or terms which are predicated on the known thing or refer to it.[5] Very often Avicenna used *intentio* merely in the sense of the meaning of a word.

In this way extra-practical intention was explicitly introduced into medieval philosophy and became one of the foundations of High Scholasticism. A detailed description of the stages of this process is here neither possible nor indicated. In specific cases the history of meanings is tangled; the interpretations change considerably. *Intentio* represents, indeed, one of the most problematic terms in Scholasticism. All I shall attempt here is to exhibit, by means of a few cross-sections, the structural character and the place of extra-practical intention in this philosophy.

Thomas Aquinas is particularly suited to such an attempt. Simonin has already done some very creditable preliminary work on his concept of intentionality.[6] Thomas, too, is familiar with the broad meaning of 'extra-practical intention' prevalent in Avicenna, for example in his commentary on the 'Sentences'. Mostly, however, we encounter a narrower meaning, in which the intention is distinguished from the known object, the *res*, which elsewhere was regarded as the *intentio prima*. *Intentiones* are, then, the likenesses, *similitudines* or even *imagines*[7] absorbed in the soul that represent the *res* or make it present again. Furthermore, he uses *species* or *forma rerum* as almost synonymous with *intentio*.[8] Thus *intentiones* are, here, first and foremost, imprints of things, cognitive images in the human mind which terminate the (sensory or intelligible) knowledge and at whose production this knowledge aims. They are, thus, the means for grasping the objects to be known, not the known objects themselves. It is clear, therefore, that this *intentio* is very closely bound up with the Thomistic theory of knowledge, the so-called species theory.

In addition there is a series of subspecies of this extra-practical *intentio*, which, however, are only fully comprehensible and meaningful within the context of the whole Thomistic conception of knowledge. The one most seldom spoken of is an *intentio sensibilis* (or *intentio formae sensibilis*):[9] it coincides with the *species sensibilis*, the form of the perceptual object which is received into the mind without the *materia*, in the case of sense perception. More often we encounter the *intentio intelligibilis*, which is identical with that *species intelligibilis* which corresponds in the *intellectus* to the *species sensibilis*. Still a third kind of *intentio* is mentioned in the *Summa Contra Gentiles*, the

5. The distinction between *prima* and *secunda intentio* in Arabic philosophy, as I can only hypothesise, has to do with the doctrine of primary and secondary substances in Aristotle. The *secundae intentiones*, like secondary substances, have only a derivative and, to that extent, secondary being. This is expressed most clearly by Averroes, who says of the *secundae intentiones* (or *intelligibilia*), 'quorum esse est in intellectu tantum' (*Metaphysica*, I, 1, *Venet*, 1550f., 169b59).

6. H.D. Simonin, 'La notion d' "intention" dans l'oeuvre de Saint Thomas d'Aquin', *Revue des sciences philosophiques et theologiques*, vol. 19 (1930), pp. 445, sqq.

7. *Summa Contra Gentiles* IV, 11, 'Est autem . . .'

8. This becomes particularly evident by combining the passages I, 58, and VI, 11, in the *Summa Contra Gentiles*.

9. *Summa Theologica* 1, 1 78a, 3c.

intentio intellecta.[10] It is here the final cognitive image (*terminus*) in which the knowledge ends, which the intellect actively forms from the passively received *species intelligibilis* ('id quod intellectus in se ipso concipit de re intellecta'). This *intentio intellecta*, too, is a likeness, a *similitudo* or *imago*. In this respect we would certainly be justified in claiming a close relationship between extra-practical intention in St Thomas and the copy theory of knowledge. This does not mean, however, that this copy has to be fully intuitable by the senses. This is shown, for example, by the fact that the *intentio intellecta* is also designated as *verbum interius*, meaning inner word or concept, and is presented as the product of an abstraction.[11] In a more formal ontological sense Thomas also frequently speaks of *intentiones logicae*. They coincide materially with the earlier *intentiones secundae*, the basic logical concepts, which include, above all, the Aristotelian categories. *Intentio logicalis* is, indeed, a basic term in Scholastic logic.

As is well known, the Thomistic theory of knowledge did not dominate the entire period of the Middle Ages. Particularly in later Scholasticism, completely novel conceptions of knowledge developed alongside the older ones. In many ways, however, one has the impression that the whole doctrine of extra-practical intention, including the distinction between *prima* as well as the *secunda intentio*, had become somewhat of an embarrassment. They really did not know what to do with it anymore, especially after the doctrine of species increasingly began to be displaced by terministic conceptions in theory of knowledge. Sometimes it almost seems as if *intentio* means the same as 'content', or 'object of thought' or 'presentation', or 'concept', in a very vague sense, to be found so frequently today (as, for example, in *intentio generis*, an expression which is virtually synonymous with 'genus'). Thus it is not surprising that the term *intentio* in its extra-practical meaning was not carried over (like so many other Scholastic terms) into modern philosophy.

For a preliminary, though still rather simplified, picture of the variety of the competing theories on extra-practical *intentio* at that time, one had best turn to the 23rd *Distinctio* in the first book of the 'Sentences' by Peter Aureol. If one tries to group these theories, the one which is particularly new is that of the extra-practical *intentio* as an act, i.e. as an *actus rationis* (*actus intellectus*). This conception appears for the first time in Duns Scotus, though his concept of extra-practical *intentio* wavers a good deal. In general, he upholds the traditional doctrine of the *intentio prima* as *res intellecta* and the *intentio secunda* as the object of logic proper;[12] at times he simply takes over the Aristotelian-Thomistic species doctrine of knowledge.[13] He is thus somewhat inconsistent when he develops the traditional doctrine and then, abruptly, at the end of the 'Questions', designates the discursive act of

10. In the *Summa Theologica* (1, q 85q 1 ad 4) only the *intentio intelligibilis* or *species intelligibilis* appears.

11. *Summa Contra Gentiles* IV, 11. On the doctrine of the *verbum interius* see also *Summa Theologica*, 1, q. 27 al c, and 1. 34 a. 1 c, 1: 'Illud ergo proprie dicitur verbum interius quod intelligens intelligendo inquit.'

12. *Super lib.* I *Posteriorum* 1. 46 *Item* . . .

13. Prantl, *Geschichte der Logik*, vol. 3, sect. XIX, nos 107 and 109.

inference as an *intentio secunda*, which, as *actus rationis*, or *intellectus*, leads to the *primae intentiones*. Such a conception would be more understandable with the Thomist Hervaeus Natalis, who only partially accepted the act theory. For him, *intentio* is first and foremost everything that is found in the subject that represents the object and that leads to it. Naturally the *actus intellectus*, too, is one of these entities which represent the object.[15] While disregarding some less important advocates of this conception, who, for the most part, depend chiefly on Scotus, we must pay some attention to William of Ockham. He, too, however, is inconsistent; just after he has characterised the *res realiter existens* as an *intentio prima*, he designates, at the end of this same *Quodlibet*, the *res* as well as the *intentio secunda* as mere *actus intelligendi*, indeed even as *animae passiones*.[16] The basis for this conception is characteristic; it is arrived at merely on the basis of the Principle of Parsimony.[17] What is noteworthy is the clarity with which Scholastics such as Giles of Rome· (Aegidius Romanus)[18] or Peter Aureol[19] opposed such psychologistic conceptions, especially of the objects of logic (of the *secundae intentiónes*), by pointing out their non-mental nature.

Others interpret the extra-practical intention as a *relation*. This interpretation, too, originated in incipient form in Duns Scotus, e.g. when he, at one point, presented the *intentio secunda* as the relation of that which is predicable to that of which it can be predicated.[20] The main advocate of this theory is Hervaeus Natalis. Yet in his case, too, the *intentio* is not so much a genuine relation as a relational property in the object known. It does not denote a relation between the known and the knowing, but rather a characteristic on the side of the known (but by no means on that of knowing!) in relation to knowing.[21] The *ens intellectum* here seems to be almost identical

14. '... triplex est operatio intellectus. Una est intelligentia simplicium; alia est compositio vel divisio ... Tertia est operatio discursiva a praemissis ad conclusiones, at ille discursus est intentio secunda et est actus rationis per quem ducimur in cognitionem primarum intentionum et aliarum scientiarum'. (*Super lib.* I, Post, q. 46).

15. 'Uno modo dicitur intentio ex parte ipsius intelligentis omne illud quod per modum alicuius repraesentationis ducit intellectum in cognitionem alicuius rei, sive sit species intelligibilis sive actus intellectus sive conceptus mentis' (Prantl, vol. 3, sect. 19, no. 396).

16. *Quodlibeta*, IV, 19.

17. 'Frustra fit per plura quod fieri potest per pauciora ... ergo praeter actum intelligendi non eportet ponere aliquid aliud' (Prantl, vol. 3, sect. 19, n. 768).

18. 'Logica non est de actibus sed est de intentionibus et conceptibus qui formantur per huiusmodi actus ... Dilectica ergo, quae proprie rationalis est, magis erit de huiusmodi conceptibus quam de ipsis actibus' *ibid.*, vol. 3, no. 371).

19. 'Logica non coniungit actum intellectus actui intellectus sed conceptus secundarios conceptibus primus ...; ergo manifestum est, quod secunda et prima intentio non sunt actus intelligendi sed obiectivus conceptus' (Prantl, vol. 3, n. 705).

20. '... intentio secunda quae est quaedam relatio rationis in praedicabili ad illud de quo est praedicabile ...' (Prantl, vol 3, sect. 19, no. 106).

21. '... qui quidem respectus non tenet se ex parte actus intelligendi vel ex parte scientiae in ordine ad rem intellectam sed magis e converso, respectu rationis, tenens se ex parte rei intellectae in ordine ad intellectum ipsum' (according to Peter Aureol in Prantl, no. 701).

with the fully known object,[22] and is then designated by *intentionalitas*. The possession, the having, of such *respects rationis* is also characterised as a *habitudo rei intellectae*.[23]

Finally I should mention the conception of Peter Aureol himself, who discussed all of the previously mentioned conceptions of *intentio*. For him it is a mere *conceptus mentis*, namely one which, originating from the objects, is formed only by means of an act of intellect. Yet, in the last analysis, he believes that this *conceptus* should include as an indistinguishable part the *conceptio passiva* of the object and the conceived object itself, which only increases the difficulties of the *intentio* doctrine.[24]

Characteristic of the conceptions of extra-practical intention at the end of the Scholastic period are the definitions of concepts in the *Lexicon* of Goclenius, a Marburg disciple of Petrus Ramus at the beginning of the seventeenth century. At first he talks about an intention in the proper sense (*intentio formalis*) as *actus mentis, quo tendit in obiectum*. Only in the loose sense does the *intentio* also designate the *obiectum in quod actus mentis tendit*, the so-called *intentio obiectiva*. In this sense the *actus mentis* is always a cognition, an *actus intellectus, quo obiectum suum percipit* (*quo obiectum cognoscimus*) and correspondingly, the *intentio obiectiva* is always the object of a cognition (*id quod per astum cognoscitur*.)

Thus the picture of extra-practical *intentio* that the late Scholastics give us is highly complex. Nevertheless, the great diversity of the medieval conceptions stays within certain bounds, which accounts for their relative unity compared with the modern conception. Here is one common unifying feature: regardless of the differences between the late Scholastic and the High Scholastic versions of intention, whether as an objective entity (object, relation or concept) or as an act, it was always closely associated with knowledge.

Furthermore, it should be mentioned that this cognitive meaning of the term 'intention' in no way remained restricted to philosophy; it seems to have been used effectively even in languages other than Latin. There is no doubt that Dante is still wholly under the influence of Scholastic philosophy when he writes about the *intenzione* which is drawn out of things by the power of conceptualisation (*apprensiva*) and which is incorporated by the soul ('tragge intenzione et dentro voi spiega'. *Purgatorio* Canto XVIII. Vers 22f.). It is interesting to note that it was only at that time that the Latin

22. 'Prima intentio . . . non est aliud quam esse intellectum'. Peter Aureol, in 1, Sent., dist. 23, art. 1.

23. 'Alio modo dicitus intentio, quod se tenet ex parte rei intellectae et hoc modo dicitus intentio res ipsa quae intelligitur inquantum in ipsam tenditur sicut in quoddam cognitum per actum intelligendi, et, intentio sic dicta formaliter et in abstracto dicit . . . terminationem quae est quaedam habitudo rei intellectae ad actum intelligendi . . . Prima intentio concretive et materialiter dicit illud quod intelligitur . . . Intentio, prout se tenet ex parte rei intellectus, dupliciter potest accipi scil. in abstracto ipsa intentionalitas et in concreto pro eo cui ista intentionalitas convenit' (Prantl, n. 396).

24. 'Intentionalitas (or intentio: note 532) est ipsemet conceptus obiectivus per intellectum formatus claudens indistinguibiliter conceptionem passivam et rem quae concipitus per ipsam, et idem est dicta intentio quod conceptus' (Prantl, n. 539).

word *intendere* took on the new meaning of the Italian *intendere* and the French *entendre*, in the sense of understanding.[25] The Scholastic *intentio* in the sense of a cognitive image may have played a role in the appearance of this peculiar new meaning of the Latin *intendere* as well as in the new development of the Italian and French meanings.

3. Intention in Husserl

What is the situation with regard to the meaning of the term 'intention' in contemporary philosophy? Bearing in mind the distinction between 'intention' and 'intentionality', it should be made clear that Franz Brentano did not revive the independent term 'intention', at least not in those of his writings published so far. As I will point out, he spoke only of intentional objects and intentional relations. Presumably someone who knew the Scholastics as well as Brentano did had a reason for avoiding the expression *intentio*, which was all too reminiscent of the various theories of knowledge connected with this term, and, in particular, of the Thomistic species doctrine.

Thus the actual term 'intention' first re-emerges, as far as I can see, in Edmund Husserl. It is not very easy to determine clearly his conception of the essence of intention. At times we must go beyond Husserl's own statements, since he himself offers no final account of the question. What follows is an attempt to work out an exegesis of what is essential in the Husserlian conception by way of a somewhat free and extrapolating approach.

It is best to start from the fact that the Husserlian intention appears in two different places – in meaningful signs (words) and in very specific kinds of experiences; the subclasses of these intentions are disregarded here as inessential.

(1) The Verbal-Intention (*Wortintention*).[26]
This intention is by no means identical with the word itself. However, it has the closest relationship with what is designated as the meaning of a word, insofar as this is not understood as the object meant. The intention, like the meaning, is something that belongs to the word, it is something that is directed from the word to an object. Metaphorically, one could speak of the verbal intention as a beam or an arrow shooting out from the word toward the object. What is behind the image of such an intentional beam is the assumption that a peculiar, non-real, ostensive pointer issues from the word to an object, and that one has to follow it if one wants to understand the word one has heard. The verbal-intention is, thus, the non-real pointer beam emanating from the word (as from a sign post).[27] Of course this beam

25. The first example of this meaning is, according to Ducange-Henschel, *Glossarium mediae et infimae latinitatis, sub voce intendere*, in the *Vita* of St Catherine of the fourteenth century: *Prophetarum cum discretione intendenda*.

26. Cp. especially *Logical Investigations*, vol. 2, no. 1; English edition trans. J.N. Findlay, pp. 269–336.

27. R. Ingarden speaks here of an 'intentional direction factor' (*Richtungsfaktor*) in *Das literarische Kunstwerk* (Halle, 1931), pp. 61ff.

is not an independent entity; it is attached to the word from which it emanates, tied to it as its source of radiation. Such a phenomenon is attributed to it, bestowed upon it; on the basis of such an assigned intention pointing toward a thing, the word 'has' the meaning of this thing as a property, yet it does not 'have' the intention itself, the intentional beam, for this beam cannot form a property. Meaning is, accordingly, the property a word has of possessing, not as a property *per se* but as a kind of ideal, external accessory, an intentional beam which emanates from it and points to a definite object.

(2) The Experiential Intention (*Erlebnisintention*).[28]

Husserl calls experiences that possess this sort of intention, act or intentional experiences. Occasionally even such acts themselves are called 'intentions'.[29] Strictly speaking, this is still an improper phrase, a *pars pro toto*. Acts have the 'essential character' (*Wesenscharakter*), the 'peculiarity of intention, the relation to an object through representation or an analogous mode'. Intention, thus, is something pertaining to an act, not the act itself. So perceiving or wanting are not intentions in themselves, but they include intentions directed toward the object of perception, toward the target meant. The essence of this experiential intention, however, is never clearly delimited by a definition in Husserl. Yet from the context it becomes clear that for him intention is the 'character' of an act, its peculiarity by virtue of which it relates to, is directed toward, or aims at an object. Intention is like the central thread woven into every act, aiming at the object belonging to each act. Intention is, therefore, a dependent component of an act, a dependent part thereof.

One might suppose that there are also independent acts of intending in addition to those mentioned thus far. Intention in this sense is often identified with the .act of meaning (*meinen*). The German expression *meinen* itself has a variety of meanings: the most common one being to believe. Yet when it simply refers to the pointing toward something, to the making something an object ('I mean this one, no other') then it must be noted that such a *meinen* makes possible sense only in connection with other acts. Furthermore, such an explicit *meinen* cannot be traced in acts of perceiving, feeling or wanting; the most common and at the same time most important acts include no explicit independent meaning intentions (*Meinungs-intentionen*). Thus the meaning of Husserl's original·act-intention is that of a peculiar function of pointing at something. There is reason to place special emphasis on this specific function because more recently Husserl[30]

28. Cp. especially *Logical Investigations*, trans. J.N. Findlay, vol. 2, no. 5, esp. § 18; pp. 533–659, esp. pp. 580–1.

29. Not taken into consideration are the equivocations that Husserl himself distinguished as well as intention in the narrower sense, i.e. the act of the non-intuitive or empty aiming at an object which corresponds to the intuitive experience that fulfils it.

30. As in *Formale und transzendentale Logik* (Halle, 1929), see esp. p. 183 (*Wesen der Intentionalität als konstituierende Leistung*) and p. 216, and E. Fink, *Die phänomenologische Philosophie Edmund Husserls in der gegenwärtigen Kritik* (Berlin, 1934); 'Studien zur Phänomenologie 1930–1939', *Phaenomenologica*, vol. 21 (1966), p. 143.

himself describes this function of the intention as a process of constituting, of constructing, the objects, even as a productive creation which, by the way, brings extra-practical and practical intention into immediate proximity again. The question may remain undecided to what extent a demonstration of such functions is possible at all. At any rate, they are not distinctive functions necessary for the essence of general act intentions.

What, then, is the relation between verbal intention and experiential intention? Certainly it is not a case of an equivocation if both are called 'intentions'. A common feature of both is, above all, the fact that the carrier of the intention (word or act) points to an object as well as the fact that these intentions are dependent upon their carriers. To be sure, the difference in carriers is not the only difference between verbal-intention and act-intention. Going beyond Husserl's treatment of the question, one will also have to note differences in the structure of the intentions themselves. Thus the verbal-intention is an artificially assigned attribute of the word, its connection with the word is non-real (*ideell*) resulting from the act of attribution, while experiential intention, being mental directedness independent of such acts of attribution, has a real existence in the act itself. Connected with this is the further difference that verbal intentions are located, as it were, outside of the real body of sound, thus forming a kind of non-real (*ideell*) appurtenance, whereas act-intentions are parts embedded in the acts themselves. These differences, however, do not exclude the possibility that the 'pointing beams' of words as well as acts constitute a common, basic characteristic of Husserl's two types of intention.

4. A comparison between intention in the Scholastics and in Husserl

What, then, is the relation between intention in Husserl and intention in the medieval Scholastics? Let us first briefly point out the main differences in parallel columns:

(1) Extra-practical intention in the Scholastics is a self-contained entity, and is, in this sense, an independent entity, regardless of whether we mean a mere likeness of a thing, a thing, or an intellectual act; the only case where this differs is where we interpret *intentionalitas* as a relational property (*habitudo*).

(1) In Husserl the verbal intention is a dependent entity, an *accidens*. Only acts of a mere intentional *meinen* would be relatively independent; but even they must be distinguished from intellectual acts in general.

(2) The Scholastics have extra-practical intention only in cognitive acts.

(2) In Husserl, on the other hand, it also occurs in non-cognitive acts, e.g. in representational acts or believing, and particularly in emotional and practical acts (for example, delight at something or striving for something).

(3) We encounter the term 'intention' in the Scholastics only in the fields of logic and in epistemology.

(3) Husserl uses it throughout the entire realm of philosophy, especially, also, in general psychology, phenomenology and philosophy of language.

(4) In the High Scholastics the doctrine of *intentio* usually occurs in close connection with the species doctrine of knowledge, a special form of the copy theory.

(4) Husserl's use of the term is not based upon any special theory of knowledge.

(5) Even in the conception of *intentio* as act, the element of directedness toward the object is not elaborated at all or is not elaborated as such; the conception of relational property regards it at best as a relation of the object to the act.

(5) In Husserl's conception the essential element of verbal and experiential intentions is the pointing relatedness of the word and the act to the object.

The only thing the Scholastics and Husserl might have in common with regard to intention is, perhaps, the connection with mental acts in general. But this connection is too general to provide the foundation for an essential relationship in structure. At any rate, on the basis of the findings above, we cannot speak of a common Scholastic and phenomenological concept of extra-practical intention.

If this is true, then we are justified in asking why Husserl re-introduced the Scholastic term at all. The answer can be given only in the light of the history of the expression 'intentional'. Historically speaking, as I want to re-emphasise, both terms have been used in a closely parallel fashion, and it is only for systematic reasons that I considered it appropriate to loosen up their tight linkage.

5. *The intentional in the Scholastics*

Obviously the term 'intentional', too, goes back to the Scholastics. To my knowledge its first occurrence has not yet been traced, yet it is already used by Thomas Aquinas. He contrasts the *esse intentionale*, characteristic of every likeness, every *similitudo* in the transmitting medium (e.g. the *similitudo coloris in aere*, the likeness of colour in the air) to the *esse reale* of the original (the *esse coloris in pariete*, the being of colour on the wall); in a similar fashion the expressions *secundum intentionem* or *intentionaliter* and *secundum esse* or *realiter* are contrasted; the expression *esse in intentione* is also used. Thus 'intentional', in this context, means a certain mode of existence, the characteristic irreal kind of being attributed to likenesses, the extra-practical as well as to the practical intentions, the goals of an intention to do something as opposed to the being of real objects.[31] *Esse intentionale*, therefore, does not simply mean

31. Brentano's historical remark in his *Psychology* concerning Thomas Aquinas, to the effect that not only what is thought of is intentional in the thinker, but also that

the same as 'to be an *intentio*' which is sometimes called *intentionalitas*, but rather 'to have an existence of the sort that the *intentio* has'.

The late Scholastics formulated the conception of intentional existence even more radically: *esse intentionale* now becomes an existence that depends solely on the act, even on the act of will of the subject. A typical example is Durandus de S. Porciano's differentiation between an *esse intentionale* in a primary sense and the *esse reale*. The former he attributes to those objects which owe their existence solely to an act of the intellect (non sunt nisi per operationem intellectus); among them he lists genus, species, and, in general, the *logicae intentiones*, but he (like Thomas) does not include the image present in the medium, which is in *this* sense real. In a secondary sense he uses 'intentional' for everything that possesses a weak, inferior kind of existence (*esse debile*) insofar as it has not yet reached the full development of its *essence* (quia deficit a perfectione propriae speciei) as, for example, the light and the *species coloris* in the conveying medium.[32] This secondary meaning, however, gradually recedes into the background and the conception of the intentional existence as a subjective existence dependent upon the act takes precedence.[33]

We should bear in mind that according to this Scholastic conception of the *esse intentionale*, certainly not every *intentio* forms an *ens intentionale* with an *esse intentionale*. Thus the *intentio prima*, in its most commonly accepted meaning as direct object of knowledge, is not simply intentional; in Ockham, for example, the *intentio prima* was characterised almost as *res realiter existens*.[34]

6. Brentano's intentional inexistence

Among modern philosophers it was, indeed, Brentano who resumed the use of the term 'intentional', and, in so doing he referred explicitly to the Scholastic usage of the term. But his students and commentators in particular have paid too little attention to the context in which it was introduced. In general it should be stressed that in the works of Brentano which have been published so far (and these are the only ones which can be used as references here) the term intentional is very seldom used.

the object of love is in the lover and the thing desired in the desirer, turns out to be correct for the *esse intentionale* (as distinguished from the *intentio* itself).

32. In Sent. 1, dist. 23, art. 1 (ed. Romae, 1595, vol. 1, p. 530): 'Esse intentionale' is comparable to the 'esse obiectivum tantum et ficticium seu apparens' and is differentiated from the 'esse reale et fixum extra verorum (probably: rerum)naturam, absque omni apprehensione', 'per quod patet quod esse intentionale non est aliud quam visio aut apparitio obiective.' 'Illud quod non est existens in rerum natura nec habet esse fixum extra secundum quod huiusmodi, illud inquam est quid intentionale' (Prantl, p. 592, notes 530 and 532).

33. 'Scholastici ens intentionale appelant ens quod sola conceptione et consideratione inest, seu ens quod est intra animam per notiones, cui opponitur reale quod reperitur extra animae notiones' (Goclenius, *Lexicon philosophicum*).

34. Likewise his follower Armandus de Bellovisu: 'Ipsa ergo res intellecta materialiter et in concreto dicitur intentive sive res intellecta sive ens reale ut humo, lapis et huiusmodi' (Prantl, vol. 3, sect. 19, note 631).

Brentano re-introduces the term in *Psychology from an Empirical Standpoint*, and he does this in connection with the attempt at a more exact differentiation between mental and physical phenomena. This fact by itself shows that this is a matter of general psychology and no longer, as before, a matter of epistemology and logic.

Furthermore, it is striking that the word 'intentional' in Brentano's *Psychology* is always used as a direct or indirect attribute of 'object'. In Brentano every mental phenomenon (such as presentation, judgement, love) is characterised by that which, in his opinion, 'the Scholastics of the Middle Ages called the intentional (or even mental) inexistence of an object, and what we might call, though not wholly unambiguously, reference to a content (which is not to be understood as meaning something real), or immanent objectivity. Every [mental phenomenon] includes something as object within itself . . . This intentional inexistence is characteristic exclusively of mental phenomena.' These can be defined as 'those phenomena which contain an object intentionally within themselves'.[35]

It is of no conern here just to what extent such a conception of mental acts *per se*, and not just of cognition, is a Scholastic or Thomistic one. One thing is clear, however: in Brentano the term 'intentional' is intimately connected with a conception of the experiential structure according to which all objects to which an experience relates are at the same time contained in this experience, they exist within it. The term 'intentional (mental) inexistence' expresses this immanence in the *mens* especially clearly; it seems to denote an embeddedness in the sense of a Scholastic or, in particular, a Thomistic *intentio*.

In this sense such 'intentional' objects obviously do not exist outside the *mens*. This conception originates mainly in critical realism which Brentano, too, advocated, and which regards physical phenomena such as colours from the outset as something subjective. This critical realism is certainly no copy theory of knowledge; nevertheless a relation exists insofar as it leads to a doubling of the external object in the consciousness in the form of a phenomenal correlate of the real object. In Brentano, the word 'intentional' is thus synonymous with 'immanent' and stands in contrast to 'transcendent', and 'intentional object' is synonymous with 'immanent object'. Without the underlying conceptions of immanence and transcendence, Brentano's theory of the intentional object, or, more precisely, of the intentional inexistence of the object, loses its foundation.

This becomes even more apparent from Brentano's later objections to this terminology. In a footnote in the 1911 edition,[36] he objects only to the misunderstanding that the expression 'intentional inexistence' denotes an intention to do something and the pursuit of a goal. 'In view of this I might have done better to avoid it altogether. Instead of the term "intentional" the

---

35. *Psychologie vom empirischen Standpunkt*, 2nd ed. Oskar Kraus (1925), Book II, chapter 1, sect. 5. *Psychology from an Empirical Standpoint*, English edition ed. Linda L. McAlister (London and New York, 1973).

36. 2nd ed., vol. 2, p. 8; English ed., p. 180.

Scholastics very frequently used the expression "objective".[37] This has to do with the fact that something is an object for the mentally active subject, and, as such, is present in some manner in his consciousness . . .' Here too, therefore, the intentional is nothing but that which is present, immanent, in consciousness, as opposed to that which actually exists. More importantly, Brentano, at this point, is very close to giving up the expression 'intentional' in order to throw the mental immanence of mental phenomena into even bolder relief. In an appendix of 1911, the term completely disappears. Here he only speaks of the 'mental reference to something as object'.[38]

According to Oskar Kraus,[39] however, Brentano later completely gave up the doctrine of immanent objectivity, of the mental inexistence of the objects. He maintains that only the reference to something as object remained for Brentano as characteristic of mental phenomena. Even then, however, it is significant that in connection with this the expression 'intentional', too, completely disappears.[40] For Brentano it was and remained closely connected with the doctrine of the act-immanent objects; mental inexistence, not the reference to something as object, constituted for him the essence of intentionality.

This realisation does not conflict with the claim that at the same time Brentano was the first to point out the essential relatedness of the mental phenomena to objects. The only thing that is open to dispute is whether he specifically characterised this side of the mental life by the expression 'intentional'. What he himself regarded as being equivalent to 'intentional (or even mental) inexistence of an object', namely, on the one hand, reference to a content, direction toward a (non-real) object, and, on the other hand, immanent objectivity, are two very different things. Objects toward which I direct myself do not by any means have to exist immanently. Even if both things always went together, they would still have to be distinguished conceptually. It seems that Brentano was not sufficiently aware of this difference when he combined the two phenomena under the heading 'intentional inexistence'. That the word 'intentional', in particular, is connected not with the conception of the reference to an object, but with the idea of immanence is shown clearly by the remark about the adjective 'intention (also even mental)' inexistence, in which their meaning in the sense of immanence within the mind is once again expressed.[41]

37. So Durandus de S. Porciano speaks of an 'esse in intellectu obiective' of truth as opposed to 'esse in intellectu subiective', as it belongs to the *species* or *actus intelligendi* (Prantl, note 564).

38. 2nd ed. vol. 2, pp. 133ff.; English ed., pp. 271ff.

39. 2nd ed., vol. 1, p. 269, no. 11; English ed., p. 89; and Oskar Kraus, *Franz Brentano* (Munich, 1919), pp. 23f.

40. This becomes particular clear in the Appendix mentioned above; 'Mental Reference as Distinguished from Relation in the Strict Sense'.

41. 2nd ed., vol. 1, p. 124; English ed., p. 88n. 'They [the Scholastics] also use the expression "to exist as an object (objectively) in something", which, if we wanted to use it at the present time, would be understood, on the contrary, as a designation of a real existence outside the mind. At least this is what is suggested by the expression "to exist immanently as an object", which is occasionally used in a similar sense, and in which the term "immanent" should obviously rule out the misunderstanding which is to be feared.'

Thus 'intentional' for Brentano refers to the property of an object which is immanent in consciousness in a way analogous to that in which the species are immanent in the Thomistic–Aristotelian theory of knowledge, with which Brentano had concerned himself a good deal.[42] He thus occupies a strange position on the dividing line between the medieval and the modern conception. On the one hand, his use of the term 'intentional' is highly Scholastic; on the other hand, the concept of mental reference, which does not yet bear the designation 'intentional', is modern.

This does happen, however, in two places in the very important lecture of 1889, *On the Origin of Our Knowledge of Right and Wrong*.[43] Here Brentano speaks of an 'intentional relation to something which may not be actual but which is presented as an object'. Yet there is no mention of intentional phenomena. The intentional relation is also described as a 'subjective attitude' ('subjectives Verhalten'), and thus not as a relation in the usual sense between two equal poles, but rather as something which Brentano later described as 'relation-like' ('relativlich'). An act, not an object, therefore, is 'intentional'. But in this case, too, it is made clear that that to which the act refers is primarily 'inwardly objective', i.e. 'immanent' or 'intentionally inexistent' in the sense of the *Psychology* of 1874.

Finally, Brentano also uses the expression 'intentional' to denote the merely phenomenal as distinguished from the real. Thus he talks about mental phenomena such as knowledge, joy, and longing as having real existence in addition to their intentional existence, while physical phenomena such as colours, sounds, warmth have only phenomenal and intentional being.[44]

If one were to understand 'intentional' here in the sense of 'immanent', intentional and real existence would be mutually exclusive; 'immanent objectivity' should then mean mere objectivity in the Scholastic sense, i.e. a lack of real existence.

7. The intentional in Husserl

On the basis of this evidence it no longer seems to me to be doubtful that the modern meaning of the term 'intentional', and not just that of the term 'intention', is first arrived at in Husserl. Husserl was the first to separate the concept of intentionality from the notion of immanent inexistence and interpreted it, or, speaking more precisely, re-interpreted it, as relatedness to, direction toward, the object.

This comes out with greatest clarity in Husserl's discussion of Brentano's doctrine of mental phenomena in his fifth *Logical Investigation* ('On Intentional Experiences and their "Contents"'). There he warns, in

42. Nicolai Hartmann now follows him in this, unconsciously to be sure, in his *Metaphysics of Knowledge*. For him, the intentional object is 'wholly and completely immanent' and represents, as such, the transcendent-real object (see esp. 2nd ed., p. 105ff.).

43. English edition ed. Roderick M. Chisholm (London and New York, 1969), pp. 14, 16.

44. *Psychologie*, 2nd ed., vol. 1, p. 129.

particular, of two misunderstandings to which Brentano's exposition could give rise. The first one – the possibility of construing the objective relatedness of experiences as a real relation between the ego and the object known – is of minor importance. What is more dangerous, according to Husserl, is the misunderstanding implicit in expressions such as 'immanent objectivity', 'intentional or mental inexistence', 'the object's being contained in consciousness'; this amounts to the view that the object is thought of as included in the experience as in a box. Here an essential difference between Husserl's and Brentano's conception of the intentional comes to light. For Husserl the intentional object is never immanent, but transcendent in a sense yet to be shown. What is 'immanent', an expression Husserl still wanted to avoid in the *Logical Investigations* (see *Logical Investigations*, vol. 2, Investigation V, sect. 11), for instance *real* (*reell*) data of sensation, 'appearances', are precisely not intentional.

In addition, further striking peculiarities of Husserlian intentionality appear. First, it should be noted that Husserl speaks not only, as Brentano does, of intentional object but, above all, of intentional experiences or data. No one before Husserl had done this.

In order exactly to comprehend the actual sense of the adjective 'intentional' in Husserl, one must again become somewhat specific. This will also require a more exact elaboration of some points that Husserl left in need of clarification.

For Husserl, intentional *experiences* are in the foreground. 'The qualifying adjective "intentional" names the common "essential character" of a certain classes of experiences, which relate to objects.'[45] To this extent 'intentional' means nothing but the property of an experience to possess an intention in the previously discussed sense of the term, a directedness toward an object. 'Intentional' in this sense is synonymous with 'having an intention or containing it'.

Husserl often speaks, too, of intentional relation as a characteristic of acts, in the same sense in which Brentano spoke of a relation of mental to physical phenomena. Yet the question arises whether a relation can really be the bearer of intentionality in the strict sense. There is certainly a particular relation betwen an act and the object toward which it is directed: one member of the relation, the act, is directed intentionally (through an 'intention') toward the other member, the object. The relation itself, however, is not directed toward the object. Thus the relation can at best be 'intentional' in a derivative sense inasmuch as it depends on the intentionality of the act or rather contained in the act.

Other bearers of intentionality can be *linguistic expressions*. Husserl, indeed, attributes intentional meaning to words with an intention toward objects.

With acts as well as with words, 'intentional' thus means 'having an intention', 'tending toward an object', and to this extent, 'intending'. The situation changes when we now move on to *objects* as bearers of intentionality. Here the predicate 'intentional' means, first of all, the same as 'being intended',[46] 'being the object of an intention', 'being the goal at which one aims'. Thus the opposite of the intentional is the not-intended, that which is not aimed at; in this sense, for example, one's own mental life is, normally, not intentional. In principle, every object can be intentional in this way, can become the object of an intention – regardless of whether the object is immanent or transcendent (in the sense of being beyond the limits of the given, and, to this extent, not given), real or unreal.

Besides this, the expression 'intentional' as applied to objects has a yet narrower, more specific meaning for Husserl. According to it, 'intentional' refers to everything that lies beyond the realm of experiences and their 'components', but which is still actually meant or intended by the acts as 'correlates'. Here 'intentional' is contrasted to '*reell*', the latter meaning contained in experience as a constituent part, as an independent piece or a dependent element;[47] the data of sensation are supposed to be included here as well.[48] The intentional in this sense lies, therefore, essentially outside of the experiences, and is in this respect 'transcendent'.[49] In *Ideas*, Husserl introduced the term 'noematic' for 'intentional' in the above sense, and the term 'noetic' for '*reell*'. This terminology, however, is based on a conception of the structure of consciousness, which, insofar as it presupposes the existence of sense-data, cannot be regarded as certain and binding. In this doctrine of the data of sensation, a vestige of the old species doctrine remains, according to which only correlates of objects, not objects themselves, can appear in consciousness itself.

Finally, one finds in Husserl a third meaning of the expression 'intentional' with respect to objects, one which corresponds almost completely to that of the Scholastics. It means the mode of being of such objects, which only exist thanks to consciousness, as opposed to the mode of being of reality. Husserl, then, often speaks of 'merely intentional' objects. If one starts out, however, from the new meaning of 'intention' as mere directedness toward an object, the retention of such a terminology does seem rather unfortunate. For such directedness can in no way constitute an object or maintain it in existence. On the contrary, the completed constitution of an object is presupposed before an act can direct itself toward it; one simply cannot direct oneself toward something which is not yet constituted. Thus Husserl's terminology leads to a confusion of intention as directedness and intention in the sense of constituting an object, a confusion which, especially in Husserl, had unfortunate consequences; for he interpreted the intentionality of the object more and more in the sense of being constituted by functioning intentions.

46. Occasionally Husserl himself differentiates between *intentional*, which can be used both for meaning and object, and *intended*, which can only be used for the object (see *Logical Investigations*, vol. 1, Inv. 1, sect. 30).

47. *Ideas – General Introduction to Pure Phenomenology* (1913), trans. W.R. Boyce, Gibson, sect. 88.

48. *Ideas*, sect. 98.

49. *Ideas*, sect. 61.

8. A comparison of Husserlian and earlier intentions

I shall now compare the Husserlian concept of intentionality, once again in a summary fashion, with that of his predecessors.

The last mentioned meaning of 'intentional' in contrast to *'reell'* indeed has its origin in Scholastic philosophy and is carried over almost unchanged into modern philosophy.

The situation is different with the conceptions mentioned before. Diametrically opposed to the Scholastic conception[50] is, in particular, the meaning of 'intentional' as differentiated from the *'reell'* which has no basis in Scholastic philosophy nor in Brentano. Brentano's immanent intentional object provides a link only insofar as Husserl is concerned with the same entity and designates it as intentional, yet he conceives it in an altered sense, no longer in that of immanence, but of a peculiar transcendence to the *'reell'* content of consciousness.

'Intentional' in the sense of 'intended' occurs, in the strict sense, first in Husserl. This meaning is completely absent from Scholastic philosophy. It is true that we encounter in Brentano a directedness toward an object, which thus becomes the target of this directedness; however, this object is not yet called intentional; in Brentano this term remains connected with the idea of immanence. Husserl's conception of intentionality is free from this idea of immanence, but is characterised by the element of intendedness.

A meaning of 'intentional' which we find exclusively in Husserl and which he uses most frequently is the one of an intending or meaning directedness (*intendierend-meinenden Gerichtetheit*) in the experience toward the object.

Thus the main result of our historical comparison can be stated as follows: both with regard to the meaning of the term 'intention' and to that of the derivative term 'intentional', very considerable differences remain. It may very well be that the modern conception is historically connected to the medieval one, yet at the final state of development, the differences in meaning have become so far-reaching that all that remains for a portion of the phenomena is a sameness of label and for the corresponding terms mere equivocation of meanings. Here, as in all cases, terminological agreements between medieval and modern, between Scholastic and phenomenological philosophy, must be treated with extreme caution, in the interests of both, and in the interest of the subject-matter itself. This is even more true in those cases where, on the basis of such agreement, it is claimed that there have been influences and that ideas have been taken over from the one to the other.

50. This becomes quite clear when we look back to the above-cited passage from Armandus de Bellovisu (note 35), who used 'intentional' primarily to denote what is immanent, and only in a secondary sense did he use it to denote the known object of intention.

9. Systematic concluding remarks

The main goal of the present essay has now been reached. All that was intended here was to discuss the relationship between the medieval and the modern conceptions, to show their differences and their similarities in a historical context. Systematic problems were investigated and clarified only to the extent necessary for an understanding of the history. Nevertheless, the systematic interest served as a kind of guideline for the questions posed. It seems, therefore, appropriate to add a few systematic supplementary remarks and conclusions.

The present essay has not dealt with a number of questions which would have to be taken up in a systematic investigation of intentional structures. To point out only one: the relationship between intention and consciousness which, not without reason, has hardly been mentioned so far. We can by no means assert from the very start that they are identical, as little as that the mental and the conscious are identical. We should not under-estimate how important it is to clarify these questions. It is also extremely important, particularly from the epistemological point of view, to clarify the relationship between that which is intended and that which is given, whose identity, too, must not simply be assumed.

On the basis of the preceding results, a certain terminological reform would seem to be indicated. The term 'intention' was certainly meaningful and historically justified as a means of pointing out an extremely important and thus far almost overlooked area of phenomena. But today when the complexity of the respective structures has been revealed and when, in many cases, equivocations have intruded, the foreign word has degenerated into a dangerous catchword because it is often used rather haphazardly; therefore, a simplifying adaptation of the terminology to the new situation would certainly be desirable.

Yet, as far as possible, the coining of new technical terms should be avoided. In any case preference should be given to expressions close to the subject-matter. In many cases the German word *meinen* is quite suitable; yet, for reasons indicated above (p.000), this is not always the case. I would recommend that the intentional act be designated as 'object-directed' (*gegenstandsgerichteten*) and the intentionally intended object as 'act-meant'. For in view of the problematic nature of the structure in question, it would be premature to worry over the substitution of another term for 'intentional' in the sense in which it is opposed to '*reell*'; possible formulations would be 'act-transcendent' (*aktjenseitig*) or 'experience-transcendent' (*erlebnis-jenseitig*). For the merely intentional object as contrasted with the real object, the term 'act-dependent' or 'experience-dependent' would seem appropriate. For 'intention' itself, meaning a pointing from the word or act to the object, a term such as 'object-directed' or 'object-aiming reference' will usually suffice.

Such terminological revisions, however, do not affect the importance of the subject-matter. It remains Brentano's indisputable achievement to have revealed that the mental refers to an object. One may doubt whether this phenomenon is a suitable means for distinguishing the area of psychology or the area of phenomenology from other areas. Yet this does not change the fact that object-directed acts are of fundamental importance, and not only for the comprehension of the mental as such. If we start from the study of inorganic and merely organically living nature, it is an enormous leap, something fundamentally new, to have a being that is not confined within itself, that can go beyond itself and can have something else as an object, that can refer and can be directed toward something else, and this not only in a real-causal manner, but also in a peculiarly non-real, mental manner. Here something utterly new enters the world. Dead nature rises above its self-containment and reaches out beyond itself. This signifies a turning point in the cosmic order.

Such a phenomenon is important enough to constitute a basic theme not only in psychology but in the philosophy of life, metaphysics and philosophical anthropology, as well. This is true even if consciousness or object-directed acts are already present in subhuman living beings, above all in the higher animals. This would not exclude their decisive role in the human structure. But their importance is altered and enhanced in the human being since he has the ability, to a certain extent, freely to control these object-directed acts. Such a structure, furthermore, has its own, inherent value and dignity worthy of further investigation. Finally, one can gain here basic ethical insights. Is it permissible that a being whose essence and value reach their full development only when it rises above itself should remain confined within itself, within its natural biological confines and plant-like rootedness? Is it not rather destined to start out from its specific station and reach beyond itself by utilising what nature has granted it? A thoughtful answer to these questions, which each person must work out and live for himself, will also, more than ever, determine the fate of our humanity and our civilisation.

Postscript, 1969

(1) The only essential addition in the reprint of this essay of 1936 is on p. 122. I deal here with Brentano's use of the expression 'intentional relation' in *The Origin of Our Knowledge of Right and Wrong* which I had overlooked when the original essay was written.

(2) In the light of new material, which had not been available to me before, concerning the role of 'intention' and 'intentionality' in the Scholastics, sections 2 and 5, in particular, need to be supplemented, although they are by no means out-dated. For additional material on the role of *intentio* in Ockham and Albert of Saxony, see I.M. Bochenski, *A History of Formal Logic* (Notre Dame University Press, 1961). pp. 155ff. On the origin of the differentiation between *prima* and *secunda intentio* see *ibid.*, p. 154. Compare, further, William and Martha Kneale, *The Development of Logic* (Oxford, 1962), pp. 195, 229ff.

(3) Husserl's last publications and the posthumous works published in the *Husserliana* edition would call for considerable expansion of sections 3 and 7. Yet I do not believe that this would lead to any essential changes in my interpretations. For a preliminary enlargement upon my account I refer the reader to the pertinent sections in my book *The Phenomenological Movement, A Historical Introduction* (The Hague, 1969), pp. 39ff, 117ff.

10   Scholastic Roots of Brentano's Conception of Intentionality[1]

Ausonio Marras

Statement of the problem

Much of the current interest among analytic philosophers in the concept of intentionality has grown out of Brentano's celebrated doctrine of 'intentional inexistence' as a distinguishing mark of psychological phenomena. Brentano, in turn, claimed to have derived this concept from the Scholastics. In an often-quoted passage of his *Psychology From an Empirical Standpoint*,[2] Brentano says:

> Every mental phenomenon is characterised by what the Scholastics of the Middle Ages called the intentional (or mental) inexistence of an object, and what we might call, though not wholly unambiguously, reference to a content, direction toward an object (which is not to be understood here as meaning a thing), or immanent objectivity. Every mental phenomenon includes something as object within itself, although they do not always do so in the same way. In presentation something is presented, in judgement something is affirmed or denied, in love [something is] loved, in hate [something] hated, in desire [something] desired, etc.

In his masterly book *The Phenomenological Movement: A Historical Introduction*,[3] Herbert Spiegelberg has claimed that in this passage Brentano actually gives two distinct characterisations of psychological phenomena: one in terms of the idea of 'intentional inexistence', the other in terms of the idea of 'reference to a content (or object)'.[4] 'Intentional inexistence',

1. This research was supported by Canada Council research grants (nos. S71-0224 and W73-0602). A shorter version of this paper was read at the International Congress 'Tommaso D'Aquino nel sua VII Centenario' in Rome on 18th April 1974.

2. English edition edited by Linda L. McAlister, trans. D.B. Terrell, Antos C. Rancurello, and Linda L. McAlister (London and New York, 1973), p. 88.
3. 2nd ed. (The Hague, 1969), two volumes. All references to this work will be to pp. 40 and 41 of the first volume.
4. Neither Brentano nor Spiegelberg distinguish, in this context, between 'content' and 'object'. The claim that in the passage just quoted Brentano gives two distinct characterisations of psychological phenomena is not exclusively

Spiegelberg explains, 'which literally implies the existence of an "intentio" inside the intending being', is indeed a scholastic (Thomistic) conception; but as such it is a conception that was really alien to Brentano's thought. 'Reference to an object', on the other hand, is a conception that was 'completely original with Brentano', and has no significant connection with the scholastic conception of intentional inexistence. For, Spiegelberg explains,

> the term 'intentio', as used in scholastic philosophy, signifies the peculiar image or likeness formed in the soul in the process of acquiring knowledge, thus representing, as it were, a kind of distillate from the world outside. . . . Thomas Aquinas distinguished actually an *intentio sensibilis,* an *intentio intelligibilis,* and at times even an *intentio intellecta.* . . . Never is there any suggestion of a reference to an object as the distinguishing characteristic of these 'intentions'.

Moreover, Spiegelberg continues, Brentano never

> mention[s] formal images of the scholastic type. It is true that wherever he uses the adjective 'intentional' he still betrays traces of the scholastic doctrine about the immanence of the object known within the soul. But it was this very doctrine of the mental inexistence of the object of knowledge in the soul which Brentano came to reject during what Brentano scholars call the crisis of immanence ('*Immanenzkrise*') of 1905.

Thus Spiegelberg concludes: 'It was certainly none of Brentano's doing that [his] new wholly unscholastic conception came to sail under the old flag of "intentionality".'

The aim of this paper is to show, contrary to Spiegelberg's contention, that there is in fact a very intimate connection between the two conceptions of psychological phenomena contained in Brentano's previously quoted passage, although no attempt shall be made here to determine the extent to which Brentano was actually aware of this connection. I shall hold, essentially, that the idea of reference to an object not only is not incompatible with the scholastic idea of intentional inexistence, but is in fact *constitutive* of that very idea. I shall also attempt to discredit an assumption which I believe underlies Spiegelberg's comments in the quotation before the last quotation, and that is that the doctrine of intentional inexistence commits scholastic thought to some form of *immanentistic* epistemology (opposed, at least in spirit, to Brentano's 'realistic' epistemology), in that it fails,

---

Spiegelberg's: in 'Brentano on Descriptive Psychology and the Intentional' (in E.N. Lee and Maurice Mandelbaum, eds. *Phenomenology and Existentialism*, Baltimore, 1967), Roderick M. Chisholm holds that Brentano presents here two distinct theses: an ontological thesis concerning 'intentional inexistence' and a psychological thesis about the reference to an object as a distinguishing characteristic of the mental. See also Chisholm's article 'Intentionality' in Paul Edwards (ed), *Encyclopedia of Philosophy* (New York, 1967).

allegedly, to give a coherent account of the independent existence of the object known.

Aquinas on intentional inexistence

That classical scholastic thought[5] is *professedly* committed to a realistic epistemology is too well known to deserve much elaboration. Suffice it to say that (1) it insists on the distinction between the knowing *subject*, the knowing *act*, and the *object* of knowledge ('Actus cognitionis est medius inter cognoscentem et cognitum')[6] and that (2) it typically regards the object known as something 'external to' (independent of) the knowing subject ('res cognita dictur esse cognitionis objectum, secundum quod extra cognoscentem in se ipsa subsistens').[7]

It may seem, however, as apparently it must have seemed to Spiegelberg, that this realistic commitment is inconsistent with the doctrine of intentional inexistence, which requires that the object known exist, somehow, *in* the knowing subject. How can the object known really be independent of the knowing subject, if in order to be known it must have a subjective (i.e., subject-dependent) mode of existence?

The problem, essentially, is to make sense of the claim that such ordinary objects of knowledge as tables and chairs are capable (and, moreover, simultaneously capable) of *two* modes of existence: existence outside the understanding (*esse naturale* or *materiale*) on the one hand, and existence in the understanding (*esse immateriale* or *formale* or *intentionale*) on the other. Can we make sense of this claim?

This question is all the more pressing as soon as we realise that according to the Aristotelian-Scholastic tradition real existence (as ascribed to ordinary 'empirical' substances) means *hylomorphic* existence. Now since an object of knowledge, such as a table, is said to exist in the subject only *morphically*, not hylomorphically, it must exist therein in a secondary, less-than-real – shadowy or disembodied – sense of existence. (Some have been inclined to call this sense of existence 'subsistence'.)

Now it seems to me that if the doctrine of intentional inexistence forced us to attribute two types of existence to ordinary empirical *substances* (that is, to independent particulars), then, I should say, so much the worse for intentional inexistence. For I should say, in good Aristotelean spirit, there is only one type of *substantial* existence (existence appropriate to ordinary empirical substances), and that is *hylomorphic* existence. Hence if a table, for example, were to exist immaterially in my understanding, it would have to exist in it merely morphically, not hylomorphically. But then it cannot be that the table itself, *as a* (somehow disembodied) *substance*, exists in my understanding, albeit formally. For no *substance* is capable of merely formal existence.

5. At least the classical period, roughly from Abelard to Duns Scotus. All textual evidence in this paper, however, is drawn from the writings of Thomas Aquinas, and my interpretation is intended to be strictly Thomistic.

6. *De Veritate*, 1, 9.

7. *De Veritate*, 14, 8, 5.

How, then, are we to explain the 'inexistence' of the object in the subject without invoking the principle that objects, *qua* substances, are capable of two distinct forms of existence? The scholastic answer, I believe, is as follows:

To say that an object *exists formally* (immaterially, intentionally, etc.) in the subject is merely to say that the *form* of the object exists in the subject ('Lapis autem non est in anima, sed forma lapidis').[8] As soon as we recast the original claim in this way, it becomes clear that the sense of existence postulated by the doctrine of intentional inexistence is to be assimilated not to the sense of existence in 'The Parthenon exists', nor even to the shadowy sense of existence or subsistence in 'Pegasus subsists (in some possible world)', but rather to the sense of existence in 'Redness exists in the rose'. In other words, a careful reading of scholastic texts reveals that the 'formal existence' of an object in a subject is to be understood by reference to the *attributive* or *predicational* sense of existence according to which we say that a form or attribute exists in, or is *exemplified* by, an object – the object in this case being the knowing subject himself. As the Scholastics put it, the form of the object exists in the subject as an attribute or *modification* of the subject (*sicut accidens in subiecto*).[9]

It is therefore not the case that the doctrine of intentional inexistence commits us to distinguishing two senses of existence as applicable to *substances*: it simply commits us to the well-known distinction between substantial existence and predicational existence – the existence of things and the existence of attributes *in* things. I believe that failure to realise that intentional inexistence is a form of predicational, not of substantial, existence, has been a major cause of misunderstanding of scholastic epistemology.[10] Once this misunderstanding is cleared up, the charge of immanentism can also be defused. For the inexistence of the object known amounts to the exemplification of the object's form by the subject. And, as any student of scholastic philosophy well knows, the form thus exemplified – the *species* – is not *that which* is (directly) known, but that *by means of which* the extramental object is known. (More on this later.)

However, the sense in which the form of an object can be *in* the knowing subject requires further elucidation, for it is not yet clear how the following two questions are to be answered: (1) If the form which is, e.g. in a stone (and thus which *makes* something a stone) is also *in* a knowing subject, wouldn't we have to say that the knowing subject, by virtue of *having* (exemplifying) that form, is *himself* also a stone?[11] (2) How is it that the mere

8. *III De Anima*, 13, 789; cf. *Summa Theologiae*, I, 85, 2.

9. *Quaestiones Quodlibetales*, VII, 4c.

10. Guilty of such a misunderstanding is, I suspect, R.M. Chisholm, who classifies such nonexistent but thought-of *particulars* as unicorns among the intentional objects, and who attributes to the Scholastics the belief that such objects 'have a mode of being . . . which is short of actuality but more than nothingness'; see the works cited in note 4 above. He appears to forget that intentional objects, *qua entia rationis*, have the kind of being which is appropriate to attributes, not to particulars (whether exitent or nonexistent, or whether thought-of or not).

11. This question brings us face to face with a metaphysical presupposition of Aristotelean-Scholastic epistemology, according to which it is of the nature of the

inexistence of a form in the subject (unlike, for example, the inexistence of a form in an *object*) can bring about the intentional *reference* to an object which, as Brentano correctly insisted, is a distinguishing characteristic of awareness? How, in other words, is the Brentanian idea of reference *constitutive*, as we claimed against Speigelberg, of the scholastic doctrine of intentional inexistence? It is in the context of this latter question, primarily, that I shall discuss my point of disagreement with Spiegelberg.

(1) There appear to be two ways in which the first question might be answered. The first is to suppose that the form which 'is in' the knowing subject is *analogous* to, but not identical with, the form which 'is in' the object known. That is, the attribute (or set of attributes) which characterises an object in a determinate way, e.g. as a stone, and the attribute (or set of attributes) which characterises the subject (understanding) in a determinate way, e.g. as being in the state whereby it has knowledge of the stone, are not identical but merely analogous, or structurally similar, attributes. The sense of analogy involved here, though difficult to specify precisely, is like the sense of the analogy between the blueness which characterises a blue object and the blueness which characterises the *sensation* of a blue object. Clearly the sensation is not literally blue in the same sense in which the object is blue; but it must be so in some analogous sense, for the sensation must have some structural property by virtue of which it can be a sensation of *blue* and not, say, of *red*. In other words there must be an *isomorphism* between the properties which properly characterise sensations and the properties which characterise their proper objects. Similarly, there must be an *isomorphism* between the form which characterises, say, a stone, and the form which characterises a knowing subject, by virtue of which the subject can be said to have knowledge of the stone without *being* a stone.

Alternatively, we may suppose that while the *form* which 'is in' the object known and the form which 'is in' the knowing subject are indeed identical, the sense of *being in* involved in each case is not identical but merely analogous. In other words, we ought to distinguish two kinds of 'being in', 'being in$_1$' and 'being in$_2$', although both fall under the same category of the 'being in' of exemplification. For, clearly, the property of being a stone is not exemplified by the knowing subject in the same sense in which the *same* property is exemplified by a stone; otherwise the subject would *be* a stone. However, there is a sense in which the subject must be in a 'stone-like' state, if it is to be in a state appropriate to the knowledge of a stone and not, say, of a tree.

This latter answer to the foregoing question strikes me as somewhat less plausible than the former (I can only discern *one* sense of exemplification, as

---

knower to 'take on' the form of the thing known – an ability which is said to distinguish those beings which are capable of knowledge from those which are not (cf. *Summa Theologiae*, I, 14, 1). By 'taking on' the form of the external object, the subject becomes *somehow* (i.e. formally or intentionally) *identified* with it. This, essentially, is what is encapsuled in the Aristotelean dictum in *De Anima*, that the soul is somehow everything, for its nature is to (be able to) know everything.

I can only discern one sense of (substantial) existence), although it is the one, I think, that was favoured by the scholastics.[12] It is not necessary, however, to decide here which of the two answers is the correct one; suffice it to say that either the one or the other, once details are filled in, can reasonably be taken to constitute a plausible answer to our question.

(2) In order to answer the second question it is necessary to articulate further the scholastic conception of form.

Thomas Aquinas distinguishes three aspects of form. Considering, by way of illustration, the form of a stone, he distinguishes: (a) the form of the stone as it 'exists in' the material stone (*forma lapidis in materia*); (b) the form of the stone as it 'exists in' the soul (*forma lapidis in anima*) as a mere modification of it; and (c) the form of the stone in the soul inasmuch as it *represents* the form existing in the material stone (*forma lapidis in anima inquantum repraesentat formam lapidis in materia*).[13]

'Form' without qualification normally applies to the form as it exists in the object. As such, according to Aquinas, it is a universal only in potency. It becomes an actual universal (and thus, for Aquinas, a principle of knowledge) only inasmuch as it is abstracted by the intellect from the individuating conditions of the object. As thus abstracted, the form 'resides' in the intellect and is then properly called *'species'* or *'intentio'*. But even as residing in the intellect, we must distinguish in the form or species its *esse naturale* from its *esse repraesentativum*. In the first sense the species is not an actual universal, a principle of knowledge, for it is as such only an accidental modification of a particular subject (it simply 'in-forms' the external object). It is only in the second sense, as a likeness (*similitudo*) or *representation* of the object that the form or species acquires the logical status of an actual universal and thus plays a role in cognition:

> ... non per modum quo similitudo rei habet esse in cognoscente, res cognoscitur, sed per modum quo similitudo in intellectu existens est *repraesentativa* rei.[14]

What is the sense of 'likeness' or 'representation' pertaining to the species? Aquinas is careful to contrast likeness as an 'agreement in nature' (*convenientia in ipsa natura*), such as might obtain between the fire and a hot object,[15] with likeness in the order of representation, which pertains to the species *qua* universal and which is thus relevant to cognition:

> Similitudo aliquorum duorum ad invicem potest dupliciter attendi. Uno modo secundum convenientiam in ipsa natura ... Alio modo

---

12. Compare *Summa Theologiae*, I, 84, 1.

13. See *De Veritate*, 8, 11, 3.

14. *De Veritate*, 2, 5 17. ('... a thing is known not according to the manner in which the likeness of the thing exists in the knower, but rather according to the manner in which the likeness existing in the intellect is representative of the thing.' All translations from the Latin are the author's.)

15. *Summa Contra Gentiles*, II, 46.

quantum ad repraesentationem; et haec similitudo requiritur cognoscentis ad cognitum.[16]

The likeness of representation, then, requires no natural resemblance between the species and the thing represented. Thus the species is not to be thought of as a picture, *Bild* or image reminiscent of the Lockean ideas or of the sense-data of modern representationalist theories of knowledge. Instead, the likeness of representation simply requires that the species have a certain *relation* to the thing represented:

> . . . hoc modo aliquid cognoscitur *secundum quod est in cognoscente repraesentatum*, et non secundum quod est in cognoscente existens; similitudo enim in vi cognoscitiva existens non est principium cognitionis rei secundum esse quod habet in potentia cognoscitiva, sed *secundum relationem quam habet ad rem cognitam* . . .[17]

Indeed, the representational likeness of the species is explicitly said to *be* a relation: 'Similitudo est relatio quaedum.'[18] And the relation in question, as indicated in the passage just quoted, is a *directed* relation: the representing species *bears a relation to (habet relationem ad)* the thing represented. (As a result of this role played by the species, *all* understanding as such is said to bear a relation to objects: 'Ipsum intelligere habet relationem ad rem quae intelligitur.')[19]

The relation that the species or *intentio* is said to have to objects is always expressed in terms which highlight the directional character of the relation. Thus Aquinas says that the species 'habet respectum *ad* rem',[20] 'determinat cognitionem *ad* aliquod',[21] 'importat ordinem quemdam unius *ad* alterum'.[22]

This fact, together with the previous point that the likeness of the species is not to be confused with natural resemblance, makes it plausible to suppose that the *esse repraesentativum* of the species involves essentially what Brentano called the *referentiality* or *directedness* of mental phenomena. Indeed, in the following quotation Aquinas speaks of the referential character of the species in quite unambiguous terms. Discussing the form human nature as an abstracted universal (i.e. a species in its representative being), he points out:

16. *De Veritate*, 2, 3, 9; also 8, 1. ('The likeness between two things may be considered in two ways. First inasmuch as they agree in a common nature. . . . Second, from the point of view of representation; and such a likeness of the knower to the object known is necessary.')

17. *De Veritate*, 2, 5, 17. '. . . thus a thing is known by virtue of its being represented in the knower, not by virtue of its existing in him; for the likeness existing in a knowing power is a principle of knowledge not by virtue of the being it has in the knowing power, but by virtue of the relation it has to the thing known.')

18. *Summa Contra Gentiles*, II, 11.

19. *Summa Contra Gentiles*, I, 53.

20. *De Veritate*, 10, 4.

21. *De Veritate*, 10, 4.

22. *In II Sententiarum*, 38, 1, 3.

Non est *universalitas* illius formae secundum hoc esse quod habet in intellectu, sed *secundum quod refertur ad res* ut similitudo rerum.[23]

Moreover, as soon as we recall that *qua* universal the species or *intentio* is also called *'verbum mentis'* (or *'verbum interius'*),[24] and that words (at least the categorematic ones) may be said to represent things in the sense that they *signify, stand for,* or *refer to,* things, it does not seem altogether implausible to suppose that the *esse repraesentativum* of the species belongs to a logical order *analogous* to what we would now call the *semantical* or *intentional* order of signification, reference or aboutness. Indeed, if the traditional analogy between *speech* and *thought* is to be taken seriously, it must be founded upon such a supposition.[25]

However this may be, it seems clear that according to the Scholastics the species as a representation of the object involves a *reference* to the object. And this is as it should be: for it is clearly of the nature of representation, even from a purely phenomenological point of view, that through it reference is made to an object. To represent is always to represent *something* (whether existent or not): literally, a representation is a representing *of* an object *to* a subject.

It is this intentional or referential aspect of the species *qua* representation that Spiegelberg seems to have utterly overlooked in his comments about the doctrine of intentional inexistence. To be sure he is correct in saying that this doctrine 'implies the existence of an *"intentio"* inside the intending being'; but he fails to realise that the nature of an *intentio* is precisely to *tend to,* be *directed towards,* an object. As Aquinas explains, 'Intentio, sicut ipsum nomen sonat, significat *in aliud tendere*';[26] and again: 'Intentio in ratione sua *ordinem quemdam unius ad alterum* importat.'[27] Thus Speigelberg's claim that 'never is there any suggestion of a reference to an object as the distinguishing characteristic of these "intentions"' seems altogether indefensible.

Concerned as he is with stressing the idea of *immanence* in the Scholastic doctrine of intentional inexistence, Spiegelberg obscures the point that the scholastics were talking not about mere *inexistence,* but about *intentional* inexistence.[28] The species or *intentio* does indeed inhere in the subject, but in

23. *De Ente et Essentia,* 3, 6–7. ('The universality of that form does not derive from the existence it has in the intellect, but from its referring to things whose likeness it is.')

24. *De Veritate,* 4, 1, c.

25. It is not implausible to assimilate the Scholastic *species* to Husserl's *noemata* and, by analogical extension, to the Fregean *Sinne.* In each case, a mental or linguistic act's (intentional) reference to an object is determined by (is a function of) the act's species, or noema, or *Sinn.* For an insightful account of the analogy between Husserl's *noemata* and Frege's *Sinne,* and of their analogous roles in determining an act's reference, see Dagfin Føllesdal, 'Husserl's Notion of Noema', *Journal of Philosophy* 66 (1969), 680–7; and D.W. Smith and R. McIntyre, 'Intentionality via Intensions', *Journal of Philosophy* 68 (1971), 541–61.

26. *Summa Theologiae,* I–II, 12, 1c.

27. *In II Sententiarum,* 38, 1, 3.

28. Spiegelberg says that phrases like 'intentional inexistence' and 'intentional relation' 'have no standing among the genuine scholastics'. This is certainly

playing the epistemic role of representing the object it does not merely inhere, it has no mere inexistence: it has *intentional* inexistence, for it intends, or bears a reference to, the object represented. In the following passage Aquinas stresses precisely this point by distinguishing, concerning the act of knowledge, between the '*quod insit*' (the 'being in', the inexistence) and the '*quod ad aliud sit*' (the 'being directed towards the other thing', that is, the intentional reference to the object):

> Notitia . . . dupliciter potest considerari: vel secundum quod comparatur ad cognoscentem, et sic inest cognoscenti sicut accidens in subjecto . . . : vel secundum quod comparatur ad cognoscibile, et ex hac part non habere *quod insit* sed *quod ad aliud sit*.[29]

Enough has been said, I believe, to discredit Spiegelberg's contention that the idea of *referentiality*, as applied to mental phenomena, is a 'wholly unscholastic notion' and that it is 'completely original with Brentano'. Spiegelberg's claim that 'never is there any suggestion of a reference to an object', as the distinguishing characteristic of *intentio* or species seems to contradict the ample textual evidence presented in the foregoing paragraphs. We have seen, instead, that the nature of the species or *intentio* is to be *representational* of an object, and therefore – so at least thought Aquinas – to bear a *reference* to an object. For as we have seen it is clearly of the nature of representation that through it reference is made to an object.

The idea that representation is essentially referential was also evidently clear to Brentano: in the celebrated passage already quoted, he clearly says that 'in [re]-presentation *something* is [re]presented'.[30] And lest it be thought that the referentiality or intentionality of representation is a property which representation has *qua* mental phenomenon (as intentionally defined) and not *qua* representation, we may be reminded that for Brentano representations are not merely *instances* of mental phenomena, nor are the two merely *contingently* equated. Instead, Brentano claimed, 'the following *definition* of mental phenomena is indubitably correct: they are either [re]presentations or they are based upon [re]presentations . . .'[31] In other

mistaken. The phrase 'intentional [in]existence' (*esse intentionale*) occurs in several places in Aquinas: e.g. in *II De Anima*, 24, 553, in *De Sensu*, 5, 62 and 19, 291 – although, admittedly, such synonymous phrases as '*esse intelligibile*', '*esse immateriale*', '*esse repraesentativum*' and '*esse formale*' occur more frequently. As for the phrase 'intentional relation', the phrases '*relationem ad*', '*respectum ad*', as well as such phrases as '*esse ad*' and '*quod ad aliud est*' (cf. *Quaestiones Quodlibetales*, VII, 4c), as contrasted to the phrases '*inesse*' and '*quod inest*', were commonly used to characterise the relational character of the *intentio*.

29. *Quaestiones Quodlibetales*, VII, 4c. ('An item of knowledge . . . may be considered under two aspects: either in relation to the knower, and in this way it exists in the knower as an accident in a subject . . . or in relation to the thing to be known, and what it thus has is not inexistence but reference to a thing.')

30. In the English edition of Brentano's *Psychology* 'Vorstellung' is translated as 'presentation'. A more common translation, however, is '*re*presentation'. It is so translated, for example, by Spiegelberg himself (*op. cit.*, p. 39). The difference in translation, however, is merely of stylistic interest, for, as we have pointed out, a representation is here understood, literally, as a *re*-presentation.

words, according to Brentano, all mental activity, that is, *awareness* in the most general sense, comes to the same thing as representation: awareness simply amounts to the state of *being present* of an *object* to *a* subject. As he explains in his acute phenomenological analysis of representation,

> even the 'being present' is 'being [re]presented' in our sense. And such things occur whenever something appears in consciousness, whether it is hated, loved, or regarded indifferently, whether it is affirmed or denied or there is a complete withholding of judgement and – I cannot express myself in any other way than to say – it is [re]presented. As we use the verb 'to [re]present', 'to be [re]presented' means the same as 'to appear'.[32]

The charge of immanentism

Spiegelberg also seems to intimate that any admission of immanent existence of the known object within the knowing subject tends to preclude all reference to extramental (nonimmanent) objects, with the apparent results that the scholastic doctrine of intentional inexistence tends to commit one to some form of immanentism or subjectivism. This, at least, seems to be the point of his reference to the scholastic 'doctrine about the immanence of the object known within the soul' as the 'very doctrine . . . which Brentano came to reject during what Brentano scholars call the crisis of immanence ('Immanenzkrise') of 1905' (see p. x above). As is well known, Brentano's so-called 'crisis of immanence' marked a transition in Brentano's thought from a position which some critics, rightly or wrongly, have characterized as at least in part subjectivistic or immanentistic,[33] in so far as it admitted the existence of certain ideal (mind-dependent) entities as (possibly the only) objects of reference for the mind, to a position of thoroughgoing 'reism' (as Spiegelberg, following Kotarbinski, characterizes this position), according to which the only objects of reference can be real existents (i.e. physical or psychical phenomena). Thus Spiegelberg's remark seems to intimate that the admission of such immanent entities as the scholastic species or 'intentions' is somehow an impediment to a purified realistic epistemology admitting of reference to real, nonimmanent objects.

But this again betrays a misunderstanding of the scholastic doctrine of intentional inexistence. As we have seen, the immanent existence of the object known within the subject simply amounts to the existence (recall: in the predicational, not in the substantial, sense of the word) of a form or species as *representative* of the object; and this certainly need not be regarded as an impediment to a realistic epistemology. For, as we have already

31. *Psychology*, p. 85.
32. *Psychology*, p. 81.
33. See specially Lucie Gilson, *La Psychologie descriptive selon Franz Brentano* (Paris, 1955); E. Levinas, *En decouvrant l'existence avec Husserl et Heidegger* (Paris, 1949); and R. Danzer, *Das Allgemeine und das Besondere. Zur Ontologie Franz Brentanos* (Gelsenkirchen, 1965).

pointed out (p.X), the species or *intentio* is not *that which (id quod)* is directly or primarily known by the understanding (as is the 'impression' or idea' of classical empiricism), but is instead *that by means of which (id quo)* the extramental object is known. That is, the species is the *vehicle* which carries the reference to the extramental, nonimmanent object, which alone is known primarily. The following quotation from *Summa Theologiae* suffices to make this point firm and unambiguous: 'Species intelligibilis non est quod intelligitur, sed id quo intelligit intellectus.'[34]

To be sure Aquinas does not deny that, exceptionally, the species can itself be the object of knowledge; his point is simply that it can be so only in a secondary, reflexive sense:

> Quia intellectus supra seipsum reflectitur, secundum eandem reflexionem intelligit et suum intelligere.et speciem qua intelligit. Et sic species intellectiva secundario est id quod intelligitur. Sed id quod intelligitur primo est res cuis species intelligibilis est similtudo.[35]

Indeed, the very act of self-knowledge, for Aquinas, implies or presupposes an act of knowledge of an extramental object:

> Unde mens nostra non potest seipsam intelligere ita quod seipsam immediate apprehendat; sed ex hoc quod apprehendit alia, devenit in suam cognitionem.[36]

It should be clear from the foregoing that it would be a blunder to confuse the species with Lockean 'ideas' and their respective modes of representation. For in the first place the species is not an individual entity at all (an object of perception), but a state or *attribute* of a perceiver. In the second place the species is not something which can be perceived directly and independently of the object, and by perceiving which the object is (indirectly) perceived; for, as we have just seen, an extramental object must first be perceived if the species is to be perceived at all. And in the third place, the likeness between the species and the object is not a likeness in the natural order, as might be the likeness between a picture and the thing pictured, but a likeness in the order of signification. In this respect the species is more appropriately to be compared with a *word* – and in fact the scholastics did conceive the species as somehow a *mental* word (*verbum mentis*). And certainly words are not pictures, nor are they normally the object of reference of our speech, but that which *carries* our reference to objects.

34. *Summa Theologiae*, I, 85, 2.
35. *Summa Theologiae*, I, 85, 2. ('Since the intellect reflects upon itself, by this very reflection it understands both its own (act of) understanding and the species by which it understands. And thus the intelligible species is in a secondary sense that which is understood. But that which is understood in a primary sense is the thing of which the intelligible species is a likeness.')
36. *De Veritate*, 10, 8. ('Thereby our mind cannot understand itself in such a way as to apprehend itself immediately. Instead, it is by virtue of apprehending other things that it arrives at a knowledge of itself.')

Consequently, contrary to what Spiegelberg appears to suggest, there seems to be no good reason to believe that the scholastic doctrine of intentional inexistence, despite its admission of such 'immanent entities' as species or intentions, is an obstacle to a realistic epistemology. Nor, as far as I can tell, is there any good evidence to suppose that Brentano thought so.

Postscript

This paper was written before I was able to see Spiegelberg's essay whose translation is included in this volume. Save for a certain difference in emphasis in his account of the 'immanence' aspect of Brentano's conception of the intentional, which in the earlier essay is given somewhat greater prominence than in the section of *The Phenomenological Movement* to which my paper is addressed, Spiegelberg's main thesis is basically the same in the two works: the notion of *intentional inexistence* (immanent objectivity) is, both historically and conceptually, sharply distinct from the notion of *reference to an object*. (Interestingly, Spiegelberg is willing to grant in his essay, but not in his later work, that Brentano may have regarded these two notions as equivalent.) In particular, Spiegelberg's essay underscores two claims which in my paper I take to constitute a basic misunderstanding of the Scholastics' (Aquinas') notion of *intentio* (*species*): (1) that the *intentio* is a 'self-contained, independent entity', and (2) that in the account of *intentio* the 'element of directedness is not elaborated at all'. Against the first point I have argued that the *intentio*, being an *ens rationis*, a universal and thus an *attribute*, has, unlike *particulars*, a dependent mode of existence (and is thus unsuited to be a 'discrete image' playing a role in a 'copy theory of knowledge'). Against the second point I have provided ample textual evidence to show that the element of directedness is an essential characteristic of the *intentio*.

11 'Intentional Inexistence'[1]

Roderick M. Chisholm

1

I have suggested that the locution 'There is something that S *perceives* to be *f*' may be defined as meaning: 'There is something such that it is *f*, it appears to S in some way, S takes it to be *f*, and S had adequate evidence for so doing.' And I have suggested that 'S *takes* something to be *f*' may be defined by reference to what S assumes, or accepts. I have now said all that I can about the philosophic questions which the concepts of *adequate evidence* and of *appearing* involve. Let us finally turn, then, to the concept of *assuming*, or *accepting*. The principal philosophic questions which this concept involves may be formulated by reference to a thesis proposed by Franz Brentano.

Psychological phenomena, according to Brentano, are characterised 'by what the scholastics of the middle ages referred to as the intentional (also the mental) inexistence of the object, and what we, although with not quite unambiguous expressions, would call relation to a content, direction upon an object, (which is not here to be understand as a reality), or immanent objectivity.'[2] This 'intentional inexistence', Brentano added, is peculiar to what is psychical; things which are merely physical show nothing like it.

Assuming, or *accepting*, is one of the phenomena Brentano would have called intentional. I will first try to formulate Brentano's thesis somewhat more exactly; then I will ask whether it is true of assuming.

2

The phenomena most clearly illustrating the concept of 'intentional inexistence' are what are sometimes called psychological attitudes; for example, desiring, hoping, wishing, seeking, believing, and assuming. When Brentano said that these attitudes 'intentionally contain an object in themselves', he was referring to the fact that they can be truly said to 'have objects' even though the objects which they can be said to have do not in fact exist. Diogenes could have looked for an honest man even if there hadn't been any honest men. The horse can desire to be fed even though he won't be fed. James could believe there are tigers in India, and *take* something there to be a tiger, even if there aren't any tigers in India.

1. Chapter 11 of Chisholm's book *Perceiving: A Philosophical Study* (Ithaca, N.Y. 1957), pp. 168–85.

2. Franz Brentano, *Psychologie vom empirischen Standpunkte*, (Leipzig, 1924), vol. 1, pp. 124–5. *Psychology from an Empirical Standpoint* (New York and London, 1973), p. 88.

But *physical*—or non-psychological—phenomena, according to Brentano's thesis, cannot thus 'intentionally contain objects in themselves'. In order for Diogenes to sit in his tub, for example, there must be a tub for him to sit in; in order for the horse to eat his oats, there must be oats for him to eat; and in order for James to shoot a tiger, there must be a tiger there to shoot.

The statements used in these examples seem to have the form of relational statements. 'Diogenes sits in his tub' is concerned with a relation between Diogenes and his tub. Syntactically, at least, 'Diogenes looks for an honest man' is similar: Diogenes' quest seems to relate him in a certain way to honest men. But the relations described in this and in our other psychological statements, if they can properly be called 'relations', are of a peculiar sort. They can hold even though one of their terms, if it can properly be called a 'term', does not exist. It may seem, therefore, that one can be 'intentionally related' to something which does not exist.[3]

These points can be put somewhat more precisely by referring to the language we have used. We may say that, in our language, the expressions 'looks for', 'expects', and 'believes' occur in sentences which are intentional, or are used intentionally, whereas 'sits in', 'eats', and 'shoots' do not. We can formulate a working criterion by means of which we can distinguish sentences that are intentional, or are used intentionally, in a certain language from sentences that are not. It is easy to see, I think, what this criterion would be like, if stated for ordinary English.

First, let us say that a simple declarative sentence is intentional if it uses a substantival expression—a name or a description—in such a way that neither the sentence nor its contradictory implies either that there is or that there isn't anything to which the substantival expression truly applies. 'Diogenes looked for an honest man' is intentional by this criterion. Neither 'Diogenes looked for an honest man' nor its contradictory – 'Diogenes did *not* look for an honest man' – implies either that there are, or that there are not, any honest men. But 'Diogenes sits in his tub' is not intentional by this criterion, for it implies that there *is* a tub in which he sits.

Secondly, let us say, of any non-compound sentence which contains a propositional clause, that it is intentional provided that neither the sentence nor its contradictory implies either that the propositional clause is true or that it is false. 'James believes there are tigers in India' is intentional by this criterion, because neither it nor its contradictory implies either that there are, or that there are not, any tigers in India. 'He succeeded in visiting India', since it implies that he did visit India, is not intentional. 'He is able to visit India', although it does not imply that he will visit India, is also not intentional. For its contradictory – 'he is not able to visit India' – implies that he does *not* visit India.

A third mark of intentionality may be described in this way. Suppose there are two names or descriptions which designate the same things and

---

3. But the point of talking about 'intentionality' is not that there is a peculiar type of 'inexistent' object; it is rather that there is a type of psychological phenomenon which is unlike anything purely physical. In his later writings Brentano explicitly rejected the view that there are 'inexistent objects'; see his *Psychology*, pp. 271ff, and *The True and the Evident* (New York and London, 1966), pp. 77–9.

that E is a sentence obtained merely by separating these two names or descriptions by means of 'is identical with' (or 'are identical with' if the first word is plural). Suppose also that A is a sentence using one of those names or descriptions and that B is like A except that, where A uses the one, B uses the other. Let us say that A is intentional if the conjunction of A and E does not imply B.[4] We can now say of certain cognitive sentences – sentences using 'know', 'see', 'perceive', and the like in one of the ways which have interested us here – that they, too, are intentional. Most of us knew in 1944 that Eisenhower was the one in command (A); but although he was (identical with) the man who was to succeed Truman (E), it is not true that we knew in 1944 that the man who was to succeed Truman was the one in command (B).

Let us say that a *compound* sentence is one compounded from two or more sentences by means of propositional connectives, such as 'and', 'or', 'if-then', 'although', 'because', and the like. The three foregoing marks of intentionality apply to sentences which are *not* compound. We may now say that a compound declarative sentence is intentional if and only if one or more of its component sentences is intentional. Thus the antecedent of 'If Parsifal sought the Holy Grail, he was a Christian' enables us to say that the whole statement is intentional.

When we use perception words propositionally, our sentences display the third of the above marks of intentionality. I may see that John is the man in the corner and John may be someone who is ill; but I do not now *see* that John is someone who is ill. Perception sentences, as we have seen, entail sentences about taking and assuming. And sentences about taking and assuming display the second of the above marks of intentionality. 'He takes – and therefore assumes – those rocks to be the reef' does not imply that the rocks *are* the reef and it does not imply that they are not. And similarly for its contradiction: 'He does not take – or assume – those rocks to be the reef.'

We may now re-express Brentano's thesis – or a thesis resembling that of Brentano – by reference to intentional sentences. Let us say (1) that we do not need to use intentional sentences when we describe non-psychological phenomena; we can express all of our beliefs about what is merely 'physical' in sentences which are not intentional.[5] But (2) when we wish to describe perceiving, assuming, believing, knowing, wanting, hoping, and other such attitudes, then either (a) we must use sentences which are

4. This third mark is essentially the same as Frege's concept of 'indirect reference'. See Gottlob Frege, 'Über Sinn und Bedeutung', *Zeitschrift für Philosophie und philosophische Kritik*, n.s. C (1892), pp. 25–50, especially p 38; reprinted in Herbert Feigl and W.S. Sellars (eds), *Readings in Philosophical Analysis* (New York, 1949), and Peter Geach and Max Black (eds), *Philosophical Writings of Gottlob Frege* (Oxford, 1952).

5. There are sentences describing relations of comparison – for example, 'Some lizards look like dragons – which may constitute an exception to (1). If they are exceptions, then we may qualify (1) to read: 'We do not need any intentional sentences, other than those describing relations of comparison, when we describe nonpsychical phenomena.' This qualification would not affect any of the points to be made here.

intentional or (b) we must use terms we do not need to use when we describe non-psychological phenomena.

In describing non-psychological phenomena, we do, on occasion, use sentences which are intentional by one or more of the above criteria. One may say, 'This weapon, suitably placed, is capable of causing the destruction of Boston' and 'The cash register knows that 7 and 5 are 12.' But although these sentences are intentional according to our criteria, we can readily transform them into others which are not: 'If this weapon were suitably placed, then Boston would be destroyed' and 'If you press the key marked "7" and the one marked "5", the cash register will yield a slip marked "12".'

It would be an easy matter, of course, to invent a psychological terminology enabling us to describe perceiving, taking, and assuming in sentences which are not intentional. Instead of saying, for example, that a man *takes* something to be a deer, we could say 'His perceptual environment is deer-inclusive.' But in so doing, we are using technical terms – 'perceptual environment' and 'deer-inclusive' – which, presumably, are not needed for the description of non-psychological phenomena. And unless we can re-express the deer-sentence once again, this time as a non-intentional sentence containing no such technical terms, what we say about the man and the deer will conform to our present version of Brentano's thesis.

How would we go about showing that Brentano was wrong? I shall consider the three most likely methods. None of them seems to be satisfactory.

3

Some philosophers have tried to describe psychological attitudes in terms of *linguistic* behaviour. In his inaugural lecture, *Thinking and Meaning*, Professor Ayer tried to define the locution 'thinking of x' by reference to the use of symbols which designate x. A man is *thinking of* a unicorn, Ayer suggested, if (among other things) the man is disposed to use symbols which *designate* unicorns; he *believes* that there are unicorns if (among other things) he is disposed to utter sentences containing words which *designate* or *refer to* unicorns. And perhaps one might try to define 'taking' and 'assuming' in a similar way. But this type of definition leaves us with our problem.[6]

When we talk about what is 'designated' or 'referred to' by words or sentences, our own sentences are intentional. When we affirm the sentence 'In German, *Einhorn* designates, or refers to, unicorns', we do not imply that there are any unicorns and we do not imply that there are not; and similarly when we deny the sentence. If we think of words and sentences as classes of

6. A.J. Ayer, *Thinking and Meaning*, p. 13. Compare W.S. Sellars, 'Mind, Meaning, and Behaviour', *Philosophical Studies*, vol. 3 (1952) pp. 83–95; 'A Semantic Solution of the Mind-Body Problem', *Methodos* (1953), pp. 45–85; and 'Empiricism and the Philosophy of Mind', Herbert Feigl and Michael Scriven (eds), *The Foundations of Science and the Concepts of Psychology and Pschoanalysis* (Minneapolis, 1956). See also Leonard Bloomfield, *Linguistic Aspects of Science* (Chicago, 1939), pp. 17–19.

noises and marks, then we may say that words and sentences are 'physical' (non-psychological) phenomena. But we must not suppose the meaning of words and sentences to be a property which they have apart from their relations to the psychological attitudes of the people who *use* them.

For we know, as Schlick once put it, 'that meaning does not inhere in a sentence where it might be discovered'; meaning 'must be bestowed upon' the sentence.[7] Instead of saying. 'In German, *Einhorn* designates, or refers to, unicorns', we could say, less misleadingly, 'German-speaking people use the word *Einhorn* in order to designate, or refer to, unicorns.' A word or sentence designates so-and-so only if people *use* it to designate so-and-so.

Or can we describe 'linguistic behaviour' by means of sentences which are not intentional? Can we define such locutions as 'the word "Q" designates so-and-so, in language which is not intentional? If we can do these things, and if, as Ayer suggested, we can define 'believing', or 'assuming', in terms of linguistic behaviour, then we must reject our version of Brentano's thesis. But I do not believe that we can do these things; I do not believe that we can define such locutions as 'The word "Q" designates so-and-so' or 'The word "Q" has such-and-such a *use*" in language which is not intentional.

Let us consider, briefly, the difficulties involved in one attempt to formulate such a definition.

Instead of saying, of a certain word or predicate "Q", that it designates or refers to so-and-so's, we may say that, if there were any so-and-so's, they would satisfy or fulfil the *intension* of the predicate "Q". But how are we to define 'intension'? Professor Carnap once proposed a behaviouristic definition of this use of 'intension' which, if it were adequate, might enable us to formulate a behaviouristic, non-intentional definition of 'believe' and 'assume'. Although Carnap later conceded that his account was over-simplified, it is instructive, I think, to note the difficulties which stand in the way of defining 'intension' – as well as 'designates' and 'refers to' – in non-intentional terms.[8]

Carnap had suggested that the 'intension' of a predicate in a natural language may be defined in essentially this way: 'The intension of a predicate "Q" for a speaker X is the general condition which an object y must fulfil in order for X to be willing to ascribe the predicate "Q" to y.' Carnap did not define the term 'ascribe' which appears in this definition,

7. Moritz Schlick, 'Meaning and Verification', *Philosophical Review,*, vol. 45 (1936), p. 348; reprinted in Feigl and Sellars (eds), *Readings in Philosophical Analysis*. Compare this analogy, in 'Meaning and Free Will', by John Hospers: 'Sentences in themselves do not possess meaning; it is misleading to speak of "the meaning of sentences" at all; meaning being conferred in every case by the speaker, the sentence's meaning is only like the light of the moon: without the sun to give it light, it would possess none. And for an analysis of the light we must go to the sun' (*Philosophy and Phenomenological Research*, vol. 10 [1950], p. 308).

8. Carnap's definition appeared on p. 42 of 'Meaning and Synonymy in Natural Languages', *Philosophical Studies*, vol. 4 (1955), pp. 33–47. In 'On Some Concepts of Pragmatics', *Ibid.*, vol. 6, pp. 89–91, he conceded that 'designates' should be defined in terms of 'believes'. The second article was written in reply to my 'A Note on Carnap's Meaning Analysis', which appeared in the same issue (pp. 87–9).

but from his general discussion we can see, I think, that he would have said something very much like this: 'A person X ascribes "Q" to an object y, provided that, in the presence of y, X gives an affirmative response to the question "Q?".' (Let us assume that the expressions 'is willing to', 'in the presence of', 'affirmative response', and 'question' present no difficulties.)

Such a definition of 'intension' is adequate only if it allows us to say of Karl, who speaks German, that an object y fulfils the intension of '*Hund*' for Karl if and only if y is a dog. Let us consider, then, a situation in which Karl mistakes something for a dog; he is in the presence of a fox, say, and takes it to be a dog. In this case, Karl would be willing to give an affirmative response to the question '*Hund?*' Hence the fox fulfils the condition which an object must fulfil for Karl to be willing to ascribe '*Hund*' to it. And therefore the definition is inadequate.

Perhaps we can assume that Karl is usually right when he takes something to be a dog. And perhaps, therefore, we can say this: 'The intension of "*Hund*" for Karl is the general condition which, more often than not, an object y must fulfil in order for Karl to be willing to ascribe "*Hund*" to y.' But if the occasion we have considered is the only one on which Karl has been in the presence of a fox, then, according to the present suggestion, we must say, falsely, that the fox does not fulfil the intension of Karl's word '*Fuchs*'. Moreover, if Karl believes there are unicorns and, on the sole occasion when he thinks he sees one, mistakes a horse for a unicorn, then the present suggestion would require us to say, falsely, that the horse fulfils the intension, for Karl, of his word '*Einhorn*'.

The obvious way to qualify Carnap's definition would be to re-introduce the term 'believe' and say something of this sort: 'The intension of a predicate "Q" for a speaker X is the general condition which X must *believe* an object y to fulfil in order for X to be willing to ascribe the predicate "Q" to y.' And, in general, when we say, 'People use such and such a word to refer to so-and-so', at least part of what we mean to say is that people use that word when they wish to express or convey something they *know* or *believe*—or *perceive* or *take*—with respect to so-and-so. But if we define 'intension' and 'designates' in terms of 'believe' and 'assume', we can no longer hope, of course, to define 'believe' and 'assume', in terms of 'intension' or 'designates'.

4

The second way in which we might try to show that Brentano was wrong may be described by reference to a familiar conception of 'sign behaviour'. Many philosophers and psychologists have suggested, in effect, that a man may be said to *perceive* an object x, or to *take* some object x to have a certain property f, provided only that there is something which *signifies* x to him, or which signifies to him that x is f. But what does 'signify' mean?

We cannot be satisfied with the traditional descriptions of 'sign behaviour', for these, almost invariably, define such terms as 'sign' by means of intentional concepts. We cannot say, for instance, that an object is a sign provided it causes someone to *believe*, or *expect*, or *think of* something; for sentences using 'believe', 'expect', and 'think of' are clearly intentional.

Nor can we say merely that an object is a sign provided it causes someone to be *set for*, or to be *ready for*, or to *behave appropriately* to something, for sentences using 'set for', 'ready for', and 'behave appropriately to', despite their behaviouristic overtones, are also intentional. Similar objections apply to such statements as 'One object is a sign of another provided it *introduces* the other object *into the behavioural environment*, as contrasted with the physical environment, of some organism.'

If we are to show that Brentano's thesis as applied to *sign* phenomena is mistaken, then we must not introduce any new technical terms into our analysis of sign behaviour unless we can show that these terms apply also to non-psychological situations.

Most attempts at non-intentional definitions of 'sign' make use of the concept of *substitute stimulus*. If we use 'referent' as short for 'what is signified', we may say that, according to such definitions, the sign is described as a substitute for the referent. It is a substitute in the sense that, as stimulus, it has effects upon the subject which are similar to those the referent would have had. Such definitions usually take this form: V is a *sign* of R for a subject S if and only if V affects S in a manner similar to that in which R would have affected S.[9] The bell is a sign of food to the dog, because the bell affects the dog's responses, or his dispositions to respond, in a way similar to that in which the food would have affected them.

This type of definition involves numerous difficulties of which we need mention but one – that of specifying the respect of degree of similarity which must obtain between the effects attributed to the sign and those attributed to the referent. This difficulty is involved in every version of the substitute-stimulus theory. Shall we say that, given the conditions in the above definition, V is a sign of R to a subject S provided only that those responses of S which are stimulated by V are similar in *some* respect to those which have been (or would be) stimulated by R. In other words, should we say that V is a sign of R provided that V has some of the effects which R has had or would have had? This would have the unacceptable consequence that all stimuli signify each other, since any two stimuli have at least some effect in common. Every stimulus causes neural activity, for example; hence, to that extent at least, any two stimuli will have similar effects. Shall we say that V is a sign of R provided that V has *all* the effects which R would have had? If the bell is to have all the effects which the food would have had, then, as Morris

9. Compare Charles E. Osgood, *Method and Theory in Experimental Psychology* (New York, 1953), p. 696: 'A pattern of stimulation which is not the object is a sign of the object if it evokes in an organism a mediating reaction, this (a) being some fractional part of the total behaviour elicited by the object and (b) producing distinctive self-stimulation that mediates responses which would not occur without the previous association of non-object and object patterns of stimulation. All of these limiting conditions seem necessary. The mediation process must include part of the same behaviour made to the object if the sign is to have its representing property.' Some of the difficulties of the substitute stimulus concept (qualification (a) in this definition) are met by qualification (b), which implies that the subject must once have perceived the thing signified. But (b) introduces new difficulties. Since I have never seen the president of the United States, no announcement, according to this definition, could signify to me that the president is about to arrive.

notes, the dog must start to eat the bell.[10] Shall we say that V is a sign of R provided that V has the effects which *only* R would have had? If the sign has effects which only the referent can have, then the sign *is* the referent and only food can be a sign of food. The other methods of specifying the degree or respect of similarity required by the substitute-stimulus definition, so far as I can see, have equally unacceptable consequences.

Reichenbach, in his *Elements of Symbolic Logic*, has applied this type of analysis to the concept of taking; but the consequences are similar. To say of a subject S, according to Reichenbach, that S *takes* something to be a dog is to say: 'There is a z which is a bodily state of S and which is such that, whenever S is sensibly stimulated by a dog, S is in this bodily state z.'[11] In other words, there are certain bodily conditions which S must fulfil in order for S to be sensibly stimulated by a dog; and whenever S satisfies any of these conditions, then S is taking something to be a dog.

But among the many conditions one must fulfil if one is to be sensibly stimulated by a dog is that of being alive. Hence if we know that S is alive, we can say that S is taking something to be a dog. The difficulty is that the bodily state z, of Reichenbach's formula, is not specified strictly enough. And the problem is to find an acceptable modification.

In reply to this objection, Reichenbach suggested, in effect, that 'S takes something to be a dog' means that S's bodily state has all those neural properties which it must have – which are 'physically necessary' for it to have – whenever S is sensibly stimulated by a dog.[12] But this definition has the unacceptable consequence that, whenever S is sensibly stimulated by a dog, then S *takes* the thing to be a dog. Thus, although we can say that a man may be stimulated by a fox and yet take it to be a dog, we can never say that he may be stimulated by a dog and *not* take it to be a dog.[13]

Similar objections apply to definitions using such expressions as 'dog responses', 'responses specific to dogs', 'responses appropriate to dogs', and the like. For the problem of specifying what a man's 'dog responses' might

10. See Charles Morris, *Signs, Language, and Behaviour*, p. 12, and Max Black, 'The Limitations of a Behavioristic Semiotic', *Philosophical Review*, vol. 56 (1947), pp. 258–72.

11. This is a paraphrase of what Hans Reichenbach formulated in special symbols on p. 275 of *Elements of Symbolic Logic* (New York, 1947).

12. Reichenbach suggests this motification in 'On Observing and Perceiving', *Philosophical Studies*, Vol. 2 (1951), pp. 92–3. This paper was written in reply to my 'Reichenbach on Observing and Preceiving' (*ibid.*, pp. 45–8), which contains some of the above criticisms. In these papers, as well as in Reichenbach's original discussion, the word 'perceive' was used in the way in which we have been using 'take'. Reichenbach used the term 'immediate existence' in place of Brentano's 'intentional inexistence'; see *Elements of Symbolic Logic*, p. 274.

13. This sort of modification may suggest itself: Consider those bodily states which are such that (i) S is in those states whenever he is sensibly stimulated by a dog and (ii) S cannot be in those states whenever he is *not* being stimulated by a dog. Shall we say 'S takes something to be a dog' means that S is in this particular class of states? If we define 'taking' in this way, then, we must say that, in the present state of psychology and physiology, we have no way of knowing whether anyone ever *does* take anything to be a dog, much less whether people take things to be dogs on just those occasions on which we want to be able to *say* that they take things to be dogs.

be is essentially that of specifying the bodily state to which Reichenbach referred.

Of all intentional phenomena, expectation is one of the most simple and, I think, one which is most likely to be definable in terms which are not intentional. If we could define, in non-intentional terms, what it means to say of a man, or an animal, that he expects something – that he expects some state of affairs to come about – then, perhaps, we could define 'believing' and 'assuming', non-intentionally, in terms of this sense of 'expecting'. If we are to show that Brentano is wrong, our hope lies here, I think.

For every expectancy, there is some possible state of affairs which would *fulfil* or *satisfy* it, and another possible state of affairs which would *frustrate* or *disrupt* it. If I expect the car to stop, then, it would seem, I am in a state which would be fulfilled or satisfied if and only if the car were to stop – and which would be frustrated or disrupted if and only if the car were not to stop. Hence we might consider defining 'expects' in this way:

'S *expects* E to occur' means that S is in a bodily state *b* such that either
(i) *b* would be fulfilled if and only if E were to occur or (ii) *b* would be disrupted if and only if E were not to occur.

Our problem now becomes that of finding appropriate meaning for 'fulfil' and 'disrupt'.

Perhaps there is a way of defining 'fulfil' in terms of the psychological concept of *re-enforcement* and of defining 'disrupt' in terms of *disequilibration, surprise,* or *shock.* And perhaps we can then provide an account of the dog and the bell and the food in terms which will show that this elementary situation is not intentional. It is possible that the dog, because of the sound of the bell, is in a state which is such that either (i) his state will be re-enforced if he received food or (ii) it will be disequilibrated if he does not. And it is possible that this state can be specified in physiological terms. Whether this is so, of course, is a psychological question which no one, apparently, is yet in a position to answer. But even if it is so, there are difficulties in principles which appear when we try to apply this type of definition to human behaviour.

If we apply 'expects', as defined, to human behaviour, then we must say that the appropriate fulfilments or disruptions must be caused by the occurrence, or non-occurrence, of the 'intentional object' – of *what* it is that is expected. But it is easy to think of situations which, antecedently, we should want to describe as instances of expectation, but in which the fulfilments or disruptions do not occur in the manner required. And to accommodate our definition to such cases, we must make qualifications which can be expressed only by re-introducing the intentional concepts we are trying to eliminate.

This difficulty may be illustrated as follows: Jones, let us suppose, *expects* to meet his aunt at the railroad station within twenty-five minutes. Our formulation, as applied to this situation, would yield: 'Jones is in a bodily state which would be fulfilled if he were to meet his aunt at the station within twenty-five minutes or which would be disrupted if he were not to meet her there within that time.' But what if he were to meet his aunt and yet *take* her to be someone else? Or if he were to meet someone else and yet *take* her to be his aunt? In such cases, the fulfilments and disruptions would not occur in the manner required by our definition.

If we introduce the intentional term 'perceives' or 'takes' into our definition of 'expects', in order to say, in this instance, that Jones *perceives* his aunt, or *takes* someone to be his aunt, then, of course, we can no longer define 'assume' – or 'perceive' and 'take' – in terms of 'expects'. It is worth noting, moreover, that even if we allow ourselves the intentional term 'perceive' our definition will be inadequate. Suppose that Jones were to visit the bus terminal, believing it to be the railroad station, or that he were to visit the railroad station believing it to be the bus terminal. If he met his aunt at the railroad station, believing it to be the bus terminal, then, contrary to our formula, he may be frustrated or surprised, and, if he fails to meet her there, his state may be fulfilled. Hence we must add further qualifications about what he believes or doesn't believe.[14]

If his visit to the station is brief and if he is not concerned about his aunt, the requisite re-enforcement or frustration may still fail to occur. Shall we add '. . . provided he *looks for* his aunt'? But now we have an intentional expression again. And even if we allow him to look for her, the re-enforcement or frustration may fail to occur if he finds himself able to satisfy desires which are more compelling than that of finding his aunt.

We seem to be led back, then, to the intentional language with which we began. In attempting to apply our definition of 'expects' to a situation in which 'expects' is ordinarily applicable, we find that we must make certain qualifications and that these qualifications can be formulated only by using intentional terms. We have had to introduce qualifications wherein we speak of the subject *perceiving* or *taking* something to be the object expected; hence we cannot now define 'perceive' and 'assume' in terms of 'expect'. We have had to add that the subject has certain *beliefs* concerning the nature of

14. R.B. Braithwate in 'Belief and Action' (*Aristotelian Society*, suppl. vol. 20 [1946] p. 10) suggests that a man may be said to believe a proposition *p* provided this condition obtains: 'If at a time when an occasion arises relevant to *p*, his springs of action are *s*, he will perform an action which is such that, if *p* is true, it will tend to fulfil *s*, and which is such that, if *p* is false, it will not tend to satisfy *s*.' But the definition needs qualifications in order to exclude those people who, believing truly (*p*) that the water is deep at the base of Niagara Falls and wishing (*s*) to survive a trip over the falls, have yet acted in a way which has not tended to satisfy *s*. Moreover, if we are to use such a definition to show that Brentano was wrong, we must provide a non-intentional definition of the present use of 'wish' or 'spring of action'. And, with Braithwaite's definition of 'believe', it would be difficult to preserve the distinction which, apparently, we ought to make between *believing* a proposition and *acting upon* it (see *Perceiving* chapter 1, sect. 2). I have proposed detailed criticisms of a number of such definitions of 'believe' in 'Sentences about Believing', *Proceedings of the Aristotelian Society*, vol. 56 (1955–6), pp. 125–48. Some of the difficulties involved in defining *purpose* non-intentionally are pointed out by Richard Taylor in 'Comments on a Mechanistic Conception of Purpose', *Philosophy of Science*, vol. 17 (1950), pp. 310–17, and 'Purposeful and Nonpurposeful Behaviour: A Rejoinder', *ibid.*, pp. 327–32.

the conditions under which he perceives, or fails to perceive, the object. And we have referred to what he is *looking for* and to his other possible *desires*.

It may be that some of the simple 'expectancies' we attribute to infants or to animals can be described, non-intentionally, in terms of re-enforcement or frustration. And possibly, as Ogden and Richards intimated, someone may yet find a way of showing that believing, perceiving, and taking are somehow 'theoretically analysable' into such expectancies.[15] But until such programmes are carried out, there is, I believe, some justification for saying that Brentano's thesis does apply to the concept of *perceiving*.

15. C.K. Ogden and I.A. Richards, *The Meaning of Meaning*, 5th ed. (London, 1938), p. 71.

12 Chisholm and Brentano on Intentionality*

Linda L. McAlister

1

Franz Brentano's *Psychology from an Empirical Standpoint* first appeared in 1874, but due to various accidents of history it was ninety-nine years before the publication of an English translation of this important work.[1] In the meantime, many recent English-speaking philosophers have become acquainted with Brentano's thought through the writings and translations of Roderick M. Chisholm, who is today surely the foremost living Brentano scholar, in addition to his many other philosophical activities. Chisholm has, for example, published explications of Brentano's famous doctrine of 'intentional inexistence' or 'intentionality' on several occasions, and his interpretations have been extremely suggestive and influential.[2] Brentano had introduced the notion of intentionality into modern philosophical discussions in the following famous paragraph from his *Psychology from an Empirical Standpoint*:

> Every mental phenomenon is characterised by what the Scholastics of the middle ages called the intentional (or mental) inexistence of an object, and what we might call, though not wholly unambiguously, reference to a content, direction toward an object (which is not to be understood here as meaning a thing), or immanent objectivity. Every mental phenomenon includes something as object within itself, although they do not all do so in the same way. In presentation something is presented, in judgement something is affirmed or denied, in love loved, in hate hated, in desire desired and so

---

1. *Psychologie vom empirischen Standpunkt* (Leipzig, 1874); 2nd complete German edition ed. Oskar Kraus (Leipzig, 1924); English edition, *Psychology from an Empirical Standpoint*, ed. Linda L. McAlister, trans. D.B. Terrell, Antos C. Rancurello and Linda L. McAlister (London and New York, 1973). References are to English ed.

2. See Roderick M. Chisholm, 'Intentionality and the Theory of Signs', *Philosophical Studies*, vol. 3, no. 4 (June 1952); *Perceiving* (Ithaca, N.Y., 1957), ch. 11; the Introduction to his anthology *Realism and the Background of Phenomenology* (New York, 1960); the articles entitled 'Franz Brentano' and 'Intentionality' in the *Encyclopedia of Philosophy*, ed. Paul Edwards (New York, 1967); and elsewhere.

* Reprinted from *The Review of Metaphysics*, XXVIII, no. 2 (Dec. 1974), pp. 328–38.

on . . . This intentional inexistence is characteristic exclusively of mental phenomena. No physical phenomenon exhibits anything like it.[3]

I believe, however, that Chisholm's interpretation of Brentano's intentionality doctrine is not wholly accurate, and that while the doctrine he sets forth as Brentano's is an interesting and provocative one, it gives a misleading impression of what Brentano's views actually were, by obscuring almost entirely the specific nature of the question Brentano was trying to solve, and by misreading the answer Brentano gave. If only for the sake of historical accuracy a corrective should be given, but of course, taking another look at Brentano's particular way of construing the mind/body problem and the solution he put forth may also prove to be suggestive in its own right.

In this paper I will first show that there is no textual basis for the interpretation of Brentano's intentionality doctrine that Chisholm gives, and I will discuss briefly how, in light of that fact, Chisholm might have thought that there was. Then I will point out instances in which the version of intentionality that Chisholm attributes to Brentano conflicts with other views that Brentano held at the time. Out of these discussions emerges a different interpretation of Brentano's intentionality thesis, and, I hope, a more accurate one.

2

In the chapter entitled 'Intentional Inexistence' in this book *Perceiving*, Chisholm purports to give an explication of Brentano's intentionality doctrine; he says he is attempting, not to set forth a different thesis, but 'to formulate Brentano's thesis somewhat more exactly'. He says:

> The phenomena most clearly illustrating the concept of 'intentional inexistence' are what are sometimes called psychological attitudes; for example desiring, hoping, wishing, seeking, believing, assuming. When Brentano said that these attitudes 'intentionally contain an object in themselves', he was referring to the fact that they can be truly said to 'have objects' even though the objects which they can be said to have do not in fact exist. Diogenes could have looked for an honest man even if there hadn't been any honest men. The horse can desire to be fed even though it won't be fed. James could believe there are tigers in India, and *take* something there to be a tiger, even if there aren't any tigers in India.
>
> But *physical* – or non-psychological – phenomena, according to Brentano's thesis, cannot thus 'intentionally contain objects in themselves'. In order for Diogenes to sit in his tub, for example, there must be a tub for him to sit in; in order for the horse to eat his oats, there must be oats for him to eat, and in order to James to shoot a tiger, there must be a tiger there to shoot.[4]

3. *Psychology*, pp. 88–9.
4. *Perceiving*, p. 169; see above, p. 140.

It seems clear that Chisholm thinks the crux of the distinction Brentano is drawing between physical and mental phenomena is that mental phenomena refer to objects which may or may not exist, while physical phenomena refer to objects that must exist. Hence Brentano's intentionality thesis is interpreted as a thesis about the required existential status of the objects of mental and physical phenomena respectively; the objects of the former need not exist, the objects of the latter must.

Schematically Chisholm's version of the distinction is as follows:

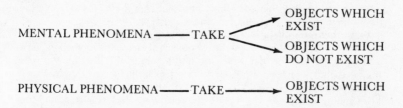

MENTAL PHENOMENA ——— TAKE 〈 OBJECTS WHICH EXIST / OBJECTS WHICH DO NOT EXIST

PHYSICAL PHENOMENA ——— TAKE ——→ OBJECTS WHICH EXIST

But where, exactly, does Chisholm find this distinction in Brentano's passage? If we look back to the original text quoted above and try to find where Brentano says that the distinction between mental and physical phenomena lies in the respective existence requirements of their objects, we will look in vain. Brentano mentions nothing of the sort explicitly. In fact, his emphasis seems to be in another direction entirely. He says merely that mental phenomena refer to, are directed toward, objects, but this is not true of physical phenomena. Schematically, then the distinction that Brentano seems to have been making is not the one Chisholm attributes to him, but, rather:

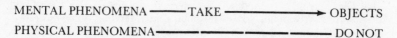

MENTAL PHENOMENA ——— TAKE ————————→ OBJECTS
PHYSICAL PHENOMENA———— ——— ——— ——— —— DO NOT

One way a person might arrive at such a misconstruction of Brentano's point would be through a misunderstanding of Brentano's parenthetical remark – the only place in the passage in question where he even mentions the objects of mental phenomena. What Brentano says about them is:

> *worunter hier nicht eine Realität zu verstehen ist.*

Chisholm renders this in *Perceiving* as:

> *which is not here to be understood as a reality.*[5]

If one draws no distinction between existence and reality, such a remark could easily be construed in the way Chisholm has construed it. Unfortunately, however, 'eine Realität' does *not* mean the same as 'something that exists' for Brentano, and to interpret it in this way would be

5. P. 168, see above, p. 140; as opposed to the less literal, but also less misleading version of the English edition of the *Psychology*: 'which is not to be understood here as meaning a thing' (p. 88).

an error. Brentano talks about *realia* and *irrealia* (*Realitäten* and *Nichtrealitäten*), *and* about what exists and what does not exist, and he means something different in each case. For Brentano, a *reales* or a *Realität* is a particular individual thing, while an *irreales* is a non-thing, as, for example, a universal, a species, a genus, a state of affairs or values. Brentano maintained that something could be a *Realität*, i.e. an individual, a thing, even if it did not exist. A unicorn or a hippogriff, for example, would be particular individual things, and hence *realia*, even though they do not exist. So 'eine Realität' does not mean 'something that exists' and it is wrong to interpret the remark that something need not be a *Realität* as meaning that that something need not be understood as existing.

What that parenthetical remark does mean, as I understand it, is simply that non-things, *irrealia*, too, can be the objects of mental phenomenon just as well as things can – a view which Brentano held at the time he wrote the *Psychology*, but which he was later to reject in favour of the view that only things, *realia*, can be the objects of mental phenomena.

Chisholm, oddly enough, is perfectly well aware that 'eine Realität' does not mean 'something that exists'. In fact, it is he who suggests, in the Preface to his translation of Brentano's *The True and the Evident*, that the least misleading translation of 'Realität' is 'thing' rather ·than 'reality', specifically to prevent people from making this mistake. Perhaps the answer is that he himself had made the mistake in his earlier expositions of Brentano and in this later translation (1966) has revised his opinion.

At any rate, the suggestion that Brentano's parenthetical remark provides the justification for interpreting his paragraph the way Chisholm repeatedly interprets it in his earlier treatments of Brentano's intentionality thesis must be rejected.[6] Because I can find no other hint of a justification for it in Brentano's passage, and because the alternative interpretation I have suggested is the more straightforward and apparently fitting one, I conclude that Chisholm's interpretation is incorrect. In the next section I shall call attention to three points where Chisholm's interpretation is demonstrably in conflict with various positions Brentano takes in other sections of *Psychology From an Empirical Standpoint*.

3

One of the most striking instances in which Chisholm's formulation of the intentionality doctrine differs from what Brentano actually said has to do with physical phenomena. In his Introduction to *Realism and the Background of Phenomenology*, Chisholm says:

> The things upon which [mental] activities are directed or to which they refer, need not exist in order thus to be directed upon or referred

6. Nor should it be thought that the very term 'intentional *in*existence' suggests objects that may not exist; the prefix 'in-' is not, in this case, one of negation, but rather one of location, a vestige of the Scholastic doctrine that a *simulacrum* of the object of, e.g. thought or love, came into being *in* the mind when the object was thought of or loved.

to. No physical phenomenon, according to Brentano, has this type of freedom; the objects of our physical activities are restricted to what does exist. We can desire or think about horses that don't exist, but we can ride only those that do.[7]

Notice that his example of a physical phenomenon here is a physical activity, namely, riding. In the passage from *Perceiving* quoted earlier his examples of physical phenomena were sitting, shooting and eating, again all physical activities.

Compare Brentano:

> Examples of physical phenomena ... are a colour, a figure, a landscape which I see, a chord which I hear, warmth, cold, odour which I sense; as well as similar images which appear in the imagination.[8]

For Brentano, physical phenomena are obviously not physical activities at all, but sensible qualities.[9] This would seem to be a clear indication that Chisholm's formulation of Brentano's thesis has somehow gone awry.[10]

We must remember that in *Psychology from an Empirical Standpoint*, Brentano, obviously, was writing a book about psychology, which he defined as the science, not of the mind or of the soul, but of mental phenomena,[11] just as, at that time, the natural sciences were often referred to as the sciences of physical phenomena. In order to delimit the range of his subject-matter in a systematic way, it was incumbent upon him to find some unified principle or definition which distinguishes between mental and other phenomena. But what did Brentano mean by 'phenomenon' and what other sorts of phenomena are there? As is also obvious from the title of his book, he was an empiricist and believed that all of our knowledge, all of our concepts, are derived from what we perceive. He believed, further, that human beings have two kinds of perception: external perception through the sense organs, and a form of direct inner perception. Phenomena are the objects of both of these two kinds of perception, and in both categories there are certain ultimate, basic objects which constitute the simplest elements out of which more complex structures are constructed. The job of the empiricist, as he sees it, is to discover these most basic of our objects of perception, and show how they form the more complex constructs. Mental phenomena are the objects of inner perception, i.e. they are what we are

---

7. *Realism*, p. 4.

8. *Psychology*, pp. 79–80.

9. His friend and editor Oskar Kraus points out, apparently correctly, that the inclusion of 'a landscape' in this list is simply a slip on Brentano's part. See *Psychology*, p. 79n.

10. Anthony Kenny, too, in *Action, Emotion and Will*, p. 195, construes physical phenomena as physical activities, and launches what he takes to be a criticism of Brentano, when he is in fact only criticising a Chisholmian version of Brentano; his complaint against Brentano is easily answerable when one sees what Brentano actually meant by 'physical phenomena'.

11. See *Psychology*, pp. 8ff.

conscious of when we introspect,[12] and the three basic classes of mental phenomena are presentation, judgement, and acts of emotion and will. Physical phenomena, by the same token, are the objects of our acts of external or sense perception, and Brentano was interested in what he takes to be the most basic objects of external perception, the sensible qualities out of which more complex objects are constructed. Brentano does not ordinarily use the term 'phenomenon' for anything but these most basic objects of inner and external perception. He would not call physical objects such as horses, chairs or guns physical phenomena, much less activities such as riding, sitting or shooting. Hence when Brentano begins Book 2 of his *Psychology* with the words, 'All the data of our consciousness are divided into two great classes – the class of physical and the class of mental phenomena', he is saying that the only two kind of phenomena there are, are mental acts on the one hand, and sensible qualities on the other – the most basic objects of our two kinds of perception.

Brentano saw his task in this chapter of his *Psychology*, entitled 'The Distinction Between Mental and Physical Phenomena', as that of drawing a distinction between mental acts and sensible qualities. Now these are obviously quite different sorts of thing, and it is easy enough in practice to tell the one from the other; that is not the problem. What is not so easy is to find a single principle that is true of all mental acts and false of all sensible qualities. Brentano tries several principles, but he finds none wholly satisfactory until he arrives at the principle of intentionality, i.e. that all mental phenomena – mental acts – take or are directed toward objects, but no physical phenomena – sensible qualities – do so.

Chisholm's mistake in construing physical phenomena as physical activities rather than as sensible qualities is not unconnected with his previously discussed mistake of interpreting intentionality as the doctrine that mental phenomena take objects which may or may not exist while physical phenomena take objects which do exist. If that is the position you are discussing, then, of course, you would have to choose as your examples of physical phenomena things that might reasonably be supposed to take objects, and physical activities which are expressed by transitive verbs are the most obvious source of examples. But as I have pointed out, that interpretation is incorrect, and the fact that it leads to this second discrepancy is further confirmation of the error.

There are two other related discrepancies between Chisholm's account of Brentano's thesis and the thesis itself which should be noted. Chisholm says in his Introduction to *Realism and the Background of Phenomenology*:

> Brentano's criterion of the psychological or mental might be put in this way: From the fact that a certain thing is the object of an intentional act or attitude, one cannot infer either that the thing

12. Brentano distinguishes between inner observation – introspection in the usual sense – in which the attempt is made to focus attention on one's own mental acts, and inner perception, wherein attention is focused on something else and one becomes aware of one's own mental acts only incidentally. He believes the former is impossible. See *Psychology*, pp. 29–30.

exists or that it does not; from the fact that a·proposition is the object
of an intentional act or attitude, one cannot infer that the proposition
is true or that it is false.[13]

Brentano would say that these two claims hold true in general or for the
most part, but he would admit a major exception to each of them, yet
Chisholm's formulation gives us no inkling of this. In the first case, where
Chisholm says that from the fact that something is the object of an
intentional act you cannot infer whether it exists or not, Brentano's
exception lies in the case of the mental phenomena which are the objects of
acts of *inner* perception. According to Brentano, an inner perception is a
judgement; it is not an ordinary fallible judgement, however, but rather an
evident, i.e. self-evidently true, judgement. And all judgements, according
to Brentano at that time, were existential in nature, that is to say, they were
all either affirmations or denials of the existence of their objects.[14] In the
particular case of inner perception, the affirmation of the existence of the
object, the mental phenomenon, in question was thus held by Brentano to
be self-evidently true, and so, from the fact that it is the object of *this sort* of
intentional act, one *can* infer that the object exists.

Chisholm also says Brentano maintained that if a *proposition* is the
object of an intentional act or attitude you cannot infer either that that
proposition is true or false. But again, Brentano would allow of an
important exception. Once more it has to do with his doctrine of *Evidenz*; if a
proposition is the object of an *evident* judgement, then, although it is the
object of an intentional act or attitude, it does follow that that proposition is
true. Another way of putting this is to say that knowing is pre-eminently a
mental phenomenon; still, from the fact that one knows a proposition, it
does follow that the proposition is true. To give an interpretation of
Brentano's doctrine that suggests either that Brentano did not consider
knowing a mental phenomenon, or that he did not hold that knowing X
implies that X is true, is to give a misleading picture of Brentano's position.

4

What view of Brentano's intentionality thesis then emerges from the
foregoing criticisms of Chisholm's interpretation? First, that Brentano
meant it not primarily as a thesis about the objects of mental phenomena,
but about the fact that mental phenomena are by their very nature
relational while physical phenomena are not.[15] It is not, however, simply
that mental phenomena are relational while physical phenomena, i.e.
sensible qualities, are not. That would, at any rate, be false. For, as a matter
of fact, physical phenomena are capable of standing and do stand in all sorts

13. *Realism*, p. 4.
14. *Psychology*, pp. 210ff.
15. In my earlier paper, 'Franz Brentano and Intentional Inexistence', *Journal of the
History of Philosophy* (October, 1970), under the influence of Chisholm's interpretation,
I gave a rather different account of Brentano's thesis. I do not think the two are
mutually exclusive, but I do think that the present version gives a more accurate
picture of what Brentano wanted to emphasise in his *Psychology*.

of relations: temporal, spatial, relations of magnitude, etc. For example, sound A can stand to sound B in relations such as 'temporally prior to', 'louder than', 'more piercing than', and so on.

Nor does the difference between mental and physical phenomena consist in the fact that the former are necessarily relational while the latter are only contingently so. In order to make a case for this claim one would have to maintain not only that it is logically impossible for there to be a mental phenomenon that stands in no relations whatsoever (which Brentano does claim), but also that it is logically possible for there to exist a single sensible quality which stands in no relations whatsoever to anything. Presumably this latter condition would require one to maintain that there is a possible world which consists in its entirety of a single sensible quality, there being absolutely nothing else, not even a consciousness which senses it, with which it could enter in a relation. While I believe that Brentano is committed, whether he realised it or not, to such a view,[16] it is certainly not the crux of his intentionality doctrine.

The crucial difference between mental phenomena and physical phenomena, i.e. between mental acts and sensible qualities, as Brentano saw it, is that the former enter necessarily into a *particular kind of relation* which is wholly foreign to the realm of physical phenomena. What are these relations? They are relations to something *as object*, and this is a kind of relation which a sensible quality could not possibly enter into, except as the object term. It could never be the subject term. Sound A could be louder than B, or subsequent to B, or similar to B, or whatever, but in no such instance is either A or B the object of the other. And although A or B could be the object of a mental phenomenon, they are wholly incapable of having, or being directed toward, an object. Physical phenomena simply lack this directional nature which is a logically necessary characteristic of mental phenomena.

Brentano himself goes hardly any further into the analysis of this unique kind of relation in the *Psychology* of 1874[17] except to classify its many various sub-categories, i.e. presentations, judgements, loves, desires, etc. and to try to establish how they are related to one another. But it is clear that a deeper understanding of Brentano's insight is needed and must be sought through the analysis of what it is to refer to, to point to, to mean, or to intend something in the broadest sense. Much of twentieth-century philosophy has been devoted to the investigation of this very question in one guise or another, and I do not presume even to make an attempt to answer it here.

16. Compare *Psychology*, pp. 92–3: 'It is undoubtedly true that a colour only appears to us when we have a presentation of it. We cannot conclude from this, however, that a colour cannot exist without being presented.'

17. Later on he does say of this relation that it is not really a relation but rather something 'relation-like' because he believes that both the subject and the object of a genuine relation must exist, and he has, by then, begun to emphasise the point which Chisholm has tried to incorporate into Brentano's original view, namely that the objects of (some of) these intentional relations need not exist. The exceptions that I mentioned above, however, are still valid; if one knows X, X must be true, and if one has an inner perception, what is perceived must exist. See the Appendix to the *Psychology*, 'Mental Reference as Distinguished From Relation in the Strict Sense', pp. 271ff. (1911).

What I have done is simply to offer a corrective to one seemingly inaccurate presentation of Brentano's thesis in order to cast light on what I take to be his real insight, in the hope that it will be of interest and perhaps of help to other philosophers to see the specific form and context in which the issue was originally raised.

13 Brentano's Theory of Correct and Incorrect Emotion[1]

Roderick M. Chisholm

What affirmation and negation are in thinking, pursuit and avoidance are in desire; so that since moral virtue is a state of character concerned with choice, and choice is deliberate desire, therefore both the reasoning must be true and the desire right, if the choice is to be good, and the later must pursue just what the former asserts. Now this kind of intellect and of truth is practical; of the intellect which is contemplative, not practical nor productive, the good and the bad state are truth and falsity, respectively (for this is the work of everything intellectual); while of the part which is practical and intellectual the good state is truth in agreement with right desire (Aristotle, *Ethics*, VI, 2).

1

Brentano's theory of correct and incorrect emotion is based upon the analogy he believes to hold between what he calls the sphere of the intellect and the sphere of the emotions. What he has to say about this presumed analogy seems to me to be very important indeed. Even where his views are controversial, they are extraordinarily suggestive, not only for ethics, but also for the theory of preference and for philosophical psychology. I shall attempt to expound some of his views here in the hope that this exposition may lead others to look into the work of Brentano. It must be emphasised, however, that a presentation of this sort can hardly do justice to the details of Brentano's theory.

Brentano usually describes the analogy in question as one that holds between 'judgement', on the one hand, and 'love and hate', on the other. But he uses the terms 'love' and 'hate' very broadly to refer, not only to what we might call 'pro-emotions' and 'anti-emotions', but also to what Aristotle, in the passage above, called 'pursuit' and 'avoidance'. We may put the analogy, in somewhat over-simplified form, first by noting certain facts about judgements and then by noting the corresponding facts about 'love and hate'.

1. Revised by the author. Reprinted from *Revue Internationale de Philosophie*, vol. 78 (1966), fascicule 4, pp. 395–415.

Judgements are either positive or negative; they are either affirmations or denials. They are also either correct or incorrect; or, as one usually puts it, they are either true or false. There is a very close connection between the correctness and incorrectness of judgements, on the one hand, and *existence* and *non-existence*, on the other. For to say of an object that it *exists*, Brentano suggests, is to say that it is *correct to accept* that object, and to say of an object that it *does not exist* is to say that it is *correct to reject* that object. The latter point may also be put by saying that an object exists if and only if it is worthy of being accepted or affirmed, and that an object does not exist if and only if it is worthy of being rejected or denied.[2]

And now, *mutatis mutandis*, Brentano thinks, we may say much the same thing about emotions, about 'love and hate'.

Emotions are either positive or negative; they are either pro-emotions or anti-emotions, love or hate. Love and hate may be correct and they may also be incorrect. There is a very close connection between the correctness and incorrectness of emotions, on the one hand, and *goodness* and *badness* on the other. For to say of an object that it is *good*, Brentano suggests, is to say that it is *correct to love* that object, and to say of an object that it is *bad* is to say that it is *correct to hate* that object. The latter point may also be put by saying that an object is good if and only if it is worthy of being loved and that an object is bad if and only if it is worthy of being hated.

But to put the analogy this way, as I have said, is to over-simplify Brentano's doctrine. And, as he concedes, there are also fundamental points of disanalogy that hold between the intellectual and the emotive spheres.

2

One might ask whether *any* instance of love or hate could be said to be correct or to be incorrect. How could one *defend* the doctrine that there are correct emotions and incorrect emotions? To understand Brentano's attitude toward this question about emotive phenomena, we should consider its analogue in application to *intellectual* phenomena. What if one were to ask whether there are any judgements or beliefs that could be said to be correct or incorrect, to be true or false? How could one defend the doctrine that some beliefs or judgements are true or correct and that others are false or incorrect?

It is not difficult to see that if there is a procedure by means of which we can defend the doctrine that there are correct judgements and incorrect judgements, then there will be an analogous procedure by means of which we can defend the doctrine that there are correct emotions and incorrect emotions.[3]

2. For the details of this view, see Brentano's *Wahrheit und Evidenz* (Hamburg, 1958); first published in Leipzig in 1930), ed. Oskar Kraus. The English edition is *The True and the Evident* (London 1966), ed. Roderick M. Chisholm.

3. It is significant to note that, in his lecture 'On the Concept of Truth' (1899), Brentano appeals to the concept of the correctness of *emotion* in order to illuminate the concept of the correctness of judgement, rather than conversely. See *Wahrheit und Evidenz*, p. 25; *The True and the Evident*, p. 21.

Brentano's procedure, in the case of intellectual phenomena, is to appeal to those judgements and beliefs that we *see*, directly and immediately, to be correct; or, as he puts it, those judgements and beliefs that are experienced as being correct or manifest themselves as being correct (those judgements and beliefs that are '*als richtig charakterisiert*'). These include judgements of 'inner perception'; for example, the judgement that I am now thinking of a certain thing, the judgement that I seem to see such-and-such, or the judgement that I seem to remember so-and-so. The judgement that I now seem to see a cat, Brentano would say, is one that manifests itself as being correct. But it is the judgement that I *take* there to be a cat, and not the judgement that I do in fact see a cat, that thus manifests itself as being correct. There are also certain 'truths of reason' – for example, that there are no round squares – which are also experienced as being correct. (These 'truths of reason', according to Brentano, are all negative; they tell us merely what does not exist and what cannot exist. Every affirmative judgement that is seen to be correct is a judgement about oneself and one's psychological activities.)[4]

It is in virtue of such directly evident facts as these, according to Brentano, that one first acquires the concept of correctness. The way in which we thus come to understand what it is for a belief or judgement to be correct is thus like the way in which we come to understand any other empirical concept: we are presented with something that manifests that concept. Then, once having the concept of correctness and the correlative concept of incorrectness, we are able to derive, by what is sometimes called 'intuitive induction', certain general principles about correctness and incorrectness; for example, that no judgement is both correct and incorrect; that if a judgement is not correct then it is incorrect. We shall consider such principles in more detail below. They are all 'apodictic' and '*a priori*'. 'But when we say that a certain type of knowledge is *a priori*, we do *not* mean to imply that the concepts which it involves can be given without perception and apperception.'[5]

The correctness and incorrectness of emotion, Brentano says, are similar in these respects to the correctness and incorrectness of judgement. In *Vom Ursprung sittlicher Erkenntnis*, Brentano cites the following examples of emotions that 'manifest themselves as being correct'. First of all, the love or pleasure that we take in *insight* is a love or pleasure that we experience as being correct. So, too, the love that we have for joy – unless, Brentano significantly adds, 'it be joy in what is bad'. (We shall return to this qualification below.) *Correct emotion* itself provides another example. Love of

4. See *Wahrheit und Evidenz*, p. 148ff.; *The True and the Evident*, p. 130ff.

5. Franz Brentano, *Vom Ursprung sittlicher Erkenntnis*, 3rd ed. ed. Oskar Kraus (Leipzig, 1934), p. 111. The first edition of this work (Leipzig, 1889) was translated into English by Cecil Hague and published as *The Origin of the Knowledge of Right and Wrong* (London, 1902). Subsequent German editions of Brentano's book contain much important material, including the selection from which the above quotation is taken, not included in the English edition. This new material is included in *The Origin of Our Knowledge of Right and Wrong* (London, 1969), trans. Roderick M. Chisholm and Elizabeth Hughes Schneewind; references in the present paper to the English edition are to the 1969 edition.

love that is correct is itself love that is correct. And, finally, every *thought or idea* is something that is good in itself, and 'with every enrichment within the sphere of our ideas, regardless of the good or bad results that may happen to follow, the good within us is increased'.[6] Love for this type of intellectual enrichment also manifests itself as being correct.

These emotions, then, and others to be discussed below, present us with the concept of a *correct emotion*. The best statement of Brentano's views about the way in which we acquire this concept is one that Brentano sets forth himself in a letter written to Oskar Kraus, on 21 March 1916. Brentano writes:

> What does it mean to say of a judgement or of an emotive attitude [*Gemütsbezeihung*] that it is correct? You say that this question has not been answered. And, according to you, we cannot see that such correctness obtains unless we have knowledge of an *adaequatio rei et intellectus* and of an *adaequatio rei et amoris*. But to me nothing could be easier than to show that this last is false. If it is necessary to have knowledge of an *adaequatio rei et intellèctus*, then we find ourselves in an absurd *regressus in infinitum*. For how is one to know that there is a correspondence between the intellect and reality without first having knowledge both of the intellect and of reality? The correct answer, as I stated long ago, is this. The concept of correctness is made manifest to us in precisely the way in which other concepts are made manifest to us. We consider a multiplicity of things each of which exemplifies the concept and we direct our attention upon what these things have in common. Whenever I perceive that I judge with evidence I am aware of myself as someone who is judging correctly. The evidence of my own judgement also enables me to speak of the correctness of the judgements of other people: if anyone, however arbitrarily, arrives at an opinion which coincides with that of my own evident judgement then his opinion is correct, and if anyone arrives at an opinion that contradicts it then *his* opinion is not correct. And now, so far as the correctness of our emotive attitudes is concerned, we find that the situation is completely analogous. We know with immediate evidence that certain of our emotive attitudes are correct. And so we are able to compare these various attitudes and thus to arrive at the general concept of a correct emotion. Here, too, we will find that there are others whose emotive attitudes correspond with our own. If their attitudes should happen to be only a matter of habit or instinct, we may still say that they are correct but not that they are experienced as being correct [*als richtig charakterisiert*]. I cannot see any ground at all for reservations or misgivings about this. One can never find the criterion of correctness in an *adaequatio rei et intellectus vel amoris*; it can

6. *Vom Ursprung sittlicher Erkenntnis*, 3rd ed. p. 23; *The Origin of Our Knowledge of Right and Wrong*, p. 23. The final example – the value of enriching the sphere of our ideas – is developed in considerable detail in Brentano's writing on aesthetics. See Franz Brentano, *Grundzüge der Ästhetik* (Bern, 1959), ed. F. Mayer-Hillebrand, pp. 142–69.

be found only in those attitudes which we know with immediate evidence to *be* correct.[7]

3

According to Brentano's view, when we contemplate those *judgements* which are 'experienced as being correct', we are able to abstract certain general 'apodictic' principles about correctness. These principles form the basis of what is traditionally called logic and what also might be called 'the theory of correct judgement'. The same thing holds, he believes, for correct emotion and accordingly there is also 'the theory of correct emotion'.

Omitting certain details that are involved in Brentano's theory of judgement, we may formulate some of what he takes to be the basic principles of the theory of correct judgement in the following way:

(1) It is impossible for there to be anything which is such that it may be correctly affirmed and also correctly denied.

(2) It is impossible for there to be anything which is such that it may be incorrectly affirmed and also incorrectly denied.

(3) It is impossible for there to be anything which is such that it may be correctly affirmed and also incorrectly affirmed.

(4) It is impossible for there to be anything which is such that it may be correctly denied and also incorrectly denied.

(5) It is impossible for there to be anything which is such that it may be neither incorrectly affirmed nor correctly denied.

(6) It is impossible for there to be anything which is such that it may be neither incorrectly affirmed nor incorrectly denied.

(7) It is impossible for there to be anything which is such that it may be neither correctly affirmed nor incorrectly affirmed.

(8) It is impossible for there to be anything which is such that it may be neither correctly denied nor incorrectly denied.

These principles are objective and universal. Thus we may construe the first as telling us that, for *any* persons S and S', it is impossible for there to be anything which is such that it may be correctly affirmed by S and correctly denied by S'. S and S' may be the same person, in which case the principle tells us that it is impossible for there to be anything which is such that there is anyone who may correctly affirm and also correctly deny it. Or S and S' may be different persons, in which case the principle tells us that it is impossible for there to be anything which is such that there is one person who may correctly affirm it and another person who may correctly deny it. And analogously for the other principles. Brentano has sometimes been accused of what Frege and Husserl called 'psychologism'; but the fact that

7. The letter is published in full in Franz Brentano, *Die Abkehr vom Nichtrealen* (Bern, 1966), ed. F. Mayer-Hillebrand, pp. 291–4; the passage here translated is on pp. 293–4. Compare also pp. 207–8, 305–6. The letter was also published in part in Oskar Kraus, *Franz Brentano: Zur Kenntnis seines Lebens und seiner Lehre* (Munich, 1919), pp. 31–3.

he recognises the universality and objectivity of such principles as the above indicates that the charge is unjustified.[8]

Following one traditional usage, we may say that principles (1) through (4) constitute the ground of *the law of contradiction* and that principles (5) through (8) constitute the ground of *the law of excluded middle*. Brentano's terminology is not orthodox, unfortunately, and he cites a version of (2) as being 'the law of excluded middle'.[9]

There is no doubt, according to Brentano, that the first four of these laws, those that we are calling the basis of the law of contradiction, have their analogues in the sphere of the emotions. Hence we may say that it is impossible for there to be anything which is such that it may be correctly loved and also correctly hated, or such that it may be correctly loved and also incorrectly loved, or such that it may be correctly hated and also incorrectly hated. Brentáno refers to the first of these principles as the 'law of antagonism' and to the second, i.e. the principle according·to which it is impossible for there to be anythihg which is such that it may be incorrectly loved and also incorrectly hated, as 'the law of excluded middle for the sphere of the emotions'.[10] And here, too, 'psychologism' is false. For any subjects S and S', it is impossible for S to love correctly what S' hates correctly; and similarly for the other versions of the first four principles.

But what of the emotive analogues of the second four principles, i.e. (5) through (8), those principles which (unlike Brentano) we are associating with 'the law of excluded middle'?

In *Vom Ursprung sittlicher Erkenntnis*, Brentano had said: 'Of the two opposing attitudes, love and hate, being pleased and being displeased, in every instance one of them is correct and the other incorrect.'[11] But Brentano was subsequently to revise his opinion.[12] And according to his later view, principles (5) through (8) do not hold for the sphere of the emotions. When it is reported, as it sometimes is, that Brentano did hold a version of 'the law of excluded middle' for the sphere of the emotions, it must be kept in mind that this was his term for the emotive version of (2), not for the emotive versions of (5) through (8).

---

8. On Brentano and the charge of 'psychologism', see Brentano's letter to Husserl in *Wahrheit und Evidenz*, pp. 153–9, and compare also pp. 63–4 and pp. 124–5 (*The True and the Evident*, pp. 135–8, 54–5, 110–11), as well as Oskar Kraus's Introduction.

9. See Franz Brentano, *Die Lehre vom richtigen Urteil* (Bern, 1956), ed. F. Mayer-Hillebrand, p. 175.

10. See *Die Lehre vom richtigen Urteil*, p. 175. In the manuscript from which this section of *Die Lehre vom richtigen Urteil* was taken, Brentano cites a number of alternative labels for the emotive version of the first principle; viz. 'Gesetz des Antagonismus (des Widerstreits), Widerstrebens, Gegengefühlens, des Gegenstimmens, Gegengefühls, des Abneigens.' The manuscript, listed as EL 4 in Brentano's *Nachlaß*, is entitled 'Zur Axiomatik', and dated 16 February 1916.

11. 3rd ed. p. 19; *The Origin of our Knowledge of Right and Wrong*, p. 17–18.

12. Anton Marty, in the biographical sketch of Brentano he had prepared for the English edition of the *Ursprung*, i.e. *The Origin of the Knowledge of Right and Wrong*, called attention to this change in Brentano's views, pp. 121–2. Unfortunately there is no indication in the book that this essay *was* written by Marty. The German version appears in vol. 1 of Marty's *Gesammelte Schriften* (Halle, 1916), p. 97ff.

Hence the *indifferent* – that which is neither good nor bad – provides one important point of disanalogy between the sphere of judgement and the sphere of the emotions. Brentano seldom discusses the indifferent, but it is not difficult to see how this category would fit into his scheme. If the good in itself if that which it is correct to love and incorrect to hate, and if the bad in itself is that which it is correct to hate and incorrect to love, then the *indifferent* in itself is that which it is neither correct nor incorrect to love and neither correct nor incorrect to hate. We should remind ourselves, therefore, that 'not correct', in the sphere of the emotions, does not imply 'incorrect', and that 'not incorrect' does not imply 'correct'.

And there is a second respect in which the sphere of the emotions differs from that of judgement. A compound or conjunction of the true and the false is false, no matter how much the true that is in it may outweigh the false. But a compound or whole that is made up of goods and evils may be good, provided that the good outweighs or otherwise makes up the presence of evil.

We have been discussing *intrinsic* goodness and badness – what is 'good in itself' and 'bad in itself'. Brentano noted, however, that the terms 'good' and 'bad' are not always used to mean the same as 'good in itself' and 'bad in itself'. They are also used more broadly to mean, respectively, 'either good in itself or good as a means [*nützlich*]' and 'either bad in itself or bad as a means [*schädlich*]'. Taking the terms in this broader sense, he said we may affirm that everything is either good or bad; i.e. everything is either such that either it is good as an end or good as a means or such that either it is bad as an end or bad as a means. Otherwise, he said, there would be some things that God would have had no sufficient reason for creating.[13] 'Love' and 'hate' may also be used in this broader sense to mean respectively 'love something either for its own sake, as an end, or as a means to something further that is loved for its own sake' and 'hate something either for its own sake, as an end, or as a means to something further that is hated for its own sake'. And if we take 'love' and 'hate' in this broader sense then we may affirm emotive analogues of principles (5) through (8) and hence an emotive analogue of the law of excluded middle.

4

Some things that are good, Brentano points out, are *better* than other things that are good, and some things that are bad are *worse* than other things that are bad. But nothing that is true is *more true* than anything else that is true, and nothing that is false is *more false* than anything else that is false. And *a fortiori*, nothing else that· exists, and nothing that does not exist is *less existent* (or *more non-existent*) than anything else that does not exist. Here, then, we have another point of disanalogy between the spheres of judgements and that of the emotions.

If A is better than B, or if B is worse than A, then we may say, as Brentano does, that A is *preferable* to B. 'A is preferable to B', therefore, will

13. *Die Lehre vom richtigen Urteil*, p. 176.

not imply either that A is good or that B is bad. How, then, are we to interpret this locution?

Brentano quotes Descartes' remark that whatever is worth loving at all is worth loving in the highest degree. We cannot say, therefore, that 'A is prefereable to B' means that A is *worthy of more love*. Nor can it mean, as G.E. Moore suggested, that A is *more worthy of love* than B.[14] For correctness, and therefore correct love, is not a quantitative concept. 'A is preferable to B', according to Brentano, can mean only that it is *correct to prefer* A as an end to B as an end.[15]

Preference, like love and hate, according to Brentano may be experienced as being correct. In *Vom Ursprung sittlicher Erkenntnis*, he cites a number of principles of correct preference, or preferability, which he says we can see to be true. The first three principles that he formulates are uncontroversial. They are:

(1)   For any two things A and B, if A is good and B is bad, then A is preferable to B.

(2)   For any thing A, if A is good, then the existence of A is preferable to the non-existence of A.

(3)   For any thing A, if A is bad, then the non-existence of A is preferable to the existence of A.

But if the principles are uncontroversial, they are yet subject to misinterpretation. One is easily led to suppose, mistakenly, that if A is good then the non-existence of A is bad, or that if A is bad then the non-existence of A is good. But although joy (more exactly, a certain type of joy) is good and sorrow is bad, the non-existence of joy is not itself anything that is positively bad and the non-existence of sorrow is not itself anything that is positively good.[16]

14. See G.E. Moore's review of *The Origin of the Knowledge of Right and Wrong*, in the *International Journal of Ethics*, (1903), pp. 123–8 [ch. 14 below]. Moore wrote in the Preface to *Principia Ethica*: 'When this book had already been completed, I found, in Brentano's "Origin of the Knowledge of Right and Wrong", opinions far more closely resembling my own, than those of any other ethical writer with whom I am acquainted.' *Principia Ethica* (Cambridge, 1903), pp. x-xi. We shall see below that, by implication at any rate, Brentano accepted Moore's 'principle of organic unities'. In the lectures he gave on ethics at the University of Vienna from 1876 to 1894, Brentano appealed to considerations like those that Moore appealed to in connection with 'the naturalistic fallacy'. Brentano wrote: 'If something is recognised as being a correct goal or purpose, then there is no longer place for the question: "Do I do the right thing, do I act reasonably, in following that goal?" ... Hence we have a condition of adequacy [for any definition of correct goal or purpose]: 'The concept of a correct goal or purpose must not be construed in such a way that we can still ask such a question of something that we know to fall under that concept.' Franz Brentano, *Grundlegung und Aufbau der Ethik* (Bern, 1952), ed. F. Mayer-Hillebrand; trans. Elizabeth Hughes Schneewind as *The Foundation and Construction of Ethics* (London, 1973).

15. *Vom Ursprung sittlicher Erkenntnis*, p. 26; *The Origin of our Knowledge of Right and Wrong*, p. 26.

16. For clear discussions of this point see Oskar Kraus, *Die Werttheorien* (Brünn, 1937), pp. 226ff., and Georg Katkov, *Untersuchungen zur Werttheorie und Theodizee*

The next two principles that Brentano lists may be more controversial. Brentano says that a good is preferable 'to the same good with an admixture of the bad', by which I take him to mean:

(4)   For any two things A and B, if A and B are wholly distinct and if A is good and B is bad, then A is preferable to the larger whole, or *conjunctivum*, A and B.

On the other hand, 'a bad thing with an admixture of the good' is preferable to the bad thing itself; or, as I would put it:

(5)   For any two things A and B, if A and B are wholly distinct and if A is good and B is bad, then the *conjunctivum*, A and B, is preferable to B.

Brentano next refers to the case where we correctly 'prefer the whole of a good to its part', which I think may be formulated as follows:

(6)   For any two things A and B, if A and B are wholly distinct and if A is good and B is good, then the *conjunctivum*, A and B, is preferable to B.

But the next principle, according to which we correctly 'prefer the part of something bad to its whole' is one that Brentano later repudiates:

(7)   For any two things A and B, if A is wholly other than B and if A is bad and B is bad, then A is preferable to the *conjunctivum*, A and B.

After the publication of the first edition of *Vom Ursprung sittlicher Erkenntnis*, in 1889, Brentano was inclined to hold that the evil that is involved in retribution may yet make a bad situation less bad than it would have been without retribution. Thus he said, in one unpublished fragment, that wickedness accompanied with sorrow is better than the same wickedness accompanied with pleasure; this, he added, justifies the sorrow that is involved in repentance and throws some light upon vindictive punishment.[17] In other words, if A is a wicked deed and if B is the suffering involved in the sinner's retribution, then the two evils, A and B, may be preferable to A without B. In holding this, Brentano accepts, at least by implication, what

(Brünn, 1937), pp. 67ff. In a number of recent formulations of the logic of preference, the following theorems occur: 'p is good if and only if not-p is bad' and 'p is bad if and only if not-p is good'. But these principles, as Brentano, Kraus and Katkov saw, do not hold of intrinsic goodness and intrinsic badness. For an attempt to formulate a logic of intrinsic goodness, badness, and preferability, see Roderick M. Chisholm and Ernest Soṣa, 'On the Logic of "Intrinsically Better"', *American Philosophical Quarterly*, vol. 3 (1966).

17. '1. Bei gleichem Maß von Lust, Unlust, sittlicher Güte und Schlechtigkeit erscheint die Welt besser, wo die Lust den Guten und die Unlust den Schlechten zukommt als umgekehrt, am besten die, wo in Proportion. 2. Ja, es scheint gleiche Schlechtigkeit mit Leid besser als gleiche Schlechtigkeit mit Lust. 3. Hieraus bekommt das vindikative Strafprinzip eine gewisse Bedeutung. 4. Auch der Reueschmerz erhält Berechtigung. (Büßerleben)...' The fragment, listed in Brentano's *Nachlaß* as Ethik 1, is entitled 'Vom Guten, das in der Zuordnung liegt'. Brentano wrote to Kraus in 1908 that one of the respects in which he had revised his

G.E. Moore called 'the principle of organic unities', the principle that Moore formulated by saying that the value of a whole 'bears no regular proportion to the sum of the values of its parts' and hence 'must not be assumed to be the same as the sum of the values of its parts'.[18] In one unpublished manuscript, probably from the year 1908, Brentano wrote: 'It is not merely the summation of the elements in an order that is to be considered as good; the order itself must be taken into consideration.'[19] To illustrate this point, he cites the principles of the *bonum progressionis* (see below) and he notes the relevance of these facts to the problems of theodicy ('a consideration of the whole explains why it is that physical as well as psychical and moral evil and so-called metaphysical evil is allowed in the world').

Given the principle of organic unities, one may wonder whether there are not other exceptions to principles (4), (5) and (6) above.

Brentano next formulates two principles which, I believe, can be put as follows:

(8)   For any three things A, B, and C, if A, B and C are entirely distinct from each other, if A is good, if B is good, and if C has the same value as A, then the *conjunctivum*, B and C, is preferable to A.

(9)   For any three things A, B, and C, if A, B and C are entirely distinct from each other, if A is bad, if B is bad, and if C has the same value as A, then A is preferable to the *conjunctivum*, B and C.

Principle (9), however, seems to be questionable on the same grounds that Brentano questioned (7). (The expression, 'having the same value', which I have used in formulating (8) and (9), may, of course, be defined in terms of preferability: A has the *same value* as C, provided it is neither correct nor incorrect to prefer C as an end to A.)

Here, then, we have the formal principles about preferability that

---

original views had to do with 'the law of compensation or requital [*Vergeltungssatz*], concerning which Leibniz makes some valuable observations in his *Theodicy*'; see the *Origin of our Knowledge of Right and Wrong* (1969 ed., p. 115). See Leibniz's *Theodicy*, Part I, para. 73.

18. *Principia Ethica*, pp. 27–8. I have attempted to explicate this principle and to relate it to some of Brentano's writings in the following two articles: 'The Defeat of Good and Evil', *Proceedings and Addresses of the American Philosophical Association*, vol. 42 (1968–9), pp. 21–38, and in 'Objectives and Intrinsic Value', in Rudolf Haller (ed.), *Jenseits von Sein und Nichtsein* (Graz, 1972), pp. 261–9). The first of these two papers may also be found in John Smith (ed.), *Contemporary American Philosophy: Second Series* (London, 1970), pp. 152–69.

19. 'Nicht allein Summierung der Elemente der Ordnung ist als Gut zu betrachten, sondern auch die Ordnung selbst.' The manuscript, listed in Brentano's *Nachlaß* as M18b, is entitled 'Einteilung der Philosophie'; the passage cited is one of several 'cosmological theses' set forth by Brentano. A detailed discussion of the relation of these considerations to the problems of theodicy may be found in Katkov's *Untersuchungen zur Werttheorie und Theodizee*, referred to above; the general point of view of this work is summarised in the same author's 'Zur Widerlegung des Pessimismus auf metaphysischem Gebiete', in *Zur Philosophie der Gegenwart*, Veröffentlichungen der Brentano-Gesellschaft (Prague, 1934), pp. 35–42.

Brentano sets forth in *Vom Ursprung sittlicher Erkenntnis*. (Brentano does not take the trouble to observe that preferability is transitive and asymmetrical.)

We should now add two further principles which Brentano came to emphasise after the first edition of *Vom Ursprung sittlicher Erkenntnis*. There is first the principle of the *bonum variationis* which might be formulated thus:

(10)   For any three things, A, B, and C, if A is good, if B is good, if C is good, and if B resembles A more than C resembles A, then the *conjunctivum*, A and C, is preferable to the *conjunctivum*, A and B.

Suppose, for example, that A is a beautiful painting, that B is a perfect copy of A, and that C is a beautiful piece of music; it would be better, clearly, that there be the painting and the music rather than that there be the two paintings.[20] And then there is the principle of the '*bonum progressionis*' or the '*malum regressus*' which might be put as:

(11)   If A is a situation in which a certain amount of value x is increased to a larger amount y, and if B is like A except fhat in B there is a decrease from the larger amount of value y to the smaller amount x, then A is preferable to B.

Thus Brentano writes: 'Let us think of a process which goes from good to bad or from a greater good to a lesser good; then compare it with one which goes in the opposite direction. The latter shows itself as the one to be preferred. This holds even if the sum of the goods in the one process is equal to that in the other. And our preference in this case is one that we experience as being correct.'[21]

5

Of the remaining principles of preferability to be found in Brentano's works, the most interesting and important, by far, are those pertaining to what, following Mill, we may call the *quality* of pleasure.[22]

There is a type of pleasure and a type of displeasure that may be said to take an intentional object. Just as one may say 'I *believe that* Smith is happy' or 'I *know that* Smith is happy', one may also say 'I am *pleased that* Smith is happy' or 'I am *displeased that* Smith is happy'. Here we have four different ways of being intentionally related to one and the same object – to Smith's

20. The example is adapted from Katkov, *Untersuchungen*, p. 56.

21. *Grundlegung und Aufbau der Ethik*, p. 214; *The Foundation and Construction of Ethics*, pp. 196–7.

22. Brentano also sets forth these principles: that of two goods of equal value, the more probable is to be preferred (and hence also, presumably, that of two evils of equal value, the less probable is to be preferred); that positive knowledge, or knowledge of what exists, is better than negative knowledge, or knowledge of what does not exist; and, analogously, that a positive emotion, i.e. love or any pro-attitude, is preferable to a negative emotion, i.e. hate or any anti-attitude. See the *Grundlegung und Aufbau der Ethik*, pp. 212–13; *The Foundation and Construction of Ethics*, pp. 196–7.

being happy.[23] For pleasures and displeasures that thus have intentional objects, there is an obvious way of making qualitative distinctions: the quality of the pleasure or the displeasure will be a function of the quality of the intentional object. And how are we to assess the qualities of the various intentional objects? Simply by appealing to the principles we have already laid down.

Let us assume that you are pleased that Smith is pleased, but that I am pleased that a certain other man is displeased. Now the intentional object of your pleasure is better than the intentional object of my pleasure; for the intentional object of your pleasure is a man being pleased and the intentional object of my pleasure is a man being displeased.

And so we may say, more generally, that one pleasure is better than another pleasure if the intentional object of the one is better than the intentional object of the other; and that one displeasure is worse than another displeasure if the intentional object of the one is better than the intentional object of the other. For if I am displeased that Smith is happy, and you are displeased that Jones is sad, then the intentional object of my displeasure is better than the intentional object of your displeasure (for Smith being happy is better than Jones being sad) and therefore my displeasure is worse than your displeasure.

Brentano does not put the matter in just the way that I have put it. But he considers and contrasts the four possibilities, 'pleasure in the good', 'pleasure in the bad', 'displeasure in the good', and 'displeasure in the bad'. On the basis of what he says, one could formulate a general theory of the qualities of pleasure. Let us consider one possible theory, which seems to accord with Brentano's own.

As we have seen, Brentano recognises a category of the indifferent – of that which is neither good in itself nor bad in itself. Hence we could begin with the following principle (though Brentano does not mention it, so far as I know):

(1)   Pleasure in the indifferent is good.

If a man is pleased, say, that there are flowers in the world, where there being flowers is something that is intrinsically indifferent, then his innocent pleasure is good. And analogously for displeasure:

(2)   Displeasure in the indifferent is bad.

(But (2) differs from (1), in that whereas (1) implies the existence of a good and does not imply the existence of an evil, (2) implies the existence of an evil and also the existence of a good – namely the existence of consciousness, someone being aware of something. Brentano's view seems to be that all evil involves some good whereas it is not the case that all good involves some

23. Brentano believed that the apparent reference to a state of affairs, in the above examples to Smith's being happy, may always be paraphrased away and replaced by reference merely to concrete things, or *realia*, such as Smith. This reistic phase of Brentano's philosophy is set forth in detail in *Wahrheit und Evidenz* (in *The True and the Evident*) and in *Die Abkehr vom Nichtrealen*. See the Introduction to the latter work by F. Mayer-Hillebrand; also Georg Katkov, 'Bewußtsein, Gegenstand, Sachverhalt: Eine Brentanostudie', *Arhiv für die gesammte Psychologie*, Bd. 75 (1930), pp. 459–544.

evil.[24] Here, then, is another point at which the analogy between the sphere of judgement and the sphere of the emotions is incomplete: the existence of evil always implies the existence of something that is good, just as the false always implies something that is true; but whereas the existence of what is good may also imply the existence of what is evil, the true never implies anything that is false.)

Given principles (1) and (2) above, we may go on to say, as Brentano does:

(3)　　Pleasure in the good is good;
(4)　　Displeasure in the good is bad.

If you are pleased that Smith is pleased that there are flowers in the world, then your pleasure is good; and if I am displeased that Smith is pleased that there are flowers in the world, then my displeasure is bad.

We could now add the following four principles of preferability:

(5)　　Pleasure in the good is preferable to pleasure in the indifferent;
(6)　　Displeasure in the bad is preferable' to displeasure in the indifferent;
(7)　　Pleasure in the good is prefereable to pleasure in the bad;
(8)　　Displeasure in the bad is preferable to displeasure in the good.

Brentano does not discuss principles (5) and (6), but he explicitly affirms (7) and (8).

What are we to say of pleasure in the bad – my pleasure, say, that Smith is experiencing unjustified pain? Brentano says: 'Pleasure in the bad, to the extent that it is pleasure, is something that is good, but to the extent that it is at the same time an incorrect emotion, it is something that is bad. It it not purely bad, but it is predominantly bad. In avoiding it as being something bad, we are not exercising a simple act of hate; rather, we are exercising an act of preference.·We prefer being free from what is bad in this situation to being in possession of what is good. Here we have an act of preference which is seen to be correct and which justifies our avoidance of pleasure in the bad. We say to ourselves: Better that there be no pleasure at all than to take pleasure in the bad.'[25]

Should we say, perhaps, that pleasure in the bad is *both* good and bad, though predominantly bad? Not if what Brentano called 'the law ˙of anatagonism' is valid. For according to this law nothing is such that it may be both correctly loved and also correctly hated. And therefore, given Brentano's definitions of 'good' and 'bad', nothing is such that it is both

---

24. See *Religion und Philosophie*, pp. 173–9, and *Grundlegung und Aufbau der Ethik*, pp. 184, 192 (*The Foundation and Construction of Ethics*, 169–70, 176–7). Another version of the relevant material in *Religion und Philosophie*, is published as 'Optimismus', in Samual Hugo Bergmann, 'Unbekannte Manuskripte Franz Brentanos', in *Horizons of a Philosopher: Essays in Honor of David Baumgardt*, ed. J. Frank, H. Minkowski, and E.J. Sternglass (Leiden, 1963), pp. 34–49; 'Optimismus' appears on pp. 35–9.

25. *Grundlegung und Aufbau der Ethik*, p. 213 (*The Foundation and Construction of Ethics*, p. 196). Compare *Vom Ursprung sittlicher Erkenntnis*, p. 85. (*The Origin of our Knowledge of Right and Wrong*, p. 90).

good and bad.[26] Hence we must take a more positive stand toward pleasure in the bad and say of it either that it is good, or that it is bad, or that it is indifferent. And there seems to be no doubt about Brentano's view. He would say:

(9)　Pleasure in the bad is bad.

What about displeasure in the bad? This, Brentano says, is not purely good, but it is predominantly good.[27] It seems clear, then, that he would say:

(10)　Displeasure in the bad is good.

Hence, if we are justified in attributing principles (9) and (10) to Brentano, we may also attribute to him the following:

(11)　Displeasure in the bad is preferable to pleasure in the bad.

6

There is still another qualitative dimension of pleasure and displeasure. Plato says in the *Philebus* (64) that 'in that mixture which is most precious, there should be truth as well as pleasure'. Of the pleasures and displeasures that we have been considering, namely, those that take intentional objects, some may be called 'true' and others 'false'. We could say that a true pleasure, or a true displeasure, is one such that its intentional object exists, and that a false pleasure, or a false displeasure, is one such that its intentional object does not exist. If I am pleased, say, that peace overtures are being made, then my pleasure is true if and only if peace overtures are being made, and false if and only if they are not being made.

Brentano suggests that, all else being equal, true pleasures are better than false pleasures. Suppose I believe, incorrectly, that my father has performed certain magnificent deeds and suppose I take pleasure in what I believe that he has done. Brentano says that in such a case 'the love is correct, but the form that the pleasure takes is not correct'.[28] Or, as we may put it, the pleasure is correct but false. Brentano is clear that such a false but correct pleasure is one that it would be better not to have – this because of the intrinsic evil that error involves. Presumably also, false but correct displeasures would be displeasures that it would be better not to have.

And so we have, in effect, really *three* relevant qualitative dimensions of pleasure: (1) We may ask, first, whether the pleasure or displeasure is *correct* or *incorrect*. (2) We may ask, secondly, about the *quality of its intentional object*. Is it a pleasure (or displeasure) in the good, in the bad, or in the indifferent?

26. Compare *Vom Ursprung sittlicher Erkenntnis*, p. 150 (*The Origin of our Knowledge of Right and Wrong*, p. 145).

27. Compare *Grundlegung und Aufbau*, p. 214 (English ed. pp. 196–7); *Vom Ursprung*, p. 85 (English ed. pp. 90–1).

28. 'Obwohl hier die Liebe eine richtige ist, ist doch die Form der Freude nicht die richtige' ('In these instances the pleasure takes the wrong form, even though the love is correct'), *Grundlegung und Aufbau*, p. 187 (English ed. p. 172).

(3) And we may ask, finally, whether it is *true* or *false*. Does its intentional object exist or not? By considering the various ways in which these dimensions may be combined with each other, one could formulate certain further basic questions of the theory of intrinsic preferability.

7

We have considered, then, the basic theses of Brentano's theory of correct and incorrect emotion. To see the way in which he now makes the transition to practical philosophy, let us consider, very briefly, the way in which he utilises the traditional distinction between 'the antecedent will' and 'the consequent will'.

Brentano first distinguishes an act of *love, simpliciter*, from an act of *love that involves a preference*. If two situations, *each* of which, taken as such and as if alone, is an object of my love, pro-emotion, or favourable inclination, I may yet *prefer* one to the other. I may be happy to see Mr Smith receive a sudden stroke of good fortune; I may also be happy to see Mr Jones receive a sudden stroke of good fortune. Each of these occurrences, considered in itself and apart from its consequences, is an object of my favourable inclination. But of these two things that I thus love, I may yet *prefer* Mr Jones receiving good fortune to Mr Smith receiving good fortune. Here, then, we have an act of love that involves a preference.

Brentano next distinguishes a *wish that involves a decision* from an act of *love that involves a preference*. Though I may prefer Mr Jones receiving good fortune to Mr Smith receiving good fortune, when I consider these two things by themselves and apart from their consequences, I may yet decide that, when all other relevant things are considered, I would prefer to have it the other way around. In such a case, I will have considered the two situations in the contexts of what I take to be their total consequences and then I will have arrived at a preference with respect to these two larger situations. Hence, Brentano says, a wish that involves a decision is related to a love or preference that does not involve a decision in the way in which, according to St Thomas and Leibniz, the 'consequent will' of God is related to the 'antecedent will' of God. Both Mr Jones' good fortune and Mr Smith's good fortune were objects of my antecedent love. Mr Jones' good fortune, but not Mr Smith's, was also the object of my antecedent preference. But the total situation to which (I believe) Mr Smith's good fortune would lead, and not that to which (I believe) Mr Jones' good fortune would lead, is the object of my consequent preference. Or, more exactly, the total situation which I believe would follow upon Mr Smith's good fortune is one that I prefer to the total situation which I believe would follow upon Mr Jones' good fortune.[29]

With this concept of a wish that involves a decision, Brentano goes on to define what he calls an *act of will*. Coming to a decision, he observes, need not involve an act of will. Though I may have reached a decision about the relative merits of Jones' and Smith's good fortunes, the matter may be

29. Compare *Grundlegung und Aufbau*, pp. 218ff (English ed. pp. 200ff.); *Vom Ursprung*, pp. 122–15, 156–8 (English ed. 113–16, 150–2).

entirely out of my hands and thus involve no act of will. What distinguishes an act of will from what is merely a wish that involves a decision is

> always something we ourselves have to bring about. We can will only those things that fall within our power, or, at any rate, those things that we earnestly believe to be within our power . . . Thus we can define an act of will as a wish or a want that involves a decision and which has as its object something that we are to bring about ourselves and that we confidently expect will result from the desires that we then have. Hence one might say that an act of will is a want or a wish such that we have arrived at it by coming to a decision and such that we believe it can be realised by our own endeavours.[30]

The complex concept of an act of will thus contains a multiplicity of elements: love, conviction, preference, and causation. The first four elements are psychological, and the fifth – that of causation – occurs only as part of the intentional object of the second. Here we have a paradigm case of what Brentano called 'descriptive psychology'.

Applying now the concepts of *correct* and *incorrect* to acts of will, Brentano proceeds to construct his practical philosophy.

---

30. 'Wir können das Wollen also definieren als ein entscheidendes Wünschen, das etwas von uns selbst zu Verwirklichendes zum Gegenstand hat und von uns als Wirkung unseres Begehrens überzeugt erwartet wird. Es ist m. a. W. ein Wunsch, für den wir uns entschieden haben und an dessen Realisierbarkeit durch unser Eingreifen wir glauben' (*Grundlegung und Aufbau der Ethik*, p. 219; English ed. p. 201).

14   Review of Franz Brentano's
The Origin of the Knowledge
of Right and Wrong[1]

G. E. Moore

This is a far better discussion of the most fundamental principles of ethics than any others with which I am acquainted. Brentano himself is fully conscious that he has made a very great advance in the theory of ethics. 'No one', he says, 'has determined the principles of ethics as, on the basis of new analysis, I have found it necessary to determine them' (p. x); and his confidence both in the originality and in the value of his own work is completely justified. In almost all points in which he differs from any of the great historical systems, he is in the right; and he differs with regard to the most fundamental points of moral philosophy. Of all previous moralists, Sidgwick alone is in any respect superior to him; and Sidgwick was never clearly aware of the wide and important bearings of his discovery in this one respect. Brentano is both clearer and more profound; and he avoids Sidgwick's two fundamental errors. It would be difficult to exaggerate the importance of his work.

His main proposition is that what we know, when we know that a thing is good in itself, is that the feeling of *love towards* that thing (or *pleasure in* that thing) is '*right*' (*richtig*). Similarly, that a thing is bad, is merely another way of saying that *hatred of* that thing would be '*right*'.

The great merit of this view over all except Sidgwick's is its recognition that all truths of the form 'This is good in itself' are logically independent of any truth about what exists. No ethical proposition of this form is such that, if a certain thing exists, it is true, whereas, if that thing does not exist, it is false. All such ethical truths are true, *whatever the nature of the world may be*. Hence, in particular, none of them are either identical with any *subjective* proposition (e.g. 'So-and-so has this feeling or desire or cognition') or such that, if it be true, *any* subjective proposition whatever need be true   Thus

1. This review, which appeared in the *International Journal of Ethics*, vol. 14 (October1903), pp. 115–23, is of the first English translation of Franz Brentano's *Vom Ursprung sittlicher Erkenntnis*, a work which was originally published in German in 1889. This first English translation was by Cecil Hague and was published in London in 1902, and has long been out of print. Subsequently, a second English edition appeared with a new translation by Roderick M. Chisholm and Elizabeth H. Schneewind, entitled *The Origin of Our Knowledge of Right and Wrong* (London and New York, 1969). I have changed Moore's page citations so that they refer to the second English edition, which is more likely to be accessible to present-day readers.

Brentano recognises fully the *objectivity* of this fundamental class of ethical judgements. 'No one,' he says, '[except Herbart] has so radically and completely broken with the subjective view of ethics' (p. x.).

Nevertheless Brentano is wrong in supposing that the conception 'rightly loved' or 'worthy of love' is the fundamental ethical concept which we mean by 'good in itself'. Sidgwick was right in holding that that concept is unanalysable; and it is, in fact, the concept which Brentano denotes by the word 'right', when he says that a thing is good in itself, if the love of it would be *right*. Brentano recognises *two* very important concepts when he recognises both the concept of what it is right to love and the *rightness* which belongs to love of such things; and the question which of these is properly denoted by the words good in itself might seem to be merely a verbal question. But it is not a merely verbal question, if, as Brentano rightly does, we take what is good in itself in the highest possible degree to be that of which it our *duty* to promote the existence. For whereas the degree in which a thing possesses the quality which he calls 'right' must be taken into account in considering what is that greatest possible good which it is our duty to effect, the degree in which things are 'worthy to be loved' is not a measure of our duty to effect their existence. It is certain that many things, e.g. inanimate beautiful objects, possess the quality of being worthy to be loved, in a higher degree than they possess that of 'rightness'; it may even be doubted whether they possess the latter at all. And it is our duty to effect that which is the most 'right' possible, not that which is most worthy to be loved. Though therefore we can agree with Brentano that everything which is good in itself is worthy to be loved, we cannot agree that everything which is worthy to be loved is good.

Brentano makes a similar mistake with regard to the definition of 'true' in the sense in which that word is applied to the *object* of a belief. He says that, just as an object is good, if it be rightly loved, so it is true if it be rightly believed. The definition of truth has the same rare merit as the definition of good, namely, that it is *objective*. But that it is false appears to be plain from the fact that we can raise the question whether it *is* 'right' to believe everything that is true: that is to say, we are immediately aware that 'true' and 'rightly believed' are two distinct concepts, one of which, 'true', is an unanalysable property belonging to some objects of belief. But it is important to raise a second question with regard to this definition of 'true'. Is the 'rightness' which Brentano attributes to belief in the true the *same* quality which he attributes to love of the good, or is it not? He speaks of 'right' love as if it were merely *analogous* to 'right' belief (pp. 17–18); and this suggests that he thinks the 'rightness' is *not* the same quality in the two cases. In that case he is calling two different unanalysable qualities by the same name; and that he should not have expressly noticed whether he is doing so or not, illustrates the insufficient attention which he has given to the question what he means by '*rightly* loved' – a defect in his inquiry, which will be illustrated again later, and which will help to explain his failure to perceive that *this* quality which he denotes by 'rightness', and *not* the 'rightly loved', is the fundamental ethical concept properly denoted by 'good in itself'. In fact, I am unable to perceive that there is any unanalysable quality which we attribute to belief in the true except the very one which we attribute to love of what is worthy to be loved. In other words, Brentano's judgement that belief in the true is 'right' *is* a judgement that belief in the true is always good in itself – a proposition which does not seem to be true. If it is not true, it follows not only that 'true' does not mean 'rightly believed', but also that just as what it is good to love is not always itself good, so, it is not always good to believe what is true. The incorrectness of this definition of 'true' is further proved by the fact that, as will be shown, the quality meant by 'rightness' has degrees, whereas, as Brentano himself rightly maintains, no one thing is *more* true than another (p. 26).

Another doctrine of Brentano's also illustrates the insufficient attention which he has paid to the nature of that 'rightness' the reference to which constitutes the merit of his definitions of good and true. His belief in this doctrine seems indeed to be the main cause why he has given so little attention to the nature of this fundamental concept. It is the doctrine which explains why he has given to this inquiry the unfortunate title of an inquiry into 'The *Origin* of the Knowledge of Right and Wrong'. Brentano holds, namely, that (as Hume thought) all our conceptions are derived from 'concrete impressions' – impressions, which, he says, are either 'of physical' or 'of psychical content' (pp. 13–15). This doctrine may be perfectly true in one sense; but in the sense naturally conveyed by the words it includes a most important error. Obviously the conception of 'good', as Brentano defines it, cannot be derived merely from the experience of *loving*, but only from that of '*right* loving' – from the perception of the *rightness* of love: its *origin* cannot be merely the perception of a love which *is* right, but in which this quality is not perceived, it can only be a perception in which it is itself *contained*. But whereas the experience of loving *has* all the marks which are suggested by calling it a 'concrete impression of psychical content', the 'experience of right loving' – i.e. the perception of the *rightness* of love – has *not*. The quality of 'rightness' is *not* a psychical content and the perception of it is *not* an impression in the ordinary sense of these words. A single mark is sufficient to distinguish it: by a 'psychical content' we always mean at least *an existent*, and by 'impression' the cognition of *an existent*, and 'rightness' is not an existent. Brentano is certainly not sufficiently attentive to this distinction between the experience of loving and the experience of right loving. He says he belongs to the 'empirical school' (p. 10); and he here shows himself to be under the influence of empiricism, in a sense in which empiricism is certainly erroneous.

The same inattention to the nature of the quality which he means by 'rightness' is further shown in the account Brentano gives of our knowledge that one thing is *better* than another. His first suggestion is that since '*good*' means 'worthy to be loved', '*better*' must mean 'worthy of *more love*' (p. 25). It does not seem to have occurred to him that it must mean '*more worthy* of love', that is to say, his attention is directed only to that element of his definition, which is a 'concrete psychical content', namely the love, *not* to the more important element 'rightness', which is not. In asserting that a thing is rightly loved with a *greater love*, you do not assert that it possesses the quality of *being rightly loved* in any higher degree than what is rightly loved with a less love; and hence if good means rightly loved, you do not assert that it is better. In short, even on Brentano's definition, if anything is to be *better* than another, that can only be because the quality which he means by '*rightness*' has degrees – a point which he has entirely failed to observe, and which proves that 'true' cannot mean 'rightly believed'. The supposition that, if 'good' means 'worthy of love', 'better' means 'worthy of more love', does in fact derive most of its plausibility from an ambiguity in the latter expression, in virtue of which it denotes not merely that a greater and a less love are each of them 'right', but that each of them is '*more* right' than some other love. If we say that one thing is worthy of more love than another, these words naturally convey the meanings that to love these things with the different amounts of love in question is '*more* right' than to love them both with the same amount: we do not merely convey the assurance that to love each with the amount of love in question is 'right', in a sense in which this assurance does not exclude the supposition that to love either of them with any other amount would also be equally 'right'. And that Brentano is actually using the expression 'worthy of more love', in the sense in which to say that one thing is worthy of more love than another is to say that one love is more right than another, is shown by the reason he gives for denying that the better is worthy of more love (for, after all, he does deny it). His reason is (p. 25) that nothing which is really good can be loved too much. And this proposition obviously only implies that no one thing is worthy of less love than another, because it asserts that a greater love of a thing is in no case *less right* than a less love of the same thing. Accordingly, whether this proposition is true or false (and it seems to be false), it makes an assertion not only about degrees of love, but also about *degrees of rightness*.

But Brentano, we have said, rejects the view that 'better' means 'worthy of more love', except, he says, 'in quite another sense' (p. 26). This 'other sense' is that 'better' means 'object of a *right preference*'. But what is meant by a 'right preference'? If, as is usual, we mean by 'preference' a *feeling*, it is obviously a feeling *only* towards the thing preferred, *not* towards the thing which is not preferred. When we say that we prefer one thing to another we usually mean either (1) that we *like* the one *more* than we like the other, or (2) that we choose the one and do *not* choose the other: there is no such thing as a single feeling, called 'preference', directed to *both* the things. But in case (1) to know that a thing is 'rightly' preferred, is only to know that it is worthy of the greater love which it receives, *not that* the other thing is *only* worthy of less; and in case (2) to know that it is 'rightly' chosen is again only to know that this choice is positively 'right', *not that* the other choice is not also and equally 'right': in neither case does the 'rightness' of the preference allow any inference as to the relative value of what is not preferred. Such an inference is only possible, if by saying that the preference is 'right', we mean that the liking or choice of the thing preferred is '*more* right' than the alternative.

The above seem to be the most important points in Brentano's theory concerning the nature of intrinsic value and intrinsic superiority. As regards intrinsic value, his theory has the almost unique merit that it defines 'good in itself', not only as an *objective* concept, but as containing that very concept which is in fact properly denoted by the words: but it is defective in that the complex property which he takes to be the required definition is not merely different from the simple property which is the true definition, but has not even the same extension; 'worthiness to be loved' is not even a correct criterion of intrinsic value. As regards intrinsic *superiority* his theory has an additional defect: he does not clearly recognise that to know one thing to be *better* than another must be to know that it has in a higher degree the very property which we mean by 'good in itself'.

If now we pass to his views on the question, 'What things are good in themselves, and in what degrees?' we find that they have corresponding merits and defects. He cannot be too highly praised for insisting that, not one thing only, but very many different things have intrinsic value; and, in particular, for emphasising the value of the immense variety of different states which belong to the class 'enjoyment of things worthy to be enjoyed' or 'right loves'. These constitute, in fact, by far the greater part of considerable goods: and Brentano does recognise that they are all good, and that, if they are so, mere pleasure or mere knowledge cannot be the sole goods. But his views have the serious defect that he ascribes value to two classes of things which have little or no value – to things which are, in both cases, necessary constituents of valuable wholes, but which seem nevertheless to have no value in themselves. The first class consists of things which his definition of 'good' binds him to consider good – things which are really worthy of love: it is certainly good *to love* all such things, but only *some* of them are also good *themselves*; as an example of those which are not, I have already mentioned inanimate beautiful objects. As examples of the second class of things to which he certainly ascribes more value than they possess, we may take *pleasure* and *knowledge*. This error is even more grave than the last, since it compels him to ascribe value to things which are not merely indifferent but positively bad; and it follows not from his definition of 'good' but from a principle which I have not yet mentioned. This principle is that no one thing is better than another, unless it contains a greater number of good or a less number of bad parts. In this book, indeed, Brentano is even inclined to maintain that all judgements of intrinsic superiority are purely *analytic* – that 'better' merely *means* 'having a greater number of good parts'. But the translator tells us, in the Appendix, that he has now definitely abandoned this view: he now recognises 'that it is by no means evident from analysis that one good plus another is preferable to each of these goods taken singly'.[2] We are told, however, that Brentano has also abandoned the views with which we are now concerned – the views that, *as a matter of fact*, not only are two good things always better than one of them, but also that no one thing is better than another *unless* it contains more good parts. From the second of these principles it would follow that all good things, which are not composed of good parts, are *equally good*; and also that any quantity of pleasure is one such good thing. For it is certainly true that a greater pleasure in a very beautiful thing is sometimes better than a less pleasure in the same; and, this being so, it follows from Brentano's principle, that what differentiates the former from the latter – namely the

---

2. First English edition, p. 122n. This remark is in a biographical sketch, not by the translator, Cecil Hague, but by Brentano's student and friend, Anton Marty, which Hague appended, with no attribution to Marty, to his English edition. It is not included in the second English edition.

excess of pleasure – is good in itself. And similarly it is certain that one state may be better than another, where it only differs from that other in containing more   knowledge; and hence it would also follow that *some* knowledge, at all events, was good in itself. But the principle from which these results follow is certainly false: that it is in an error, and a grave one, may be shown by taking a case in which it would prove to be good what is in fact positively bad in a high degree. For Brentano is bound to hold that a very great pleasure in what is wholly bad, but not very bad, is not merely *better* than a less pleasure in the same, but positively good. He must even, if the bad thing be purely imaginary, pronounce it to be *better* than a less pleasure in an imaginary thing which is wholly good. In fact, however, a great pleasure in what is bad seems certainly to be *both* a great positive evil *and worse* than a less pleasure in the same. It follows that one thing may be better or worse than another, even though it does not contain more good or bad parts respectively; and hence that the facts admitted above give us no reason for pronouncing either pleasure or knowledge to be good in themselves. It does *not* follow, indeed, that pleasure is *not* good in itself; only, if it is good, we must also dispute the principle that two good things are always better than one of them – must deny, at least, that the value of the whole formed by them is always equal to the sum of the values of its parts.

The third great excellence in Brentano's ethics is his clear recognition of the distinction between what is merely *a means* to good and what is good in itself, and of the fact that the one supreme rule of practical ethics is that we *ought* always *to do* that which will cause the whole state of the Universe to have as much *intrinsic* value as possible – that for an action to be 'right' in the ordinary sense of the word, it is both sufficient and necessary that it should be a *means* to this result. He states the consequences of this principle very clearly in several points in which they are frequently overlooked. In particular, the text of the book, which consists of a lecture delivered before the Vienna Law Society in 1889, under the title 'The Natural Sanction for Law and Morality', is arranged with a view to showing, as against the relativistic views of Ihering, that, although there is no 'natural law', in the sense of laws of which the *knowledge* is either 'innate' or universal, the above principle is a '*natural* moral law' in the sense that it is *universally valid*; and that all positive laws have 'natural sanction' or are *truly binding*, if, and only if, their observance does have the best possible results.

The book consists of this lecture, together with a number of notes, of much greater bulk than the text, and Appendices [including] a review, 'Miklosich on Subjectless Propositions', which first appeared as a feuilleton in the *Vienna Evening Post*. The longest note, which consists of a criticism on Sigwart's theory of judgement, is, like the Appendix on Miklosich and some other long notes, relevant to the subject of the lecture only in that it serves to confirm Brentano's theory of judgement and of the analogy between belief in the true and love of the good. Many notes, again, are directly historical. Nevertheless, owing to Brentano's extraordinary clearness with regard to the precise relevance of all he says, the contents of the book are far more easy to grasp than is usual with books of the most regular form: there seems no reason to wish that he had arranged his matter differently . . .

15 Was G.E. Moore Mistaken About Brentano?[1]

Gabriel Franks

'When this book had been already completed,' G.E. Moore states in the Preface of *Principia Ethica*, 'I found, in Brentano's *Origin of the Knowledge of Right and Wrong*, opinions far more closely resembling my own than those of any other ethical writer with whom I am acquainted.'[2] When he later wrote a review of Brentano's book for the *International Journal of Ethics*, he praised it in the following terms:

> This is a far better discussion of the most fundamental principles of ethics than any others with which I am acquainted . . . In almost all points in which [Brentano] differs from any of the great historical systems, he is in the right; and he differs with regard to the most fundamental points of moral philosophy. Of all previous moralists, Sidgwick alone is in any respect superior to him; and Sidgwick was never clearly aware of the wide and important bearings of his discovery in this one respect. Brentano is both clearer and more profound and he avoids Sidgwick's two fundamental errors. It would be difficult to exaggerate the importance of this work.[3]

The parallels which Moore discovered between his ethical notions and those of Franz Brentano are matched by an even more striking similarity in the role they played and position they held in the development of modern British and Austro-German philosophical schools respectively. Like Moore,

1. Reprinted from *The New Scholasticism*, vol. 43 (1969), pp. 252–68.
2. G.E. Moore, *Principia Ethica* (Cambridge, 1903); latest reprint 1959, p. xi. This work will henceforth be referred to as *PE*.
3. G.E. Moore, review of Franz Brentano's *The Origin of the Knowledge of Right and Wrong* (see above, pp. 00).
   The main part of Franz Brentano's *Vom Ursprung sittlicher Erkenntnis* consists of a lecture which Brentano delivered in 1889 before the Vienna Law Society under the title 'The Natural Sanction for Law and Morality'. In its published form, it has been augmented with numerous notes and appendices. The third German edition (Leipzig, 1934) contains an Introduction and many notes which were written by Oskar Kraus. (The second English edition, *The Origin of our Knowledge of Right and Wrong*, ed. Roderick M. Chisholm (London and new York, 1969) will be cited throughout.)

Brentano marked a turning point in philosophical thought. Some historians trace to Brentano the roots of both logical positivism – and its aftermath – (through his pupil, Alexius Meinong, who in turn influenced Russell and Wittgenstein) and existentialism (through his pupil Husserl).[4] Oskar Kraus, editor and annotator of the third German edition of Brentano's *Vom Ursprung sittlicher Erkenntnis*, maintains that the works of Max Scheler and Nicolai Hartmann in the field of ethics are traceable directly to Brentano, however much they may disagree with some of his basic tenets.

Just as Moore initiated the revolt against the Anglo-Hegelian idealism which dominated English thought at the close of the nineteenth century, and favoured a return to typically English empiricism, so Brentano fostered a return to the pre-Kantian tradition of German philosophy. He looked to Aristotle and even scholasticism for inspiration, but Descartes, Hume, and Leibnitz also influenced him.[5] In fact, it has been said that Brentano is largely responsible for the circumstance that so much in recent philosophy resembles the eighteenth century in its prime, rather than any part of the nineteenth. While he had much in common with empiricism, he rejected much of Hume, but with quite original tools utterly unlike those of Kant.[6]

Principles of Brentano's philosophy

The heart of Brentano's philosophical system is his psychology, which in turn centres about the revived scholastic theory of intentional existence which, however, he considerably modified. On his view the essence of a knowledgeable soul is to refer. Our experience is always *of* something other than itself, and we are acquainted with ourselves only and always in the exercise of this referential function. Our 'inwardness' is the inwardness of 'outward'-directed beings.[7]

According to Brentano's psychology, all concepts are derived from certain concrete impressions (as Hume thought) and the concept of good is no exception.[8] But the impression from which it arises is not one with physical content (*physischer Inhalt*) but rather one with psychic content (*psychischer Inhalt*). Impressions (*Vorstellungen*) with physical contents are distinguished by the fact that they show us sensory qualities while those with psychic content refer to consciousness,[9] which is, according to his

4. Cf. John Laird, *Recent Philosophy* (London, 1936), pp. 199ff. and 183, and also Ueberweg, *Grundriß der Geschichte der Philosophie* (Berlin, 1928), Teil IV, p. 497: 'Ausser seiner engeren Schule (Marty, Kraus) sind auch Husserl, Meinong, und Stumpf von ihm ausgegangen.'

5. Ueberweg, *Grudriß* . . ., and Laird, *Recent Philosophy*.

6. Laird, *Recent Philosophy*.

7. *Recent Philosophy*, p. 110. Cf. Brentano, *Origin*, par. 19.

8. *Origin*, p. 13: 'This concept [of the good], like all our others, has its origin in certain intuitive presentations.'

9. *Origin*, p. 14: 'The common feature of everything psychological, often referred to, unfortunately, by the misleading term "consciousness", consists in a relation that we bear to an object.'

notion of consciousness, an intentional relationship to an object, which may be only internal and not real.[10]

According to his theory of psychic impressions or representations (*Vorstellungen*), which he derives from Descartes' Third Meditation, these representations are to be divided into three main classes. The first of these are the images of things, which Brentano calls 'representations in the widest sense', and of which Descartes had written: 'Some of these [thoughts] are like the images of things and to these alone does the name "idea" properly belong, as when I think of a man, or of a chimera, or of heaven, or of an angel, or of God.' The second class of psychic impressions is that of judgements (*Urteile*), which adds a second intentional relationship to the object imagined, namely that of affirmation or denial (*Anerkennen oder Verwerfen*). Finally, the third class is that of the emotions, whose characteristic intentional relationship is that of loving or hating (*Lieben oder Hassen*) or, differently expressed, being pleased or displeased (*Geffallen oder Missfallen*).[11]

The last two classes of impressions share in common the characteristic that they can be right or wrong. Having established his psychological groundwork, Brentano says:

> Now we have reached the point where the concepts of good and bad, as well as those of true and false, which we have been seeking, have their source. We say that something is true when its relation of affirmation is right. We call something good when its affirmation of love is right. That which is to be loved with a right love, that which is worthy of love, is good in the widest sense of the word.[12]

Development of the principles

Brentano, like Moore, divides the notion of good into good in itself and good as a means, and like him, considers the former to be fundamental, and the latter derivative.[13] Pursuing further the notion as to what desires are characterised as right and why, he again draws a parallel between judging and valuing. Just as there are some judgements which are blind, instinctive, prejudicial, and open to error, so are there judgements of a higher sort, which are self-evident. The principle of non-contradiction, the judgement that I now think and will, are examples of such self-evident judgements. The distinctive note of such self-evident judgements is not their degree of conviction, but their clarity.[14]

10. *Origin*, p. 14.
11. *Origin*, p. 15 and note p. 50ff.
12. *Origin*, p. 18: 'And now we have found what we have been looking for. We have arrived at the source of our concepts of the good and the bad, along with that of our concepts of the true and the false. We call a thing *true* when the affirmation relating to it is correct. In the broadest sense of the term, the good is that which is worthy of love, that which can be loved with a love that is correct.'
13. *Origin*, p. 18.
14. *Origin*, pp. 26–7.

Analogous to such judgements, the rightness of whose affirmation is evident, there are, according to Brentano, cases of love and hatred, whose rightness is equally self-evident. He gives three examples of such value judgements: (1) All men naturally seek knowledge; no one seeks error for its own sake;[15] (2) Joy is preferred to sorrow; (3) The love of good is good, and the love of evil is evil.[16] These are, of course, not the only good things, for they are probably legion, and we have no assurance that we can know them.

The notion of good now having been established as that which is rightly loved, the groundwork is ready for discerning the goal which is the criterion of ethical behaviour: 'the highest practical good'. This brings us to his concept of 'the better'.

According to Brentano, 'better' does not mean (as many have supposed) 'that which is rightly loved with a greater love', but rather 'that which is rightly preferred'. Some of these preferences, like some judgements of truth and good, are self-evident. Among the self-evident preferences are the following: (1) Something good must be preferred to something bad; (2) The existence of a good thing is to be preferred to its non-existence, and the non-existence of a bad thing is to be preferred to its existence; (3) A whole good is to be preferred to something equivalent to one of its parts.[17]

From (2) Brentano derives the principle[18] that a whole is as good as the sum of its parts. It is to this principle (borrowed, as he mentions, from Aristotle), that he looks for the final and concrete developments of his ethical theory. For while it is true that self-evident judgements about good and preferences are few, and though ethics would be extremely vague if restricted to such principles, yet he considers them adequate for the foundation of a utilitarianism which will fill the gaps in practical ethics.[19] This utilitarianism is neither hedonistic nor egoistic; it rests on the principle that the highest practical good – whether our own or that of another – is that which is to be preferred and furthered.[20]

Brentano's principle is stated in the following passage:

> After having seen how much the necessity of fulfilling desire is involved in the attaining of the highest practical good, we must also examine the origin of duty. The union among men, which renders possible a division of labours, is the only condition which makes feasible the attainment of the highest possible good, as we have recognised it. Man is therefore morally bound to live in society. And it is easily demonstrable, that restrictions must be laid on everyone's free actions, so that one person will not be more of a hindrance than an aid to another; and furthermore, these restrictions (as usual, there is much here which springs from mere natural considerations)

15. Example furnished by Aristotle in the first lines of his *Metaphysics*.
16. *Origin*, p. 20.
17. *Origin*, pp. 26–9.
18. This principle would seem to follow more logically from (3).
19. *Origin*, p. 32.
20. Cf. Kraus' note, *Origin*, p. 33.

require a more precise determination and more thorough-going guarantee by governmental sanction.[21]

Moore's criticism of Brentano in Principia Ethica

As has already been mentioned, Moore wrote two criticisms of Brentano, the first being that contained in the Preface of *Principia Ethica*, the second being a book review published in the *International Journal of Ethics*.[22] The very concise evaluation in *Principia Ethica* mentions four points of agreement between Moore and Brentano, and several of disagreement:

> Brentano appears to agree with me completely (1) in regarding all ethical propositions as defined by the fact that they predicate a single unique objective concept; (2) in dividing such propositions sharply into the same two kinds; (3) in holding that the first kind are incapable of proof; and (4) with regard to the kind of evidence which is necessary and relevant to the proof of the second kind. But he regards the fundamental ethical concept as being, not the simple one which I denote by 'good' but the complex one which I have taken to define 'beautiful'; and he does not recognise, but even denies by implication, the principle which I have called *the principle of organic unities*. In consequence of these two differences, his conclusions as to what things are good in themselves, also differ very materially from mine. He agrees, however, that there are many different goods, and that the love of good and beautiful objects constitutes an important class among them.[23]

His second point refers to the fact that Brentano, like Moore, divides ethical propositions into those referring to things good in themselves, and to those which are good as a means. As to the third point, namely, that things good in themselves cannot be proved to be such, Moore seems to imply that Brentano, like himself, regards goodness as a quality which can be directly intuited, and that all propositions about things good in themselves are synthetic. It is quite true that the goodness of things as Brentano conceived it cannot be proved, but the reasons why this is so are quite different in Moore's case from those given by Brentano. This is a very important question, which we will examine at length: that for Brentano, what is

---

21. *Origin*, pp. 33–4: 'Now that we have been able to see how so many duties toward the highest practical good arise, let us turn to the source of our legal duties. One indispensable condition for bringing about the highest practical good is that we so live that a division of labour will be possible. It is morally necessary, therefore, that man live in society. From this it follows that each person should be to a certain extent restricted in his activities; otherwise he will bring more harm than good to those around him. These restrictions can be made definite only by positive legislation (though much can be accomplished merely by the simple exercises of good sense), and they need the security and support of public authority.'

22. Ch. 14 above.

23. *PE*, p. xi.

experienced is not the goodness of things, but only the rightness of our judgements about goodness. The fourth point refers to the fact that both Brentano and Moore agree that good actions are determined by their relation to intrinsic good.

Moore seems to have been quite wrong, however, in maintaining that Brentano identifies the intrinsically good with the beautiful. As a matter of fact, this is a point which Brentano specifically denies.[24] We shall show how Moore was led to this conclusion by a false interpretation of Brentano's use of the term 'right'.

Moore's criticism in his book review

The review which Moore wrote of Brentano's book for the *International Journal of Ethics* contains six points of comparison between their respective views. (1) Moore praises Brentano for recognising that 'all truths of the form 'This is good in itself' are logically independent of any truth about what exists'.[25] (2) Nevertheless, he maintains that Brentano is wrong in supposing that the conception 'rightly loved' or 'worthy of love' is the fundamental ethical concept which we mean by 'good in itself'.[26] (3) He holds that Brentano is mistaken in identifying the quality of 'rightness' as a psychical content and the perception of it as an impression.[27] (4) He disagrees with Brentano's analysis of 'better'. (5) He says that Brentano 'cannot be too highly praised for insisting that, not only one thing, but very many different things have intrinsic value', but points out that Brentano's false definition of 'good in itself' led him to accept many things as having intrinsic value, which *de facto*, have none.[28] (6) The third great excellence in Brentano's ethics is his clear recognition of the distinction between what is merely a means to good and what is good in itself, and of the fact that the one supreme rule of practical ethics is that we ought always to do that which will cause the whole state of the Universe to have as much intrinsic good as possible.[29]

The second and third points merit closer examination, because they not only present the areas in which Moore disagrees with Brentano, but also those in which Moore has least understood Brentano. In addition, a consideration of these questions will reveal that there were differences much greater than those recognised by Moore between the two systems.

Moore identifies 'good' and 'right'

Let us examine, first of all, Moore's criticism of Brentano's analysis of

24. *Origin*, p.10.
25. Ch. 14 above, p. 176.
26. Ch. 14 above, p. 177.
27. Ch. 14 above, p. 178.
28. Ch. 14 above, p. 180.
29. Ch. 14 above, p. 181.

'intrinsic goodness' as that which it is 'right to love'. Moore interprets 'right to love' seemingly in the light of his own principles, and as a result of this interpretation, reaches some strange conclusions about Brentano's philosophy which are hardly justified. The following passage illustrates Moore's principal error:

> Brentano is wrong in supposing that the conception 'rightly loved' or 'worthy of love' is the fundamental ethical concept which we mean by 'good in itself'. Sidgwick was right in holding that that concept is unanalysable; and it is, in fact, the concept which Brentano denotes by the word 'right', when he says that a thing is good in itself, if the love of it would be right. Brentano recognises *two* very important concepts when he recognised both the concept of what it is right to love and of the *rightness* which belongs to the love of such things; and the question which of these is properly denoted by the words good in itself might seem to be merely a verbal question. But it is not a merely verbal question, if, as Brentano rightly does, we take what is good in itself in the highest possible degree to be that of which it is our *duty* to promote the existence. For whereas the degree in which a thing possesses the quality which he calls 'right' must be taken into account in considering what is that greatest possible good which it is our duty to effect, the degree in which things are 'worthy to be loved' is not a measure of our duty to effect their existence. It is certain that many things, e.g. inanimate beautiful objects, possess the quality of being worthy to be loved, in a higher degree than they do that of 'rightness'; it may even be doubted whether they possess the latter at all. And it is our duty to effect that which is the most 'right' possible not that which is most worthy to be loved.[30]

Moore's first error is the identification of 'good in itself' with 'right', instead of the whole complex, 'right to love'. It seems that Moore was led into this error by virtue of the previous identification he had made in *Principia Ethica* of Brentano's 'good', which is 'right to love' with his own concept of 'beauty', which is that which it is 'good to admire'.[31] If to admire is equivalent to 'to love', then 'right' should be equivalent to 'good'. By making this identification Moore has lost the most obvious interpretation of 'right', namely, that in Brentano's sense it means 'correct'.

Moore's interpretation of what Brentano meant by right led him to attribute certain doctrines to Brentano which would indeed have followed from such an interpretation, but which conclusions were at least not explicitly affirmed by Brentano. Thus he interprets Brentano's definition of truth as that which is 'rightly believed' as meaning 'that which it is good to believe'.[32] Well might he doubt whether it is good to believe all truths! On the other hand, Moore's interpretation has the merit of justifying the notion

---

30. Ch. 14 above, p. 177.
31. *PE*, p. 201.
32. Ch. 14 above, p. 177.

of obligation which Brentano later injects without basis into his system.[33] If 'right to love' means merely 'correct to love' it can be said to imply 'justified to love', but hardly 'obligatory to love'.

Origin of the concept of rightness

In criticising Brentano's view that 'rightness' arises from impressions with psychical content, Moore seems to take rightness in the sense we have been maintaining he should have understood it, and in this way came quite close to recognising the most fundamental difference between himself and Brentano. He states that:

> This doctrine may be perfectly true in one sense; but in the sense naturally conveyed by the words it includes a most important error. Obviously the conception of 'good', as Brentano defines it, cannot be derived merely from the experience of *loving*, but only from that of 'right loving' – from the perception of the *rightness* of love: its *origin* cannot be merely the perception of a love which *is* right, but in which this quality is not perceived, it can only be a perception in which it is itself *contained*. But whereas the experience of loving *has* all the marks which are suggested by calling it a 'concrete impression of psychical content', the 'experience of right loving' – i.e. the perception of the *rightness* of a love – has not. The quality of 'rightness' is *not* an impression in the ordinary sense of these words. A single mark is sufficient to distinguish it; by a 'psychical content' we always mean at least *an existent*, and 'rigthness' is not an existent. Brentano is certainly not sufficiently attentive to this distinction between the experience of loving and the experience of right loving. He says that he belongs to the 'empirical school'; and he here shows himself to be under the influence of empiricism, in a sense in which empiricism is certainly erroneous.[34]

It is true that Brentano does not always make it clear just what is the impression with psychical content which gives rise to the concept of good. In note 27 of his book, for example, Brentano speaks of that which distinguishes self-evident judgements as being an 'inner quality belonging to the act of insight itself', and identifies this quality with their clarity. In paragraph 27, in the Cecil Hague translation, that which characterises those tastes and pleasures which are analogous to self-evidence in the sphere of judgement is their *rightness*, but in note 31, in which the translator explains this phrase, he notes that this is how he has rendered the German phrase, '*als richtig characterisiert*'. But there is a great difference between the saying that the impression which gives rise to the concept of right love is their quality of rightness, and of saying that this quality is that they are characterised as being right. And it should be equally clear that an

33. Brentano first mentions duty in *Origin*, p. 33.
34. See Kraus' note, *Origin*, p. 75.

existential or value judgement may be psychologically characterised as being right without actually being right at all.

Differences and qualifications

Brentano's manner of setting forth his ideas, together with the inexactness of Hague's translation apparently led Moore to overlook the most important difference between his value theory and that of Brentano. For Moore, intrinsic good is actually to be found in things – it is a quality (non-natural, to be sure) which is in the objective order of things, and is discovered by intuition. But according to Brentano, this is either not clear, or is denied. In the notes which he wrote for the third German edition, Oskar Kraus points out that Brentano had not really made up his mind about this point when he wrote *Ursprung*, and actually makes contradictory statements.

This is evident if notes 23 and 25 are compared. In the latter, Brentano criticises the correspondence theory of truth, but admits that the scholastic formula of 'adequatio rei et intellectus' (roughly: a similarity between the thing and the intellect) is true 'in a certain sense', and states that 'concepts of existence and non-existence are the correlates of the concepts of the truth of (univocally) affirmative or negative judgements'.[35] On this view, 'good' should be a correlate of 'right to love', or rather, 'rightness' would be, on Moore's view.

Kraus maintains however that this view does not represent Brentano's 'definitive and correct' teaching. Not only did Brentano reject the correspondence theory altogether in his later published and unpublished works, but even in note 23 (corresponding to paragraph 20) of *Ursprung*, which was concerned with Sigwart, 'reasons for the denial of the theory of adequation are given in detail'.[36] Even in note 25 itself, Kraus points out that Brentano states that 'Whether I say, an affirmative judgement is true, or its object is existing; whether I say a negative judgement is true or its object is non-existing, I say one and the same thing in both cases.'[37] Kraus states that this opinion 'is not correct because existence and non-existence are correlates of the truth of affirmative and negative judgements, but because these linguistic expression (e.g. the sentences: "The judgement that 'There is a sun' is true" and "A sun exists") mean or express the same thing. The proposition that an affirmative judgement is true, means the

35. *Origin*, p. 74: 'The concepts of *existence* and *non-existence*, respectively, are correlates of the concepts of the truth of the (unitary) affirmative judgement and the truth of the (unitary) negative judgement.'

36. CF. *Ursprung*, p. 61 (not included in the second English edition), 'In der Anmerkung 23 ... wird die Ablehnung der Adequationstheorie ausführlich begründet.'

37. *Origin*, note, pp. 74–5: 'To say that an affirmative judgement is true is to say no more nor less than that its object is existent; to say that a negative judgement is true is to say no more nor less than that its object is non-existent. It is one and the same logical principle that tells us, in the one case, that either the simple affirmative judgement or the simple negative judgement is true, and in the other case, that the object of the judgement is either existent or non-existent.'

same thing as to say that an intuitive judgement about the object of that judgement could be nothing but affirmative.'[38]

To put the whole consideration in a slightly different light, Kraus notes in the Preface which he wrote as editor of the third German edition of *Ursprung*, that 'good' and 'value' are no more properties or characteristics of things than existence. Even less can there possibly be a Platonic 'kingdom of eternal truths' or a 'kingdom of eternal values' as some modern German philosophers, notably Nicolai Hartmann, have concluded.[39]

Kraus raised an objection in a letter to Brentano, which he reproduces in the first appendix to the third German edition of *Ursprung*. He asks if it is not true that 'It is to be taken with a grain of salt that, in ethics, we number ourselves among the empiricists?'[40] The reason he gives for this conclusion is that ethics is not derived from concepts (*Begriffe*), but from insights (*Erkenntnisse*), themselves derived from concepts, and are merely analytic and *a priori* in much the same way in which mathematical concepts are.[41]

Brentano replies that whether he is to be considered an empiricist or not depends on how one understands the term.[42] Ethical concepts are derived from experience, yet this is also true of mathematical concepts, which are not usually considered as being empirical. Brentano denies, however, that there is a strict parallel between mathematical concepts and ethical concepts, for although they are both in a sense *a priori*, ethical propositions are not merely analytical in the way e.g. $2 + 1 = 3$ is. A purely intellectual being would recognise this mathematical truth, but would not realise the self-evident truth of the proposition that 'knowledge is good' because, to arrive at such knowledge 'still another knowledge [other than that of the meaning of the terms] is necessary, namely that out of the concept of

38. Kraus adds to *Ursprung*, note 25, p. 62 (not included in the second English edition): 'It is certainly correct . . . but not because existence and non-existence are correlates of the truth of affirmative and negative judgements, but because these linguistic expressions (e.g. the propositions "The judgement 'There is a sun' is true;" and "A sun exists") both say or mean the same thing.'
Moore's affirmation of the correspondence theory of truth is very evident in the article 'Is Existence a Predicate?', originally published in the *Proceedings of the Aristotelian Society*, supplementary volume 15 (1936), pp. 175–88, and republished in *Logic and Language*, Second Series (Oxford, 1953), ed. Anthony Flew, pp. 82–94.

39. *Origin*, p. 161.

40. *Origin*, p. 111: 'We call ourselves empiricists in ethics, but this is to be taken with a grain of salt.'

41. *Origin*, p. 111: 'The concepts of *good* and *preferable* have their source in inner experience, in just the way in which the concept of *necessity* has its source in inner experience – and just as the concepts of *large* and *larger* have their source in so-called "external experience". But ethics is not based upon concepts; it is based upon certain *cognitions* (for example, the cognition that there can be no knowledge which, as such, is worthy of hate). These cognitions are acquired through consideration of the concepts that they presuppose. Hence they are "analytic" or "*a priori*" in exactly the way in which the axioms of mathematics are "analytic" or "*a priori*". The only difference between the two cases is that the concepts of mathematics – those of geometry in particular – are "ideal concepts" or fictions.'

42. *Origin*, p. 111: 'Obviously the answer depends upon the sense in which we take "empirical".'

knowledge, a love toward it arises, which is immediately characterised as right'.[43] The reason why a purely intellectual creature could not have this love is that it is not something contained in the concept of the thing loved.[44]

Brentano's conclusion is that:

> I think it is altogether justified to protest against the notion that the knowledge of the way a love must be lived and experienced must be called empirical. It is rather *a priori*; but at the same time the notion must be denied that the concepts employed are given without perception or apperception, as is indeed always the case. In contrast to many other cases, there is one thing peculiar to this, i.e. that acts of love must also be perceived and apperceived, not only acts of knowledge.[45]

To this Kraus laconically concludes: 'Ethical principles are therefore *a priori*, even according to Brentano.'[46] He believes that this solution assures an objective status to ethics[47] far more capable of resisting ethical scepticism than the 'kingdom of values'.[48]

It is difficult to see how an *a priori* principle which corresponds to no extra-subjective reality is a factor very reassuring to an objective ethic. Certainly we may doubt whether this is all that is meant by the sort of objectivity which Moore praised in his review of Brentano's book.[49] If it is true that a principle which 'follows from' the concept of good – and may, in a certain sense, be called analytic – such as Moore's principle that the good 'ought to be done' or Brentano's that the good is 'rightly loved' may be maintained without reference to extramental reality and yet be termed objective, this cannot be said of the statements about things which are good. And yet Brentano implies that principles of the first sort, and even the logical principle of non-contradiction[50] are 'self-evident' in exactly the same

43. *Origin*, p. 112: 'Thus still another experience is needed. The concept of knowledge must give rise to an act of love, and this love, just because it does arise in this way, is experienced as being correct.'

44. Cf. *Origin*, pp. 111–12: 'Now it is certain that the concept of *good* cannot be included in everything that is good;...."Knowledge is good" is not like the law of contradiction; the concepts, just by themselves, do not enable us to see that it is a true proposition.'

45. *Origin*, p. 113: 'And so I think we should protest against calling this knowledge empirical – despite the fact that, in order to acquire the knowledge, it is necessary to feel and experience love. The knowledge that we have here is *a priori*. But when we say that a certain type of knowledge is *a priori*, we do *not* mean to imply that the concepts which it involves can be given without perception and apperception. What distinguishes the present type of *a priori* knowledge from the others is the fact that one must perceive and apperceive certain acts of *love* and not merely certain intellectual cognitions.'

46. *Ursprung*, p. 112n (not included in second English edition); 'Die ethischen Prinzipien sind also nach Brentano a priori.'

47. *Origin*, pp. 9–10, 30–1.

48. Kraus, 'Introduction to 1934 Edition', p. 161.

49. Ch. 14 above, p. 177.

50. *Origin*, pp. 76–83.

way as value judgements about good things, for both sorts of judgements are rendered clear solely by the fact that they are characterised as right.[51]

Moore himself has hinted that an *a priori* principle may be necessary for the recognition of the goodness in things,[52] but he has always maintained (if we overlook his brief flirtation with the emotive theory of the logical positivists)[53] that intrinsic good is really intrinsic, and in no way depends on anyone's subjective state for its existence.

Conclusion

The findings of this study of the relationship between Brentano and Moore may be summed up as follows: Although there are similarities between the two ethical systems, the similarities are not as great as either Moore or his critics have thought them to be. This is true principally because (1) Moore consistently misunderstood the sense in which Brentano uses 'right', thus involving himself in a maze of contradictions and (2) their different epistemologies led them to have quite different ideas about what is meant by 'good in itself', and about how we know that some things are good.

51. *Origin*, pp. 75–6.

52. Cf. G.E. Moore, 'An Autobiography', p. 66, and 'A Reply to My Critics', p. 592 – both in Paul Arthur Schilpp (ed.), *The Philosophy of G.E. Moore*, 2nd ed. (New York, 1952).

53. In his 'A Reply to My Critics', in *The Philosophy of G.E. Moore*, p. 546, Moore wavered toward acceptance of the emotive theory of ethics of the logical positivists, but in a personal converstaion I had with him, on 7 September 1955, he told me that he had definitely rejected such a view. This rejection is confirmed by A.C. Ewing, who has recently reported that at some date after 1953, Moore said that 'he still held to his old view [that ethical statements have cognitive meaning], and further that he could not imagine whatever in the world had induced him to say that he was almost equally inclined to hold the other view' (*Mind*, vol. 71 (1962), 251).

16   Franz Brentano as Reist[1]

Tadeusz Kotarbinski

The term 'reism' was coined when I wrote my book on formal logic and the methodology of science entitled *Gnosiology*, which first appeared in 1929.[2] Let me quote what I wrote at the end of chapter 1, paragraph 12, of the first part of this book,

> We have in turn to concern ourselves with that category of *things*. At the present stage of the exposition of the subject-matter of this book, it does not call for lengthy explanation. Let us only repeat here that it is in Aristotle that we can trace the distinction, within the category of things, namely, of first and second subtances. Those second substances, universals, are the first to fall victim to eliminating analysis as carried out by nominalism; it must be said it was only concerning them that nominalism succeeded in convincingly proving their non-existence by a *reductio ad absurdum*. On the other hand, first substances, things in the primary sense of the word, and for us simply things, fared in exactly the opposite way, since the entire reduction of categories, as outlined above, took place precisely to their benefit. That reduction completed it turns out that there remains only that category of objects – that is, there are no objects other than things, in other words, every object is a thing, whatever exists is a thing. When the metaphorical, abbreviated, picturesque, in a word, substitutive, formulations are eliminated and replaced by the basic formulations, interpreted literally, the latter will include no phrases which would appear to be names of something other than things. They will be statements about things only. But it must be emphasised here that by things we do not mean only inorganic solids. Things are inorganic and organic, inanimate and animate, and 'endowed with psychic life' – that is, they are both things in the narrower sense of the words, and persons, too. So much for the reduction of categories of objects to the category of things. The stand taken in favour of such a reduction might be called *reism*.

---

1. Translated from the French by Linda L. McAlister and Margarete Schättle. Reprinted from the *Revue Internationale de Philosophie*, vol. 20, no. 78 (1966), pp. 459–76.

2. *Elementy Teorii Poznania, Logiki Formalnej i Metodologii Nauk* (Lvov, 1929; 2nd ed. Wroclaw, Warsaw and Cracow, 1961). English translation, *Gnosiology, The Scientific Approach to the Theory of Knowledge*, trans. Olgierd Wojtasiewicz, translation ed. G. Bidwell and C. Pinder (Oxford and New York, 1966).

At the time I wrote this I was unaware that the scope and substance of this reism had already been formulated and put forth earlier by Franz Brentano, especially in the appendices to the supplement to his major work *Psychology From an Empirical Standpoint*. This supplement, entitled *The Classification of Mental Phenomena* appeared in 1911 together with the above-mentioned appendices. In 1924 (Vol. I) and 1925 (Vol. II), after the death of the author the second edition of the complete work appeared, supplemented by new additions, notably by a number of dictations by the author between 1915 and 1917, after he had lost his sight.

How is it possible that I did not know of Brentano's thought when I wrote my *Gnosiology*? I was, after all, a student of Professor Kazimierz Twardowski, who was himself a student of Brentano's. There is a very simple explanation of this puzzle. Brentano was not a very faithful follower of his own doctrines; on the contrary, in his later years he completely changed his whole point of view. Therefore his followers went in two different directions: one group continued to work on the typology and the structural analysis of so-called intentional entities which are intangible objects perceived only through the act of thinking; the other group (by adopting the essential sense of the word 'exist') was converted to the belief that things are the only existing objects and, at the same time, are the only things that can be the objects of thought. The second group, Brentano's reist followers, consisted, among others, of Oskar Kraus, editor and annotater of the above-mentioned second edition of the *Psychology*, and also the editor and annotator of numerous posthumous writings of the master. The first group consisted of Meinong, Husserl and many others, among them Twardowski; his treatise on 'acts and products' shows, above all, that Twardowski firmly maintained a nonreist point of view in the controversy between logic and ontology.

There are also other reasons why I did not come across Brentano's reist writings in the course of my readings. During that period I had very little interest in scientific psychology; I devoted myself, rather, to the study of formal logic which displayed the anti-psychologist attitude which it still exemplifies today. No one who followed this line of thought would have dreamed of looking for ideas in the supplement to a work on psychology by an author who was such a vigorous believer in the thesis that psychology is the basis for philosophy as a whole, including logic. In the Gospels it is written 'Search and ye shall find', and this is true in a certain sense. It is also usually true that if you do not look you will not find, but just the opposite happened to me. I found a predecessor in the field of reism without looking for one. After the publication of my *Gnosiology* I received a letter from Professor Twardowski, pointing out to me that my reism had been conceived in the above-mentioned supplements and the appendices to Brentano's *Psychology*.

But even Brentano was not the first reist, and he was aware of this, because he cited Leibniz on the subject. Leibniz had said in his *Nouveaux Essais*, Book 2, chapter XIII, para. 1, in the words of Philalethes [*sic*]:[3]

---

3. These words are actually said by Theophile; cf. Leibniz, *Sammtliche Schriften und Briefe*, VI (Berlin 1962) p. 217.

It is rather the *concretum*, as, e.g. something known, warm, shining, which comes to our mind, and not the *abstractions* or qualities (because it is they which are substantial in the object and not the ideas) such as knowledge, warmth, light, etc. which are much more difficult to understand. One might even question whether these accidents are true beings, if they are not most of the time simply relations. We also know that these abstractions cause the greatest difficulty if one wants to examine them closely; as people know who are acquainted with the Scholastics, in whom the greatest difficulties occur all at once, if one is ready to exclude the abstract beings, and one decides to talk only of concreta and to admit in the demonstrations of science only those terms which represent substantial objects.

On the basis of this quotation, with reference to the term *concretum* which is used here, I propose the term 'concretism' which I have often substituted for the term *reism*, at least since 1958, because those who are somewhat familiar with philosophical terminology tend to confuse the term 'reism' with the term 'realism', which has another meaning.

But enough of preambles. What we are concerned with is what Brentano taught, and the words he used to formulate his observations. For this purpose, the best method is simply to re-read the extremely significant article contained in one of the appendices to the *Classification of Mental Phenomena*, mentioned above, which dates from 1911, entitled 'On Genuine and Fictitious Objects'. Here is the translation of the fragments which are of interest to us:

All mental references refer to things.

In many cases, the things to which we refer do not exist. But we are accustomed to saying that they then having being as objects. This is a loose use of the verb 'to be', which we permit with impunity for the sake of convenience, just as we allow ourselves to speak of the sun 'rising' and 'setting'.

Especially in connection with the mental act of making judgements, there has been talk of a content of judgement as well as an object. If I judge, 'A centaur does not exist', it is said that the object is a centaur, but that the content of the judgement is that a centaur does not exist, or the non-existence of a centaur.

A content is never presented in the sense of being object of the presentation . . . But absolutely the only thing which is presented is a person who is making the judgement concerned, and we judge that insofar as we are thinking of such a person, we are thinking of someone who judges correctly. Strictly speaking, therefore, we are not even expressing ourselves quite accurately if we say we deny that the content of a judgement exists. We ought rather to say we deny that anything exists for which the word 'content' is a name, just as words like 'of' and 'but' have no meaning by themselves and do not name anything. 'An of does not exist', 'A but does not exist', make no more sense than 'A Poturi-Nulongon does not exist'. But it does, indeed, make sense to say, 'There is no thing which is named by the preposition "of" or the conjunction "but" (pp. 293–4).

Hence we are certain that . . . nothing else can ever be, like a thing, that to which we mentally refer as an object – neither the present, past nor future . . . nor existence and non-existence, nor necessity . . . neither possibility nor impossibility . . . neither truth nor falsity . . . nor good nor bad. Nor can the so-called actuality . . . or Form . . . of which Aristotle speaks, and which we express in our language by means of such abstractions as redness, shape, human nature, and the like, even be the objects of a mental reference . . . (p. 294).

. . . anyone who studies carefully a case in which one might be inclined to assume the contrary, will discover that we always have things as objects in those cases too . . . And he will discover further that for every sentence which seems to have one of the items just mentioned as its subject or predicate, he can form an equivalent sentence in which subject and predicate are replaced by things. Leibniz knew this, particularly as concerns the so-called *nomina abstracta* . . . (p. 294).

This is not to deny that in many cases the fiction that we can have something other than a real thing as an object . . . proves to be innocuous in logical operations; and in fact these operations can even be facilitated by this fiction because it simplifies our form of expression and even our thought processes themselves. It is similar to the way in which mathematicians benefit from the use of the fiction of numbers less than zero . . . (p. 295).

Thus we can see that in 1911 the basic outline of reism had already taken shape in Brentano's mind. In order to complete this picture it will not be superfluous to mention some thoughts found in Brentano's last writings, dictated in 1917, the year in which the old teacher died.

On 6 January 1917 for example, Brentano returned to the problem of substitution, pointing out 'locutions which make words the subject and predicate of propositions which do not refer to real things in and of themselves', and declaring with respect to all such locutions that there is reason to 'show how each of them is related to the linguistic expressions which express the same thought in such a way that the names of real things become the subject and the predicates' (p. 367). Then he adds, 'Naturally, this variety of locutions arises from complications in our thinking. They make possible abbreviated discourse which is highly advantageous' (p. 367). Here we have the formulation of the programme of verification of the reist conception of language.

But it is neither language nor the sphere of possible objects of thought which preoccupies our philosopher. What perhaps interests him most of all is the sphere of being. We come across very clear statements to that effect. Brentano for instance asks 'whether concepts, presentations . . . judgements, images . . . inferences . . . plans . . . hopes . . . have being in the strict sense' (p. 331). Then, with the same comment as above, he asks 'whether a universal . . . a kind, a species . . . has being in the strict sense of the word'

(p. 331). And his answer is: 'Nevertheless, from the very beginning there seems to be hardly any doubt but that we are dealing with "being" in a loose and improper sense, for reasons which stem from what we have said about being as an object, and at best some new reasons will be added' (p. 332). An example follows; 'It is the sphere not the spherical shape which has being in the strict sense and so too it is the thing which has size not the size' (p. 333).[4]

But let us get back to essentials. We should bear in mind how Brentano saves the generality of indispensable general propositions in the act of thinking despite his conviction that only individuals are things which exist in the strict sense of the word. He believes that only individuals exist, but that one thinks of them in a general way. When we think of a thing, we always think of it in the same way and no other, and other things can be the same. Furthermore, we think of a thing in a more general or less general way, because when we think of it as a thing X or a thing Y, we think of it in a more detailed way and, therefore, in a less general way than when we think of a thing X. Here we have one of Brentano's own statements concerning the above-mentioned questions: 'Without general ideas it would not be possible to have general judgements or demonstrative proof' (p. 315).

'We can still very firmly maintain that everything which is must be individual' (p. 314). 'Whoever is thinking ... something ... is thinking of something as something ... for example ... of a man as a ... living creature' (p. 321). 'Something which is conceived in specific terms is more fully conceived than something conceived in general terms, and ... every new specific differentiation supplements the concept and hence restricts its range' (p. 314). It is superfluous to add that through the introduction of the terms 'idea', 'supplement', 'restriction', Brentano makes use of stylistic liberties in order to abbreviate his explanations. It might be useful also to quote the following passage; 'For example, both the concept of something coloured and the concept of something red are general, but not equally so, for the concept of the coloured comprehends the blue as well as the red, and so on' (p. 320).

Finally we have to discuss something without which Brentano's reism would be incomplete. I am thinking of the problem of a more precise formulation of the meaning and the application of the terms 'thing', 'that which is real', which occupy a crucial position in his system. These terms are used in his texts as synonyms; this can be explained by the fact that 'thing' is *res* in Latin. A number of examples show that in Brentano's sense material bodies are things, e.g. houses, trees, apples. Numerous other examples show that he considers thinking beings to be things. It is clear that bodies and thinking beings are both regarded as concretes, in such a way that the term 'concretum' ('Konkretum') although seldom used, denotes 'thing' and 'that which is real'. The spatial dimension is indicated as the property of the body, the temporal dimension as the property of all that is real. One assumes that it is possible that there are minds which have no spatial dimension. Is it man (a synthesis of the soul and the body) who is

---

4. The next paragraph, in which Kotarbinski comments on certain aspects of his translation of the original German text into French, has been omitted.

this thinking concretum, or is it rather the soul of man? We must remember that Brentano was an ecclesiastic, a Catholic theologian, who, it is true, had revolted against certain elements of the established ecclesiastical order, but who also retained some of the presuppositions typical of minds shaped by this order. He would certainly have rejected as incoherent the concept of thinking bodies.

With regard to spatial concreta, Brentano is preoccupied with two problems: first, can one consider a whole which is composed of things as a thing? Here the answer is an affirmative one: 'So the theory that a number of things cannot be a thing does not seem very acceptable. But the claim that several things can be a thing is no more contradictory than the claim that several groups can be a group, which no one denies' (p. 342). Second, he engaged in long meditations – which are not always easy to summarise – on the topic of whether or not the parts of an entire continuum and especially different points of solid bodies, are things. Here, too, his answer is affirmative: '[In the case of] things which have continuity . . . every part of the continuum is a real thing' (p. 353).

As concerns the question of points, the following statements are conclusive. 'The point which belongs to a spatial continuum existing in terms of its totality is something only in virtue of belonging to the continuum . . . Anyone who conceives of it . . . etc.' Or again: 'The spatial point cannot exist or be conceived of in isolation. It is just as necessary for it to belong to a spatial continuum as it is for the moment of time to belong to a temporal continuum' (p. 356). Brentano's treatment of this difficult topic lacks his usual clarity of exposition. It is as if his mind, too, is struggling here with a lack of clarity. We never get a decisive 'yes' or 'no' to the question, 'Can we say that any part of a continuum which is a thing is itself a thing?' On the other hand, even though no very convincing reasons are given, the reader is informed in a very decisive manner that there exist no actual infinities, that there only exist all kinds of potential infinities. I quote an important affirmation of this point: 'Now it is not difficult to show that it is impossible to assume these without absurdity. Those who assume them would have to deny many self-evident truths, as, for example, that the whole is greater than the part, that a quantity to which nothing is added and from which nothing is taken away does not change . . .' (p. 352).

We are coming to the end of our account of Brentano's reism. Has anything of importance been omitted? To make certain, I looked into the following sources in addition to Oskar Kraus' introductions and comments in the first two volumes of the second edition of *Psychology:* Alfred Kastil's 1951 monograph entitled *Die Philosophie Franz Brentanos*; the comments of these two, so to speak 'grandsons' of Brentano's (they were students of Anton Marty) and true adherents of reism; chapter V of Lucie Gilson's work entitled *Psychologie descriptive selon Franz Brentano* (Paris, 1955); and also a conscientious and well documented article by Gajo Petrovic entitled 'Uz Brentanova o predmetu misljenja', in *Jugoslovenski casopis za filozofiju i sociologiju*, no. 1–2 (Belgrade, 1958). Finally, I skimmed through Jan Srzednicki's work entitled *Franz Brentano's Analysis of Truth* (The Hague, 1965); this work gives a genetic deduction from the earlier to the later phrase of Brentano's views. I am convinced that I have taken into account all the essential elements of his reism. It could be useful, however, to devote a moment to a certain selected problem. One could ask in effect, why, according to this view, the word 'centaur' is the name of something that we can conceive of in thought whereas the words 'substance' or 'judgement', as well as the words 'of' or 'or' are not, despite the fact that none of these words refer to any existing thing. Here is the difference: we can think of a centaur because we would be thinking of a thing, an inexistent one, but a thing all the same, which is not true in the other cases. According to its definition a centaur is a creature which is half man and half horse, i.e. a whole composed, in some fashion or other, of things, just as many things are sometimes composed of parts which are themselves things. Neither 'concept' nor 'or' nor other similar words have such a definition. But let the author explain himself:

> But we have the ... ability to unite the most diverse objects ... with one another whether they are compatible with each other in reality or not, and we thus arrive at an integral object ... For example, I am capable of thinking of ... a white stallion which is black ... (*Psych.*, p. 281).
>
> An objection could be made with respect to *certain absurdities* (*Absurda*) as for example when someone makes a round square an object ... But here too we find that nothing but real elements are employed in the absurd composite, indeed if a cubical sphere did exist in reality, it would be a sphere and cubical and consequently for the one reason and the other, it would be a thing (pp. 346–7).

We have just shown above that Brentano was the first to develop a reistic philosophy, more than a decade before the system had a name. We might ask why he was attracted to this doctrine in particular. In order to answer this question one must be aware, in rough outline at least, of the evolution of his thought.

Brentano was a great student of Aristotle. Aristotle answered 'it is', to the question whether or not it is true that no triangle has angles whose sum is greater than two right angles, as if 'it is' meant the same in this case as it does when you say of a thing that it is.[5] If this were so, then we could think of other objects beside things; we could think, for example, of 'A is B', i.e. of states of affairs, or contents of judgements ... Aristotle distinguished ten kinds of 'somethings' which we can think of and which it is impossible to reduce to the same category. In addition to things, we can think, for example, of size, quality, relation, place, etc. But our thinker could not continue to agree with this view. Insofar as meditation leads us to believe that the presentation of the concept of something that is thought is a uniform one, 'the simple observation of facts' leads to the firm conviction that only real things can be objects of thought (p. 322). Fictitious names such as 'size', 'quality', 'relation', 'place', refer to nothing; they are not the names of anything. Only the words relating to the first category are really the names of something, i.e. the names of realities, or things, of the only

5. See Brentano's letter to Kraus, in Kraus' Introduction to *Psychology*, p. 383.

objects of which we can think. These realities include only separate things, individuals, because the 'universals' (an internal contradiction) could not exist. Here Brentano gives as an example, proof of the contradiction between a real 'triangle as such' and a 'triangle in general' (p. 275).

The following exposition by Oskar Kraus shows us what is particularly essential to adherents of the venerable Brentano's reist doctrine:

> The future will decide which of the directions that have been taken will bring us nearer the goal of knowledge – Brentano's older school which adheres to the earlier doctrines and outdoes them in its belief that it cannot dispense with *entia rationis* (with 'propositions in themselves', 'facts', 'ideal objects', 'objectives', 'images', 'values', and so on), or Brentano's younger school.
>
> It is now incumbent upon the opposing sides to come to terms with Brentano's claims and, in particular, to explain why every sentence which contains an *ens rationis* or an abstraction can be translated without change of meaning into a sentence using only concepts of things and no such mental fictions! (*Psychologie vom empirischen Standpunkt*, vol. 2 (1925), p. xxii. Not included in the English edition.)

I do not propose at this point to make a detailed comparison of the venerable Brentano's doctrine and my own logico-ontological view, which I have called reism. Anyone who wants to acquaint himself with it would have to go through my *Elementy Teorii Poznania, Logiki Formalnej i Metodologii Nauk*, as well as the additons appended to the second edition (1961), among which the article entitled 'Fazy Rozwojowe Konkretyzmu' ('The Stages of the Development of Concretism') is especially important for the understanding of the short but rather dramatic history of the forging of this idea in the fire of critical controversy. Toward the end of 1966, the Pergamon Press published the English translation of the above-mentioned book and its appendices as *Gnosiology, The Scientific Approach to the Theory of Knowledge*. The whole theory was also presented in a 1935 article in *Przeglad Filozoficzny*, and reprinted in English in Tarski and Rynine's translation in *Mind* [Vol. 64 (1955), pp. 488–500].

The differences lie in the way we approach the subject, the store of ideas, the terminology, and the emphasis. It seems to me that I began by objecting to the suggestions of Berkelian philosophy and derivative schools, who want to view the objects of external experiences as complexes of sensory qualities, thereby eliminating substances independent of all perception. On the contrary! There are physical bodies independent of us which act upon our sense organs and are perceived! If one examines attentively the propositions which seem to deal with other so-called categories of being, for example, qualities, relations, events, we very often seize upon flagrant examples of clearly metaphorical, descriptive, or substitutive locutions, even when we know, for example, that the qualities pertain to things, or that they are inherent in them. When someone says that the quality of sphericity pertains to the earth he is saying, in a metaphorical and descriptive way, that the earth is spherical. Now, we are trying to take all such propositions, those that contain the names of distinctive signs, qualities, constructions, concepts, ideas, relations, dispositions, events, states of affairs, places, tendencies, and other obstructions of various sorts, such as substitutive locutions, which are often useful because they are very brief – and replace them with equivalent sentences which clearly contain only the names of concrete things. The enterprise is often successful and proves itself useful for didactic ends, for very frequently you can thus explicate – by means of immediately comprehensible propositions – enigmatic propositions, bristling with subtle scientific terms. Could we not actually operate in this way? Is it not, as a matter of fact, possible, because there are, in reality, no other objects which we could know and, in general, no objects other than things? Could it be that each object is a thing?

How is reism, as I conceive it, correctly to be understood? It is a programme of substituting for all propositions containing onomatoids or apparent names (names which are not the names of things), propositions containing – in addition to prepositions, conjunctions, and other words which are not names – only real names, that is to say, names of things which could be either general names (such as 'the horse' 'the stone'), or individual names (such as 'the earth' 'Aristotle') or non-referring names (such as 'a centaur'). As regards things, the thing thus conceived is a physical body and thinking subjects are regarded as bodies.

That this view has certain essentials in common with Brentano's view, as well as what their main differences are, is clearly shown in the above resumé. They share the guiding hypothesis of substitution, but they interpret 'thing' differently. Here I return to Alfred Kastil, who, in 1951, wrote the following:

> Kotarbinski recognises Brentano expressly as the 'originator of reism' in this century. Yet he himself gives the proposition that we can only think about what falls under the general concept of a thing a materialistic interpretation, and this is closer to modern physicalism than to Brentano, for whom the name 'thing' refers to immaterial as well as material things just as Descartes had spoken of the non-dimensional soul as a *res cognitans*. [Alfred Kastil, *Die Philosophie Franz Brentanos* (Munich, 1951), Introduction, p. 24].

The years have passed and reism – Brentano's as well as my home-grown variety – has duly met the difficulties of which it was conscious, and the reproaches it received from time to time. The idea of things demands very detailed explication from the physical point of view, if it is to include not only bodies but also molecules, and the objects spoken of by physics in general. (What attitude is to be adopted by a somatism which identifies things and bodies with regard to fragments of the electro-magnetic field?) But the most violent challenges to the deftness of reism are raised against the theory of the whole, which successfully narrows the term 'whole' while vehemently opposing the identification of the whole with the body.

We could establish that, since Kraus' above-mentioned appeal, the onus of proof has been shifted to the other side in the controversy. In fairness, which of the contending parties is assigned the task of supplying valid reasons for its claim? In general today it is not demanded that the adversaries of reism explain why it is possible to eliminate apparent names from all propositions; rather, the adherents of reism are asked to prove that it is possible to do so.

17 Brentano's Argument for Reismus[1]

D.B. Terrell

Philosophers in the English-speaking world who have paid any attention to Franz Brentano at all have tended to be preoccupied with the *Psychologie vom empirischen Standpunkt* (1874) and *Vom Ursprung sittlicher Erkenntnis* (1889). These are important works and they do make interesting contributions to philosophy. The attention they have received from English-speaking philosophers and the influence they have exerted have been if anything less than they have deserved. To suppose, however, that Brentano's work had been accomplished before the last decade of the past century had begun is an error of considerable proportions. It is also a very common one.

For more than a quarter century after the publication of *Vom Ursprung sittlicher Erkenntnis* Brentano continued an active and fruitful philosophical career. After 1895, he no longer held an academic position; nevertheless, by correspondence and conversation and occasional publication he continued to labour at the development of a philosophy truly scientific and its defence against high-flown metaphysical speculations. The affinities of Brentano's philosophical style with the dominant traditions of British philosophy were apparent from the beginning; they are still more striking at the end. While some British philosophers who took pride in their 'robust sense of reality' were still lured by the secrets of Meinong's jungle, Brentano had set out to defoliate it, no matter that its seeds had first been nurtured on his own earlier views. The cutting edge of his attack was linguistic analysis, *Sprachkritik*. The outcome was the plain philosophy of 'Reism': *only things can exist and only things can be objects of thought*. This is the dominant theme of Brentano's philosphical activity during this century. To ignore it would be comparable to ignoring all that Wittgenstein had written since the *Tractatus*.

Now, with the publication of Roderick Chisholm's English edition of *Wahrheit und Evidenz*,[2] it is to be hoped that there will develop a wider appreciation of Brentano as a twentieth-century philosopher. In both *The True and the Evident* and *Die Abkehr vom Nichtrealen* the dominant positions of *Sprachkritik* and *Reismus* in Brentano's later thought are unmistakable. No one who has read the material in either book can continue to accept the

1. Reprinted from *Revue Internationale de Philosophie*, vol. 20 (1966).
2. *The True and the Evident* (London, 1966). Attention should also be called to *Die Abkehr vom Nichtrealen*, ed. F. Mayer-Hillebrand (Bern and München, 1966).

interpretations of his earlier writings that have been projected to us through the distorting lenses of phenomenology and *Gegenstandstheorie*.

Various sorts of considerations can be advanced in support of such a doctrine as reism. Since it is intended to exclude from the world and from our thought certain alleged entities,[3] Ockham's razor (or the principle of *Denkökonomie*, as German idiom puts it) can be called upon directly. But the razor is never by itself sufficient. It can cut only what has been shown to be unnecessary. This is the typical role of *Sprachkritik* in Brentano's later philosophy. Even though language appears to contain names that designate all sorts of irreal objects, we can show by linguistic analysis that our thought can afford to do without them. All such references can be eliminated by translation into a language containing only the names of *realia*, i.e. persons and physical things.

Brentano also attempts to support reism by arguments independent of either Ockham's razor or linguistic analysis. Most of them are indirect arguments in which an absurdity or an infinite regress is shown to be implied by the assertion of an irreal entity of some sort. There is only one general and direct argument for reism, as Reinhard Kamitz acknowledges in his painstaking study of Brentano's attempts to establish his position.[4] Professor Mayer-Hillebrand also gives priority to the same argument on which Dr Kamitz places such emphasis, the proof from the univocal significance of *vorstellen*.[5] Both Professor Mayer-Hillebrand and Dr Kamitz attribute to me certain objections to this argument.[6] In the remainder of this article I shall expand upon these objections and explore some of the features of Brentano's theory which are brought to our attention by them.

The argument from the univocal significance of the word 'thinking' is repeated on numerous occasions in Brentano's correspondence and manuscripts. I give a version taken from *Wahrheit und Evidenz*, as it appears in Chisholm's translation: 'The expression "to think" (*vorstellen*) is univocal. To think is always to think of *something*. Since "to think" is univocal, the term "something" must also be univocal. But there is no generic concept that can be common both to things and to non-things. Hence if "something" denotes a thing at one time, it cannot denote a non-thing – an impossibility, say – at another time.'[7] In attacking this argument, I do not mean to lend

---

3. Brentano, unlike Kotarbinski, who coined the expression *Reismus*, was never a physicalist. Both persons and physical things are *realia*. Excluded are objects of thought as such (e.g. Lockean ideas), abstractions formed by hypostasising adjectives, the existence or the possibility of anything, and so on. For brief accounts of the distinction between *realia* and *irrealia*, see Professor Mayer-Hillebrand's Introduction to *Die Abkehr vom Nichtrealen* (pp. 92ff) and Professor Chisholm's Introduction to *The True and the Evident* (pp. vii-viii).

4. Part II of *Franz Brentano's Lehre vom Wahren Urteil*. Dissertation (Innsbruck, 1961).

5. *Abkehr*, p. 37: Unter den Argumenten gegen die Vorstellbarkeit nichtrealer Geganstände überhaupt nimmt die erste Stelle das aus der Einheit des Begriffs des Bewußtseins geschöpfte ein.

6. *Abkehr*, pp. 399–400, note 69, and *Franz Brentano's Lehre vom Wahren Urteil*, pp. 188–97.

7. *The True and the Evident*, p. 108; p. 122 in *Wahrheit und Evidenz*.

support to the doctrine of non-things or *irrealia* in any of its many forms. I mean only to show that it lends no support of its own to Reismus, alongside the principle of *Denkökonomie* and the practice, case by case, of *Sprachkritik*. But no additional support may be needed.

Neither do I mean to question the importance that Brentano himself attached to the argument. It is clear that he thought very highly of it. In one of the letters included in *Wahrheit und Evidenz*, having stated the argument in much the same form as above, he wrote: 'I would say that this proof is absolutely decisive.' It is interesting, however, that he immediately goes on to say that 'one may verify the result, again and again, by analysing those cases in which a non-thing appears to be the object of a person's thought.'[8]

The argument from the univocal significance of 'thinking' has two essential presuppositions. They are the targets of my objections to the argument. One is that 'something' (*Etwas*) has, in the intentional context, an independent meaning. 'Thinking of something' designates a complex concept of which its meaning is a constituent. The other is that there is no common genus that comprehends both things and non-things, *realia* and *irrealia*. Neither of these assumptions is axiomatic; both are open to reasonable doubt.

Brentano's pupil and friend, Anton Marty, did not accept Brentano's radical *Reismus*. Much of what we know of Brentano's thinking on the subject is to be found in the later years of their forty-year correspondence. Marty's pupil, Oskar Kraus, shared his acceptance of *irrealia*, but under the pressure of Brentano's arguments abandoned the view. Apparently the line taken by Marty shortly before he died (in 1914) was that we *could* conceive of a common genus for both *realia* and *irrealia*. I begin, therefore, by considering the objections that can be made to Brentano's assumption that this is not so.

If Brentano's thesis is false, we must be able to identify some still more comprehensive class than the class of *realia*. We must be able to identify some characteristic which can belong equally to *realia* and *irrealia*. Marty made two related but distinct proposals toward a more comprehensive interpretation of 'something'.[9] First, the *Etwas* in *Etwas-vorstellen* is taken to mean the *Vorgestelltes* – what is thought about. 'Someone thinking' is equated in meaning to 'someone thinking about something' and then to 'someone thinking about something being thought about'. If we can think about *irrealia*, they will fall under the general concept of 'things which are thought about'. So interpreted, 'something' remains univocal although it can range over both things and non-things.

Brentano is quick to point out that when one is said to be thinking about a horse, 'horse' does not mean 'horse being thought about'. If that were the case, he continues, someone who believes that there are horses would only be believing in horses being thought of, more accurately, in someone who is thinking about horses. A further objection to Marty's interpretation of

8. *The True and the Evident*, p. 95; *Wahrheit und Evidenz*, p. 106. The same letter is included in *Die Abkehr vom Nichtrealen*, p. 249.

9. See *The True and the Evident*, pp. 94–8; *Wahrheit und Evidenz*, pp. 105–8; *Abkehr*, pp. 250–5.

Etwas emerges upon constructing an analogous interpretation in the context of denial. If the analogy is legitimate, when we say of someone that he denies something, 'something' should be understood to mean 'something denied'. This will not do, Brentano insists: '. . . nothing could be more obvious than the fact that, if a man rejects or denies a thing, he does *not* reject or deny it as something rejected or denied; on the contrary, he knows it is something which he himself does reject or deny'.[10]

Marty's second proposal was that 'something' ranges univocally over the class of 'what is thinkable'. It is met by much the same line of augmentation that was addressed to the identification of 'something' with 'what is thought of'. There is suggested, however, a different sort of objection. Brentano poses a rhetorical question: 'Who would want to take "being thinkable" as a generic characteristic, common to stone, horse, forest?'[11] The objections considered before could consistently have been made while admitting that 'thought of' and 'thinkable' are generic characteristics. The difficulties arose only from attempting to identify them with the significance of 'something' in 'thinking about something'. Now we seem to be told that they cannot be considered generic characteristics at all, quite apart from the meaning of 'something'.

Surely it is generally true of stones, horses, forests that they are all thinkable. Whatever thought can be about must be capable of being an object of thought, must be thinkable. If 'being thinkable' is acceptable as a characteristic at all, it must indeed be a characteristic that applies generally to everything of which anyone can be said to be thinking. There are only two ways in which Brentano's objection can be understood. Either 'being thinkable' is not really a characteristic of anything or, even though it is a characteristic of everything, it is not a generic characteristic in the sense that it does not establish a common genus.

The only plausible way of expanding on the latter interpretation would reduce the objection to the sort we have previously considered. In order for a characteristic to enter into the process of abstraction that produces general conceptual thinking, it must not only be true of something but also enter into our distinct idea of it. The idea of the genus must be included in the distinct idea of anything falling within the genus, Brentano holds. It is true of horses, forests, stones that they are thinkable, but it is not the case that our distinct idea of any horse, forest or stone includes the characteristic of being thinkable. We think of a racehorse as something living, animal, equine, swift. No doubt there are other characteristics that should be included, but 'thinkable' is not among them. We can not, then, think of racehorses as belonging to the genus of 'thinkable things'.

The distinctive interpretation of Brentano's question is the one on which 'being thinkable' is denied to be a characteristic of anything. It is only a pseudo-characteristic, a *denominatio extrinseca* that can be unmasked by analysis and shown to be a linguistic fiction. To say of something that it is

10. Both of these objections are raised in the letter of 8 November 1914 to Oskar Kraus, pp. 95ff. in *The True and the Evident*. See citations above.

11. This proposal of Marty's is discussed in the letter dated 16 November 1914, pp. 97ff. in *The True and the Evident*.

thinkable is to say that there is someone capable of thinking of it. Despite appearances, when we assert that racehorses are thinkable, we are not really referring directly to racehorses, but to people thinking about racehorses.[12] But all of this is an appeal to *Sprachkritik*. The force of the objection to Marty's proposed common genus depends on the reductive analysis of the particular expression used, 'being thinkable'.

There are relative determinations that are not subject to reductive linguistic analysis. These could serve as a basis for abstraction to more and more general concepts. It is difficult, however, to conceive of any genuine relational characteristic which, like the pseudo-characteristic of 'being thinkable', could be asserted of anything we might think of. But even if there were such a characteristic, a line of reasoning which should by now be familiar would exclude it from constituting the common genus signified by 'something'. The fact that a given thing can be in a certain relationship and can be thought of as such does not imply that the relationship must be included in every occasion of thinking about it. 'Being in some relation to something else' is true, no doubt, of everything we think about, but it need not be included in every idea of anything. If we take it to define an all-inclusive class, the class of things related to other things, there is still an obstacle to identifying it with the meaning of 'something' in 'thinking of something'. 'Someone thinking about something' is not synonymous with 'someone thinking about something relative to something else', even on the assumption that everything we think about is related to something else.

Unless we adopt the doctrine of internal relations, and Brentano did not, we can have some distinct ideas of things without including their relations to other things. Generic concepts formed by abstraction from distinct ideas of this kind will not include relational constituents and so will not be species of the general concept of 'something related to something else'. One possibility is not disposed of by that line of argumentation, however. If there is a genuine relation that everything has to itself, the argument will not apply. That we can have a distinct idea of something without having an idea of its relations to other things does not entail that we can have a distinct idea of anything without including some relation to itself. If our distinct idea of anything did include such a relation, not only would it define a class to which everything belongs but it could remain as the final product of the abstractive process.

There is at least one candidate for the role that has just been outlined, the relation of self-identity. It is unlikely that there are any others. Let us consider, then, the prospect of taking the highest class under which falls everything we think about as the class of *things identical with themselves*. First of all, if this expression is admitted as the designation of a class, it is surely a class that includes everything we think about. Moreover, unlike the concept of the relational taken non-reflexively, it is difficult to understand how we could have a distinct idea of anything without thinking of it as that thing which it is, as self-identical. The objections encountered before do not apply

---

12. This is not an adequate account of Brentano's analysis of such expressions and others in which possibility or capacity is involved. See *On Ens Rationis*, Supplementary Essay in the *Psychology*.

when we propose to substitute 'something identical with itself' for the simple 'something' in 'someone thinking about something'. *Vorstellender, Etwas Vorstellender* and *Ein-mit-sich-selbst-identisches Vorstellender* are all synonymous, varying only in explicitness.

A question still remains, however. The fixed assumption of Brentano's argument has been throughout that the concept of thinking is univocal and that it can be univocal only if there is a generic class common to everything we think about. Is 'something identical with itself' just to be equated with Brentano's *Reales*, or will it include *irrealia* as well? If *irrealia* are to be counted among things identical with themselves, are they so in the same sense as *realia*? If we ban them from the range of the self-identical, this proposal hardly constitutes a threat to the argument for Reism; it reinforces it. If *irrealia* are self-identical, but in a different sense from *realia*, to admit them as objects of thought would violate the univocal significance of 'thinking'.

There is a *prima facie* case for saying that the class of things identical with themselves, if there is one, is a higher class than the class of *realia*. If 'the existence of A' can be permitted to stand in a context involving identity at all, it would seem permissible to assert that it is identical with itself. Brentano does insist that if his opponent speaks of '*the existence of A*' he must deny that it is the same as A.[13] If such a denial can be meaningfully asserted, we must be permitted to say 'The existence of A is the same as the existence of A'. If so, the existence of A must be counted among things identical with themselves (and distinct from other things). We can not suppose that the expression 'identical with' applies in one sense to A and in another sense to the existence of A. Otherwise, the judgement with which we began, the denial that the existence of A is identical with A, would have neither of the distinct senses of 'identical with'. It would either be meaningless or it would require still a third sense of identity. It is much more the acceptable course to admit that there is a common significance. In that case, the concept of things identical with themselves applies to all things univocally, real and irreal, and constitutes a common genus for both sets.

Dr Kamitz and Professor Mayer-Hillebrand appeal to the process of abstraction in order to reject the possibility of a common genus for *realia* and *irrealia*. Their point is that all of our general concepts are derived from more specific ones and ultimately from intuitive presentations (*Anschauungen*). If there are no intuitive presentations of *irrealia*, there can be no general concept of *irrealia*; and if there is no general concept of *irrealia*, there can be no still more general concept that includes *irrealia*, as a species. They are correct in insisting that an argument along these lines is required by

13. Brentano makes the distinction between them the basis of an infinite regress argument; this is one of his favourite weapons against certain classes of alleged *irrealia*. For example, in the letter to Kraus dated 16 November: 'If I ask whether the being of this person is to be distinguished from the person himself, then, of course, you will say yes; and similarly you will have to say that the being of this person is distinguished from the being of the being of this person . . .' *The True and the Evident*, p. 98.

Brentano's theory of the relation between intuitive presentations and general concepts. They are also correct in ascribing to Brentano the doctrine that all of our intuitive presentations have *realia* as their objects. What they fail to take sufficient account of is that the argument, when cast into this form, either begs the question or makes the distinctive feature of Brentano's original argument quite irrelevant. If Brentano had insisted that we can not think of *irrealia* at all and therefore have no intuitive presentations of *irrealia*, the circle is plain to see. Suppose that there are independent grounds for rejecting intuitive presentations of *irrealia*. Then the argument to the denial of irreal objects of thought generally becomes a straightforward appeal to concept-empiricism. We have no ideas not based on intuitive presentations; we have no intuitive presentations of *irrealia*; therefore we have no ideas of *irrealia*. The univocal character of the expression 'to think' has no function in such an argument; it is entirely irrelevant. The resort to concept-empiricism and the denial of intuitive presentations of *irrealia* may be conclusive. It may enlighten our understanding like the light of day; but like the light of day it pales the other stars into invisibility. Such is the fate of Brentano's argument from the univocal significance of *vorstellen*.

It is doubtful whether it is entirely appropriate to interpret the *Etwas* of *Etwas-vorstellen* as the univocal name of a highest general class in any case. It makes no real difference whether we take that class to be the class of *realia*, with Brentano, or some other, still more comprehensive class, such as the class of things identical with themselves, understood to include *irrealia* as well. Not every word can be plucked out of its context and defined as an independent unit of meaning. That is a lesson that could have been learned from Brentano before it was learned from some others who are more often given credit for it. That *Etwas-vorstellender* is univocal requires that *Etwas* be univocal only on the presupposition that the *Etwas* has some independent meaning of its own. The alternative is to consider it a synsemantikon. Then Brentano's argument from the univocity of *Etwas-vorstellender* is cut off at the outset.

According to Dr Kamitz's detailed analysis of the argument[14] the second premise (after the one that asserts the univocal significance of 'thinking') is a proposition to the effect that the expression 'someone thinking' is synonymous with the expression 'someone thinking of something' (*Etwas-vorstellender*). Apparently, then, in this context the word *Etwas* can be dropped without loss of meaning. If so, we have reason to regard it as a synsemantical fragment of the expression in which it occurs. Alfred Kastil offers the following argument in the Introduction to the *Kategorienlehre*, which he edited: 'Da man nun aber, ohne Sinnesänderung, statt "A ist" immer auch sagen kann "A ist ein Seiendes", so ergibt sich, daß das Wort Seiendes nicht immer als Name fungiert, sondern unter Umständen synsemantisch . . .'[15] If *Etwas-vorstellender* and *vorstellender* are synonymous, the same argument is applicable here and indicates that the word *Etwas*

14. *Franz Brentano's Lehre vom Wahren Urteil*, pp. 143ff.
15. *Kategorienlehre*, p. vi.

does not always function as a name, but functions synsemantically in some contexts.

It is clear from Brentano's continued debate with Kraus that he had a more sophisticated view of the role of *Etwas* than has been suggested in the preceding discussion. In a letter dated March 1915, he wrote to Kraus: 'Sie schreiben mir die Meinung zu, "Etwas" könne nur Reales bedeuten. Keineswegs! Etwas ist kein Substantiv oder Adjectiv, sondern ein Pronomen, das auf Substantiva oder Adjektiva stellvertretend sich beziehen kann, die keine Dinge bezeichnen. Meine Behauptung war nur die, daß es nicht in demselben Fall stellvertretend für Dinge und für Nichtdinge stehen könne, ohne equivok zu sein.'[16]

This passage requires an adjustment in Professor Mayer–Hillebrand's rejoinder to the suggesteion that *Etwas* is not an independently meaningful portion of the expression, *Etwas-vorstellender*. She relies on the abstraction process, as illustrated by the transition from 'X is thinking of a red apple' to 'X is thinking of an apple'. In each case, she quite correctly observes, 'red apple' and 'apple' function as auto-semantic terms, the linguistic expression of concepts. Her argument continues, as Dr Kamitz describes it, as follows: 'Und genau dieselbe Situation liegt in allen weiteren Fällen vor, in denen X abstrahiert und daher vor. Die Worte "Frucht", "Etwas" fungieren in allen diesen Redewendungen autosemantisch: sie sind ja nichts anderes als sprachliche Bezeichnungen der Dinge, auf die sich X vorstellend bezieht.'[17] This understanding of the function of *Etwas* requires that it be regarded as a subtantive of the same sort as 'red apple', 'apple', 'fruit', etc. This is contrary to Brentano's insistence in the passage quoted above that *Etwas* is not a substantive or an adjective, but a pronoun that can stand as the representative of substantives or adjectives. He plainly intends to draw a distinction between the role of *Etwas* in *Etwas-vorstellender* and the role of *Apfel* in *Apfel-vorstellender*.

To say that *Etwas* has the function of a pronoun suggests that its role is more like that of a blank to be filled in than that of a term with an independent meaning of its own. It may seem to do the work of words like 'apple', 'fruit', in the context of such an expression as 'someone thinking of . . .' but the difference in function becomes obvious in other contexts. We can say of anyone who is thinking that he is thinking of something. It does not follow that whenever we ask a question about someone, 'What is he thinking of?', 'something' is an appropriate response. On the contrary, such a response is but a way of evading the question. If I tell someone that I am thinking of an apple, I do not expect him to respond by asking, 'What are you thinking of?' If he does ask that question, I take it to be a sign of inattention or a hearing disability. My reply is likely to be, 'An apple, as I just told you.' But if I indicate merely that I am thinking about something, I take the same question to be an expression of interest. To reply to it as I did in the former case, by saying, 'Something, as I just told you,' would be ill-mannered as well as uninformative. It is quite clear that when we compare 'thinking of an apple' with 'thinking of something', the situation is not the

16. *Abkehr*, p. 283.
17. *Franz Brentano's Lehre vom Wahren Urteil*, p. 190.

same as with the comparison between 'thinking of apples' and 'thinking of fruit'. Professor Mayer-Hillebrand is mistaken in representing them to be the same.

Even if we were to accept the interpretation proposed by Professor Mayer-Hillebrand and Dr Kamitz, it would not be to the advantage of Brentano's argument, however. The relation between thinking of a red apple and thinking of an apple is nòt necessarily parallel to the relation between 'red apple' and 'apple'. As Professor Mayer-Hillebrand and Dr Kamitz describe the process of moving from *roten Apfel-vorstellender* to *Etwas-vorstellender* they would indeed not be parallel. The concept of someone thinking in more general terms is not a more general concept of someone thinking. Someone thinking of a red apple is a member of the class of persons thinking of an apple with some colour or other. He is not a member of the class of persons thinking of an apple without regard to its colour. Neither of these two classes is a genus within which the other is a species. So it is with *Etwas-vorstellender*. If we insist upon treating *Etwas* as a name of the highest level of abstraction, and not as a pronoun that can be replaced by a substantive with a higher or lower level of generality, *Etwas-vorstellender* serves to identify just one species within the general class designated by *vorstellender*. It stands for the class of those who are thinking of something at the utmost level of abstraction. Persons who are thinking of apples do not belong to that class, nor persons who are thinking of red apples. On such an interpretation, *Etwas-vorstellender* cannot be synonymous with *vorstellender*, since they do not even have the same extension. *Etwas-vorstellender* can be synonymous with *vorstellender* only if *Etwas* is interpreted as a pronoun that assumes meaning only upon being identified as the representative of some substantive or other, without restriction as to specificity or generality.

Brentano's argument does not collapse if the *Etwas* in *Etwas-vorstellender* is assigned the pronominal function of a blank to be filled in. In the letter of 9 March 1915, in which he himself described it as a pronoun, he then went on to add this: 'Meine Behauptung war nur die, daß es nicht in demselben Fall stellvertretend für Dinge und für Nichtdinge stehen könne, ohne, aequivok zu sein. Das wäre nur dann nicht richtig, wenn Reales und Nichtreales ein und demselben höheren Begriff als Gattungsbegriff unterständen . . .'[18] We come back then to the question of whether 'something' can be replaced by either the name of a real thing or an irreal without being equivocal. The answer to that question depends on the answer we give to the question as to whether there is a common genus to which both *realia* and *irrealia* belong. And that question we have already discussed.

18. *Abkehr*, p. 283.

18 Brentano's Theory of Induction[1]

Hugo Bergman

It is a remarkable fact that Hume's problem of the validity of the incomplete induction did *not* disquiet most of the logicians of the nineteenth century. They studied the logical mechanism of induction, but the problem as discovered by Hume, that is, as an epistemological issue, was scarcely realised as existent. To quote one example, F.F. Apelt's *Theorie der Induktion* (1854), a book of great merit in many respects, virtually disregards the incomplete induction as such, and treats complete and incomplete induction as being on an equal footing.

The exception, of course, is John Stuart Mill, whatever may be our opinion of the answers he offers to the question. On the European continent, Franz Brentano found himself grappling with the problem from the beginning of his philosophical thought. His *Versuch über die Erkenntnis*, edited from his literary remains by Alfred Kastil in 1925, is in essence a theory of induction.

1

Brentano starts his inquiry with a distinction between induction in a broader and induction in a narrower sense. This distinction, however, has nothing in common with the difference between complete and incomplete induction. Brentano's 'induction in a broader sense' seems to be very close to Husserl's 'essential intuition'.[2] Brentano's definition is:[3] 'We carry out an induction in a broader sense whenever we draw a general law from an experienced fact, even if this is done without any inferential process; the reason for the fact becoming immediately evident from the distinct apperception of the concept.' Such an induction in a broader sense was carried out by Helmholtz when he discovered the *general* truth that every vowel contains certain 'overtones', which bestow its character upon it. This was *not* an empirical law which may be invalidated by supplementary experience; the distinct apperception of the phenomenon produced the law

---

1. Reprinted from *Philosophy and Phenomenological Research* (1944), no. 5, pp. 281–307.

2. Marvin Farber, 'A Presuppositionless Philosophy', *Philosophical Essays in Memory of Edmund Husserl*, p. 57.

3. *Versuch über die Erkenntnis*, p. 81.

at a single stroke with complete certitude.[4] In his *Origin of our Knowledge of Right and Wrong*, Brentano speaks of the cognition of a general truth without induction (in a narrower sense), and mentions Herbart's 'very remarkable' theory of a sudden mounting (*Erhebung*) to general ethical principles. Oskar Kraus, probably influenced by Husserl, has put special emphasis on this theory of Brentano's.

Brentano contrasts this 'induction' with the 'induction in a narrower sense', which 'derives a general law from one or several experienced facts' and in which the cognition of the law is not absolutely certain (as it was above), but only probable, because we have no immediate insight into the reason for the fact.

2

In approaching this problem of 'induction in a narrower sense', Brentano starts with examples taken from a field to which induction is not indigenous. He asks whether induction can be used in *mathematics*. Take this example. Someone does not know that the sum of the angles in a triangle is 180°. But by exact measurement of a specific given triangle he finds that the sum of the angles of *that* specific triangle is equal to two right angles. And now he asks whether this is a peculiarity of the specific triangle measured by him or whether he has succeeded, by determining the sum of the angles of *one* triangle, in discovering a general law which pertains to all triangles. If the former is the case, then by chance he has chosen from a countless multitude of triangles with different sums of their angles, *one* triangle with a surprisingly simple relation between the sum of its angles and the right angle. If the latter is the case, however, this simple relationship is not accidental but has a necessary connection with the triad of sides of a figure. He does not yet know what this relation may be, but he has seen 'a thousand times' that certain regular features are connected with other regular features; and so he reaches the conclusion that it is infinitely more probable that he has discovered a *law* than that he has stumbled across an accidental quality of an accidental triangle. One exact measurement has furnished him, in this way, with a geometrical law of, if not absolute certainty, at least infinite probability. He has carried out an induction.

Should the triangle, chosen at random, itself show special peculiarities – should it, for instance, be isosceles or equilateral – then the induction too would be limited to triangles of this special kind, and no inductive extension of the inference to triangles in general would be justified.

Brentano quotes examples from the history of mathematics. Archimedes discovered certain geometrical laws by such an empirical process. The result of these inductions, though granting only high probability, afterwards directed him in his endeavours to find an exact demonstration of these laws, which he had first observed through induction.

How can the basic principle of this induction be formulated? Brentano

4. I do not enter into details. Kraus, in his edition of Brentano's *Psychology* (1924), speaks about an *a priori* psychology corresponding to *a priori* mathematics.

does not answer the question explicitly, but we might define it in roughly this way. If we find a certain simple regularity in a haphazardly chosen geometrical figure, it is *infinitely* more probable that the reason for this regularity lies in a law of the general character than that the established regularity is peculiar to the figure we have chosen at random.

3

Brentano begins the expositions of his theory of induction in a narrower sense with this mathematical example, because it demonstrates in a simple way that the passage from singular case to universal statement is justified by the assumption that the universal statement – let us call it u – is a *general law* from which the singular case s necessarily ensues. The central point of the induction is this relation $u \rightarrow s$ of a general law to the special assertion s implied in that law. The judgement s asserts that one concept (sum of angles = 2R) is connected in a single case with another concept (triangle). The judgement u tells us that this connection is necessary, and it is this necessity which is the *vera causa* of s.[5]

Now in mathematics this law u is (according to Brentano's view of mathematics, which is contrary to that of Kant) an analytic proposition. But if we use induction outside mathematics in the factual sciences – physics, history, etc. – this aspect changes. The law u aimed at by our induction is no longer analytic, but synthetic. Netheless, induction is made possible in this field also by an assumption of a law u, so that the singular case s can be considered (with great probability) as a result of u.

Different inductions will lead to different synthetic laws u, but all are possible only on the basis of the general law of causality. This law is the ultimate reason of all induction in the factual sciences.

Thus, induction in mathematics and induction in the factual sciences show many common features, but also important differences. If I understand Brentano rightly (he does not refer explicitly to this difference), the consideration of probability is necessary *once* in mathematics, but *twice* in the field of the factual sciences. In mathematics the supposed law (if it exists at all) is *analytically* true. The probability does not refer to the law u as such, but only to the question whether the observed regularity s is the consequence of a law u or only accidental. In the realm of the factual sciences the situation is far more complicated. The assumed general law of causality is *not* analytically true but synthetically; and Brentano, as we shall see at once, uses the calculus of probability in order to demonstrate it. On the other hand, the connection between the singular judgement s and the supposed law u is again only probable. So the appeal to probability makes its appearance *twice* – once, as in mathematics, for the relation $s \rightarrow u$, and once (*not* as in mathematics) for the proof of the universal law u itself.

4

In induction applied to mathematics, u is an analytic judgement possessing

5. *Versuch*, p. 107.

full certainty. In the factual sciences *u* stands for different synthetic laws in different inductions – laws of nature, of social life, etc. Brentano replaces all these special synthetic laws by the one general law of causality. For if we can prove the general law of causality, the scientist, when relating a given singular phenomenon to a general law, will stand on firm ground and will be concerned only with the explanatory value and the intrinsic probability of his law. But if we are unable to prove the general law of causality, then all the laws assumed in different branches of science remain unfounded, and all induction of laws is doomed. Hence, every theory of induction must set out to refute Hume, to establish the general law of causality and thus justify induction. No task of this kind is incumbent on induction in a broader sense, nor on induction in a narrower sense when *applied to mathematics*.

5

Brentano uses the calculus of *probability* for the solution of Hume's problem. This is the centre of his theory, and he has tried again and again to give the most cogent form to his argument.

He formulates the law of causality in the following way.[6] 'Nothing contingent (*Zufälliges*) comes into existence; everything not necessary (and thus not independent of a cause) is, when it starts, determined in its becoming a cause.'

He deduces this law from the concepts 'coming-into-being' and 'contingent' with the aid of probability-calculus. The concept of 'coming-into-being' contains the concept of time, and in a double sense – the time when the thing is and the time when it has not yet been. Whatever starts to be, has not yet been before. Thus 'coming-into-being' contains the concept of a *limit*. Now the nature of a limit implies that the limit cannot exist for or of itself; it requires a continuum, whose limit it is, no matter how small this continuum may be. Hence, it follows that nothing can begin and end at the same time. There must be an interval between beginning and ending, and this interval, however small, contains in itself an infinity of temporal moments.

The concept of coming-into-being does *not* contain the concept of causation. Contingent, non-caused becoming is not contradictory. But we can say this. If something can come into being contingently, it comes into being without any conditions; thus at every moment when it had not come into being it was as possible as it is now, when it has sprung up; and inversely, it could likewise not have come into being at the moment when it – accidentally – did come into being. Were there equal chances for both possibilities or were there not? In answering this question we have to distinguish several cases. The simplest is that there are only two possibilities: the coming-into-being and the not-coming-into-being of a certain *x* at a certain moment. The case becomes more complicated if we have to consider more than one positive case: *x, y, z*, etc.

We start with the simple case of two possibilities only. Since *ex suppositione* there is no reason for either possibility becoming real, both the coming-into-

6. *Versuch*, p. 126.

being and the not-coming-into-being are of equal probability $= \frac{1}{2}$ in every single indivisible moment. And now we ask: How probable is it that x, which could come into being without reason, did *not* happen *during a certain time*? This question has, according to Brentano, to be answered in the following way. Since the probability for not-becoming (as also for becoming) in every indivisible moment $= \frac{1}{2}$, and since there is an infinity of indivisible moments in every stretch of time (however small), the probability of the not-coming-into-being of x during a certain time is $= (\frac{1}{2})^\infty$ – and that is an abyss of improbability. Therefore, the assumption that something which could happen without reason did *not* happen within a stretch of time, however small, is infinitely improbable. Whatever stretch of time we choose, this x, which could happen without reason, must have existed during this time. In other words, since it existed, it could not *become*. It must have existed from eternity. We are therefore justified in denying any coming-into-being without reason. Thus, the law of causality has been demonstrated.

Brentano supports the basic idea of this demonstration by referring to the testimony of common sense.[7] 'I have often asked simple people whether they are certain that something cannot happen without cause. When they asserted their certainty, I asked them, why were they so certain about it, and repeatedly I was told: 'Why, of course! If it could become without cause, why has it not been there before?' This reply of the common man contains the nucleus of Brentano's theory.

6

This reflection, Brentano continues, becomes even more unfavourable toward the indeterminist if we suppose that there are not merely two contradictory possibilities – as the becoming and the non-becoming of x – but many positive possibilities, contrary to one another, as p, e, x, y, $z \cdots$ in a finite number. Through this assumption the probability of the not-coming-into-being of x is lowered.

The following example seems to correspond to Brentano's ideas. Let us assume that a certain colour x could come into being at a certain spot without cause. How probable is it that this colour, since it could come into being without reason, did *not* emerge during a past stretch of time? We assume that all the other colours, y, z, $\cdots$, could also appear on this spot without cause and their number is n. Then there are $n + 1$ possibilities: the coming-into-being of x, of y, etc. and finally the not-coming-into-being of any one of these colours. Thus, the probability of the coming-into-being of a certain colour x at a certain indivisible moment without cause is $= 1/n+ 1$, and against it the probability of its not-coming-into-being is $n/n+ 1$. The probability that no colour at all emerged at this indivisible moment, is $1/n+ 1$, whereas, under the former assumption of two possibilities only, the probability of the not-coming-into-being at one moment was $\frac{1}{2}$. If we again seek the probability during a certain time, however small, we find the answer: The probability that *no* colour appeared during a certain stretch of time, however small, if it could appear without reason, is $(1/n + 1)^\infty$. Thus,

7. *Versuch*, p. 125.

it is as good as certain that one of these colours appeared during any time, however small.[8]

If we finally assume that the number of the positive instances contrary to each other is infinite – and not finite $= n$, as we previously assumed – the question becomes more complicated. Let us ask, for instance, how probable it is that a certain red colour should emerge at this or that point of the *infinite* number of points on a certain surface, if it can happen without any cause. Thus far Brentano has inquired into the probability of the *not*-coming-into-being of a certain x. But if the number of possible positive cases is infinite, as here, it is from the very beginning infinitely *im*probable that one determined possibility x will be realised, whereas in the two former cases it was infinitely probable that the case in question would be realised during some stretch of time. Thus, Brentano here reverses his question.[9] He does not ask in this case, what is the probability of *not*-coming-into-being, but the probability of the coming-into-being of one of the infinitely many possible species; and this probability is $1/\infty$ for one indivisible moment. The probability that the species should *preserve* itself during a stretch of time, however small, is $(1/\infty)^\infty$, that is, practically an impossibility. Thus in this case, when there is an infinite number of species excluding each other, the probability that one of them will come into being, and continue even for the shortest time, is practically nil. In any moment, the abrupt change of the species is infinitely more probable than its continuation.

7

The basis of Brentano's line of argument is the contradiction between absolute contingency (*Zufälligkeit*) and continuity. 'Being-in-time postulates continuity, contingency contradicts it.' On the one hand, even something which came into being accidentally necessarily has to continue for a time; on the other hand, since there is an infinity of moments in any length of time, the resulting probability for the continuation is $(\frac{1}{2})^\infty$ or $(1/n + 1)^\infty$. Thus, the synthesis of being and contingency is impossible. Brentano also expresses this impossibility by saying that a contradiction exists between what *can* be and what *must* be. What must be is the *continuation* both of the being and the not-being, once it started. What can be – if everything is contingent, accidental – is the interruption of the being and not-being at every moment, and this 'can' is infinitely more probable than the 'must', i.e. the continuation.[10] If you assert absolute contingency and at the same time assert continuity of time, you have to assert, on the one hand, that for every moment the abrupt change is infinitely more probable than the continuing duration; and further you have to assert that the continuing duration is infinitely more frequent than the abrupt change. There is an insoluble contradiction between these two statements, which can be solved only by abandoning the assumption of absolute contingency.

8. *Versuch*, p. 129. The details above are not given by Brentano.

9. In this published book, Brentano gives only hints (*Versuch*, pp. 123, 130). I follow Antòn Marty's lectures on metaphysics.

10. *Versuch*, pp. 131, 153, 201.

8

Brentano stated this argument against indeterminism in repeated fresh and revised forms. The editor of the *Versuch*, Alfred Kastil, tells us that besides the published variants of the argument there are many left unpublished.[11] Here we wish to quote only a few variants published by Kastil.

Absolute contingency not only contradicts the law of the continuity of time, but also another principle held by Brentano: the impossibility of an actual infinity of existing things.[12] The contradiction becomes apparent in the following way. If *one* individual could come into being without cause, then equally a second, third, fourth, etc. could. Since every given number N is one of an infinity of numbers, it is infinitely improbable that the number of accidentally emerging things will be just N. Hence, the coming into existence of an infinity of things is infinitely more probable than the emergence of any given finite number. Thus we again reach the same result. What 'must' be, according to an *a priori* law, is shown to be infinitely improbable, while the infinitely more probable cannot be.

The same argument can be extended to infinite space.[13] Under the assumption of absolute contingency the probability that every single point will be full or vacant equals $\frac{1}{2}$. And again it is infinitely more probable that the whole of infinite space will be filled than any given finite part of it. But an infinite filled space is absurd. Thus we come to the same contradiction that the logically absurd is the infinitely probable.[14]

9

Another variant tries to show that the assumption of an absolute contingency – or, as Brentano also puts it, of an 'absolute facticity' – contradicts the law that contrary opposites cannot exist together.[15] A point cannot be black and red at the same time. Now again the probability of the two colours is equal under the given assumption. But if black and red can start equally *in sensu diviso*, they can start equally *in sensu composito*. One colour cannot prevent the emergence of the other, since it is not yet in existence. So they may start together, and if they start together, they must continue together for a certain time. Thus, a point would for a certain time be black and red, which is against the law of contrary species excluding each other.[16]

10

Thomas G. Masaryk, a disciple of Brentano, said of his master that his

11. *Versuch*, p. 198.

12. *Versuch*, pp. 136, 203. For Brentano's arguments against actual infinity, see *Versuch*, p. 207. See also my *Das Unendliche und die Zahl* (1913).

13. *Versuch*, p. 155.

14. See also Marty's objections, *Versuch*, p. 199, and Brentano's reply, p. 203.

15. *Versuch*, pp. 136, 204.

16. Brentano himself thought this argument 'very risky' (*Versuch*, pp. 203–4) and nearly yielded to Marty's objections, but in the end maintained the argument.

mind was a sharp as a razor. Brentano's arguments against indeterminism show this acumen, and it is not easy to disprove them. If Brentano had succeeded in producing an unimpeachable proof for the validity of the law of causality, it would have marked a turning-point in the development of philosophy. But it seems to me that Brentano's argument cannot stand criticism.

In the first place, it is impossible to meet Brentano on his own ground. He says repeatedly that it is logically impossible for something to come into being without continuing for a time. A boundary cannot exist for or in or of itself. It demands a continuum, whose external or internal boundary it is.[17] One might, therefore, argue against Brentano: If something has happened (without cause) at a certain moment, it *must* continue to exist for *logical* reasons. These logical reasons, it is true, cannot explain why it continues during a certain time t and not during $\frac{1}{2}t$ or $2t$. But to this it could be replied that since we suppose absolute contingency, we cannot and need not explain the length of time, which is *accidental*; all that is logically necessary being that the thing in question, once it has emerged accidentally, must continue for a time.

But this argument against Brentano does not reach the root of the matter. There is a far more fundamental question. Can the law of causality be demonstrated with the help of the probability-calculus?

11

To answer this question, let us refer again to Brentano's important distinction between the use of induction in the field of mathematics and in the field of the factual sciences (see above). The use of induction in the field of geometry, as illustrated by the example of Archimedes, seems entirely justified to us because we are from the very beginning quite certain that geometrical relations are subject to strict laws. Therefore, it seems, in a concrete case, when a certain regularity has not been demonstrated deductively but found empirically – it seems in such a case quite legitimate to inquire with the aid of the probability-calculus whether the regularity, which has been discovered empirically, is the expression of a law, or is only peculiar to an accidentally chosen figure. We are sure about the laws of geometry in general, and our probability-consideration affects only the question whether a special regularity discovered accidentally can or cannot be derived from these geometrical laws. Thus, the consideration of probability is conducted within the general framework of geometrical laws.

This situation changes entirely if we try, with Brentano, to demonstrate the law of causality itself with the aid of the probability-calculus. No general framework of valid laws is assumed in this case; on the contary, such a general framework itself remains to be proved by the calculus of probability. It seems to me that this imposes a burden on the calculus which the latter cannot carry.

The probability-calculus is an aggregate of purely analytic, i.e. tautological operations, which have nothing to do with the reality of things.

17. *Versuch*, p. 127.

When we say, there is a 1/6 chance that by throwing a die we shall throw the number '2' – this proposition is entirely analytic. There are six possibilities, and the possibility '2' is one of the six. Nothing has been said as to how often the face '2' will appear when we actually throw the die. We can pass over the modern frequency-theory of probability, given by Mises and others, which was not known to Brentano. That the die, when actually thrown, shows one or another regularity, would be a synthetic, a physical, law. But no synthetic proposition can be derived from an analytic proposition unless we make additional suppositions of a synthetic nature.

It is often assumed that the so-called law of great numbers – the law of Bernoulli – can fill this gap. It is interpreted to mean that if we know the analytic chances of any set of events, we do really know the character of the *actual* events which are to take place. Hence, the law of great numbers would be a law about *empirical* facts. Thus Brentano says:[18] 'The law of great numbers teaches us that the more we repeat events, the less will their average results depart from the law which we have established on the strength of the demonstrative analysis of the conditions.' But no empirical fact can be deduced from an analytic-tautological proposition. The so-called law of great numbers is itself an analytic proposition referring to 'probabilities', i.e. to possible combinations, not to empirical facts.

The transformation of the analytic law of great numbers into a physical, empirical law of the behaviour of actual events cannot be achieved without additional assumptions as to the experience itself, and these necessary additional assumptions in themselves *partake of the character of the law of causality*. For that reason, the calculus of probability cannot be used to demonstrate the law of causality itself.

12

We have no right to assume that in a supposed chaotic world of absolute contingency things would behave according to the law of great numbers. It would therefore be impossible to use the calculus of probability to predict the empirical events. I have asserted this against Brentano in a previous book.[19] Kraus has replied:[20] 'In the same way one could say that in such a world of contingency the laws of arithmetic or the law of contradiction would cease to be valid. This alone is true that in a world of pure contingency the law of great numbers as well as other axiomatic evidence would lead to absurd results. But this in itself proves that the assumption of a world surrendered to chance is absurd. And this absurdity is what is demonstrated by the use of the calculus of probability.'

Let us think over this vindication of Brentano's argument by his great, lately deceased disciple. I did not say that the laws of probability become senseless or invalidated in such a world; they become useless. No empirical conditions whatsoever can make analytic propositions false, but they may become useless in certain situations.

18. *Versuch*, p. 96.
19. *Der Kampf um das Kausalgesetz in der jüngsten Physik* (1929).
20. Oskar Kraus, *Wege und Abwege der Philosophie* (1934), p. 152.

Arithmetic, as well as the probability-calculus, is first and foremost an analytical calculus constructed by ourselves. It is an ideal creation of our mind, and there is at the outset no guarantee for the existence of empirical correlates, as has been shown by Husserl again and again. This ideal creation of our mind serves us in constituting the determining empirical reality and in rendering our *subjectives* synthesis of apprehension *objective*. Thus the ideal, be it an analytical calculus or other ideal creations of the mind, confers upon our subjective representations the new character of the relation to the object.[21]

But ideal relations cannot unconditionally be transferred to the reality. '2 + 2 = 4' is an indisputable analytical proposition. But if we have two equal weights on a scale and we add two further equal weights, it will not be demonstrable from arithmetic alone that the result will be equal to four weights. This is a physical fact, not an arithmetical proposition.[22] We could think without contradiction that the result of our weighing would be not four, but five.[23] Would this prove that arithmetic is false? Not at all. It would only show that when using arithmetic we have to make certain provisions to meet the laws of experience. It would be the same if we were to find out that by adding two drops to two drops, we would get not four, but three drops. Neither arithmetic nor its function for building objective reality would be abolished, but it would be necessary to correct the ideal results in accordance with the laws of physics.

We use the probability-calculus in the same way as an instrument for the construction of reality. The calculus in itself is an analytical, ideal creation of the human mind. We apply it to reality in order to find out whether a given reality is present in 'random distribution' and, therefore, does not need explanation by supposing a special causal law, or whether we have to assume the working of *special causes* to explain an ordered, non-random distribution.[24] Let us take a simple example. If we throw a die and find that in a series of throws each face turns up in approximately one sixth of the run, we conclude that the distribution is a random distribution and does not need the assumption of any special law. But, if we find that the series does not correspond to the probability-fraction and that one of the faces appears

---

21. Ernst Cassirer, *Philosophie der symbol. Formen*, vol. 3, p. 490.

22. N.R. Campbell, *Physics: The Elements* (1920), pp. 278, 298.

23. Cf. C.J. Lewis, *Mind and the World-order*, p. 250. Mill asked us to suppose a demon sufficiently powerful and maleficent so that every time two things were brought together with two other things, this demon should always introduce a fifth. The conclusion which he supposed to follow is that under such circumstances 2 + 2 = 5 would be a universal law of arithmetic. But Mill was quite mistaken. In such a world we should be obliged to become a little clearer than is usual about the distinction between arithmetic and physics, that is all. We should simply find ourselves in the presence of an extraordinary physical law. But the laws of mathematics would not be affected. It is because this is true that arithmetic is *a priori*. Its laws prevent nothing. They are compatible with anything which happens or could happen in nature.

24. Cf. Moritz Schlick, *Gesetz und Wahrscheinlichkeit* (*Gesammelte Aufsätze*, 1938), p. 328: 'Zufällig nennen wir Ereignisse, die den Regeln der Wahrscheinlichkeitsrechnung gehorchen.'

more frequently than the other five, we would be obliged to seek the *cause* of this deviation from the law of great numbers. Thus the calculus serves us in determining those cases where *special causal explanations* are necessary. In this way it is an instrument for the construction of the real law-bound physical world from the data of sensual experience.

All this *presupposes* that the world can be constituted as a world reigned over by laws. But a world of absolute, pure chance, not being subject to any laws – if it can still be called a world at all – is *ex supposito* not susceptible to any construction by laws. In an ordered world subject to the reign of laws, we are bound (and able) to explain every deviation from the 'law' of great numbers, i.e. from random distribution, by the assumption of special laws; but in a 'world' surrendered to absolute chance, we are neither bound nor able to explain anything. The most improbable may happen; the law of great numbers may cease to apply; explanation would be neither necessary nor possible in this 'world' of chaos. The calculus of probability is an instrument to build a rationalised, objective world. It cannot be used to demonstrate the impossibility of an irrational world of pure contingency. Thus, Brentano's attempt to prove the law of causality with the aid of the probability-calculus fails.

13

Nevertheless, Brentano's theory of induction is of lasting interest and value. The distinction between induction in a broader and in a narrower sense (see above), and the foundation given to the application of induction to problems of mathematics (see above) are of permanent value. So, in general, is the idea of connecting the theory of induction with the calculus of probability. The fertility of this idea has been proved by the development of the theory of induction during recent decades.

19 Toward a Phenomenognosy of Time Consciousness[1]

Oskar Kraus

Introduction

The recent edition of Edmund Husserl's *Vorlesungen zur Phänomenologie des innern Zeibewußtseins* prompted the publication of the following selections. This edition was prepared by Martin Heidegger of Freiburg im Breisgau (published in book form by Max Niemeyer (Halle, 1928), a reprint from the *Jahrbuch für Philosophie und phänomenologische Forschung*, Vol. IX).

In these lectures, which date from 1905, and in the postscripts dated up until 1910, Husserl reports on Brentano's doctrine of time consciousness based on notes he made when he attended Brentano's lectures. Husserl uses these notes to criticise the doctrine Brentano maintained at that time. That report and, in particular, the critique call for comment.

First of all, neither the author nor the editor mentions that Brentano had long since given up the doctrine that Husserl criticises, and substituted another for it. The editor should have made it clear that the polemic was directed against a theory that Brentano no longer professed. What is more, Husserl puts forward a doctrine that replaces objective differences of time (i.e. temporal variations of the object as Brentano previously taught) with 'modes of consciousness'.[2]

There are even further similarities; yet, on the other hand, there are also far-reaching differences. But these similarities concern one of the most important points: the transition to a doctrine of modes.

The editor should not have remained silent about this fact. That Husserl was aware of it is shown by the following circumstances. In 1911 Brentano published parts of his empirical psychology under the title *Klassifikation der psychischen Phänomene*, with appendices. The doctrine that time consciousness has to do with modes of consciousness, i.e. modes of presentation that carry over to the judgement, is included there. Brentano sent this book to Husserl. Therefore, he should have called the attention of his student Heidegger to the fact that the doctrine under attack had been abandoned by Brentano by 1911 at the latest. (In fact, Brentano had given it up as early as 1895, as we

---

1. From the correspondence between Franz Brentano and Anton Marty and a section of a lecture by Marty on Brentano's theory of time dating from 1895, with an Introduction and notes. Reprinted from *Archiv für die gesammte Psychologie*, vol. 75 (1930), pp. 1–22.

2. *Vorlesungen*, p. 432; book edition, p. 66.

shall see.) In 1919, *together* with Husserl and Stumpf, I published *Franz Brentano: Zur Kenntnis seines Lebens und seiner Lehre* (Beck, Munich); Stumpf gives an account of Brentano's earlier doctrine of time[3] but also indicates the later change. He writes: 'This clear initial description of the facts he later "modified" in the literal sense of the word, in that he defined the transformation not as one of content, but as a change in the mode of the presentation.'

In the same book I deal explicitly with the new theory of time. Section 18 (p. 39) presents the temporal modes as '*modi obliqui*'. On 17 July 1918 Husserl asked me for the proofs of my book and he actually received them. In addition, he is naturally in possession of the book which contains his, Stumpf's, and my contributions. I criticise Husserl for having failed to draw the attention of the editors of his lectures to Brentano's doctrine of modes.

The question under consideration is of greatest importance. That Husserl devoted a special lecture course to the problem of time shows that he is well aware how important this investigation is. What we are concerned with is the phenomenognosy of time consciousness. Over the years Brentano changed his position on this question several times. At the beginning, independently of John Stuart Mill, he tried a solution that was similar to Mill's; later he understood the intuition of time as an intuition of peculiarly and continually varying differences in objects. Somewhere around the end of 1894 he gave up that doctrine. Difficulties of essentially the same sort as were later pointed out by Husserl caused him to revise the doctrine. The essential thing is this: Brentano recognised, as was already noted, that the intuitions of time differences that provide us with the presentation of 'earlier', 'later', 'present', and 'past', could not be differences of the primary objects, i.e. of what is usually called the 'content' of sensation; for reasons that are hinted at below as well as presented in the new editions and continuations of his *Psychology* (Meiner, Leipzig; three volumes have appeared so far), he recognised that the intuition of time goes back to the intuition of a continual modification of the sensory act itself, a modification that is present to us as an intuition in inner perception. You can see in this a certain similarity to Kant's doctrine, according to which we are concerned with a form of inner sense.

While, however, the 1894 theory of modes regards the intuition of time as an intuition of a continuum of differences in judgement – an instinctive belief in the sensory qualities, Brentano ultimately reached the point of transferring the modification to the *presentation*. This last stage of development had not yet been reached when he wrote the letter reprinted below. I refer you to Brentano's *Psychology* and to *Psychology III, Vom sinnlichen und noetischen Bewußtsein* (Leipzig, 1928). The same applies to the role of consciousness of the present with which we comprehend our consciousness itself in inner perception, and which is not represented below.

In the above mentioned *Klassifikation der psychischen Phänomene* of 1911 Brentano explains:

If we hear a series of sounds in a conversation or in a melody, or if we

3. See ch. 2 above.

watch a physical object which is in motion or is changing colour, the same sound, the same individual spatially and qualitatively defined coloured thing, appears to us first as present, then more and more as past, while new things appear as present, whose presentation then undergoes the same modal alteration. Anyone who took these differences to be differences of the objects involved – somewhat as spatial differences undoubtedly are when I have a presentation of something more to the right or more to the left in my field of vision – would be unable to do justice to the great difference which exists between space and time. (*Psychology*, p. 279).

We are dealing with different kinds of presentations.

But regardless of whether they are modes of judgement or primary modes of presentation, they are, in any case, modes of consciousness.

Now, by reprinting a letter of Marty's to Brentano of March 1895, and Brentano's answer, as well as a fragment from Marty's lectures setting forth the new doctrine, I can show, on the one hand, the disposition of problems out of which Brentano's later doctrine, as well as that of Husserl, evolved. On the other hand, I believe that the exemplary clarity in the posing of the questions, as well as in the attempt to solve them will be generally welcome, particularly in connection with Husserl's lectures.

Since I deal critically with Husserl's errors in the notes, I can claim that the pages which follow are not only of historical but also of current philosophical interest. All the more so because psychologists themselves, with few exceptions, are used to occupying themselves with measurements of the so-called present time and with similar tasks, yet have devoted very little attention to the analysis of time consciousness as such.

In addition, these pages may serve as a supplement to Brentano's *Psychology*, especially to the statements contained in *Psychology III* on the problem of time, and also as a prelude to the additional wealth of publications on the problem of time that are still to be expected from Brentano's *Nachlaß*.

1

Anton Marty to Franz Brentano   Prague
                                                                   9 March 1895

Dear Friend and Teacher,

I am under the pressure of time with regard to a chapter of my lectures on psychology; I have promised to lecture on the new theory of time, but I find, on the eve of the presentation, that I do not have an absolutely clear view of the matter myself. I thought I had notes on the subject that could set me right on the unclear points. But I find no such notes, and I see, with the time so short, no other way out than to ask you to rush to my aid by mail and, if possible, immediately (for I'll be up to this part by next Tuesday).

(1) What we can call our intuition of time is actually the intuition of a

special mode of judgement.[4] With the blind belief encountered in external intuition and with the evident kind in inner intuition there is connected a continuum of judgements which judge the intuited content[5] to be more and more past and temporally removed.

[Brentano's note: Ad. 1 'Cp. (e) and (f) in my letter'].[6]

(2) This continuum of judgement relations and the intuition of time that relates to it is limited. The presentation of the earlier past and of the future are conceptual constructs by analogy with what is given in that intuition, and the judgement that something will be in the future or was yesterday, is not of the same sort as that mode of judgement, rather, it only has a special object that reflection upon it presupposes.

[Brentano's note: Ad. 2 Cp. (g) and (h) in my letter].

(3) The continuum has *one* dimension.

(4) What about the non-real character of the temporal determinations? It seems that the irreality of the past is not merely a result of intentionality, for the relation to the intentional is also given in the case of the presently existing thing. What is present is that which causes the judgement: that it is.

[Brentano's note: Cp. (m) in my letter].[7]

Likewise, past is that which causes this special mode of judging. Why, then, isn't 'past' also merely an aorist as 'existing' is?

If it is a modifying predicate, then there must be another reason for it.

(5) What about the elimination of the modifying abstraction, which you also mention?

[Brentano's note: I do not understand the question. Maybe (h) relates to it].

In haste, and I thank you a thousand times in advance.

Yours truly
A. Marty

4. At that time Brentano described the intuition of time as an intuition of a continuum of modes of judgement; later as a continuum of modes of presentation, which, however, carry over to the judgement that is included in every sensation as a blind belief in the qualitative-spatial ('the suggestion of reality' as Linke calls it). Cp. below, p. 238 n. 28.

5. The word 'content' = 'object'. Cp. Brentano's letter in *Philosophische Hefte*, vol. 4 (Berlin, 1929).

6. Brentano refers in this note to Marty's letter to points (e) and (f) in his reply, which follows on p. 228 below.

7. At the time of this correspondence Brentano still believed that besides things there were non-things as well. On his later, contrasting theory, cp. my lecture 'Die kopernikanische Wendung in Franz Brentano's Erkenntnis und Wertlehre', reprinted in no. 3 of *Philosophische Hefte*. Cp. also my new edition of the *Psychology*, vols. 1–3. The earlier doctrine stipulated that a past king was no king and a past sound was no sound, so that here we were presented with a modifying attribute that changed a thing into a non-thing. Brentano gives up all this in his later writings. On the basis of the point of view they held at that time, Marty's question was justified: Why is it that just the predicates 'past' and 'future' change the thing into a non-thing, if differences in time are traced back to modes of intentionality of consciousness, i.e. to modes of

Franz Brentano to Anton Marty

Vienna, Sunday evening
March 1895

Dear Friend,

Even today not yet completely recovered, I don't know whether I will fulfil your wishes satisfactorily.

My opinion is that it would be best for you to:

(a) develop the old view,

(b) point out the objections to it, in particular the objection that heterogeneous elements are supposed to form a continuum.[8] Also, that there would be less difference between a non-thing and a thing than there would be between two non-things; indeed there would be infinitesimally little difference between them!

Then,

(c) you could speak about the earlier view I once entertained, independently of Mill, but in agreement with him, and show why it had to appear untenable. (According to it, time was not a continuum at all).

Then,

(d) how, in spite of this, I revived it. But with considerable modifications.

(e) The way for the revival was paved by the view, at which I arrived quite independently of these considerations, that every sensation is bound up with an apprehension of that which is sensed. (Irrevocably; this does not even cease to apply with the knowledge that the phenomenon is not real. Comparison with higher and lower desires. This holds true also of proteraesthesis.)[9]

(f) *In the same way as one could suppose the object of proteraesthesis to be modified in a continual manner, one could also think the object was unchanged, but the apprehension that refers to it was subject to a continual transformation.*[10] (There appear to be diverse modes of apprehension, in particular, the difference between the assertoric and apodictic modes. Here one would have only one kind of mode with continually varying species.)

(g) For the rest, it seems at first that nothing has changed as compared with the earlier view. As before when we had a limited continual series of objects in the proteraesthesis, we now have a limited continual series of

---

apprehension contained in the sensation? For a reference to a mode of apprehension is given just as much in the present as in the past and in the future; in the first case to the present mode and in the other cases to the past and future modes.

Brentano's answer is to be found in his letter under (m). Today the answer would be different. But its explication cannot be given here. Cp. provisionally, *Psychology III*.

8. Husserl stresses this fact as a rather strange one on p. 378 (12) of his *Vorlesungen*. Cp. below what Marty has to say about his own old lecture notes!

9. Marty elaborates on this idea, that is only alluded to here, in the lecture reprinted below. 'Proteraesthesis' = original intuition of time = Husserl's 'retention'.

10. All italics are Kraus's.

modes of apprehension of the same object. Thus one could continue to operate in a wholly analogous way.

(h)Nevertheless it remains to be investigated whether now some things are conceivable that were inconceivable before, as, for example, a true future mode in expectation.[11] We must be careful not to disallow this prematurely. It would have a particular importance for animal psychology and for the question whether there could be any sort of presentation of the future and something related to desire and striving in animals. According to the old theory this seemed to be essentially and definitely ruled out.

(i) It is obvious that in the new theory the objections (b) really no longer apply.

(k) One could also point out that the fact that the 'time word' is the expression of the apprehension favours the view that time differences are bound together with differences of apprehension.

(l) Also the usual view certainly seems to be more compatible with the view that the object which is recognised as present or past, etc. is the same.[12]

(m) Just as something present, something existing, means something to be apprehended as such, so, the same naturally applies to something past and previously or more recently past. Obviously then, other universal concepts can also be formed, such as the concept of sometime past: *it is to be apprehended with a kind of apprehension from a wide-ranging group of kinds of apprehension*.

This is done in a hurry and is certainly far from being exhaustive. Still, I hope it is comprehensible to you. Because I am afraid my letter may arrive too late, I cannot delay in sending it off.

3. *Time*
(From Marty's lecture on Brentano's doctrine of time, 1895)

It is noteworthy that differences in time are expressed linguistically by the copula, which is, after all, the sign of acceptance or rejection. Probably relying on this, earlier philosophers have, in fact, regarded differences of time as differences of judgement.

We find as far back as Aristotle an allusion to this, although it is not clear whether he considers time to be differences in the objects or in the judgements.

Thomas Aquinas, likewise, speaks about this; he even seems inclined to establish a major classification of judgements based upon differences in time (Commentary on Aristotle's *De Interpretatione*, chapter 13). He speaks there of five viewpoints for the *divisio enuntiationum:* (1) *unitas,* (2) *qualitas,* (3) *quantitas,* (4) *tempus* (whether the *enuntiatio* is *de praesente, de praeterito,* or *de futuro*), (5) *materia (de necessitate, impossibilitate, contingentia).*

This allows the assumption that St Thomas did not consider the time difference as a mere difference in objects. In recent times John Stuart Mill,

---

11. Compare Husserl's related idea in the *Vorlesungen.*
12. Cp. *Vorlesungen,* p. 386 (20).

in Book I of his *Logic*, has very clearly stated that he considers the differences in time, i.e. present, past, and future not as differences in the objects of judgement, but as differences in the kind of judgemental attitude, similar to quality, for example. He thinks the past, present and future have to do not with the predicate but with predication.

About twenty-five years ago (1868–70) when I heard his lectures, Brentano, too, independently of Mill, set forth such a doctrine. Whoever affirms a thing as past or as future, he maintained, certainly affirms the same object, but the sort of affirmation is different in the two cases. But he soon gave up this idea, mainly because, according to this formulation of the doctrine, time would not be a continuum at all. For Mill – and at that time Brentano too – listed present, past and future as three discrete species of judgements. So, once again he began to locate time in the object of presentation.[13]

This seemed particularly clear with regard to motion in place. If you think of this pencil that I am moving around in a circle, you do not merely think of it at a point (for then you would be thinking of it at rest); rather you think of it as being situated at different points on the course, but not simultaneously (for then you would be thinking of a body as long as the stretch through which the pencil moves), but rather you think of it as having been at various points on the stretch longer and longer ago. And, to be sure, this fact that the body was there longer and longer ago is, in a peculiar way, *intuitively* present to you. This intuition is a thing pertaining to a peculiar activity of the imagination, but not an activity of the imagination in the usual sense of the word, for the latter is not really original, but is productive only through experiences and acquired dispositions; in the presentation of the past, on the other hand, we have something that is *absolutely new*, for which there is no analogue whatsoever in experience. Insofar as I think of what was present as moving further and further into the past, an absolutely new element enters my thinking, and for that reason Brentano called this activity of the imagination *original association* in contrast to acquired association.[14]

13. Marty was Brentano's student in Würzburg from the autumn of 1868 until Easter 1870. Cp. Carl Stumpf, ch. 3 above. This shows that a theory of modes was first set forth by Brentano, but because of the discontinuity of the three discrete modes it was dropped. At the same time the date of Marty's lecture can be established as 1895 at the latest.

14. Husserl, *Vorlesungen*, p. 382 (16), in a critique, raises, in addition to Brentano's self-criticism of this theory, an objection which is certainly original but which moves in the wrong direction. He says, namely: 'A sound of a tone that is experienced has just faded away, it is renewed via original association and continuously retained as far as its content is concerned. But that would mean A is . . . not past at all, but has remained present. The whole difference would consist in the fact that the association is also supposed to be creative and that it adds a new element, called "past". . . . Thus the past, insofar as it falls within the sphere of the original temporal intuition, would have to be present at the same time. The temporal element "past" would have to be a present element of experience in the same sense as the element red that we actually experience is (which is clearly nonsense).'

Husserl is misled here into accusing Brentano of saying something that is 'clearly nonsense', by the ambiguity of the word 'present'. If I think of something red [*n.b.* to

He thinks, therefore, that through so-called 'original associations', i.e. through a special innate activity of the imagination, a continual series of presentations from the imagination attaches itself to every sensory or perceptual presentation, and these presentations reproduce *and at the same time change or modify* the perceived content in such a way that they add to it the past moment, i.e. earlier and earlier past, so that it seems, as it were, temporally removed.

This activity of the imagination, which he also calls proteraesthesis, is so lively that everyone is convinced that he perceives a movement or, in

---

say that I 'experience' red is wrong; one experiences states of consciousness, but not qualities or spatial extension: cp. Husserl p. 370 (4), 'None of these are experiences'] I say, therefore, 'I think of something red', I can also say, 'Red is given', 'Red is my intentional object', 'Red is "present" to me'. In this context, however, the phrase 'Something is present to me' means exactly the same as 'It is given', i.e. 'I think of it' or 'I sense it'. The word 'present' has no function in this context other than that of the word 'given' or 'intentionally or mentally inexistent'.

According to Brentano's earlier doctrine, the temporal element was not a determining (i.e. a closer determining) characteristic but a modifying characteristic (a modifying attribute) of the content of sensation (the object of presentation, the phenomenal object); I am thus presented with or see something, e.g. something extended, as well as being presented with the determinations 'red' and 'present' (= 'now'), and then with the determination 'past', or 'had been' through which determinations the 'red-extended' is altered; i.e. from a 'presently-existing' to a 'presently-past', from a thing to a non-thing. (The red-extended is first *present* to me as now (= present), i.e. given, intentionally inexistent and connected in a continuum as present-past, i.e. given, intentional, mentally inexistent.)

You can see an 'open contradiction' in this doctrine only if you do not notice that to be present as past means the same as given as past or to be intentionally mentally inexistent. Husserl himself raises the counter-objection; 'Perhaps someone will object, A itself is past in consciousness but, in virtue of the original association, is a newer content A with the character of "past".' Well! Brentano had similar thoughts on the matter. So where is this 'open contradiction'? Completely on Husserl's side. For he continues; 'In the meantime, if a similar content A is constantly in consciousness, even if it too has a new element, then A is not past but present.' I ask: what does 'A constantly in consciousness' mean? Nothing but 'someone constantly presents A', i.e. someone is constantly an A-presenter; that which is constantly 'present' and does not go by, is the *presenting* of A, but not, however A; A does not exist at all, if it is merely presented, therefore it is neither present nor past and indeed also then it is neither present nor past when it is presented as present or past, i.e. when someone presents it for a period of time as present or past.

Husserl says in the same connection: 'What, then, are the presently experienced elements of original association? Are they perhaps times themselves? Then we come to the contradiction: All these elements are now there, are contained in the same object of consciousness; they are, therefore, all contemporaneous and yet the succession of time excludes simultaneity.' The contradiction is only an apparent one and is to be explained through the misunderstanding of the equivocal character of the little word 'is' in the expression, 'Something *is* in consciousness'. In this case the word 'is' does not express the affirmation of the presented something, but merely the consciousness of its being presented. Husserl says that the various elements of time are simultaneously in consciousness, so it is only that there exists a consciousness that thinks all of these time elements at the same time. In this there is, at least, no general, change and succession, that he sees movements, hears melodies.[15]

This continuum of intuitive presentations of the imagination is so large, that a movement which is not too slow becomes noticeable and similarly, a melody is recognisable as such. After all, it lasts not more than fractions of seconds. A whole sentence that I speak to you is not present to you in this intuitive way, let alone the whole lecture. After a very short time it breaks off and then you must reproduce that which was earlier in the usual way by means of acquired memory. I think consideration of movement clarifies the matter best.

Why do we not see the grass grow? Because the movement is too slow to fall into this peculiar intuitive activity. If this activity of the imagination that grasps what is sensed and removes it temporally were unlimited, then we would be able to see the grass grow if we looked at it long enough.

Another example. We 'see' the second hand on a clock move. Why not the hour hand? Clearly because its motion is so slow that it no longer falls within the range of that activity of the imagination that presents you with it intuitively.[16] The short piece of the past is, however, the whole of our

---

contradiction. There would only be a contradiction if you think, with Husserl, that all time elements which are simultaneously presented, from the fact that there is a consciousness that presents them simultaneously, must also somehow be simultaneous.

That 'open contradiction' of which Husserl speaks, is certainly not to be found in the assumption that a phenomenal succession appears to us simultaneously, i.e. now in the present time consciousness. This phenomenal succession is not, as Husserl supposes, to be viewed, according to Brentano, as 'temporal signs', no more than phenomenal places are to be viewed as signs of location. But just as the coloured-extended object that we see imparts to us the concept of the coloured-extended, so we get time concepts from the phenomenal time differences of the object that we see. If we ask which differences of the intuition the concepts of present and past are derived from, and if, like the later Brentano, we do not conceive of these differences as differences in the so-called primary object, they must ultimately all be given simultaneously, or else there would be no intuition of time at all. That is why it was necessary to reject the shaky objections raised by Husserl, objections which, if they were right, would apply to any phenomenognosy of time consciousness that derives these concepts from intuitions of temporal modes.

15. Marty remarks now and then: 'One cannot experience what is past'. Brentano, at any rate in his later version (printed in *Vom sinnlichen und noetischen Bewußtsein* (Leipzig, 1928), p. 48) teaches: 'A sound, for example, which has become an object of of proteraesthesis, is no longer merely a sound but a sound of the same pitch, and, I dare add, a sound of the same intensity. If it were otherwise not every aesthesis would result in a proteraesthesis, for the weaker intensity would be the result of the partial disappearance of the object given in the aesthesis. A descrescendo is just as noticeable as is a crescendo.' So says Brentano. Of course it is true that one cannot experience what is past if one means that something that is past cannot cause a sensation. But it is not true that I can have no sensation of the past, i.e. no proteraesthesis. The intuitive way one sees a movement, hears a melody, etc. proves the opposite. The following words of Marty's lecture express with absolute clarity that we intuit an earlier and a later.

16. That activity of the imagination that Brentano calls proteraesthesis bears the name 'imagination' only equivocally, just as the terms 'original association' or 'momentary memory' which have the same meaning are neither association nor

intuitive presentation of time, and we only construct conceptually the presentation of further past, and, by analogy to the 'earlier' and 'later' given in intuition, we also construct the concept of the future. This is similar to the intuition of space. What is immediately present in intuition is very little. Our field of vision is unbelievably narrow; yet we know how to reap tremendous dividends from this small capital! We extend space conceptually to infinity. And thus, starting from the small, intuitive piece of temporal intuition that the imagination interrupts, breaks off at every moment, we construct the concept of unmeasured time, and we speak of millions of years.

The whole of these determinations of time that we are given in intuition, and that we construct conceptually is the analogue of an endless line, i.e. the species vary in one dimension and, as far as possibility is concerned, into infinity. In other words, there is no final species according to nature, rather it is merely a matter of our peculiar organisation – which concrete boundaries intuition of time has – and the duration of time intuitions could be different in different individuals and in different senses.[17]

The fact that the species of time form a continuum so that many, indeed an endless number, are always given together, and are always accompanied by relations in intuition, has furthered the well-known illusion that time is something merely relative; Leibniz, for example, thought that time was succession. In truth time is by nature not succession, but the prerequisite thereof. *The earlier or later* is a temporal relation which presupposes absolute temporal determinations, quite analogous to place.[18]

---

memory in the strict sense of the words. Husserl polemicises against the doctrine that the 'original intuition of time is a creation of the imagination'. He says that it is most striking that in his theory of time intuition Brentano does not take into consideration the conspicuous distinctioin between time perception and time fantasy, which he could not possibly have overlooked. Now if 'Brentano could not possibly have overlooked this distinction', he will certainly not have overlooked it. I truly do not have to defend him here, but it suffices to point to the existing letters and lectures and that which Husserl 'could not possibly have overlooked' because it was in print right under his nose for a long time. Strangely enough, Husserl speaks himself (p. 391 (25)) of 'primary remembering or retention', without being struck by the fact that this says more or less the same as 'original association' or 'proteraesthetic imagination'. With as much or as little justice as Husserl criticised Brentano, one would criticise Husserl by saying that it is rather striking that he has overlooked the conspicuous distinction between time perception and time memory.

17. Cp. *Vorlesungen*, p. 391 (25): 'Note: *Idealiter*, is also possible for a consciousness· in which everything is retained.'

18. At that time both Brentano and Marty believed – as Husserl still does today – that absolute species of determinations of locations as well as absolute species of determinations of space are given in the intuition, just as red and blue and the notes C and D are given in intuition in the final species. But Brentano later recognised the error of this formulation and expounded it. We perceive spatial and temporal absolutes only in a very general way, never *in specie specialissima*. The respective explanations are contained in Kraus's editions of Brentano's *Psychology*, and *Sensory and Noetic Consciousness*. All I can do here is cite them.

Only one thing should be noticed: it is impossible for anyone to be justified in expressing relative determinations of something and at the same time to be justified in

Here is something else that was not given with the place! The temporal determinations that are added to presentations or perceptions in this way through proteraesthesis are *modifying* rather than *determining* predicates.

This can only be made clear by means of examples. Something red existing here or blue existing there actually are a red or a blue something. The predicates 'here' and 'there' are determining. Yet a past sound is not a real sound, yesterday's or tomorrow's rain is not real rain. You do not get wet from it. 'Past' and 'future' are modifying predicates, just as predicates such as 'painted', 'thought of', 'loved', 'hated', 'desired', etc. are.

And what is more, *all these predicates change the real into the non-real.* A thought-of 'palace' is not only no palace, it is nothing real at all. The same is true of the past as such, the future as such.

This very characteristic that the past and future are not real, constitutes, however, a serious objection to the doctrine previously set forth, that the differences in time[19] are a matter of the contents *thought* of.

If time, like space, is a continuum, then it must be true that there is a continuum made up of totally heterogeneous elements – as heterogeneous as the real and the non-real – and that is highly objectionable.[20] In such a case an actually present red must stand in a relation of continuity with the past red. And if they are united in a continuum, even though the one is real and the other not real, there is less difference between them than there is between *irrealia*; the difference between them would be infinitesimally, i.e. infinitely, small! But how can that be? Colours and sounds can certainly not form a continuum. Why not? Because they are of different species. Nonetheless, they are still closer to one another insofar as both are things. In contrast, the past and present are separated by a much greater gulf than that which separates sounds and colours.

That is the big difficulty. (In old lecture notes you can read that I stressed this as particularly serious and mysterious even when I adhered to the old viewpoint).

In order to avoid this difficulty, it would seem that one must return to the old view that time is not a matter of the thought-of *content*, but of the *mode of judgement*, and Brentano, too, is now inclined to do this, although with significant modifications. The way for this revival was paved by the conclusion, arrived at completely independently, that *every sensation is originally and indissolubly connected to the cognition of the thing sensed.*

I have often said that everything that appears to the child is regarded by him instinctively as true, on the basis of an innate necessity. On closer scrutiny, it can be seen that this instinctive belief is simply inseparable from

---

denying the final absolute determinations of the same kind which form the basis for them. In other words, nothing relative can *in fact exist* without being based upon an absolute that is determined up to the *final species* of the same kind. Yet it is true that something relative can be intuited without such *final species*.

19. What are meant here are naturally the differences of the so-called proteraesthesis, i.e. of temporal intuition. The word 'time' as used here is an abbreviation for temporal intuition.

20. Cp. Husserl, *Vorlesungen*, who raises this objection on p. 378 (12) and also on p. 382 (16) and above p. 228.

sensation.[21] It is true that this sensory believing, if I can call it such, upon which this direct belief in the external world is based, is suspended, as it were, by the higher knowledge, but cannot be eliminated. It is not an act that is superimposed, for one-sided detachability is part of the concept of superimposition. The situation is rather such that *sensation is an act* which contains two mutually inseparable parts, namely *the intuition of the physical phenomenon and the assertoric acceptance of the same*.

One might object to this by saying that we could emancipate ourselves from this sensory belief that is so clear in the case of children and sensory illusions; this is indubitably true in the case of physicists, philosophers, physiologists, and, to a certain extent even of ordinary people. The reply to this is that in the case of this so-called emancipation from the sensory belief we are actually confronted with two judgements. On the basis of rational deliberation, a rational, insightful judgement, i.e. knowledge, arises. But the instinctive judgement remains. In spite of the countervailing knowledge that the phenomenon does not really exist, the judgement persists and holds firm. In Aristotle there is a pertinent reference to the well known sensory illusion created with a little ball held between crossed fingers. You can say to yourself a hundred times that there is only *one* ball, but nonetheless the illusion that there are two persists. Helmholtz, too, has repeatedly emphasised with regard to optical illusions that they persist even after the error has been realised and one has made a rational judgement to the contrary. This is perfectly well known in cases of illusions of perspective.[22]

Such an opposition of acts of higher and lower judgement has an analogy in the sphere of the emotions, for there is an obvious conflict between higher and lower desires. Very often the same thing is both loved and hated, loved blindly, instinctively, sensuously, and hated as a result of higher ethical considerations. When the ascetic or any one of us combats certain sensuous desires and, restrained by ethical considerations, chooses the opposite, do the senuous desires cease? No, they remain. This is why the moralists' doctrine maintains that the so-called *motus primo primi voluntatis* are not sinful because we cannot master them, indeed because they are ineradicable.

Thus opposing higher and lower judgements can exist simultaneously in the same consciousness, and I believe I can maintain with complete

21. CP. Franz Brentano, *Vom sinnlichen und noetischen Bewußtsein*. Linke speaks of a suggestion of reality (*Wirklichkeitssuggestion*). Very few psychologists pay attention to this element of belief that is contained in the sensation itself. People are often of the opinion that judging is indeed a higher mental function. Yet this is certainly an error. A thorough analysis will reveal that this same kind of consciousness, this same kind of intention that is contained in higher forms of knowing and judging, is already present in the acts of sensation. In the same way the essential characteristic of loving and hating which is already contained in the affects, recurs in the higher acts of evaluation, as Marty at once explained.

22. The ball experiment (see Aristotle, *Metaphysics* 1011a33, *On Dreams* 460b20, and *Problemata* 958b14, 959a15, and 965a36) is not the best example of what is to be proved. For here additional convictions acquired by means of experience and habituation play a role in addition to the original acts of sensation. It would have been better if Marty had simply pointed to the fact that no one can free himself from the belief that he has a dark plane before him when he shuts his eyes; in short, if he had referred to the instinctive belief which all of us have in sensory qualities.

certainty that the belief in its content[23] is an inseparable and unceasing part of every sensory intuition, a part of the same fundamental act.

Such a belief exists not only in sensation but in proteraesthesis as well. In this sensory manner we believe not just in the present sound, but also in an immediately past one. *Here, too, the act of intuition incorporates the affirmative judgement as well; and now it is not too far-fetched to say that instead of thinking of the objects of proteraesthesis as being modified in a continual way, we transfer this modification to the corresponding affirmation while the object remains unchanged. The object of proteraesthesis is the same as that of sensation, but it is connected with a modified form of the affirmation. For example, red is always seen and affirmed, but this affirmation is subject to a continual transformation and it is this transformation that, as it were, makes the object temporally remote and that constitutes the source of our concept of time.*[24]

We already know that there are various modes of affirmation, e.g. the evident, a special mode that contrasts with the blind, and the motivated, a special mode that contrasts with the unmotivated. Thus the temporal affirmation, too, is a particular modification, yet in this case we are

23. 'Content' here means 'object'. We are concerned with the belief in that which is sensed.

24. This expresses in the clearest manner the doctrine that the proteraesthesis, which Husserl re-christened 'retention', consists in a continuum of modifications of consciousness (*Bewußtseinsmodifikationen*). Husserl uses the expression 'modifications of consciousness' in his 'Lectures' p. 421 (55); he also speaks there of a 'continual modification of the perception'.

If one adheres to these statements one would have to consider his theory identical with Brentano's re-formulation of the original theory. One would have to believe that Husserl's theory means that the source of the time concept is not the intuition of a characteristic change of that which is sensed, but the intuition of the modally varying sensation itself. But p. 338 (22) does not allow this interpretation. It says there: 'We distinguish between the persisting immanent object and the object in its mode of appearance of which we are conscious as actually present or as past.' Furthermore, he shows us the 'object in the mode of change'. Only one of the two is possible; either the temporal difference is a difference in *objects*, or it must be a difference of relations, of intentionality, i.e. a mode of consciousness. It is not easy to determine what sort of a difference it is according to Husserl. But from all appearances, it is a third alternative. He speaks, in fact, not only of the mode of appearing, but also of the mode of what appears.

Consciousness, according to Husserl, refers to its object by means of an appearance in which the object presents itself in its mode of appearance. But how the object can exist in its mode of appearance if this mode of appearance is not supposed to be a difference in object, is simply incomprehensible.

The talk of an 'equivocal sense of intentionality' depending on whether we are looking at the relation of the appearing to what appears, or the relation of consciousness to the 'mode in which something appears' and on the other hand to 'that which appears as such' does not make the theory any more transparent. If the 'how' something appears were a difference in object, according to Husserl, then we would have Brentano's old theory before us, whose 'original imagination of association' simply means a characteristic modification of the object. Only by completely misinterpreting Brentano's doctrine could Husserl identify the role of the so-called 'activity of the imagination' with that of 'imagination' so-called (cp. above p. 230 and note 14).

confronted with a kind of mode of affirmation that is characterised by continually varying species; the modes of affirmation form a continuum of one dimension. Furthermore, this continuum, as we also said on the earlier view, is limited, indeed quite narrowly so.

On the earlier view we had a limited continuous series of objects always being modified; here we have a limited series of modes of affirmation of the same objects.

Of course, on the new view it still remains true that time is not identical with the relations earlier and later, but that these relations are based on absolute determinations.[25] It also remains true that the limitation does not lie in the nature of the temporal species, that the continuum can be further constructed conceptually into infinity, so that it can be depicted as analogous to an endless straight line.[26]

We see, therefore, that a number of points remain the same on both the new and the old views. One thing is eliminated, however; the difficulty that made the old view so dubious to us, namely that it allowed things and non-things to form a continuum. For now what follow one another continually are the modes of affirmation, and they are all real. The object, on the other hand, remains unchanged; it is not that red comes after past red, but that red remains unchanged.[27]

Now, if one asks, 'Is there, then, still an intuition of time, and what is it?'

Should Husserl mean a third thing that lies in the direction of the 'noema' that he later discovered, we would be confronted with a fiction in comparison to which the fiction of the so-called 'immanent object' at least had the advantage of being a fiction *cum fundamento in re*. With the 'noema' and its correlative 'noesis', on the other hand, we are clearly dealing with free creations of Husserl's mind, since it is a fiction *sine fundamento in re sed cum fundamento in elocutione* to speak of 'the remembered as such', 'the perceived as such', etc. as though these 'noema' were words with a meaning of their own and not mere sentence fragments which, taken as such, are destined to awaken preparatory presentations and expectations of meaning, but which, do not have independent meaning in themselves.

Since this 'noema' is already an absurd fiction, the absurdity reaches dizzying heights if a 'noesis' is invented and added to it as a correlative which is supposed to be related to empirical thought in the same way as an 'ideal number' is related to a collective of numerable things. I feel no need whatsoever to continue any further with a critique of this newest phase of a so-called 'phenomenology' which hypostatises the 'realm of ideal numbers' a realm of 'pure', i.e. ideal, consciousness, particularly since Husserl, in calmly carrying his fantasy structure into the clouds, has not even made minimal efforts to come to terms with the devastating critique that Brentano raised against this sort of fiction (viz. *Psychology*, Book II).

25. Cp. above, note 18.

26. Cp. Oskar Kraus, *Offene Briefe an Albert Einstein und Max von Laue über die gedanklichen Grundlagen der speziellen und allgemeinen Relativitätstheorie* (Vienna, 1925) and my other earlier critiques that are mentioned there, especially *Fiktion und Hypothese in der Einsteinischen Relativitätstheorie, Sonderheft der Annalen der Philosophie; Zur Relativitätstheorie* 2nd ed. (Leipzig, 1922).

27. According to Husserl, *Vorlesungen*, p. 371, the red that we see as the object of our sensation should actually not be called red at all. 'The sensed red', he says literally 'is only called red equivocally, for "red" is the name of a real quality'. Applying this to the sounds that we hear, 'the sensed tone C is only called C equivocally, for "C" is the

The answer is, 'What deserves the name is not the intuition of *physical* phenomena, but the intuition of a *mental* phenomenon or a continuum of mental phenomena, a continually varying series of modes of judgement; and it is here that the source of all temporal concepts is to be sought. For on the basis of this intuition of a 'limited continuum of characteristic modes of affirmation one can then form the concepts of a more distant past, and the concepts of the future, of which we have no actual intuitions.[28]

One more question arises. We attribute temporal determination to things. We speak of yesterday's rain, of today's lunch, of a future examination; and these are certainly not modes of affirmation, but things of a completely different sort.

The answer to be given is this: These predicates signify references of a particular mode of affirmation to possible judgements.

Just remember the concept of existence! What did we say about what exists? What exists is what is to be affirmed. Now, just as the presently existing signifies something to be affirmed as such, the past and the more remote and more recent past signify something modified to be affirmed as such, and these predicates are not real.[29]

Of course it is then possible to form universal concepts as, for example, the concept of 'something that existed at some time or another in the past'. That simply means something that is to be affirmed with some mode of

---

name of a real quality'. A thought-of thing is only equivocally a 'thing', etc.!

Just as phenomenal places are actually only 'signs of locality', sensed qualities are actually only signs of a quality.

28. Later Brentano transferred the modification to the act of presentation itself and let it thus carry over into the act of judgement. In this connection the doctrine of the direct and indirect modes (*modus rectus* and *obliquus*) plays an important role. This theory of Brentano's had been available to Husserl since 1911 in the copy inscribed by Brentano himself, and, in addition, in the book on which Husserl collaborated, *Franz Brentano: Zur Kenntnis seines Lebens und seiner Lehre* (Munich, 1919). Cp. the introduction.

29. This description – as already mentioned – does not correspond to the latest development of the doctrine. According to the most recent version, there are no non-real predicates, nor are words such as 'existence', 'existing things', 'past things', 'future things', expressions that have their own meaning. Also there is no reference to possible judgements included; for a more detailed discussion of this see *The True and the Evident*. The reader will find some additional material on this subject in *Philosophische Hefte*, no. 3, and in my edition of Brentano's *Psychology*. But another volume *Raum, Zeit, Kontinuum* is still to be·published. One ought not believe that the above treatment has even come close to exhausting the subject. Just to raise the most important point, it includes only statements about proteraesthesis (Husserl's 'retention') which refer exclusively to primary objects. It does not deal with the question whether inner perception itself exhibits anything like proteraesthesis. Do we have presentations of hearing and seeing and thinking in temporal variations as we do of sounds? Brentano denies this and also shows why this would lead to an infinite regress and thus is not possible. Inner perception shows us our own acts always only as present – as boundaries. According to Brentano, inner perception is evident, a characteristic that is lacking with regard to external intuition and therefore also with regard to proteraesthesis. This is another important instance where significant differences between his doctrine and Husserl's emerge.

affirmation out of a wide-ranging group of modes of affirmation. This was the error that Mill and Brentano, too, earlier, had made; they thought that 'past' and 'future' are species. If that were true time would not be a continuum. What we call past is only a more general name for a wide-ranging group of species which vary infinitesimally but every one of which is different from all the others.

Bibliography of the Published Writings of Franz Brentano

Roderick M. Chisholm

1862–1869

1. *Von der mannigfachen Bedeutung des Seienden nach Aristoteles*, Freiburg i. Br., 1862, Herder.
    Reprinted in 1960 by Wissenschaftliche - Buchgesellschaft, Darmstadt.

2. 'Ad disputationem qua Theses Gratiosi Philosophorum Ordinis Consensu et Auctoritate pro Impetranda Venia Docendi . . .', Aschaffenburg, 1866, J.W. Schipner (3 pages).

3. 'Geschichte der kirchlichen Wissenschaften', in Johann Adam Möhler, *Kirchengeschichte* (ed. P.R. Gams), vol. II, 526–84, vol. III, Part Two, 103–4; Regensburg, 1867, Georg Joseph Mans.

4. *Die Psychologie des Aristoteles, insbesondere seine Lehre vom* Nous Poietikos, Mainz, 1867, Franz Kirchheim.

5. 'August Comte und die positive Philosophie', *Chilianeum: Blätter für katholische Philosophie, Kunst, und Leben*, Neue Folge, vol. II (1869), 15–37.
    Also in *Die vier Phasen der Philosophie* (1926).

1870–1879

1. 'Thomas von Aquin' (review of Johannes Delitzsch, *Die Gotteslehre des Thomas von Aquino*), *Theologisches Literaturblatt*, ed. F.H. Reusch, vol. V (Bonn, 1870), 459–63.

2. Review of Friedrich Kampe, *Die Erkenntnistheorie des Aristoteles*, in *Zeitschrift für Philosophie und philosophische Kritik*, vol. 59 (1872), 219–38, and vol. 60 (1872), 81–127.

3. (Published anonymously) 'Der Atheismus und die Wissenschaft', *Historisch-politische Blätter f. d. katholische Deutschland 1873*, vol. 72 (1873), 853–72, 916–29.

4. *Psychologie vom empirischen Standpunkt*, vol. I, Leipzig, 1874, Duncker & Humblot.

5. *Über die Gründe der Entmutigung auf philosophischem Gebiete*, Vienna, 1874, Braumüller.
Also in *Über die Zukunft der Philosophie* (1929).

6. 'Herr Horwicz als Rezensent. Ein Beitrag zur Orientierung über unsere wissenschaftlichen Kulturzustände', *Philosophische Monatshefte*, vol. 4 (1875).

7. *Was für Philosoph manchmal Epoche macht*, Vienna, Pest, and Leipzig, 1876, Hartleben.
Also in *Die vier Phasen der Philosophie* (1926).

8. *Neue Rätsel von Änigmatias*, Vienna, 1879, Carl Gerold's Sohn.

1880–1889

1. *Über den Creatianismus des Aristoteles*, Vienna, 1882, Carl Gerold's Sohn.

2. *Offener Brief an Herrn Professor Eduard Zeller aus Anlass seiner Schrift über die Lehre des Aristoteles von der Ewigkeit des Geistes*, Leipzig, 1883, Duncker & Humblot.

3. 'Miklosich über subjecktlose Sätze', review of Franz Miklosich, *Subjecktlose Sätze, Wiener Zeitung*, no. 261 (13 November 1883) and no. 262 (14 November 1883).
Also in the first edition of *Vom Ursprung sittlicher Erkenntnis* (1889), in the English translations of this work (1902 and 1969), but not in subsequent German editions; in vol. II of *Psychologie vom empirischen Standpunkt* (1924) but not in English translation.

4. 'Das Recht auf den Selbstmord', *Deutsche Zeitung*, Vienna, 6 September 1894.
Also in the second and subsequent editions of *Vom Ursprung sittlicher Erkenntnis*.

5. *Vom Ursprung sittlicher Erkenntnis*, Leipzig, 1889, Duncker & Humblot.

1890–1899

1. *Das Genie*, Leipzig, 1892, Duncker & Humblot.
Also in *Grundzüge der Ästhetik* (1959).

2. *Das Schlechte als Gegenstand dichterischer Darstellung*, Leipzig, 1892, Duncker & Humblot.
Also in *Grundzüge der Ästhetik* (1959).

3. 'Rěul ca object de poesie', *Tribuna Bucuresci*, Bucharest, June, 1892.
Translation, appearing in eight issues, of *Das Schlechte als Gegenstand dichterischer Darstellung* (1892).

4. *Über die Zukunft der Philosophie*, Vienna, 1893, Alfred Hölder.

5. 'Über ein optisches Paradoxon', *Zeitschrift für Psychologie und Physiologie der Sinnesorgane* (Bd. 3, 1892 and Bd. 5, 1893), vol. III (1892), 349–58, and vol. V (1893), 61–82.

6. 'Zur Lehre von den optischen Täuschungen', *Zeitschrift für Psychologie und Physiologie der Sinnesorgane*, vol. VI (1894), 1–7.

7. *Die vier Phasen der Philosophie und ihr augenblicklicher Stand*, Stuttgart, 1895, Cotta.

8. *Meine letzten Wünsche für Österreich*, Stuttgart, 1895, Cotta.

9. 'Vorwort', in A. Herzen, *Wissenschaft und Sittlichkeit*, Lausanne, 1895, Verlag Payot, iii–vi.
    Also in third edition and subsequent German editions of *Vom Ursprung sittlicher Erkenntnis*.

10. *Noch ein Wort über das Ehehinderniss der höheren Weihen und feierlichen Gelübde*, Vienna, 1895, Manz.
    Included in *Zur eherechtlichen Frage in Österreich* (1896).

11. *Zur eherechtlichen Frage in Österreich: Krasnopolski's Rettungsversuch einer verlorenen Sache*, Berlin, 1896, J. Guttentag.

12. *Krasnopolskis letzter Versuch*, Leipzig, 1896, J.J. Arndt. First published in *Die Zeit*, Vienna, October, 1896.

13. 'Zur Lehre von der Empfindung', *Dritter internationaler Congress für Psychologie in München*, Munich, 1897, Lehmann, 112–33.

1900–1909

1. *Neue Vertheidigung der Spanischen Partie*, Vienna, 1900, Verlag der 'Weiner Schachzeitung' (Georg Marco); reprinted from the *Wiener Schachzeitung*.

2. *Neue Vertheidigung der Spanischen Partie: Zweiter Artikel*, Vienna, 1900, Verlag der 'Weiner Schachzeitung' (Georg Marco); reprinted from the *Wiener Schachzeitung*.

3. 'Über voraussetzunglose Forschung,' published anonymously in *Münchner Neuesten Nachrichten*, no. 573 (15 December 1901).
    Also in *Die vier Phasen der Philosophie* (1926).

4. *The Origin of the Knowledge of Right and Wrong*, translation by Cecil Hague of the first edition of *Ursprung sittlicher Erkenntnis*, London, 1902, Archibald Constable & Co., Ltd.

5. 'Von der psychologischen Analyse der Tonqualitäten in ihre eigentlich ersten Elemente', *Atti del V. Congresso Internazionale di Psicologia*, Rome, 1905, Forzani, 157–65.
    Also in *Untersuchungen zur Sinnespsychologie* (1907).

6. *Untersuchungen zur Sinnespsychologie*, Leipzig, 1907, Duncker & Humblot.

7. 'Thomas von Aquin', *Neue Freie Presse*, Vienna, 18 April 1908.
    Also in *Die vier Phasen der Philosophie* (1926).

8. *Änigmatias: Neue Rätsel*, Munich, 1909, Oskar Beck.
    Second edition of *Neue Rätsel von Änigmatias* (1879).

1910–1919

1. 'Aristotles', in E. v. Aster, *Grosse Denker*, vol. I (Leipzig, 1911, Quelle & Meyer), 155–207.

2. *Aristoteles und seine Weltanschauung*, Leipzig, 1911, Quelle & Meyer.
    Reprint of 'Aristoteles' (1911) with some additional material.

3. *Aristoteles' Lehre vom Ursprung des menschlichen Geistes*, Leipzig, 1911, Veit & Comp.

4. *Von der Klassifikation der psychischen Phänomene*, Leipzig, 1911, Duncker & Humblot.
    Also in vol. II of *Psychologie vom empirischen Standpunkt* (1924).

5. *La Classificazione delle Attività Psichiche*, Lanciano, 1913, R. Curabba.
    Translation by Mario Puglisi of *Von der Klassifikation der psychischen Phänomene* (1911).

6. 'Epikur und der Kreig', *Internationale Rundschau*, Zürich, 1916.
    Also in second and subsequent editions of *Vom Ursprung sittlicher Erkenntnis*.

1920–1929

1. 'Zur Lehre von Raum und Zeit', *Kant-Studien*, vol. XXV (1920), 1–23.

2. *Vom Ursprung sittlicher Erkenntnis*, second edition, ed. O. Kraus, Leipzig, 1922, Felix Meiner.

3. *Die Lehre Jesu und ihre bleibende Bedeutung*, ed. A. Kastil, Leipzig, 1922, Felix Meiner.

4. *Psychologie vom empirischen Standpunkt*, second edition, vol. I, ed. O. Kraus, Leipzig, 1924, Felix Meiner.

5. *Psychologie vom empirischen Standpunkt*, second edition, vol. II, ed. O. Kraus, Leipzig, 1924, Felix Meiner.

6. *Versuch über die Erkenntnis*, ed. A. Kastil, Leipzig, 1925, Felix Meiner.

7. 'Religion und Philosophie', *Philosophie und Leben*, vol. I (1925), 333–9, 370–81, 410–16.
    Also in *Religion und Philosophie* (1954).

8. *Die vier Phasen der Philosophie*, ed. O. Kraus, Leipzig, 1926, Felix Meiner.

9. 'Über Prophetie' (with editorial notes by O. Kraus), *Jahrbuch der Charakterologie*, vol. II–III (1926), 259–64.

10. 'Zur Klassifikation der Künste', *Hochschulwissen*, Heft 2 (1926), 57–62.
    Included in slightly different form in *Grundzüge der Ästhetik* (1959).

11. 'La Rivelazione Soprannaturale ed il dovere di crederla' (translated by Mario Puglisi), *Il Progresso Religioso*, N. 2 (1926), 3–22.

12. *Der Sonnengesang des heiligen Franz von Assisi* (Brentano's German translation in verse), Dresden, 1926, Wolfgang Jess.

13. *Psicologia*, Madrid, 1926, Revista de Occidenti.
    Translation by José Gaos, vol. I of 1st edition of *Psychologie vom empirischen Standpunkt*.

14. *El Origén del Conocimiento Moral*, Madrid, 1927, Revista de Occidente.
    Translation, by M.G. Morente, of first edition of *Vom Ursprung sittlicher Erkenntnis*.

15. *Vom sinnlichen und noetischen Bewußtsein* (*Psychology III*), ed. O. Kraus, Leipzig, 1928, Felix Meiner.

16. *Über die Zukunft der Philosophie*, ed. O. Kraus, Leipzig, 1929, Felix Meiner.

17. 'Gegen entia rationis, sogenannte irreale oder ideale, Gegenstände' (with editorial notes by O. Kraus), *Philosophische Hefte*, vol. II (1929), 257–74.
    Also in *Wahrheit und Evidenz* (1930) and English translation (1966).

18. *Vom Dasein Gottes*, ed. A. Kastil, Leipzig, 1929, Felix Meiner.

1930–1939

1. *Wahrheit und Evidenz*, ed. O. Kraus, Leipzig, 1930, Felix Meiner.

2. Letter to Anton Marty on consciousness of time; pp. 6–8, in 'Zur Phänomenognosie des Zeitbewußtseins', by O. Kraus, *Archiv für die gesammte Psychologie*, vol. 75 (1930), 1–22.

3. *Kategorienlehre*, ed. A. Kastil, Leipzig, 1933, Felix Meiner.

4. *Vom Ursprung sittlicher Erkenntnis*, third edition, ed. O. Kraus, Leipzig, 1934, Felix Meiner.

1940–1959

1. Letters to H. Schell, in Eduard Winter, *Franz Brentanos Ringen um eine neue Gottessicht: Nach dem unveröffentlichten Briefweschsel F. Brentano – H. Schell*, Brünn, 1941, Rudolf M. Rohrer.
   Also in *Über die Perfektabilität des Katholizismus* (1971).

2. *Psicologia*, Buenos Aires, 1942, Editorial Schapire-Parana.
   Translation by José Gaos of Volume One of the first edition of *Psychologie vom empirischen Standpunkt*.

3. *Psychologie du point de vue empirique*, Paris, 1944, Aubier.
   Translation by Maurice de Grandillac of Volumes One and Two of the second edition of *Psychologie vom empirischen Standpunkt*.

4. Translation into Hebrew of *Ursprung sittlicher Erkenntis*, by Hugo Bergman, Jerusalem, 1933, The Hebrew University.

5. *Aristotles*, Barcelona, 1943, Ed. Labor S. A.
   Translation by Moises Sanchez Barrado of *Aristoteles und seine Weltanschauung* (1911).

6. 'Briefe Franz Brentanos an Hugo Bergman', edited by Hugo Bergman, *Philosophy and Phenomenological Research*, VII (1946), 83–158.

7. *Grundlegung und Aufbau der Ethik*, ed. F. Mayer-Hillebrand, Bern, 1952, A. Francke.

8. *Religion und Philosophie*, ed. F. Mayer-Hillebrand, Bern, 1954, A. Francke.

9. 'Das Franz Brentano-Gutachten Über die päpstliche Infallibilität', with editorial comments by Ludwig Lenhart, *Archiv für mittelrheinische Kirchengeschichte*, vol. VV (1955), 295–334.

10. *Die Lehre vom Richtigen Urteil*, ed. F. Mayer-Hillebrand, Bern, 1956, A. Francke.

11. *Grundzüge der Ästhetik*, ed. F. Mayer-Hillebrand, Bern, 1959, A. Francke.

1960–1969

1. *Änigmatias: Rätsel*, fifth revised edition, Bern and Munich, 1962, A. Francke.

2. *Geschichte der Griechischen Philosophie*, ed. F. Mayer-Hillebrand, Bern and Munich, 1963, A. Francke.

3. 'Unbekannte Manuskripte Franz Brentanos', in *Horizons of a Philosopher: Essays in Honor of David Baumgart*, edited by J. Frank, H. Minkowski, and E.J. Sternglass, Leiden, 1963, E.J. Brill; 34–49. Two papers ('Optimismus' and 'Übereinstimmende Sätze bei Aristoteles und Leibniz') with editorial notes by Samuel Hugo Bergman.

4.   Two letters to Ernst Mach in pp. 157–9 of K.P. Heller, *Ernst Mach: Wegbereiter der Modernen Physik*, Vienna, 1964, Springer-Verlag.

5.   'On the Concept of Truth', in John V. Canfield and F.H. Donnell, eds., *Readings in Theory of Knowledge*, New York, 1964, Appleton-Century-Crofts, pp. 261–84.
     Translation by R.M. Chisholm and Kurt R. Fischer of the first selection in *Wahrheit und Evidenz*.

6.   Six letters to A. Meinong, in R. Kindinger, ed., *Philosophenbriefe*, Graz, 1965, Academische Druck- u. Verlagsanstalt; 18–23.

7.   'Sprechen und Denken', 'Wahrheit ist eine Art von Übereinstimmung', 'Über den Sinn und die wissenschaftliche Bedeutung des Satzes, "Veritas est adequatio rei et intellectus"', 'Kurzer Abriss einer allgemeinen Erkenntnistheorie' (in English and German) in *Franz Brentano's Analysis of Truth*, by Jan Srzednicki, The Hague, 1965, Martinus Nijhoff; pp. 116–35.

8.   *Die Abkehr vom Nichtrealen*, ed. F. Mayer-Hillebrand, Bern and Munich, 1966, A. Francke.

9.   *The True and the Evident*, London, 1966, Routledge & Kegan Paul.
     Translation, by R.M. Chisholm and E. Politzer, of *Wahrheit und Evidenz* (1930).

10. *Sull' origine della conoscenza morale*, Brescia, 1966, La Scuola Editrice.
     Translation by Adriano Bausola of *Vom Ursprung sittlicher Erkenntnis*.

11. Letter to Ernst Mach in pp. 287–93 of Joachim Thiele, 'Ein Brief Franz Brentanos über Probleme der Geometrie', *Kant-Studien*, vol. 58 (1967), 385–93.

12. Letter to Ernst Mach, in pp. 294–6 of Joachim Thiele, 'Briefe Deutscher Philosophen an Ernst Mach', *Synthese*, vol. 18 (1968), 285–301.

13. *Die vier Phasen der Philosophie*, second edition, Hamburg, 1968, Felix Meiner.

14. *Über die Zukunft der Philosophie*, second edition, Hamburg, 1968, Felix Meiner.

15. *Psychologie vom empirischen Standpunkt*, vol. III, *Vom sinnlichen und noetischen Bewußtsein*, second edition, ed. Franziska Mayer-Hillebrand, Hamburg, 1968, Felix Meiner.

16. *The Origin of Our Knowledge of Right and Wrong*, London, 1969, Routledge & Kegan Paul.
     Translation, by R.M. Chisholm and E. Schneewind, of the third edition of *Vom Ursprung sittlicher Erkenntnis* (1934).

17. 'Einige Bemerkungen über die Frage: Ist es zeitgemäss, die Unfehlbarkeit des Papstes zu definieren?' (407–437); a letter to Georg v. Hertling (452–3); and 'Gesuch an das Staatsministerium . . . um

Ernnenung zum a. o. Professor'; in Theobald Freudenberger, *Die Universität Würzburg und das erste vatikanische Konzil*, Neustadt a. d. Aisch, 1969, Degener.

1970–

1. *Versuch über die Erkenntnis*, second enlarged edition, Hamburg, 1970, Felix Meiner.

2. Letters to H. Schell in Eduard Winter, *Über die Perfektabilität des Katholizismus*, Berlin, G.D.R., 1971.

3. Letter to Giovanni Vailati, in Giovanni Vailati, *Epistolario: 1891–1909*, Turin, 1971, Einaudi Editore, 268–71.

4. *The Foundation and Construction of Ethics*, London, 1973, Routledge & Kegan Paul.
   Translation by E. Schneewind, of *Grundlegung und Aufbau der Ethik* (1952).

5. *Psychology from an Empirical Standpoint*, London, 1973, Routledge & Kegan Paul.
   Translation by A.C. Rancurello, D.B. Terrell, and Linda L. McAlister, of the second edition of volumes I and II of *Psychologie vom empirischen Standpunkt* (1924).

Bibliography of Works on Brentano

BOOKS

Álvarez-Aquilina, Satué. *La Doctrina de la Intendionalidad en Brentano.* Barcelona, 1961.

Bergman, Hugo. *Untersuchungen zum Problem der Evidenz der inneren Wahrnehmung.* Halle, 1908.

Bergmann, Gustav. *Realism. A Critique of Brentano and Meinong.* Madison, Milwaukee and London, 1967.

Boring, E.G. *A History of Experiemental Psychology.* 2nd ed., New York, 1950.

Brentano, Lujo. *Mein Leben im Kampf um die soziale Entwicklung Deutschlands.* Jena, 1931.

Brentano, Peter Anton v. *Schattenzug der Ahnen.* Regensburg, 1940.

Brentano, Peter Anton v. *Stammreihen der Brentanos.* Bad Reichenhall, 1933.

Brück, Maria. *Über das Verhältnis Edmund Husserls zu Franz Brentano, vornehmlich mit Rücksicht auf Brentanos Psychologie.* Würzburg, 1933.

Chisholm, Roderick M. *Perceiving: A Philosophical Study.* Ithaca, N.Y., 1957.

Chisholm, Roderick M., ed. *Realism and the Background of Phenomenology.* New York, 1960.

Eaton, H.O. *The Austrian Philosophy of Value.* Norman, Okla., 1930.

Freudenberger, T. *Quelle und Beiträge zur Geschichte der Universität Würzburg,* Vol. 1. Würzburg, 1969.

Gilson, Lucie. *La Psychologie descriptive selon Franz Brentano.* Paris, 1955.

Gilson, Lucie. *Méthode et métaphysique selon Franz Brentano.* Paris, 1955.

Grossmann, Reinhardt. *The Structure of Mind.* Madison, Wisc., 1965.

Hartlich, *Die ethischen Theorien Franz Brentanos und Nicolai Hartmanns in ihrem Verhältnis zu Aristotles.* Leipzig, 1939.

Hauber, V. *Wahrheit und Evidenz bei Franz Brentano.* Stuttgart, 1936.

Hemlein, I. *Die Kritik der Offenbarung bei Franz Brentano.* Freiburg, i.B., 1947.

Hernandez, M. *Francisco Brentano.* Salamanca, 1953.

Hertling, Georg v. *Erinnerungen aus meinem Leben,* I. Munich, 1919.

Hillebrand, Franz, *Die neuen Theorien der kategorischen Schlüsse.* Vienna, 1891.

Husserl, Edmund, *Philosophical Investigations.* Trans. J.N. Findlay, London and New York, 1970.

Kastil, Alfred. *Die Philosophie Franz Brentanos.* Bern, 1951.

Katkov, Georg. *Untersuchungen zur Werttheorie und Theodizee.* Brünn, 1937.

Kraus, Oskar, *Franz Brentano: Zur Kenntnis seines Lebens und seiner Lehre.* Munich, 1919.

Kraus, Oskar. *Die Werttheorien.* Brünn, 1937.

Manera, Xavier Franco. *El conocimiento moral en Brentano.* Madrid, 1957.

Margolius, H. *Die Ethik Franz Brentanos.* Leipzig, 1929.

Marras, Ausonio, ed. *Intentionality, Mind and Language*. Urbana, Chicago and London, 1972.

Marty, Anton. *Untersuchungen zur Grundlegung der allgemeinen Grammatik und Sprachphilosophie*. Halle, 1908.

Meurer, W. *Gegen den Empirismus*. Leipzig, 1925.

Mill, John Stuart. *The Later Letters of John-Stuart Mill, 1849–1873*, vol. XVII. Ed. Francis E. Mineka and Dwight N. Lindley. Toronto, 1972.

Most, Otto. *Die Ethik Franz Brentanos und ihre geschichtlichen Grundlagen*. Münster, 1931.

Müller, R. *Franz Brentanos Lehre von den Gemütsbewegungen*, 1943.

Müller-Freienfels, R. *The Evolution of Modern Psychology*. Trans. W.B. Wolfe. New Haven, 1935.

Passmore, John. *A Hundred Years of Philosophy*. 2nd. ed. London, 1966.

Rancurello, Antos C. *A Study of Franz Brentano*. New York, 1968.

Reinhard, E. *Die Brentanos in Aschaffenburg*. Ashchaffenburg, 1928.

Rogge, Eberhard. *Das Kausalproblem bei Franz Brentano*. Stuttgart and Berlin, 1935.

Russell, Bertrand. *The Analaysis of Mind*. New York, 1921.

Scharwath, Alfred G. *Tradition, Aufbau und Fortbildung der Tugenlehre Franz Brentanos*. Meisenheim am Glan, 1967.

Scherg, T. *Dalbergs Hochschulstadt Aschaffenburg*, III, Aschaffenburg, 1954.

Schlick, Mortiz. *Allgemeine Erkenntnislehre*. Berlin, 1918; 2nd ed. 1925.

Seiterich, E. *Die Gottesbeweise bei Franz Brentano*. Freiburg i.B., 1936.

Skrbensky, H. *Franz Brentano als Religionsphilosoph*. Zürich, 1937.

Spiegelberg, Herbert. *The Phenomenogical Movement*. The Hague, 3rd ed. 1975.

Srzednicki, Jan. *Franz Brentano's Analysis of Truth*. The Hague, 1965.

Werner, A. *Die psychologisch-erkenntnistheoretischen Grundlagen der Metaphysik Franz Brentanos*. Hildesheim, 1931.

Windischer, H. *Franz Brentano und die Scholastik*. Innsbruck, 1936.

Winter, I. *Fünfzig Jahre eines Wiener Hauses*, Vienna, 1927.

ARTICLES

Aquila, Richard E. 'The Status of Intentional Objects', *The New Scholasticism*, vol. 45 (Summer, 1971).

Arnaud, Richard B. 'Brentanist Relations', in K. Lehrer, ed., *Analysis and Metaphysics* (Dordrecht, 1975).

Barclay, James R. 'Franz Brentano and Sigmund Frued', *Journal of Existentialism*, vol. 5 (1964).

Barclay, James R. 'Themes of Brentano's Psychological Thought and Philosophical Overtones', *The New Scholasticism*, vol. 33 (1959).

Bausola, Adriano. 'Das Problem der Erfahrung der Causalität bei Franz Brentano', *Proceedings of the 14th International Congress of Philosophy*, vol. II (Vienna, 1968).

Bergman, Hugo. 'Franz Brentano', *Revue internationale de Philosophie*, XX, nr. 78 (1966).

Brentano, Claudine, 'Jugenderinnerungen an meinen Bruder', *Monatshefte für pädagogische Reform* (Vienna, 1918).

Brentano, J.C.M. 'The Manuscripts of Franz Brentano', *Revue internationale de Philosophie*, XX, nr. 78 (1966).

Burger, E. 'Franz Brentanos pädagogische Bedeutung,' *Monatshefte für pädagogische Reform* (Vienna, 1918).

Canobbio-Codelli, F. 'Husserl: La Fenomenologia della Conscienza Temporale', *Rivista di Filosofia Neo-Scholastica*, vol. 64 (Jan.–Mar., 1972).

Chisholm, Roderick M. 'Beyond Being and Nonbeing', *Philosophical Studies* 24 (1973).

Chisholm, Roderick M. 'Brentano's Descriptive Psychology and the Intentional', in *Phenomenology and Existentialism*, ed. Maurice H. Mandelbaum and Edward N. Lee (Baltimore, Md., 1967).

Chisholm, Roderick M., 'The Defeat of Good and Evil', *Proceedings and Addresses of the American Philosophical Association*, vol. 42 (1968–9).

Chisholm, Roderick M. 'Franz Brentano', in *Encyclopedia of Philosophy*, ed. Paul Edwards (New York, 1967).

Chisholm, Roderick M. and Sellars, Wilfrid 'Intentionality and the Mental', in H. Feigl, M. Scriven, and G. Maxwell, eds., *Concepts, Theories, and the Mind-Body Problem*. Minnesota Studies in the Philosophy of Science. (Minneapolis, 1958).

Chisholm, Roderick M. 'Objectives and Intrinsic Value', in Rudolf Haller, ed. *Jenseits von Sein und Nichtsein* (Graz, 1972).

Chisholm, Roderick M. 'Sentences About Believing', *Proceedings of the Aristotelian Society* (1955–6).

Deely, John N. 'The Ontological Status of Intentionality', *The New Scholasticism*, vol. 42 (Spring, 1972).

Del Negro, W. 'Von Brentano über Husserl zu Heiddeger', *Zeitschrift für philosophische Forschung*, vol. VII, nr. 4 (1953).

Egidi, Rosaria. 'Logica e Realtà', *Giornale critico della Filosofia Italiana*, vol. 1 (April–June, 1970).

Eisenmeier, J. 'Brentanos Lehre von der Empfindung', *Monatshefte für pädagogische Reform*, vol. 18 (1918).

Fels, H. 'Brentano und Kant. Ein Beitrag zur Geschichte des platonischen Aristotelismus', *Philosophisches Jahrbuch*, vol. 43 (1930).

Findlay, J.N. 'Comments and Questions Raised by Prof. Chisholm's Paper on Brentano's Descriptive Psychology', *Proceedings of the 14th International Congress of Philosophy*, vol. II (Vienna, 1968).

Foges, M. 'Personliche Erinnerungen an F. Brentano', *Neues Wiener Journal* (March 21, 1917).

Foradori, E. 'Franz Brentanos Lehre von den Axiomen', *Archiv für die gesammte Psychologie*, vol. LXXXI (Leipzig, 1931).

Grossmann, Reinhardt B. 'Acts and Relations in Brentano', *Analysis*, vol. 21 (1960).

Grossmann, Reinhardt B. 'Non-existent Objects, Recent Work on Brentano and Meinong', *American Philosophical Quarterly* (January, 1969).

Gurwitsch, Aron. 'Bemerkungen zu den Referaten Herrn Chisholm, Landgrebe und Patočka', *Proceedings of the 14th International Congress of Philosophy*, vol. II (Vienna, 1968).

Gurwitsch, Aron. 'Toward a Theory of Intentionality', *Philosophy and Phenomenological Research*, vol. 30 (March, 1970).

Hernandez, M. 'La doctrina de la intencionalidad en la fenomenologia', *Acta Salamanticensia* (Salamanca, 1958).

Höfler, Alois, 'Franz Brentano in Wien', *Süddeutsche Monatsheft* (May 1917).

Ingarden, Roman. 'Le Concept de Philosophie chez Franz Brentano', *Archives de Philosophie*, vol. 32 (July–Sept., 1969).

Kamitz, Reinhardt. 'Acts and Relations in Brentano', *Analysis*, XXII, iv (March, 1962).

Kastil, Alfred. 'Brentanos Stellung zur Phänomenologie', *Zeitschrift für philosophische Forschung*, vol. V (1951).

Kastil, Alfred. 'Ein neuer Rettungsversuch der äusseren Wahrnehmung. Kritische Bemerkungen zu Stumpfs Erkenntnislehre', *Zeitschrift für philosophische Forschung*, vol. III (1949).

Kastil, Alfred. 'Franz Brentano und der Positivismus', *Wissenschaft und Weltbild*, vol. II, nr. 4 (1949).

Kastil, Alfred, 'Wahrheit und Sein', *Zeitschrift für philosophische Forschung*, vol. I, nr. 4 (1948).

Katkov, Georg. 'Bewußtsein, Gegenstand, Sachverhalt. Eine Brentano-studie', *Archiv für die gesammte Psychologie* vol. LXXV, nrs. 3 and 5 (1930).

Katkov, Georg. 'Descartes und Brentano. Eine erkenntnistheoretische Gegenüberstellung', *Archiv für Rechts- und Sozialphilosophie*, vol. XXX, nr. 4, (1937).

Kersten, Fred. 'Franz Brentano and William James', *Journal of the History of Philosophy* (April, 1969).

Kim, Jagewon. 'Materialism and the Criteria of the Mental', *Synthese*, vol. 22 (1971).

Kraft, Viktor. 'Franz Brentano', *Wiener Zeitschrift für Philosophie, Psychologie, Pädagogik*, vol. IV, nr. 1 (1952).

Kraus, Oskar. 'Besonderheit und Aufgabe der deutschen Philosophie in Böhmen', *Zur Philosophie der Gegenwart* (Prague, 1934).

Kraus, Oskar. 'Franz Brentanos Stellung im philosophischen Leben der Gegenwart', *Philosophische Weltanzeiger*, vol. 2, nr. 2 (1928).

Kraus, Oskar. 'Die "kopernikanische Wendung" in Brentanos Erkenntnis-und Wertlehre', *Philosophische Hefte*, vol. 3 (1929).

Kraus, Oskar. 'Über Franz Brentanos ethische Prinzipienlehre', *Monatshefte für pädagogische Reform* (Vienna, 1918).

Kubát, Daniel. 'Franz Brentano's Axiology – A Revised Conception', *Review of Metaphysics*, vol. 12 (1958).

Land, J.P.N. 'Brentano's Logical Innovations', *Mind*, o.s. (1876).

Lenhard, L. 'Das Franz Brentano-Gutachten über die päpstliche Infallibilität', *Archiv für mittelrheinische Kirchengeschichte*, vol. 7 (1955).

Linke, P. 'Intentionalität und Transzendenz', *Wissenschaftliche Zeitschrift der Friedrich-Schiller-Universität*, vol. IV (Jena, 1955).

Lycan, K. 'On Intentionality and the Psychological', *American Philosophical Quarterly* (1969).

Mandl. E. 'Aus meinen Erinnerungen an Franz Brentano', *Internationale Rundschau* (Zürich, 1917).

Mayer-Hillebrand, Franziska. 'Franz Brentanos Einfluß auf die Philosophie seiner Zeit und Gegenwart'. *Revue Internationale de Philosophie*, XX nr. 78 (1966).

Mayer-Hillebrand, Franziska. 'Franz Brentanos Lehre von den Fiktionen der Sprache', *Innsbrucker Beiträge zur Kulturwissenschaft* (1955).

Mayer-Hillebrand, Franziska. 'Franz Brentanos ursprüngliche und spätere Seinslehre und ihre Beziehungen zu Husserls Phänomenologie', *Zeitschrift für philosophische Forschung*, XIII, nr. 2 (1959).

Mayer-Hillebrand, Franziska. 'Franz Brentanos wissenschaftlicher Nachlaß', *Zeitschrift für philosophische Forschung*, vol. VI, nr. 4, 1952.

Mayer-Hillebrand, Franziska. 'Remarks Concerning the Interpretation of the Philosophy of Franz Brentano. A Reply to Professor Srzednicki', *Philosophy and Phenomenological Research*, vol. XXIII (1963).

Mayer-Hillebrand, Franziska. 'Rückblick auf die bisherigen Bestrebungen zur Erhaltung und Verbreitung von Franz Brentanos philosophische Lehren und Kurze Darstellung dieser Lehren', *Zeitschrift für philosophische Forschung*, vol. XVII (1963).

Mayer-Hillebrand, Franziska. 'Über Bedeutung und Berechtigung der Normwissenschaften', *Innsbrucker Beiträge zur Kulturwissenschaft*, vol. 5 (1955).

McAlister, Linda L. 'Franz Brentano and Intentional Inexistence', *Journal of the History of Philosophy* (October, 1970).

Merlan, Philip. 'Brentano and Freud', *Journal of the History of Ideas*, vol. 6 (1945).

Merlan, Philip. 'Brentano and Freud. A Sequel', *Journal of the History of Ideas*, vol. 10 (1949).

Morick, Harold, 'On the Indispensability of Intentionality', *Canadian Journal of Philosophy*, vol. 2, no. 2 (September, 1972).

Morrison, James C. 'Husserl and Brentano on Intentionality', *Philosophy and Phenomenological Research*, vol. 31 (September, 1970).

Nathan, N.M.L. 'Brentano's Necessitarianism', *Ratio*, vol. 13 (June, 1971).

Nettesheim, J. 'Christoph Bernhard Schlüter und Franz Brentano', *Zeitschrift für philosophische Forschung*, vol. XVI, nr. 2 (1962).

Pidoll, M. v. 'Zur Erinnerung an Franz Brentano', *Monatshefte für pädagogische Reform* (Vienna, 1918).

Puglisi, Mario. 'Franz Brentano', *American Journal of Psychology*, vol. 35. 1924.

Sanz, R. 'El problema de los valores en la teoria del conocimiento moral de Franz Brentano', *Acta Salmanticensia* (Salamanca, 1948).

Schmidkunz, H. 'Brentanos Logik und ihre pädagogische Folgen', *Monatshefte für pädagogische Reform* (Vienna, 1918).

Seiterich, Eugen. 'Die Gottesbeweise bei Franz Brentano', *Freiburger Theologische Studien* vol. 24 (Freiburg, i.B., 1936).

Soucek, R. 'Alfred Binet et l'école de Brentano', *Journal de Psychologie Normale et Pathologique*, vol. 21 (1924).

Spiegelberg, Herbert. 'The Lost Portrait of Edmund Husserl by Franz and Ida Brentano', in *Philomathes: Studies and Essays in the Humanities in Memory of Philip Merlan*, ed. Robert B. Palmer and Robert Hamerton-Kelly (The Hague, 1971).

Stumpf, Carl. 'Franz Brentano', *Deutsches biographisches Jahrbuch*, II (1917–20).

Stumpf, Carl. 'Franz Brentano', in *Lebensläufe aus Franken*, II, ed. Anton Chroust (Würzburg, 1918).

Srzednicki, Jan. 'Remarks Concerning the Interpretation of the Philosophy of Franz Brentano', *Philosophy and Phenomenlogical Research*, XXII (1962)

Srzednicki, Jan. 'A Reply to Professor Mayer-Hillebrand,' *Philosophy and Phenomenological Research*, XXIII (1963).

Srzednicki, Jan. 'Some Elements of Brentano's Analysis of Language and Their Ramifications', *Revue internationale de Philosophie*, XX, nr. 78 (1966).

Terrell, D.B. 'Franz Brentano's Axiology. Some Corrections to D. Kubát's Paper', *Review of Metaphysics* (1959).

Terrell, D.B. 'Descriptive Psychology and the Nomology of Mind', *Proceedings of the 14th International Congress of Philosophy*, vol. VI (Vienna, 1968).

Titchener, E.B. 'Experimental Psychology: A Retrospect', *American Journal of Psychology*, vol. 36 (1925).

Titchener, E.B. 'Functional Psychology and the Psychology of Act', *American Journal of Psychology* vols. 32 and 33 (1921 and 1922).

Titchener, E.B. 'Review of Brentano's *Psychologie vom empirischen Standpunkt*', *American Journal of Psychology*, vol. 36 (1925).

Utitz, Emil. 'Erinnerungen an Franz Brentano', *Wissenschaftliche Zeitschrift der Universität Halle-Wittenberg*, IV, i (December, 1954).

Utitz, Emil. 'Franz Brentano', *Kant-Studien*, vol. XXII, nr. 3 (1917).

Vanni-Rovighi, S. 'La Natura delle categorie secundo F. Brentano', *Rivista di Filosofia Neoscolastica*, vol. 30 (1938).

Windischer, H. 'Franz Brentano und die Scholastik', *Philosophie und Grenzwissenschaften*, vol. VI, nr. 6 (Innsbruck, 1936).

Wu. Joseph. 'The Problem of Existential Import', *Notre Dame Journal of Formal Logic* (October, 1969).

DISSERTATIONS

Barclay, James. 'Brentano and Freud, A Comparative Study in the Evolution of Psychological Thought.' (University of Michigan 1959).

Bear, Harry. 'The Theoretical Ethics of the Brentano School, a Psycho-epistemological Approach.' (Columbia University, 1954).

Estall, Martyn. 'Studies in the Philosophy and Psychology of Franz Brentano.' (Cornell University, 1938).

Fischer, Kurt R. 'Franz Brentano's Philosophy of *Evidenz*.' (University of California, Berkeley, 1964).

Gruber, C. 'Die Urteilslehre Brentanos. Eine Auseinandersetzung mit Most.' (University of Innsbruck, 1934).

Hughes, Elizabeth M. 'Brentano and the Nature of Ethical Judgements.' M.A. Thesis (Brown University, 1962).

Kamitz, Reinhardt. 'Franz Brentanos Lehre vom wahren Urteil. Eine kurze Darstellung dieser Theorie sowie einiger gegen sie erhobener Einwände.' (University of Innsbruck, 1961).

Kubát, Daniel. 'Bedeutung und Wandel der ethischen Grundbegriffe bei Franz Brentano.' (University of Munich, 1956).

McAlister, Linda L. 'The Development of Franz Brentano's Ethics.' (Cornell University, 1969).

Reicher, Franziska. 'Das Nichtreale als Fiktion. Franz Brentanos ursprüngliche Lehre vom Nichtrealen, ihr Ausbau durch andere und ihr Abbau durch ihn selbst.' (University of Innsbruck, 1919).

Terrell, D.B. 'Ethics, Language and Ontology.' (University of Michigan, 1956).

Würzburger, Walter S. 'Brentano's Theory of *a priori* Judgements.' (Harvard University, 1951).

INDEX OF NAMES

GENERAL INDEX